Postcards *from the* End of America

CIVIC CENTER

I

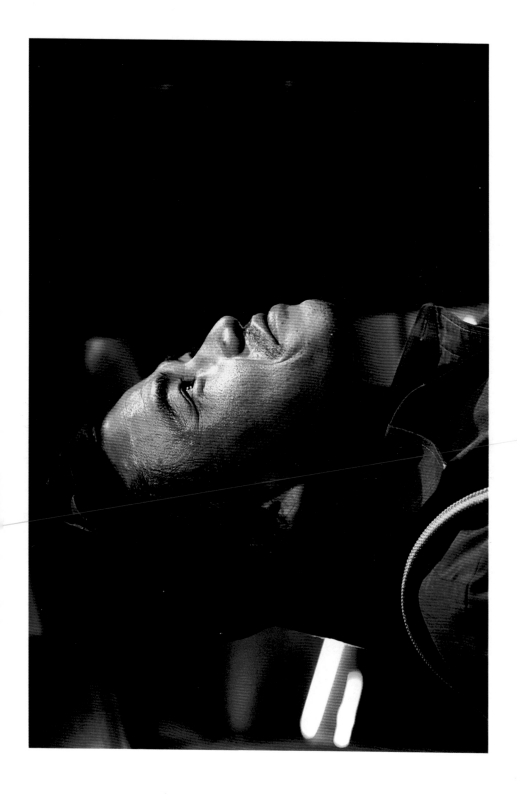

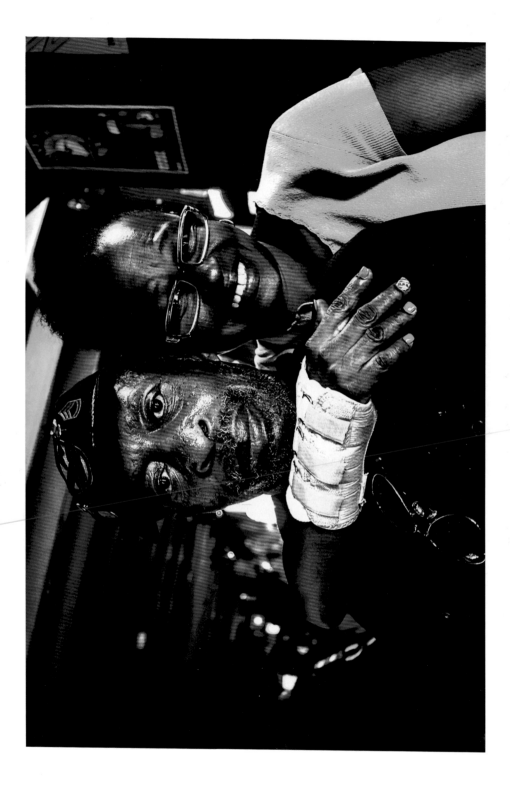

CAPTIONS

1- Richmond, VA, 2010. Sixty-four years old, Harriet worked in a thrift store. "My husband is seventy-six years old, and I will take care of him until the end. He won't be in any nursing home."

2- Savannah, GA, 2011. Eighty-three years old, he was collecting aluminum cans. "Back when I was small, I wouldn't think twice about walking a mile to buy a dollar of coal for my family. If my mom told me to do it, I'd just do it. I'd push that cart down the road to get us some coal."

3- Williston, ND, 2014. She was a bartender at DK's Lounge and Casino.

4- Wolf Point, MT, 2014. Forty-five-year-old Mervin Running Bear in Stockmans Bar. "This means we're all equal." In 2015, Mervin was arrested for stabbing a man in Arlo's, a bar across the street.

5- Portland, OR, 2014. Thirty-five-year-old Sam in Ming Lounge. Born in Laos, Sam had been a metal fabricator, welder and boat painter. Unemployed, he was homeless.

6- Boston, MA, 2011. Katie: "From the age of twelve, I've always wanted to be an animal. I stay outside as much as possible."

7- Philadelphia, PA, 2013. Chili Willie and his niece in Broad Street Tavern. Chili on fighting in Vietnam: "No, it didn't freak me out, because I had a job to do."

8- Jersey City, NJ, 2014. Karaoke at the Golden Cicada Tavern.

9- Columbus, OH, 2014. Forty-three-year-old Monroe in The Patio. Monroe was a carpenter, housepainter, bartender and valet. "Hey, you want to see my girlfriend?"

10- Kennewick, WA, 2014. Pablo in Players: "I have the smallest dick in the world, but women love me, because I know how to listen."

11- Cheyenne, WY, 2013. Fifty-three-year-old Jim in the Eagle's Nest. Jim on his nine kids: "I'm still in touch with each of them, and I've taken care of all of them."

12- On an Amtrak train going through Iowa, 2014. Fifty-seven-year-old Dean just got out of jail. "You've got to use your brain. I've always used my brain. They steal too, so I steal, but I don't rip off the little guys. I'd never steal from you. I give money to the poor. I'm stealing for Jesus."

13- Los Angeles, CA, 2013. After an all-night bus from San Francisco, I was wandering around 5th and Broadway at 5 a.m. when I ran into fifty-five-year-old Eric Hurt. Homeless, Eric had played four games in the NFL.

14- Cheyenne, WY, 2013. "You like girls? Go to the Green Door." He lived at the Pioneer Hotel.

15- Philadelphia, PA, 2011. "I'm Ahuviya Harel, twenty-six years old and female."

16- Taylor, PA, 2015. Bob Bruno at home.

17- Savannah, GA, 2011. Steven and Megan in their broken-down RV by the side of a creek. They had no heat, electricity or plumbing. Steven worked for sixteen years at the headquarters of Mellow Mushroom Pizza in Atlanta. After studying broadcasting in college, Megan was a whore for three years at the Mustang Ranch in Nevada. Drunk one night, she jumped off a bridge, so became wheelchair bound. Steven: "We fell in love over a Van Morrison song."

18- Detroit, MI, 2010. People laughed at her as she scrounged for food from a trash can outside the Greyhound station.

19- Allentown, PA, 2015. He is a veteran of Desert Storm. "Immigrants used to come here, but they came to achieve the American Dream, correct? The Muslims came also, but they didn't come to change the laws of the land. Now, they want to change the laws, just as the gays are doing. If the Muslims don't eat pork, you must cater to them. And the LBGT, the gays, since they want same-sex marriage, every state must cater to them."

20- Collingswood, NJ, 2013. Seeing me take photos at a train station, Sergeant Rambo came over, so I snapped him. "Hey, you look pretty good!" I grinned. "I've always been photogenic," he responded before telling me to beat it.

Postcards *from the* End of America

LINH DINH

Seven Stories Press

New York • Oakland • London

Seven Stories Press
140 Watts Street
New York, NY 10013
www.sevenstories.com

Library of Congress Control Number 2016961760.

Printed in the USA.

9 8 7 6 5 4 3 2 1

Many thanks to all those who supported this project through the years!

Versions of these pieces were published at *Unz Review*, *CounterCurrents*, *Intrepid Report*, *Information Clearing House* and other webzines.

CONTENTS

ENTERING CHEYENNE

4-11-13—Of all the words uttered by a person, only a few remain unforgettable. My friend Lan, for example, is reduced in my mind to a single joking sentence, "This time I'll probably have to sell my body," and I'll never forgive X for sneering, "I ain't got none!" With a public figure, the lingering words can even be misquoted, as likely was the case with the incipiently subterranean Margaret Thatcher (the Milk Snatcher). Though there's no record of it, she's repeatedly cited as having intoned, "A man who, beyond the age of twenty-six, finds himself on a bus can count himself a failure." The public likes this faux quotation because it neatly sums up Thatcher's disdain for the bottom half, for "losers," and also because it sounds pretty funny.

Well, I've seen many wars based on lies since my twenty-sixth flameout and I'm still riding the losers' express to the no-payout casino, so I'm obviously not a member of the Union League. Carless, with my Virginia driver's license long expired, I've ridden countless coaches across town, state and country. I've rolled with a vast army of losers, but as I've insisted many times, losing is not easy. To lose day in and day out requires all of your physical, mental and spiritual energy, for who bears the weight of this nasty empire, amigo? It's the bottom half that build, maintain, fight and die for this nation, that is for its ruling class, the winners who never ride buses. Soon, perhaps we will come to our senses, unite and redirect our weapons.

Recently I took a bus from Philly to Oakland, then back, with several stops each way, scheduled or not. I heard and saw much, on and off the bus. Repeatedly, I'd hear of people losing jobs or making less, much less, than just a few years ago. Yes, there were a few with improving prospects, but they were by far the minority. In St. Louis I met a fifty-two-year-old lady who hadn't found work in several years, though she had spent decades as a live-in babysitter or caretaker of the elderly. At the welfare office, she was told she'd have to wait until she was fifty-five. "So what am I going to do for three years? I still have to eat!"

From St. Louis to Terre Haute, I sat next to a forty-one-year-old manager of an Outback Steakhouse. Yes, business is down, way down, from five years ago, but this year has started out slightly better than expected, so he's keeping his fingers crossed. Joe did admit that they used to have three cooks come in the morning, each with a different set of responsibilities, but now they were down to just one. "So one guy is doing the work of three?!" I blurted out.

"Well, yeah," Joe laughed, "but he's fast."

"He's not getting paid three times as much, though."

"Of course not, but he's gotten five raises."

"You're lucky you have this guy."

"We know."

JIM GREW UP on Long Island, served two and a half years in the Airborne, studied at a culinary school in Allentown, Pennsylvania, worked as a pastry chef in Burke, Virginia, then moved to Springfield, Missouri, to be with his second wife. He was going to Allentown to see his two daughters, ten and thirteen. He had never been west of Springfield and had only driven through Chicago twice. As a grade school student he interviewed Yankees pitcher Phil Niekro, "and that's something I'll never forget." He regrets not being a cop. "If I had a chance to do it all again, that's what I'd be."

Entering Cheyenne, I saw an inquiring ad, "Missing a tooth?" Then a large billboard, "8 Million a Day for Israel. It just doesn't make any sense." I got off my coach and walked three miles into town. In summer, Cheyenne may appear more cheerful, but in early April, it was overwhelmingly gray and brown, with most of the larger buildings left over from the seventies and box-like. On Lincoln Highway, there was a line of motels advertising "clean rooms" for under $30, so I had likely overpaid for mine, booked online for $70. I had spent two nights on the bus, and would have to endure two more likewise before reaching home.

Cheyenne has long lost its intercity rail service, but there's a Depot Museum on its main square. It being winter and even colder than usual, few visitors were present, and as I photographed a John Wayne image through a store window, a uniformed soldier suggested that I should go inside for even better shots. Earlier, a man had pointed out Sanford's as a cheap yet decent drinking hole. Cheyenne folks were remarkably friendly. Presently, however, a man with bad facial skin strode up, carrying a cheap six-pack. I can't recall who said what first, or second, but in no time he had become my unofficial tour guide. Meth Visage said I could get $1 beer at the Drunken Skunk if I ordered some food. If I liked to look at dancing girls, well, there's the Green Door, just down the street. Meth boasted of once making $54 in a single day, just giving tips to tourists, mostly European, and taking photos for them. Meth had a single occupancy room at the Pioneer Hotel, and I was tempted to buy two six-packs of tallboys, which would likely gain me entry into the sparse or messy world of Meth and his buddies, one of whom was already walking beside me to act as my second unofficial tour guide. To offer unsolicited service is common in all Third World countries, so with Meth and others like him across this increasingly desperate land, we're getting a glimpse of what's to come.

Having just gotten into town, and with my bus leaving the next afternoon, I decided to pass on the Pioneer. Underdressed in a thin jacket and slacks, I was freezing as I wandered, but I toughed it out for another hour or so before ducking, finally, into the Eagle's Nest. With its proximity to the Hitching Post, my hotel, I wouldn't have to stumble too far to lie down at the end of my boozing. I planted myself on a stool near a boisterous group rolling dice on the bar. There were two pool tables and two kinds of beer on tap, Bud and Bud Light. Before long I found out that the cheerful lady next to me was named Ginger. Her easygoing boyfriend was Terry. The lanky cowboy, Jim. The bartender, Leaf.

Up to three years ago, forty-five-year-old Ginger, born and raised in Amarillo, was a manager at a video rental store, making $18 an hour, but it went out of business. She then bartended, at this very joint, but it didn't suit her, so now she works in an appliance store, making just $8 per, before tax. To add to her troubles, she and her husband of twenty-three years filed for divorce, "I never really loved him. I met him when I was just twenty-one. He got me pregnant, so we got married." She had only known two men before him, Ginger confided, and two men after, before she met Terry, "the love of my life. Now I finally know what's it's like to be loved, to be wanted. Now I finally have someone who is glad to see me at the end of each day."

Ginger has three daughters, twenty-three, twenty-two and nine years old, with the twenty-two-year-old serving in "North Korea," she said.

"You mean South Korea?"

"No, North Korea."

"It's South Korea," at least two voices chimed in. "South Korea!"

Overhearing that Ginger had only been with six men, Leaf also interjected laughingly, "Six guys?! I've been with so many more. I loved fucking."

Ginger got me a Tecate, so I bought her a Salty Dog, or maybe it was a Fuzzy Navel. In any case, things went south not long after, but we'll get to that later. Meanwhile, let's meet Jim, a lanky, Stetson-wearing fifty-three-year-old with most of his front teeth punched out, or maybe in, and he had simply swallowed them, with a chaser.

Jim was born in Oakland, where his mom died of heroin. He has nine kids that he's aware of. "I'm still in touch with each of them, and I've taken care of all of them." Maybe he has. A seasoned crane operator, Jim was in town for a new job that paid $29 an hour, big bucks in these times and parts. The work would only last a few months, however, then it's on to Casper, Wyoming. Using the internet to find gig after gig, he had bounced around the country. It's good that he had no wife and kids at home, for it would not be possible to drag them along his gypsy route. Jim had no real home, in fact, only rooms at cheap motels, and tonight, like every other night, naturally, he didn't want to sleep alone. Seeing two lovelies at a table, he grinned at me, "Are you with me? I'll get them for us."

Jim had been drinking since 10:30 in the morning, and it was creeping towards midnight, so the dude was well lubricated, and running out of money also. Jim was down to three bucks, so I gave him two for one more shot of whiskey. Earlier he had said to me, apropos of nothing, "You look like a dangerous guy."

"Me?! Fuck! I'm the biggest pussy in the world!"

Jim turned out prescient, sort of, for when I heard him refer to me as a "Chinese guy" who had just given him two bucks, I immediately hopped off my stool to strangle him, with my thumbs pressed deep into his jugular. The motherfucker froze. Now if we have been chatting then I'm no longer a Chinese, Vietnamese or any kind of ethnic guy. I'm Linh, or even Lee, if you can't quite pronounce my name. You wouldn't appreciate it either if I called you "this black dude" or "this white woman" after we've been talking.

Though my logic was sound, my action was foolish at best, if not suicidal, for I couldn't knock down a Justin Bieber standee with a right cross if you gave me three tries, but Jim, as I've already noted, simply froze, which prompted Ginger to comment, "I'm impressed." Letting go, I actually said, "Next time I won't be so tender."

Stoked by booze and Lynyrd Skynyrd on the jukebox, we had all become fast friends, though before the night was over Ginger would lose her cell phone, start to sob, "This is why I don't drink," and get into a fight with boyfriend Terry over a Doug Supernaw song, the one with mom being run over by a freight train just after being freed from prison. She thought it was hilarious. He didn't think so.

"I don't like country music. I just don't get it."

"You don't have to like country music to have a sense of humor!"

So ended my first day in Cheyenne. I saw and heard enough to know that things were rough here, as they were throughout my recent travels. Downtown there was a sign on a handsome high-rise, "THIS BUILDING IS NOT EMPTY. IT IS FULL OF OPPORTUNITY," and nearby, the art deco theater advertised movies for only $3.50. Here and there, posters warned against meth addiction.

The next morning I stepped over used syringes on my way to the bus station. The driver made us wait nearly half an hour in the cold, even though the bus was right there, with its door wide open. He treated us like losers, and we didn't dare to upset him. Had we stirred, the bossman might deny us our only chance out of ruination, if only towards another dire strait. Like Jim, I'm missing several teeth actually, for this is Uncle Ben's America. Eight million a day for Israel. Are you with me? Words, words, words. I'll get them for us.

MISSOURI DOPE

4-16-13—In Sartre's *No Exit*, hell is depicted as a room with two women and a man, which is fair enough, for a threesome is never what you envisioned it would be in the privacy of your own hell. Hell is also "other people," *"les autres,"* for in the company of another, one's vanity, smugness, extreme prejudices and fantasies, whether philosophical, political, charitable or pornographic, are rudely disrupted. One must readjust and realign one's flesh and ideas, must calibrate if not refute them, in toto and in shame, when faced with another, which in most cases is no hell at all, but a kind of heaven so awesome and humbling that we, as media-abetted cowards, must evade it constantly. OK, cheesy overture over, now get the hell away from me!

How about some choice *fromage*, my dear? Laughing Cow? Sit next to me, be my hell until Topeka do us part. Of all the lovely bodies in the world, why are we suddenly together? It must be destiny, for we are a perfectly matched couple, whether hetero, homo, transsexual or even trans-species, and thankfully race, skin tone and birthplace no longer serve as barriers, for we are together, see? Tight, tight, tight. We are a couple.

Let's see how others do it. Across the aisle is Samantha. She appears no older than twenty-two. Heading to Georgia, she got on in Denver yesterday, where the temperature never rose above 40°F, yet she had no coat on, only a thin blanket over a strap blouse. The reason, one must assume, was to show off the tattoo on her chest, a large skull with bat wings. Let's now listen to her speech. It is genteel all right. "May I ask you another question, sir?" This, on a bus where "motherfucker," "fuck off" and every other kind of "fuck" fly about freely. Her seatmate is a sixty-year-old man whose diction is nearly as formal, as in, "These candies are very good, in my opinion." A Serbian, he's teaching her basic words, at her request, "*zdravo*," "*dobro*" and "*bombona*," etc. A lovely dancing couple, they are careful not to step on each other's tongues, with the pattern they're making lurking forever in their minds, as well as mine, a mere observer, but soon, too soon, she will abruptly leave him, for this is how it usually ends, in Topeka, Kansas.

OK, OK, so traveling from Kansas City to St. Louis, I had the luck to abut a curious lady. In her mid-forties, she had hard features accentuated by severe, even aggressive makeup. She looked mean, all right, but had a calm, often soothing voice, even as she was spewing some nasty stuff. Overhearing her cell phone conversations, I gathered that she had just abandoned her apartment in St. Paul, and was heading to Kentucky, where she had family.

Her boyfriend had gotten rough on her, so she was dumping his ass, "You lay your hand on me, I'm going to waste your stupid ass, you lame-ass nigga, and I won't need a man to do it. I'll kill you myself. No, you shut the fuck up! It's over. I called 911 on you, and I'm calling the landlord, right about now. You're always acting like you're in charge, but you ain't in charge of shit! You have three days to get the fuck out of there, you hear me? You're occupying that place il-le-gal-ly. They're going to change the lock on your stupid ass."

Then she called her daughter, "What's up? I can't even hear you. Speak up! Why are you getting all sneaky on me?! Listen, listen, just listen to me. I've moved, I'm out of there, I made up my mind, so you have three days to get your ass out, you hear me? Oh, shut the fuck up! You don't know nothing about nothing. You can't do shit! You can't even fuck! All you know how to do is to eat pussies. I'm going to come back from Kentucky just to kick you the fuck out, bitch!"

Then she called her ex-landlord, "Yes, sir, I'm out of there. I know, I've been behind on the rent, but I've decided to vacate your property. There's a man in there, but he shouldn't be there, he's in there il-le-gal-ly, so you should change the lock on him. No, sir, *you* have a good day."

Note that all of the above was said in the most composed voice, and not just because the driver had warned, repeatedly, that loud noises of any kind, as well as drugs or alcohol, were not to be tolerated. Ignoring these prohibitions, a young man slipped into the tiny bathroom, and soon the entire coach was uplifted by a sweetly titillating fragrance. "A skunk," a wise man informed us, but my seasoned seatmate immediately corrected the dumbass, "No, that's some great weed."

Independently coming to the same conclusion, the driver then shouted, "You, in the far back, please come forward!" And as the young man in a DieMonsterDie T-shirt wended his way up front, the driver added, "Son, I knew grass before you knew green grass!" The toker was made to dump his stash, undoubtably for the driver to smoke later, with his wife and kids while watching *Dancing with the Stars* or some shit. Toker then had to turn around to apologize to all the other passengers. "Kick him off," my seatmate hollered, but seeing his distressed face, I decided to pipe up, "Let him go! He's only a kid!" Apparently changing her verdict, my seatmate concurred, "He don't know nothing." "Yeah, let him go," a few other voices chimed in, and the horror punk fan was spared from being stranded in the middle of heaven or hell, depending on what you're smoking.

Seriously, dude, you don't want to mess with an interstate bus driver, for as long as you're in that tight, barely reclining seat, you're subjected to their full-spectrum domination. Most are cool, no doubt, but some are certifiably world-class A-holes. In El Paso, I saw a driver berate a rider like a mother her child, and in Cleveland, two passengers were prevented from boarding for having alcohol on their breath, and I likewise for refusing to have my camera stored in the hold. When I loudly protested, this driver simply mouthed "fuck you" twice, and that was that, for he had the final say, for a driver's words are papal to those without wheels or the means to fly or ride the rails. Easing into Indianapolis, an elderly driver blessed us,

"If this is your final destination, then may you be eternally protected by the benevolence, forgiveness and wisdom of our Lord Jesus Christ."

Winding through snowy Colorado, a driver offered us a rare prospect for employment, "Greyhound is hiring. I repeat, Greyhound is hiring. If you were a friend or a family member, I'd not recommend this job, but since you are perfect strangers, I'll say that it is not such a bad job." Later, he'd spoon us more comedy, "If you are somehow unhappy with this ride, there is a form you can fill out to complain about me. For your information, my name is Sammy Taggart. Again, I am Sammy Taggart. If you are satisfied with this trip, however, and want to compliment me, my name is Chuck Hernandez."

OK, let's hop back on the bus rolling through Missouri, with a hard yet sweet woman sitting next to me, but how is she sweet you may be asking? First of all, she was sharing her cigarettes and food with all those around her, and even offered me a taco. Bought yesterday in another time zone, it was still some kind of meat wrapped in a tired shell, with hot sauce galore and a sprig of cilantro even. She was also being motherly to a young man just released from prison. He was in for "eight and a half," he confided, and I had to assume he meant months and not years, since he didn't look older than twenty-five. He hadn't eaten in three days, he added, but didn't elaborate. Though tough-featured and well-built, he appeared very subdued, even meek.

Seeing this kid, I was reminded of a garbageman turned crack dealer I knew back in Philly. He went from making $1,200 a month to $600 a day, so what did he do but slosh around in lots of pussies and booze for a couple of months, before he was caught and sent to jail for five and a half years. His demeanor changed whenever he recalled being locked up. I mean, on the face of it, it didn't sound half bad, with not much to do and cable TV, besides, at only $14 per month, way better than the outside, for sure, an excellent deal that included all of the Phillies, Flyers, Eagles and Sixers games, and certainly worth committing a felony or two for, with or without collateral damages. But the constant violence he saw in there scared the living coitus out of him. Like my late buddy Tony, he talked of guys having their assholes slit with a razor, so that tradition is still going strong apparently, at least in Pennsylvania.

The hard woman sheltered a daughter and her man, and simply slogged along, rent unpaid and all, until he raised his hand to her, provoking this latest drama, which she handled with considerable equanimity and aplomb, I must say. For many of the lower class, life lurches from crisis to crisis, with frequent slides into disaster. If this were an airplane, such an overheard tale would draw irritated looks, if not indignant complaints, but here no one gave a flying Twinkie, for each had his own harrowing sequence to hash over or, more likely, forget.

Let's meet another survivor, a man I had encountered in Kansas City a month earlier, on my way west. A blizzard had stranded over a hundred people at this modest bus terminal. Minus the handful who were willing or able to pay for a taxicab and hotel room, we just slept wherever we could, or not at all. I lay on a steel bench, with my lower legs draped over its end, and the thickness of my hoodie serving as the thinnest pillow. It did keep my ears warm. Though my eyes were closed, I never lost the consciousness that I was stuck in Kansas City, with no clear timeline for escape. Unable to drift into dreams, I'd get up repeatedly to wander around the brightly lit station, with its TV tuned to CNN nonstop, and its benches and floor sprawling with bodies, including kids and the very old, as in nearly morgue-ready. Hell is the American mainstream media earnestly beaming charades, mirages and spins 24/7, though thankfully the volume was kept low.

Seeing a squatting man, I immediately knew he was foreign, but only after we started talking did I realize he was Vietnamese like me. We then switched from English to our native tongue. Of mixed race, Tung likely had American blood in him from the Vietnam War, though there were Aussie and New Zealander troops there too, as well as contractors and reporters from dozens of other countries. A mild man, Tung sported a mustache and donned a cheap-looking, dun baseball cap featuring an eagle perched on the stars and stripes. Forty-three years old, he had been in the US eleven years, and was working as a boner at a pork processing plant in Greenbush, Minnesota, making $16 an hour, for $400 net a week. Previously, he had been at a beef plant in Sioux City, Iowa, but that place only paid $300 per week.

Greenbush is near the Canadian border, and the region is almost entirely white, but from Tung I learned that 80 percent of the workers at this pork plant are nonwhite, with many Africans, Mexicans and Asians, with the Burmese so adept at this grueling work, they're allowed to chew betel leaves on the job, with trash cans nearby to catch their spittle. Saving what he could from his modest pay, Tung had returned to Vietnam eight times, with six months his longest stay. Back in tropical Can Tho in the Mekong Delta, he would eat and drink well, and idle his time away, but that too would get tiresome, and his dollars would evaporate, so back to frozen Minnesota he would fly. Recently he passed out at the slaughterhouse and woke up in an emergency room, but since it happened just before he clocked in, even before he had a chance to put on his gloves, it wasn't considered a workplace incident. Tung spoke wistfully of a fellow Vietnamese who had gotten clipped by a forklift. The lucky man broke his chin, so thereafter was assigned the easiest tasks, on top of his medical compensation.

In the morning, with my bus still unscheduled, I trudged through the snow into town. There I saw several fine examples of empty buildings being jazzed up to entice elusive tenants. All over America, this has become an art, and a booming business for graphic designers. In the past this cosmetic would be a waste of money for any prime piece of real estate would soon be rented, but now even a well-appointed edifice in an excellent location might stay empty for years, if not permanently. Behind plate glass windows, handsomely suited men and women are shown surveying and marching towards a bright future, "RETAIL SPACE FOR LEASE," and on the signboard of yet another empty store, "YOUR NAME HERE." In St. Louis, white letters are painted onto a window, "BEAUTIFUL HISTORIC BUILDING. $6 BASE RENT. Will Design / Build Interior Space. Let's Talk!"

With so many Americans unemployed, shouldn't people like Tung be kept out of the country? With a smaller labor pool, wages would go up, and the tougher jobs would become more attractive, or at least more worthwhile, though consumer prices would spike. The problem in Tung's case, however, is that America's foreign policies have resulted in him being here at all, and I don't mean just the country, but the earth itself. Further, since our military and banking tentacles have such a wide reach, many other immigrants can rightly claim to be a bastard of Uncle Sam, although he may not have been, literally, their motherfucker.

Let's meet, then, such a person. Traveling from Salt Lake City to Reno, I sat across the aisle from a darker-skinned middle-aged man in a Bulls knit cap. We had just passed the Lovelock Correctional Center, which the driver pointed out was the residence of one O.J. Simpson. Hitchhiking was prohibited in this area, announced a billboard. Presently, Bulls Knit walked forward to ask another passenger something. This second man had on an Army Airborne cap. He said, "Man, you've got to learn how to speak English better if you're going to do business in this country. Not everybody is going to be as nice as me."

Airborne then dialed a number to ask why Bulls Knit's phone card didn't work. Done, he spoke very slowly to accommodate the foreigner, "They said you spent the minutes already. They said you spent your minutes calling Afghanistan. Hey, are you from Afghanistan?"

"Yes," the war refugee blurted in a tiny voice.

"Afghanistan! Man, I love that country!"

So there you have it. If only we would stop loving so many countries, the Bulls Knits of the world won't have to come here in ragged droves to ride our hellish buses and snag our worst jobs, and our goofy young men won't have to assist the very people they had just bombed or droned. Our young ladies also won't have as many chances to learn how to mispronounce "hello," "good" and "candy" in Serbian, Arabic, Urdu or Somali, etc., but that's a loss I think we can handle.

With killing and looting making up the DNA of any empire, however, we won't veer from our bloody ways, at least not of our own volition, though with the US of A rapidly winding down and entering its autophagous phase, state-sponsored butchering and mugging will be increasingly performed in your face and on your body. Hell has come home.

LEGGING IT IN LOS ANGELES

4-19-13—Sightseeing buses are for those who deeply dread the places they're visiting. You can't really see a city or town from a motorized anything, so if you claim to have driven through Los Angeles, for example, you haven't seen it. The speed and protection of a car prevents you from being anywhere except inside your car, with what's outside rushing by so fast that each face, tree and building is rudely dismissed by the next, next and next. You can't pause, come closer, examine, converse, sniff or step on something, so what's the point of visiting Los Angeles like this, except to say that you've been there.

Like television, the private automobile was invented to wean us off our own humanity. From each, we've learned how to amp up our impatience and indifference towards everything, and with life itself. Anything that's seen through a screen or windshield becomes ephemera, with its death nearly instant. You don't have to switch channels or run over it, it will disappear by itself. All screens and windshields have been erected to block us from intercourse. Of course, I'm writing this on a screen, and you may read it, patient reader, while staring at a screen. Screen-bound, then, let's visit Los Angeles.

UC Berkeley hosted me for a month, and I used my time in Northern California to explore a bunch of places, but with my academic responsibilities done, I decided to take a Megabus to Los Angeles, a city I had only visited a handful of times, and knew hardly at all. Evelyn Waugh wrote, "There is no place that isn't worth visiting once." I'll amend that to say, "There is no place that isn't worth visiting a bunch of times, with each subsequent visit richer than the last."

My coach rolled into Union Station at 3 a.m., and right outside I encountered the homeless, with their belongings stored in trash bags or beat-up suitcases. I then crossed LA Plaza, where many more homeless slept around a statue of a priest brandishing a crucifix. From afar I assumed it was Saint Francis Xavier, the dude who brought the Inquisition to India, complete with slow and methodical mutilation of children, with their parents' eyelids removed so they could not shut out the blessed spectacle, and women raped by rapiers, and men's penises hacked off, you know, the entire package, but thank God, up-close I discovered it was only Father Junípero Serra, who merely beat his Indians, as far as we know. American Indians, East Indians, whatever, all you can do is convert them to Catholicism, blue jeans, knife and fork, happy hours, Monsanto, a lousy cheeseburger or neoliberalism. It's all good.

Crossing Main, I then saw perhaps a hundred people lying on the grounds of Nuestra Señora Reina de Los Ángeles, a beautiful church founded in 1784. Some folks were in tents but most were just under a blanket, prone or curled up on cardboard, with shopping carts, bags and the occasional bicycle parked near them. Blue, green or yellow tarps were tied to fences to make up half-assed lean-tos. In the dark, a handful of souls were rising. One man quietly pissed. Waiting for a free breakfast at 5:30, another gent asked me what time it was. On Spring, I encountered dozens of tents on both sides of the street. In late 2009, I had been precisely here but hadn't see any of this, so these tents had only accrued in the last few years, with many more coming, I'm sure, unless the authorities decide to raze, with their occupants chased to another part of town. Magnificent City Hall was only two blocks away.

Across the country, I've seen many small flags stuck to tents, as if to declare that this, too, is America, and of course it is, and becoming more representative by the day. Though they flaunt no political signs, these tents on concrete or city grass are no less of a statement and indictment than the Occupy encampments. In fact, I'd say that they are more so, since you don't have to read anything to understand exactly what they mean. No joking or contradictory messages distract from the fact that hundreds of thousands of Americans have been reduced to living like savages in this self-proclaimed greatest country on earth.

In Oakland, a man in his early sixties said to me, "Human beings are not supposed to live like this. Look at the birds and squirrels. They can go where they want and sleep where they want. These animals can piss and shit where they want and still look civilized. Man, I'd rather be an animal!"

Many of our homeless are also in wheelchairs, so this is how we treat our lame, feeble and sick, even the horribly injured or diseased. In Berkeley, there's a diaper-wearing homeless man with a huge blood and pus-caked wound on the right side of his head, yet he's forced to be outside from before dawn until early evening. Around the Downtown Berkeley station he hovers each day, to be ignored, mostly, by the thousands who walk by him, the way one instinctively averts one's eyes from a piece of shit on the ground.

Our criminal bankers, meanwhile, are kept in high style with billion-dollar bailout after bailout, as served up, shuffling and grinning, by our criminal politicians, with the entire criminal enterprise sanctioned by American voters, whether conservatives, liberals or progressives, and explained away or ignored by our moronic or dishonest intellectuals. It's no wonder we're bankrupt. Critical thinking is dead in this country, at least in the public sphere, for the most serious and urgent questions are never asked, or only briefly aired to be ridiculed.

Iconic LA City Hall is something to behold, all right. Erected in 1928, it was retrofitted in 2001 to be "base-isolated," that is, it can now withstand, supposedly, an 8.2 earthquake, so as Los Angelenos freebase from Burbank to Gardena, City Hall itself is hovering over nothing while running on fumes. Bankrupt by the crooked banks, it has also seen its manufacturing, residents and even porn stars fleeing to less arid pastures. LA's unemployment rate is among the highest in the nation.

It was still predawn when I made it to 5th and Broadway, and who did

I run into but the appropriately named Eric Hurt. Born in Compton, Hurt went to San Jose State and was signed by the Dallas Cowboys as an undrafted free agent. A cornerback, he played four games on special team, and returned four kickoffs for an average of 17.8 yards, with a long of 24 yards. Several injuries ended his career after one season. Hurt is now fifty-five years old and homeless. To prove that he was an NFL player, Hurt carries, at all times, a Cowboys team photo from 1980. Hey, at least this still confident-looking man got to cradle that fabled pigskin four times before he got knocked stupid into 2013.

Across the street from Hurt I saw two people sleeping in front of Rite Aid, then half a block away, an old, white-bearded guy lying in front of a shuttered store, and what was his name but "Storm."

"Storm?!"

"Yeah, like the weather. That's my name."

Not to sound superstitious, but, parents, please don't tempt fate by naming your child Earthquake or Mudslide, especially if you live in LA, and if you're an aspiring athlete and your first or last name is Hurt, Spavin, Concussion or Lame, then maybe you should consider changing it. Of course, just calling your offspring Richard or Jewel doesn't mean that he or she won't end up on Skid Row.

It was now around 5:30, so buses were already delivering workers downtown. Many got off one, just to wait for another. Most of these early risers were Hispanic, I noticed. In the orange glow of the still lit street-lights, they hurried past Broadway's clothing stores, electronics shops, restaurants and botanicas. A black sanitation worker swept, while a white cop on a Segway woke up a sleeping woman, "You have to move on." She sat up groggily, a middle-aged woman all alone on a dirty sidewalk, but plopped right down as soon as he was gone. To prevent it from being stolen, she was lying on the handle of her collapsible shopping cart.

It was now light, and I had made my way to Skid Row. Nearly five thousand homeless people live here. On sidewalk after sidewalk, they have set up their crude dwellings made up mostly of tarps and cardboard. I saw shopping carts all over, and a few bicycles. Bodies lay on cardboard, bed-ding or sometimes just concrete, but trash was generally confined to trash cans. There was a commotion at 5th and Gladys, with cops and an ambulance, and people were speculating that it might have been a stabbing.

I talked to Fred, a Hispanic man in his mid-forties, and he said he would have to move to another block since one of his neighbors was too volatile, and perhaps not quite right in the head, "I just don't feel safe around that guy." I offered to buy him a beer, but he said he had stopped drinking. "If I had one, then I'd need another, then another," he chuckled. Then how about a coffee? No, he said. He didn't need anything.

On LA's Skid Row, destitution is on vivid display and goes on for block after bustling block. Warmly lit by the Southern California sun, squalor is bright and lively here. Even in winter, a light coat is sufficient, and most folks don't need to wear two or three pairs of pants to keep warm. Stores and restaurants are few and not of the best quality, of course, but you can also get what you need from an underground economy. If your pants are too raggedy, you can buy a new pair for no more than $5 from this man right here, and this upstart entrepreneur ambling around with a slightly used blanket will let you have it for $2, after some haggling. I saw a security guard buy a charity shirt from a homeless guy, which didn't surprise me in the least, for the rent-a-cop lived on a fixed budget too. One pink slip and he might end up on Skid Row.

I walked for a few blocks but could find no store that sold beer, for having eaten only a Boston Kreme for breakfast I was getting hungry again, and since I didn't want to waste time in some eatery, at least not yet, a cold, tall can of yeast would have to do. I hollered at a random dude, "Yo, where can you get some beer around here?" Follow me, he said, then led me to a fat man sitting on a folding chair next to a cooler, from whom I bought a Colt 45 for me and a Steel Reserve, alcohol content 6 percent, no less, for my guide. They cost but $1.50 apiece, though after dark, it would be $2.

It was thus I met Jay, who told me he had worked all sorts of jobs, at a store, in a factory making aluminum siding, and as a security guard at a warehouse. He had a wife who stayed at home and had a lover, or lovers, he suspected, for she was becoming increasingly distant towards him, and when he got home early one day, said to him, "What are you doing here?" in a way that irritated him no end, and from which he never recovered. He finally placed his wedding ring and a brief yet carefully worded note on his pillow, and left before she woke up. They never saw each other again. Jay then boasted of other women, and of a threesome escapade, after which he was tipped $200 by one of his lovers.

"What about the other one?"

"She liked it too."

"But two hundred bucks?! Man, come on, you got to be shittin' me!"

"You know what they say, Once you try black, you'll never go back."

Oh, why was I born a scrounging shadow of a poet, and not a resplendent, strutting gigolo? And with my luck, my threesome would have me permanently locked in a room, *No Exit* style, with my mother and mother-in-law, Herr Doktor Freud.

Continuing my interrogation, I then asked, "Hey, how do you get pussy on Skid Row?"

"For you?"

"No, for you."

"Shit, man, it is easier to get pussy here than it is to get food!" Jay did add, "It won't be high-grade pussy, but it is still pussy."

Leaving Jay, I thought I had exhausted this line of inquiry, but then I met Johnny Velasco. Clean and trim, Johnny looked younger than his fifty-three years, and his living area was also neat and clean. Mike, in a blue muscle T and blue Nike cap, worn backwards, sat on a canvas chair. Peacefully dozing, he never got up to burp a single word, even as Johnny waxed insanities about him. Per Johnny, Mike was the coolest guy in the world, practically, "He's like the Dos Equis man! Women come down from Brentwood to pick him up!"

"If he's so cool, what the fuck is he doing on Skid Row?"

"He's just chillin', man, he doesn't need to be here. He's just relaxing."

So here we had our second gigolo, one still extant, and not reminiscing. Like paunchy middle-aged guys scampering to Bangkok, or Japanese broads landing in Java, a few Brentwood housewives or caress-less bachelorettes have discovered the comforts of really cheap loving. At this rate, they can hang on to their cuddly toy for a week or more, or until they get sick of their chatty dildo, all without having to endure jet lag or airport groping. Why fly to the Third World when it is already here, and becoming more pronounced by the day?

For those with lots of cash stashed away, the coming years will be an orgy of cheap thrills dished up for next to nothing by a ballooning army of increasingly desperate Americans. They won't just screw us figuratively, then toss us a penny. They will do it literally.

CONCRETE OAKLAND

4-24-13—Other people's lives come fluttering to us in the tiniest fragments, and these we gather, when we bother to, into an incoherent jumble of impressions we pass off as knowledge. Further, our ears, eyes and mind are all seriously defective and worn-down, making intelligence a dodgy proposition, at best. Our memory also crashes daily, if not secondly, our verbal skills poor, and when we examine ourselves, there are the added distortions of endless exculpation and vainglory. In short, no one knows ish about ish, though some ish does get much closer to the real ish. One thing for sure, amigo, if you ain't aiming for ish, you ain't gonna get ish.

From behind my cranium, a reflective voice, "As you get older, more things happen, you know what I mean, and it's not much fun either." The speaker is a middle-aged white male, talking to another suspect of a similar description. They have both committed a list of crimes, small, large and unspeakable, too long and various to summarize here. Eager to please, speaker has a sweet tendency to laugh uproariously at the slightest joke or witticism hacked up from any vocal cord, no matter how stupidly inspired or ineptly delivered. Speaker is traveling from Denver to Elko, Nevada.

Four feet behind my brain stem, another voice, on another bus, "Dude, I lost my virginity in a sedan, and it was like the most gnarly experience ever. I don't know how people have sex in a car. Dude, you might as well get out and lay on the ground. I'd rather have sex on fuckin' mud!"

Speaker is a young white male chatting up a young black female. It is unclear why he keeps addressing her as "dude."

Now, permit me to hand you a chunkier fragment of life. We have just passed Winter Park, Colorado, and sitting next to us is a white male in his late thirties. From Denver to Salt Lake City, he will not buy food or drink at any rest stop, but only smoke. If you look down, you will see a loaf of Bimbo in his duffel bag. White bread is all he has chewed on since Tulsa, and will eat until Boise, where he has a sister. Siblings will then drive to Vegas, where they can blow at least part of the sister's $4,000 tax return, "We won't gamble much, maybe just $30 or $40 at a time." Fun over, they'll head to Bakersfield, California, to see relatives. He will be away from home three weeks. Now, any man who can be gone that long is likely unemployed, and broke too, obviously, unless he is a rabid fan of Bimbo, for whom nothing but Bimbo will do.

Now, excuse me for a sec, for I must reach inside my shirt and pants to scratch myself. When you sit on a bus for too long, whatever skin issues you have simply blossom! Tissues flake, scale, crack and even ooze something like Hawaiian Punch gone bad. Thus gross and itchy, I decided to get radical back in Kansas City, and, no, I didn't bomb its Federal Reserve Building. My solution was strictly personal, discreet, though *en plein air*. It had been snowing hard for hours, and the streets were mostly deserted. Having not washed in days, I decided to leave the bus station, filled as it was with blizzard and economic refugees, to crouch down by the side of a nearby building, take my pants off and rub snow on my inguinal regions. That's a fancy phrase to indicate my second, more candid head and adjacent backdoor, the one leading to the lugubrious dumpster. I froze my nuts off, but felt super clean afterwards, cleaner than I had ever been, in fact, on this phantasmagoric earth.

Constantly exposed, thus deprived of privacy, for just a few days, I was already getting weird, so it's hardly surprising that many who have to be outside all the time are borderline mad, if not ravingly so. Denied the silence and space to reflect, they often argue with themselves out loud, as if to shut up and shut out the unceasing white noise. In Oakland, I saw a young woman, draped with a thin comforter, who'd crouch down often to pick something from the ground. At first I thought she was scavenging cigarette butts, then I realized she was picking up anything that wasn't stuck to the sidewalk, a tiny scrap of paper, a dry leaf, a match stump, a candy wrapper . . . Not content to pick up the pieces, she'd kneel down on the concrete to arrange them, to give them order and meaning.

Grinning goofily, she danced jerkily for half a minute. She had on a hooded plaid jacket, black pants, blue sneakers and a dangling plastic earring. Her hair was sheared short. For nearly an hour, she loitered in front of an all-night convenience store, the one with Marilyn Monroe and the King of Pop on its walls, and Obama and lottery ads in its window. The proprietors, an Indian couple, had to keep their eye out for shoplifters and those sneaking coffee refills. Thinking a passerby had addressed her, she answered him, but the dude coldly replied, "I wasn't talking to you." A man tossed a still longish butt on the ground, so I pointed it out to our dancing scrounger. She snatched it. Wanting to find out what's up, I decided to buy two tallboys of Tecate from a store half a mile away. None was closer. "Sweet," she said when I finally handed her a beer. We were sitting in a bus shelter. It was chilly enough that night.

"What's your name?"

"Jillian," she grinned. "Jill."

"How old are you?"

"Twenty-seven."

"You don't look twenty-seven. You look maybe twenty-two, twenty-three."

"I'm twenty-seven."

"How long have you been on the streets?"

"Two and a half months."

"You should go home. Oakland's fucked up. Where are you from?"

"Oregon."

"Where in Oregon? What town?"

"It's near Canada."

"Canada?!" I laughed. "Canada is not next to Oregon. Where are you really from?"

"Here and there. I've lived in Riverside."

"Riverside is not in Oregon. Where's your mom?"

"I talk to my mom every day."

"Oh yeah? How do you talk to her, with a phone card?"

"I talk to her in my head."

A man in his forties came by and offered Jill cigarettes for what remained of her beer, less than half a can. Without hesitation, she gave it up for two cigs. He swigged, then shared that he was getting off the streets the very next night, having found a single occupancy room in San Francisco for $135 a week.

Jill's face may be in post offices across the country, as "MISSING," or probably not. Maybe no one's missing her. Up in Berkeley, there are hundreds of young people living on the streets, but those tend to band together, or at least pair up. This one was alone. I bought Jill a warm coffee from the lousy store, and she gave me a green pill. She popped three, so I ate mine, for it is impolite to refuse anything that someone else deems appropriate for her own mouth and body, be it possum, field rat or whatever American youths feel they must ingest to endure an absurd present and rudderless future, as wrecked by their elders.

Of course that was stupid, for I don't even do drugs, and am adverse to all pills, even the common aspirin. In fact, I dread, fear and deeply, deeply despise all chemicals, chemistry and even chemists, and never pass one without giving him the meanest look. My potassium, sodium, chloride and phosphorous-laden blood rapidly boils at the sight of any periodic table. If I see a pharmacy, I cross the street. (Are you happy now, Mrs. Reagan, or should I say, Are you, by chance, high on your pills, ma'am?) Yes, sometimes you must say no, but all in all, you should say yes to just about everything that's offered without malice or commerce in mind. Great travel writer Paul Theroux doesn't eat meat, and V.S. Naipaul doesn't drink alcohol, so they are missing out on a very important bonding ritual with their subjects, I think. If you come to my resplendent mud hut, you better swallow what I slop in front of you.

When Jill started to walk north, away from relatively safer downtown,

I shouted after her, "You should stay at the square," meaning Frank Ogawa Plaza, where the Occupy encampment was, by the way, "You shouldn't walk that way." But she kept going and going, while picking up pieces of nothing along the way.

What is madness, anyway? I mean, who isn't insane in various ways, none all too subtle, for there is no person who isn't farcically deluded and mad, none except me, of course, though I'm foggily aware of Ben Franklin's foggy observation, "Each mofo walks around in a fog, but since the air seems clear around each, he doesn't know he's in a fog." Who's to argue with Philly's greatest MC ever? Of course, Ben's right. We're all fogged up, and being exposed to the elements day and night, and in constant danger of being robbed, raped or killed, won't likely clear up anyone's head. Near Oakland's Lake Merritt, I saw a man trying to cross the street in a wheelchair, so I gave him a push.

"Where are you going?"

"That bus stop right there."

"OK, I'll push you. It's a lot easier for me."

"You got that right."

Jeff was his name, and he had lost his right foot in a motorcycle accident. In Daly City, I'd see a bumper sticker, "OUR NATIONAL HEALTH PLAN. DON'T GET SICK!" And don't get amputated or brain-damaged either, not even for Uncle Sam, for you may end up on your local sidewalk after leaving your mind, limbs or mama maker in Iraq. The parade's over, if there was one. In Richmond, I'd run into a poster, "I left the nightmare of war only to find myself in a [sic] another. Are you a homeless veteran?"

"Hey, man, you want a beer? I'll cross the street to get us some."

"No, that's all right, I already have beer, and you can have one too if you like. It's in my bag."

"No, man, I'm not going to take your beer."

Though not a veteran of the explosive streets of Baghdad, but merely the shaded and elegant promenades of picturesque Oakland, as stewarded by the just, wise, measured and upright Jean Quan, Jeff had clearly gone mad, for he slurred, "I have two houses, man, and you can stay in one if you like. It's a little small but it's nice. We'll take the bus there. It's only ten minutes away."

"If you own two houses, what are you doing on the streets?"

"No, man, I'm not on the streets. I'm not. Do you want a beer? I have beer."

It was awfully cold that evening, and Jeff was shivering as he spoke. A bus came, but Jeff made no effort to get on. I'm not sure he would be allowed to board it, in any case, not that he had anywhere to go, really. Though he didn't look terribly dirty, Jeff did reek of days-old sweat and urine. He smelled homeless. Another bus came, then another, but Jeff would stay outside all night, as he had so many nights.

I went back to the same area on other days, but never saw Jeff again. I did encounter "the guided one," however, a man in his sixties with stringy salt-and-pepper whiskers, and a cap over his hoodie. Mahdi's belongings were stacked on two shopping carts and a most unusual, highly modified bicycle, and they weren't together but in three spots, over some distance. I'd think that if you didn't have a door and lock, you'd want to keep all your stuffs within immediate reach, to prevent them from walking away, but clearly Mahdi was willing to sacrifice this security to stake out a vaster territory. In his own way, he was practicing imperial overreach.

Of course, Mahdi's no emperor of anything, not even of ice cream. He has lost all but a few scraps, with even his ideas stolen from him, "I see these houses all over Oakland painted in the color scheme I came up with years ago. People are making lots of money from these fancy houses, but they're using my color scheme, and I'm not getting a penny from it."

"What color scheme are you talking about?"

"It's purple, green and brown. You see it everywhere, but, you know, sometimes they change it slightly. I came up with this color scheme years ago, decades ago! It has spiritual significance, for it brings harmony to all those who dwell within. You will feel calmer, you hear me, just by looking at it. Remember: purple, green and brown. I call it my Intergalactical Cosmic Color Scheme."

If Mahdi had three drummers behind him, you might mistake him for

Sun Ra. OK, I'm sorry, Mr. Ra, for you are the man! And a Philly badass, no less, just like B. Franklin!

Not content to steal Mahdi's color scheme, the ungrateful world will soon snatch from him an even greater invention, Mahdi's magnificent sleeping bicycle. Attached to the frame is a cubicle, made of cardboard and milk crates, where you can actually lie down. You can't pedal while reclining, however, but then an RV owner can't sleep and drive either. In any case, Mahdi's invention is surely the RV of the future. After Social Security is finally wiped out, a retiring worker can be sent off with one of these tiny apartments on wheels, and when he dies, it will also serve, conveniently and economically, as his coffin. Seeing Mahdi's ingenious bike, smartasses had dubbed it all sorts of insulting names, "One guy called it the ghetto train, but this isn't a train, and it's not ghetto. Once they've stolen my idea, they'll mass-produce my bike and make lots of money. You will see it all over Oakland, and all over America."

You won't see any bizarre homeless contraption in Jack London Square, however, for it is spic-and-span and dominated by upscale restaurants. Should London's ghost amble from his Klondike Gold Rush cabin, now preserved on the square, this friend of the downtrodden would be aghast to be surrounded on all sides by bankers, stockbrokers, lawyers, "civic leaders" and assorted war profiteers kicking it back in luxurious surroundings, while enjoying filet mignon, lobster and Chardonnay, as served up by the loveliest daughters of the working class, of course, while their uglier cousins are left huddling in tents, not half a mile away.

Chased by the sky-high rent in San Francisco, not to mention Berkeley, yuppies and hipsters alike are fleeing to Oakland, fueling a mini boom in select neighborhoods, but much of the city is still a desolate mess, with homeless people everywhere. Pushing shopping carts, they scavenge for plastic and aluminum. Outside the Alameda County Administration building, they set up tents each night, and remove them each dawn, with their area hosed down by custodians, before the first clerks and secretaries arrive. Overflowing from San Francisco's Chinatown, Asian immigrants, mostly Chinese, have also given Oakland an economic boost, with hundreds of stores and restaurants opening. Oakland's Chinatown's cheap eats have naturally attracted the homeless. I saw a man buy some lo mein, with bits of vegetables and pork, for just $1.50, haggled down from two bucks. The owner, a Vietnamese woman, said that at the end of each day, she'd give food to three homeless guys, one black, one white and one Chinese. At another dirt cheap joint, I saw a homeless man enjoy rice gruel with traces of chicken and preserved egg, plus a decent pork bun, for just $1.75 and 55 cents, respectively. The self-served tea was free and unlimited. On three chairs at his table were trash bags holding his possessions.

In Oakland's Chinatown, then, our destitute mingle with their more fortunate neighbors and with tourists. Some sleep on its sidewalks, while more dwell in tents, on its fringe. A family has wisely placed their tent on the other side of a fence meant to keep pedestrians from straying onto a freeway exit ramp. This fence now protects, among other things, their little girl's pink bike.

Another sad and increasingly common feature of American life also makes a daily appearance in Chinatown. Each morning, at 8 a.m., at least six full buses depart for various casinos. Years ago, one had to trek to Reno to lose one's shirt, but now, there are "gaming facilities" all over Northern California, and the Chinese, long susceptible to gambling, are only too eager to get burned. Solemnly they return from their wallet-emptying excursion, with that free bowl of duck noodles their only winning for the day. Soon, though, they will head back to the slots and tables, to get fleeced again and again.

For a taste of local entertainment, I went to a *Tourettes Without Regrets* show. Hugely popular with those in their twenties and thirties, this episodic event is split in two parts, with the first billed as a "psychotic erotic vaudeville showcase." It turned out to be a series of monologists stridently defending their sexual orientation, access, performance and misery. It was all about sex, and terrible sex at that, yet judging by the many hoots, hollers and appreciative laughs, it was very cathartic for the audience. The second part was a poetry slam, with aggressive rhymers pitted against each other to boast and trade insults. Again, the tone was insanely strident. This night's one focus, its lone star, so to speak, was a petty and narcissistic ego that had to scream to the world that it was indeed happy and somehow fuckable. Under no disguise did love or any emotion akin to it make an appearance that night, and "you" was nearly always accompanied by an insult or accusation. The social and political were also no-shows. It was all about the solipsistic self, and the defiant defense of such. To many of us today, that's social and political enough.

SAN JOSE SHEEN

5-1-13—As every story is a meandering road, each road is also a story, or, more accurately, an infinity of stories. An abandoned trail that leads from nowhere to nowhere, with no wayfarers, only a rare roadrunner, snake or javelina, would still be an endless source of human-interest tales, or, more likely, tails. Haven't you heard of the ancient saying, "Even the fool is wise after the Interstate," especially if he drives off its exits often? Though a stuttering man of few sentences, terrible eyesight and beer-fizzled memory, I have managed to drag back a sackful of observations from my snooping around San Jose's Story Road.

Each of my visits to San Jose is a kind of homecoming, for my father, brother and, uh, absolutely composed, considerate and non-screaming stepmother are still here, and have lived here for decades. Though I have no sentimental attachment to this place, I also don't hate it. Personal crap can be tedious, and I'm not trying to bore you, only clarifying that I have my own rather lengthy Story Road in San Jose.

When I arrived in San Jose in 1978, it wasn't yet the much-lauded Silicon Valley, but simply a dozing, loudly snoring place, with orange groves even, a kind of Gilroy but with the ten-story Hotel De Anza.

My family lived on Locke Drive, a longish cul-de-sac facing the city dump. You could smell it day and night, saw it the moment you stepped outside. At a nearby creek, my brother and I caught crawfish which we brought home to be cooked, then ate with relish, *including* the shells. Those were our Red Lobster nights. Dumbass immigrants. We were on food stamps. My father operated an unlicensed bodega from his garage, kept ducks in the backyard, even pigeons in a homemade cage. Whenever a customer pointed to a specific bird, it was my job to catch the fleeing fowl. To clear the brush for his duck venture, my father, without a doubt the most solipsistic man I've ever encountered, used a flaming rolled-up newspaper as tinder and almost torched the neighborhood. It was the Fourth of July, so Angelo, our Puerto Rican neighbor, shouted when the fire truck arrived, "Goddamn kids with their firecrackers!" Angelo was one of the few non-Vietnamese left on a street dubbed *xóm rác*, the garbage ghetto. Imagine all the toxics leaching into the ground, creek, then crawfish. If not for the Jameson treatment I liberally applied in my twenties, I would be aglow with poisons.

I watched minor league baseball, inspected faux Egyptian artifacts. There was even less art and culture in San Jose back then, as if that's possible. On television, a somber message, "The San Jose Art Museum. Ignore it and it will go away." Down in Monterey, they claim John Steinbeck, and up in Oakland, there's a huge upscale-dining complex named after Jack London, but San Jose has no native writers to mummify, trot out or turn into a piñata for tourists to whack at. That's because no writer has ever lived in San Jose, and no notable artist either. (Yes, Mark Tansey spent some time here, but that's about it, and that's super lame for a major American city.) Now, I'm not saying that as soon as a bona fide wordsmith steps foot in San Jose, all the air will rush from his body, and all the blood too, but the Bay's crotch has been creatively impotent.

By 2007, the computer industry has transformed San Jose into the wealthiest metropolis in the entire country, and with all this cash came a sheen of sophistication. Not only didn't the San Jose Art Museum slink away, it now regularly features pretty hip shows, as with its current exhibits of Eric Fischl and contemporary Chinese photography. Downtown, the charmingly seedy dives have been replaced by bistros, gastro pubs and martini lounges, and in the beautifully designed and manicured Santana Row, sexy people come out to browse Guccis, Ferragamos and Teslas. Cushioned armchairs and couches are placed outside, under shady trees. Roses, tulips and daisies bloom. Here, even a toilet scrubber is decently attired, though there's nothing you can do about the lowlife tourists who infiltrate to ogle and buy nothing, save perhaps a cup of joe from Peet's. Draped in markdown merchandise from Ross, the "Dress for Less" store, they annoyingly blight this gorgeous tableau. There ought to be a law, people, a dress code to shoo away these corny riffraff, though the snapshots they post on Flickr do provide free advertising. It's not worth it.

Suddenly I remember that I was supposed to give you a quickie tour of Story Road, so let's go there, right now, and begin with the charmingly named Chot Nho Café, which in Vietnamese means the "Suddenly Remember Café." No city outside Vietnam has as many Vietnamese as San Jose, where they make up 10.4 percent of the population. Like the Indian-run convenience store, Vietnamese nail salons have become a national institution, familiar to Americans from Anchorage to Key West, but the Vietnamese nudie coffee houses are, so far, limited to California. A what coffee house? Well, let's go in and find out.

It is just before noon, and the place is packed. Five nearly naked women, four Vietnamese and one white, are walking around serving hot and iced coffees, at $5 a glass, and free hot and iced tea, frequently refilled. Eighty five percent of the clientele are Vietnamese men, with most over forty years old, including a handful of white haired elders. At a central table, a Hispanic and a black guy are playing cards, and along one wall, there are a dozen video poker machines. What really overwhelms the senses are the loud hip-hop and the twenty TV screens around the walls, showing sports nonstop, with one reserved for CNN. As if this weren't enough, you can also order a plate of rice or noodles. So sit back and enjoy Premier League and Serie A soccer, endless ESPN analysis of anything that was tossed, thrown or bounced last night, Anderson Cooper looking so earnest, Lil Wayne hollering, "I don't use rubbers, and I don't plan no kids, girl," an iced coffee with way too much ice, and shadowy flesh fluttering by. Don't stare too hard, now. Presently, one of the women is dancing on the brightly lit counter and flashing her touching assets. In Silicon Valley, she's showing off her silicone peaks.

With its emphasis on staring, and not touching, talking or any other kind of interaction, not even eye contact, and with its insane bombardment of the senses, what's happening in this café is essentially an American phenomenon, in spite of its Vietnamese cosmetic touches. In a Saigon sex café or karaoke bar, a male client would talk, grope and sing along with his hostess, they would have to deal with each other as individuals, no matter how phony or bizarre their interactions, but here both partners are relieved of this physical and psychic intercourse. Here, we dread the face-to-face contact, for the face, any face, is too intense for us. We flee each other's faces by hiding our faces in Facebook. Oh please, don't make me look at your face again, for it is simply too sexy, beautiful, sad and grotesque, and please, don't look at my eyes, nose, mouth and forehead with your mercy or judgment. Look at my photos, and I'll look at yours, OK?

Across the street from Chot Nho Café are two spiffy shopping centers, Grand Century and Vietnam Town. They are owned by the same man, Tang Lap. Let's quickly examine the ups and downs of this developer's resume, for they reflect larger economic trends. Grand Century opened in 2001 and quickly became the center of Vietnamese commercial and social life in San Jose. Pumped by its success, Tang and other Vietnamese-American investors then bought a struggling mall, Vallco Fashion Park, for $80 million in 2005. Vallco only had a 24 percent occupancy rate, but Tang clearly thought he could revive it. He was wrong. The economic crash that began in late 2007 only made matters much worse. Original investors bailed out, others dove in, and by 2009, Tang and his crew were desperately trying to dump their disaster on any sucker. With no fools nearby, Tang was forced to cast his nest wide, and who did he snare but a food processing magnate in distant Ho Chi Minh City, one Tram Be. Be paid Tang $64 million cash. His nose still bleeding, Be can now boast to his boozing buddies that he owns an American shopping mall, one with Macy's, Sears, JCPenney, a sixteen-screen AMC theater and a "glow in the dark" bowling alley. His mall has the "making of an international lifestyle center," he can slur, quoting his own brochure, before he's cut off by a wiseass, "Hey, Be, on my recent trip to San Jose, I stopped by your mall to admire it, but I saw almost no one in there. I thought I had walked in on a bomb drill or something, for all I could see was a few security guys. The food court was empty, the stores were empty, so what's up with that, Be?"

Swallowing the recovery jive dished up daily by the US mainstream media, Be probably still thinks he will get the last laugh, for when the US economy is back on its feet again, his dismal mall will be filled with frolicking consumers shoving and stepping on each other to buy anything and everything. His merchants won't be months late on their rents, and the food court will be overflowing with jiggly folks washing down mounds of fried stuff with rivers of fizzy corn syrup.

Tang knows better. Though he was lucky to salvage a hubcap or two from his Vallco wreck, he was still stuck with Vietnam Town, his most ambitious project ever. This huge mall of 185 units was supposed to be finished in 2007, yet stands mostly empty even now. The bank that funded it went bankrupt itself, and the new bank that took over the debt started to foreclose on Tang, which forced him to declare bankruptcy. Prospective merchants who had forked over huge deposits couldn't cover their balances, for banks' lending standards had stiffened and housing prices had plummeted, making less available as collateral. What a mess is right, though driving by on Story Road, you might think that all is well, that here is a salient example of the Vietnamese-American success story.

Vietnam Town is adjacent to Grand Century, so it was obviously conceived by Tang to be an extension of his older mall, but why would you want to concentrate so many Vietnamese businesses in one place? If you line up, say, five pho joints in a row, the competition among them will drive prices down, hurting their bottom line, then knock out the weakest, but what's terrible for business is often great for consumers. Cutthroat competition also forces innovations, and since we're already in Vietnam Town, let's step inside Pho 90° to sample some unusual dishes such as oxtail pho, pho with Kobe beef or pho with smoked veal. Yum, yum, yum. I know that's a lot of food, but don't worry, it's my treat.

On the back wall of Pho 90° is a large mural of Florence, with its unmistakable Brunelleschi dome and Palazzo Vecchio. You might think that this is some leftover from a pizza joint, but no, it was commissioned by the current Vietnamese owner. Though this is as ridiculous as seeing a painted panorama of Hanoi in an Italian restaurant, none of the Vietnamese diners find it odd. Vietnamese have a penchant and high tolerance for the culturally incongruent. In most Vietnamese-American homes, you'll find videos of a Vietnamese variety show called *Paris by Night*, which is usually filmed in Las Vegas. In a Hanoi home, I saw a large portrait of Napoleon on a horse, though the owner, a well-known journalist and poet, no less, cared nothing about the Corsican. Nguyen Huy Thiep has a fictional nineteenth-century Frenchman observe that Vietnam has been raped by Chinese civilization, but it's also true that it has been raped by several other civilizations as well, including French and American, and here I should clarify that one need not invade or occupy a country to rape or impose one's sweating, huffing heft on it. Forced to repeatedly absorb the foreign on a massive scale, Vietnamese have adapted by eagerly adopting the alien, if only very superficially. I mean, most, if not all, of these diners don't know or care that this is Florence or even anywhere in Italy, and on a *Paris by Night* video, you might find Vietnamese dressed up as Mexicans and pretending to play mariachi.

Now we continue down Story Road, and it's odd to be walking, I agree, for no one walks in San Jose except the homeless. We've seen a few homeless people already, panhandling on median strips near Grand Century, but now we come upon tents lurking in the woods around Coyote Creek. Driving by, you might fleetingly glimpse a tent or two, but you must get out of your car and risk walking into the bushes to realize how large this encampment is, how damning this evidence of our economic, political and social collapse. Entire families live here, many with children. Look at that crib lying in the shade. Intending to stay a while, if not permanently, people have erected barriers and fences for privacy and to protect their few belongings. They use ice chests to keep food cold, cook with propane stoves. Thanks to San Jose's mild climate, no one risks freezing to death, but as in all tent cities, of which there are now hundreds, if not thousands, across this great, indispensable nation, sanitation is a huge problem. When not shooed away by a security guard, some of these homeless bathe at the fire hydrant at Story and Roberts, and the woods provide a breezy or sun-splashed bathroom. You can let everything hang out as you bequeath to this earth a portion of yourself, a kind of down payment towards death. If you decide not to go green, however, there are the nearby shopping malls. Sometimes these homeless even stray into Chot Nho Café to survey, if only too briefly, even more atavistic baring and bearings, before they're finally booted out.

San Jose is tolerating the Story Road tent city for now, but in March its police tore down a more conspicuous encampment near the airport. It's all about appearance, of course, for you can't have out-of-town visitors see destitution or squalor as their first impression of San Jose. Before the last Super Bowl, New Orleans also cleared out a large homeless community living by its train and bus station. As a nation, we also have no plans to fix our economic problems, only cosmetic touches to disguise them, such as the fixed unemployment and inflation rates, and constant media assurances that the recovery is on course, or even accelerating. Meanwhile, costly wars continue, as well as job outsourcing, dressed up as "free trade" agreements.

Between the splendor of Santana Row and the wretchedness of these tent cities, there is the ordinary San Jose of tacky strip malls and mostly pleasant-looking houses, and in these life is still going on as usual, no? Look again. Take Jay, who lives in this $400K house with his wife, Tracy. Born in 1970 in New Hampshire, Jay earned an engineering degree from Carnegie Mellon, then served nine years in the Navy, where he rose to become a commander of a nuclear submarine based in Philadelphia. Discharged, Jay moved to San Jose in 2002, where he worked for Digital Equipment Corporation, Compaq, Hewlett-Packard and, finally, AQT, from 2007 until now. (For reasons that will be obvious, I've disguised Jay's current employer.) Though a small company, AQT was raking in the bucks, and up until four years ago, had twenty-five well-paid employees. Jay was making $120,000 a year. With revenues down, the firing started, however, and now AQT is reduced to five workers, with their salaries slashed. Jay is only making $60,000 a year, not much in expensive San Jose, with its $4 gas and sky-high real estate, yet his boss, whom Jay sneeringly calls Ho Chi Kevin, sees this as a huge favor, for Jay's being paid for doing next to nothing. (Neither man is Vietnamese, by the way, but balding white guys, just in case you're wondering about the Ho reference.) To keep Jay occupied, Ho Chi Kevin often sends him out on stupid errands, "The other day he had me buy some apples for him but when I brought them back he said they weren't the right kind of apples!" Looking at me bug-eyed, Jay shook his head several times, "So I said, 'Well, what kind of fuckin' apples do you want?!' Actually, I didn't say fuckin', I just said, 'Well, what kind of apples do you want then?!'" And guess what, he couldn't even tell me! He just sent me out to get a different kind of apple, and I had to try several times before I got it right. Did I get an engineering degree for this? I used to run a nuclear submarine! Do you need an engineering degree to buy freakin' apples?!"

To be misused or unused has become our common lot. In nearly every field, corporate, military, civic, media, entertainment and academic, talent and integrity are wasted, if not punished, as ruthless crooks, groveling connivers and grinning morons rise to the top. Jay and I were sitting at an outdoor table outside AQT. It was working hours, but Jay was clearly not missed, for there was next to nothing for him to do inside. Hey, for 60 grand a year, most people wouldn't mind running back and forth to the supermarket for Fuji, Cortland, Granny Smith, Golden Delicious, Red Delicious, Blue Crappy, Pacific Rose, Gala, Ginger Rose, Monsanto Mutant or 666 Snake-Endorsed Special, whatever, boss, I'll get it for you! The ax can slam on Jay's neck at any moment, however, so he doesn't know if today will be his last at AQT. For four years now, Jay's been frantically trying to find another job, entry-level, whatever, but nothing has come through. "So what's Plan B?" I asked.

"I don't have a Plan B, but Plan C is to move to Taiwan to teach English." Jay's wife was born in Taipei. "I really don't want to do that. I am an American. I want to live in my own country."

Ho Chi Kevin is hanging onto his skeletal crew because he believes a recovery is just around the corner. Be, too, is waiting for a recovery, as are his tenants in their empty stores. In downtown's Cesar E. Chavez Plaza, the homeless also wait, but for what, they're not quite sure. Even as job applications are sent into the void, mortgage payments ignored, bankruptcies filed and tents spread in shadow or sun, San Jose still gleams from afar, or as you speed by in your car.

SLEEPWALKING IN CAMDEN

6-27-13—With 77,000 people, Camden has one public library left, and in a city where Walt Whitman spent nineteen years and is buried, there are exactly two bookstores, a Barnes and Noble serving Rutgers Camden students, and, not too far away, La Unique African American Books & Cultural Center, with *The Master Game*, *The New World Order*, *The Unseen Hand* and *Say It Like Obama* in its window. Camden has no hotel, and only one downtown bar, The Sixth Street Lounge. Hank's closed in 2010 after half a century in business. Now, if you can barely drink in the heart of any American city, no matter how tiny, you know it's seriously messed up.

Just off downtown, there's also Off Broadway, however. The first time I entered, four years ago, I noticed "NO PROFANITIES" on the wall, yet the very stern barkeep had this T-shirt on, "PRACTICE SAFE SEX. GO FUCK YOURSELF." You're finally home, I thought. On that occasion, I was able to make the acquaintance of Jamaal, a sixty-five-year-old former math teacher. A jazz lover, he told me his favorite concert ever was Art Blakey and the Jazz Messengers at NYC's Blue Note. We talked about Mickey Roker, who used to be the house drummer at Philly's Ortlieb's. I once had a cassette of Roker keeping time behind Dizzy and Ray Brown, but it was erased by an embittered, life-hating middle-aged Korean art student I had lent the tape to. I should be awarded a peace prize, or some chintzy ribbon at least, for not strangling this motherfucker. A bottle of Rolling Rock in Off Broadway was, and still is, only $1.50. Jamaal informed me, "This place is all right. It has an older crowd. You can go home at the end of the night."

"What's the alternative?" I asked.

"Someone beats you up or shoots you."

"I'd rather just go home."

"Me too."

In Camden, I had seen Wynton Marsalis at a free concert by the river. Like Baltimore, Camden has a safe tourist section, with a much smaller, grayer fish version of the celebrated aquarium. People who come to this protected enclave don't need to see the real Camden, not that they want to. They can even arrive and leave via a ferry from Philly.

Lying outside Camden's tiny bullet-free zone, the Walt Whitman House, on Martin Luther King Boulevard, gets almost no visitors, not that Americans are flocking to pay homage to their writers. Even during its days, this "coop" or "shanty," in Whitman's own words, was called "the worst house and the worst situated," and Camden was thriving back then, with its best decades still ahead. By the 1940s, Camden would become an industrial powerhouse, with many factories employing blacks and whites, and the largest shipyard in the world.

"Yo, Chris Rock, I'm at the Walt Whitman House."

"Run!"

In 2011, Ken Rose wanted to interview me by phone on July 4th, so I decided to do it in front of the Whitman House. On the day this country was born, I would not be in Philly, its birthplace, but Camden, its prototypical morgue. A habitually lawless government has no business celebrating the Constitution, and with this country being deliberately tortured and drowned by its rulers, accompanied by the flag-waving acquiescence of deranged voters, each Fourth of July has turned into a sick and sad spectacle. Across the street was the Camden County Jail, and on the next block, ABC Bail Bonds. Before Ken called, some guy shuffled up and said he was the caretaker of the Whitman home, but as we chatted, I soon realized he didn't even know who Walt Whitman was. He referred to Whitman in the present tense, as in, "He owns this entire row, including the parking lot right here." Predictably, he wanted me to give him some change.

Yes, some Camden folks will ask you for cash, but many will also offer you cigarettes, dope or sex. Here, illicit dealing is king. Also in 2011, I met Abdul, who was selling body oils, perfumes, knit hats and boxer shorts from a table set up in front of a fried chicken joint. After peddling stuff for seven years, business was getting worse and worse, so Abdul was planning on moving to Senegal, where he had a wife. Years ago, he had been busted for drugs, a wrongful conviction, he claimed, and locked up for three and a half years. In prison, he converted to Islam. Released, he visited Senegal. As he walked into a Western Union, the lady behind the counter exclaimed, "You're my husband! I saw you in a dream."

His wife was forty years old and "doesn't have a bad thought," Abdul said. "She can't be any better!" Since she didn't want to come to the States, he would go to her. He was having a house built over there for $20,000. He sent her boxes of old clothes to sell. "American clothes are popular in Senegal," he explained. "Even used clothes."

"Where do you get old clothes? Where do you buy them?"

"I don't buy them. I get them from my relatives!"

In 2012, I met another Black Muslim man, thirty-eightish, who also sold on the sidewalk, in his case socks from a wheeled cart. Across the street were the ruins of the Carnegie Library, so I said, "That was a beautiful building once!"

"I hear they're gonna fix it up."

"Really?! But the city is broke. Camden is broke."

"Camden is broke?"

"Yeah, man, Camden is broke. Philly is broke. The whole country is broke! Didn't you hear about all the cops they laid off?"

"They got money." He then read from the inscription on the building. "Nineteen-oh-four. Man, that building is old. How old is that? Thirty, forty years?"

"It was built in nineteen-oh-four, so it's over a hundred years old."

"Really?"

He told me about a cop who had given him a ticket for selling on the street, "The judge will throw it out, though, because I was sitting in a restaurant when he busted me."

"Yeah, but you'll still have to waste your time in court. What an ass-hole! Doesn't he have better things to do than to bust people trying to make a living? This city is so fucked up and he's busting you, and you're not hurting anybody."

"There is a lot of complaints about this guy."

"Is he an older guy?"

"No, a young cop, a young, white cop."

Whoever this cop was, he's gone, because Camden has laid off its entire police force. That's right, all 270 cops who survived previous layoffs were let go in April of 2013, though 50 were immediately hired by the county police that's now in charge of keeping Camden, um, safe. Announcing this restructuring, the mayor said, "We cannot sit back and allow our children and families to experience another 2012." Or another 2011, 2010 or 2009, etc., for year in, year out, this post-industrial city ranks as one of the deadliest in America. With its cops trimmed and shuffled, little has changed on Camden's streets, though there's a mobile observation tower across from the bus terminal. Inside that box is an anxious man with his head rotating nonstop, or a dozing schmuck, or no one at all, but you wouldn't know, would you? Instant panopticons are sprouting up everywhere, from theme park parking lots to your next mass protest. The Guardian Angels also made a cameo appearance in Camden, but have wisely disappeared. Unarmed, they'd stand an excellent chance of being peeled off the sidewalk, then rolled, posthaste, into Cooper Hospital, Camden's one world-class institution. Come to Camden, where you can be cut up or expire with distinction! World-class hands will stitch you up!

"Work here. Play here. Live here," shout the "LIVE CAMDEN" bill-boards, but until recently Baltimore also declared itself, "The Greatest City in America," and Milpitas, a place most people have never heard of, drapes banners all over its blink-and-miss downtown, trumpeting, "MILPITAS A Great American City." Whatever. What is Juarez' slogan, I wonder? Or Kabul's? Speaking of Cooper, I must tell you about Paul Matthews Young, whom I met in 2012 at the Broadway train stop. On a plate glass window, this fiftyish man had taped his New Jersey ID, Social Security card and about eight sheets of paper showing his "Monetarial Earning Assessment." It wasn't clear what he was trying to convey, to whom, or if it was some kind of protest. When he told me he had eighteen children, I asked, "With how many women?"

"None."

"What do you mean none?!"

"I had them by myself."

He said his eighteen kids were born microscopically from the tip of his penis. The doctors at Cooper had something to do with this, but I couldn't get him to explain fully the procedure beyond the fact that Paul had to pleasure himself quite energetically.

Hearing Paul's story give you that old, most generic notion? Now that you've got your cheap, discount sox made in China, you want some flesh also? Are you, by chance, versed in gonorrhea? You speak syphilis? Can you spell AIDS? It's not so much a carnal need, you say, but simply an ethereal desire to assist, or rather, nudge up, the local economy? See her, that's Angela. She looks about fourteen, but she might be as old as seventeen. Walking unsteadily, her eyes are practically closed, but she can see enough to tell that you're not serious. She'll keep walking because she has no time to lose. Each day, she can easily go through five or six bags of dope, plus some powder for variety, plus she has to eat, too, and maybe down a few cans of Steel Reserve to flush that lousy Chinese food, bought from Yuk's, yes, that's really the name, at 827 S. Broadway. I'm not making anything up. Why would I? No one knows anything about Angela, not even her best friend. Thirty-three-year-old Michelle regularly gives Angela food and dope, but Angela still won't say nothing about herself, and don't you give me that shit about her being too drugged to remember, because on one level or another, none of us ever forgets anything.

I won't forget walking with Michelle when she said, "That's my baby daddy," and she pointed to some guy across the street. Squinting, the dude was probably thinking, "What's my side piece doing with that chink [or fuckhead, or asshole]?" You know, anything but "gentleman" or "Asian American," per the *New York Times* stylistic guidelines. To think is already to compose, and thus to dissimulate and cover up, and to write is to further distort, nearly always, what we pretend to think, but writing, paradoxically, can be used to hint at the rawness beneath all this culture, this domestication, this farce, this composition. This half-assed exposé almost never happens, however. Maybe it has never happened. Looking hazy, dude kept squinting as if he had a hard time recognizing his lay even.

"It's Rashid's birthday!" Michelle shouted.

"Huh? What?"

"Rashid! It's Rashid's birthday today!"

Showing no emotion, no smile, no grimace, dude gave Michelle one final squint, then kept walking.

"He doesn't remember his son's name?" I chuckled.

"No, he remembers. Lamon's just a little out of it today."

"How old is Rashid?"

"Eight! He's eight years old!"

"And he stays with you?"

"No, with my mom."

"So your mom is not so bad after all."

"She might as well do something for him, since she didn't do shit for me!"

Though Michelle is one-quarter Okinawan, it's hard to see any Asianness on her white face. She was mostly raised by her Japanese grandma, but at sixteen, she moved to Camden. Already a cokehead, she got hooked on heroin at nineteen, thanks to her junkie uncle. Unable to pay for her daily treat, she started to trick, "I've been raped and beaten. Look," she opened her mouth, "these are dentures. I don't like to go with young black guys. They're fucked up! There are, like, nine guys who go around beating up girls."

"Just for the hell of it?"

"Yeah, just for the hell of it. This is Camden!"

"So what are you going to do? What's your next move?"

"I'd like to get into rehab, maybe go to Florida."

"What's in Florida?"

"I dunno. There's a good rehab place in Florida. My sister told me about it. I need to get out of Camden, that's for sure."

Her pale arms showed purple needle marks, and so did the tops of her hands. Her veins have collapsed. A blue-headed pin pierced her upper lip, a large hoop dangled from one ear, and her hair had been dyed a burnt siena or, more likely, was just a red wig. It was a very hot day, yet she was draped in a charcoal-colored hoodie, and her faded blue tank top had been rendered lumpy by a cheap, ill-fitting bra. For someone living rough for so long, Michelle still appeared fresh, so I said, "You know, you don't even look thirty-three years old. You actually look younger!"

"You think so? I used to be beautiful." She pulled two IDs from her cloth sack, showed them to me.

Holding one up against her face, I pronounced, "No, I think you actually look better now, but you better get the fuck out of Camden soon."

She smiled. Her dentures were newish, for they weren't too yellow. Maybe she had just gotten punched? Michelle then volunteered that Lamon may be pissed because she had been seen with another guy.

"Some guy you like? Some guy you love?"

"It does get lonely out here . . . Hey, you want to hear something weird? Just last night, this one girl got so fucked up, she took her clothes off and ran down the street."

The same night, twenty-year-old De'quan Rodgers was shot dead, and another young man, 19-years-old, was found with multiple bullet wounds. About three hours before I chatted with Michelle, three more men were perforated. Shootings are nearly daily occurrences here, but a young naked woman running down the street is goofy enough to be remarked upon, if only for the next 24 hours or so.

All over town, there are RIP messages spray-painted onto walls, near where a loved one has died, whether targeted or hit by stray slugs. Sunrise, sunset. Sunrise, sunset. You live and talk much shit until Jesus, Allah, Bruce Lee or Liberace texts you, "Kum home, losr." You strut about and blather *beaucoup de merde* until Glock, SKS or Bersa Thunder taps you on the shoulder and whispers, "Hiya!" Even as you crawl on all fours, sightless and toothless, with your liver, spleen and entrails hanging out, it's still too early to call it a night. Is it last call already? On a memorial for Izzy and Cunt, someone has scrawled, "Heaven is where we go but hell is where we live." On shop windows and doors are flyers begging for information on Camden's disappeared. Some have come to buy drugs, never to be seen again. Some were just strolling to the bodega or the Chinese joint's bulletproof window. Yuk's, it's so yummy!

Sorry, man, all you wanted was a beer and here I am dragging you down with talk of bullets, blood, gurneys, scalpels, needles and more blood, so much blood, blood geysers, showers of blood, so let's head straight into Off Broadway, without further delay. As if to negate the chaos outside, this dump has so many rules, dude, as in:

NO T-SHIRTS OR VEST
NO HATS TURNED AROUND BACKWARDS
NO SCARVES
NO HOODS OR SKI CAPS
NO BAGGY PANTS

ALL TEE-SHIRTS OF ANY COLOR
MUST HAVE LOGO'S THAT ARE VISIBLE
MUST BE NAVEL HIGH
LOGO MUST BE ON YOUR
CHEST OR BACK

PLEASE DO NOT YELL OR SHOUT
ACROSS THE BAR
THANK YOU

ATTENTION BAR PATRONS
PLEASE DO NOT STAND
ON CHAIR RAIL

PLEASE PLEASE ANYONE CAUGHT TOUCHING
TV WILL BAR YOURSELF PERMANENTLY

ANYONE TOUCHING APPLIANCES BARRED
YOURSELF NO EXCEPTIONS

EMPLOYESS HAVE THE RIGHT TO CHECK
BATHROOMS AT ALL TIME

And, of course:

BE AWARE
THESE PREMISES ARE UNDER 24 HOUR VIDEO
SURVEILLANCE INSIDE & OUT

Well, I'm glad I have a dress shirt on, and no pantaloons, and I'll do my best not to get touchy-feely with that television. Watching a news story of five guys stealing seventeen Rolexes after smashing its display case, the barflies whoop with astonishment and delight, but they are blasé about a school shooting simulation. As I eat a sad cheesesteak, with its dispirited meat, cheese and bread, bits of conversation drift to me.

"Yes, there was this girl born without a rectum, and she's alive still. They haven't fixed her yet, but they will."

"You never had possum hash?"

"No, I'm a city boy. I don't know nothing about that. My cousins in North Carolina might, though."

"Possum is sweet. It's an all right meat. And muskrat is OK too. You ought to know what's edible, and what's not, because it might come in handy one day."

"No, ma'am, I'm happy with my chicken and my steak, thank you. I don't need no squirrel, no rabbit, no raccoon, no possum. Why should I bother about any of that, when I can just go to the store?"

Surrounded by rules, we aren't any safer, for a dickhead or two can just come in to make everyone lie on the ground, then relieve us of wallets and purses. Most patrons are bunched up at the far end, however, so they'll have a better chance to see what's what should shit happen. (Sign on a Camden wall, "If you believe shit happens, park here.") Several of these lushes are probably packing.

Three Beyoncé tunes in a row tells me it's time to get the fuck home. Soon I'll stagger into the dusk, into a half-feral city of aimless men and women dwelling in rotting row houses, abandoned shells shrouded by vines and shrubs, or tents, like those clustering by the freeway, across from the long-shuttered Sears and beyond a billboard pitching $5,000 Yurman watches to passing motorists. Living apart in a squalid tent down a dirt path blocked by plywood, branches and lumber, ex-factory worker Beasto can choose between bacon, hot dog or pork chop, all stored unrefrigerated in a sack of rice, and all reeking, of course. Fifty-seven, he's been away from Puerto Rico forty-three years. Meanwhile, junkie Tina has left her tent, cleaned herself up and reconciled with her mom, so of course, of course, a cheerful respite, or recovery, if you will, is temporarily possible, within the larger framework of tempered hope, outright disappointment and, naturally, unmitigated horror. Staggering on, I will pass by Cooper, where wizardly doctors can give each of us a cleaner, fresher asshole, to pump up our always suspect vanity and confidence, or I might run into lovely Michelle or Angela, for they will still be out there. All night long, she'll sleepwalk from one john to another, just so she can score and score, until she finally disappears.

UNMAKING CHESTER

8-1-13—Traveling by train to Philadelphia, going north, you will pass by Chester, Pennsylvania, a city that has been in decline for more than half a century. Founded in 1682, the same year as Philadelphia, Chester was a major manufacturer of US Navy ships from the Civil War until World War II. It also made ammunitions and automobile parts. Despite its relative small size, with a peak population of 66,039 in 1950, Chester was an industrial powerhouse.

In 1926, Mrs. Marin Garvey won a $160 washing machine for coming up with an enduring slogan for her city, "WHAT CHESTER MAKES MAKES CHESTER." This was fashioned into a huge electric sign that impressed countless rail passengers until 1973, when it was dismantled. Who can forget the sight of Mr. D'Ancona taking down the S, T, E and R? Many have sobbed to this day. Though Chester no longer produces anything, save babies and premature corpses, the same slogan adorns bright blue banners in its mostly derelict downtown. Entire buildings are abandoned and falling apart, its windows boarded up with graying plywood or left hollow. Others have first floors occupied by gasping businesses offering cheap clothes, wigs, way too expensive sneakers or Obama posters and T-shirts. "WE WON!" "HOPE WON!" "YES WE DID!" On sidewalks, black marketeers offer incense, body oils, bead necklaces, underwear and socks. The Cambridge Restaurant has been put out of its misery, thank you, Lord, for I sure won't miss their home fries, but Italian Brothers is still hanging on. They do make decent hoagies. It is claimed that Chester's Catherine DiCostanza made the world's very first in 1925, to feed a starving gambler ambling over from Palermo's Bar down 3rd Street.

Lots of Italians back in the day, as well as Irish, Poles, Jews and Ukrainians. With Chester's industries gone, they have mostly scattered. Recently, though, I walked by a downtown storefront and saw all white people inside, a truly rare sight in contemporary Chester. It turned out to be an art opening, with tentative or frustrated watercolors and oils of a snowy pine tree, a pensive cat, a covered bridge or Cubistic jazz musicians . . . On pedestals, lumpy ceramics. A shy charcoal nude lounged on a smudgy charcoal sofa. A man waved at me to come in, so I did, "Hey, what a surprise to see an art opening! Is everybody here from Chester?"

"Not all of us, but we live nearby."

A woman appeared, "Did you sign our guess book? Come, come, sign our guess book."

As I printed my first name, though, she said, "We do have a suggested $5 donation."

I have attended many art openings, from SoHo to art school, to suburban old ladies' watercolor society, but I have never encountered an admission fee, and five bucks also means two Rolling Rocks at the Gold Room, one block over. Seeing me cringe, the lady added, "It's for the wine and cheese."

"Forget it, forget it," I crossed my name out, and walked out to her "No! No!" At many art openings, you do see hungry art students, an odd bag lady or a clearly homeless guy stuffing their faces with cheddar and crackers while draining Yellow Tail Shiraz or Duck Pond Chardonnay, so the five-buck fee may be a measure to prevent undesirables from crashing this schlockfest.

What made that art bad wasn't so much execution as orientation. Rootless, it was indifferent to its surroundings, that is, it didn't pay attention to Chester, didn't care at all for it. No art is worthless if it reflects in any way its place of origin, so no painting, photo, poem or short story about

Chester can be bad if it reveals any aspect of this place, but to do this, one must first pay close attention. Folk art is never without charm and interest, but much of cosmopolitan art is mediocre since it is removed, in time and distance, from its original moment of inspiration. This cosmopolitan art may be partly salvaged by its backwoods dilution, distortion or bastardization, however, but the pleasure is likely mild, the humor unintentional. Seeing a show of Canadian Impressionist paintings in Ottawa, I remember thinking, Why? And would you care for Thai Suprematism, Ugandan Constructivism or Fijian Neo-Geo? With globalism unraveling, we can return to the local in each sphere of our lives, and that means a revival of regionalism in all the arts. We've been jerked about by the distant media long enough, teased and dictated by distant cultural centers. It's time we observe and listen to what's right in front of us.

It was a Saturday evening but Chester's main drag, the Avenue of the States, was mostly empty. Even fifteen years ago, there would have been many shoppers, or loiterers at least. Now there was hardly a parked car to break into. On both sides of the street for an entire block, there was only one business open, Huddle Barbershop. On this scorching night, two box fans were kept on high. The owner/barber would work until 10 p.m., at least. In his window, a flyer with "Get to Know Your Candidates. 'Let's Get Back to Progress,'" with the faces of two smiling, suited yet unnamed individuals, one man, one woman, with the man much taller.

Wanting to meet or at least see some people, I decided to go to the Gold Room. On the way, I walked past the old Excelsior Saving Fund, with its sign reduced to "UND." The Gold Room is large and cool, with three pool tables and five televisions. Once settled at the bar, one will notice two shelf altars featuring incense, the Vajaradhara and a beer-bellied Chinese God of Wealth, so is the owner Asian? No, just a black Buddhist. I came in as the daytime bartender was finishing her shift. Walking out, a middle-aged white guy hollered, "Your husband must be a wonderful man, because you are a wonderful lady!" She smiled, naturally. Minutes later, she said to some young guy, "Ah, you look wonderliscious today! That's a new word. I'm gonna patent it!" Then she complimented some giggling and boobiliscious apparition, hovering at the far end of the bar, backlit by a Southern Comfort light from heaven or hell, "You're so sexy. I can just hug you!" A man in his late twenties then chimed in with a false note, I think, "I'd love to spend money on both of y'all."

This verbal orgy finally stopped with the new bartender, but she also gushed in her own way, with a low-cut dress that flaunted a glittering, burning skull on her buttocks, and "MISFIT" in bold black on her back. What a pun, eh, with a skull as pelvic girdle, or dead head as live bottom, with the anus where the mouth should be? "From my booty, death will rise," she emitted wordlessly. "You may think you're staring at my ass, but you're just seeing your own cracked skull, sucka. I mean, sugar."

Thirty years old, Misfit was born in Chester, but left at seventeen to work in a home for retarded people in Williamsport, in the idyllic Poconos. It didn't pay very much, but it got her out of Chester. After nine years doing that, however, she took a $950 course to become an emergency medical technician, that is, an ambulance attendant, for which she was paid less than $2,000 a month, take-home, then she was let go. She tried hard, but couldn't land a similar job anywhere else, so she settled for this bartending gig. Misfit admitted that business was also down at the Gold Room, and no one she knew was doing well, "But we're in a recovery nationally, right?"

"No," I said, "and it's only going to get worse."

"You think so?"

"Yes, I travel all over the country, and it's the same shit all over, and everyone I talk to says they're not doing well. Well, eight or nine out of ten, anyway. Almost no one is doing well."

"So what should we do?"

"You just have to cover your own ass, that's all."

I should have said, "You just have to cover your own skull, that's all," or better yet, "We just have to cover each other's flaming skulls, that's all." As the only bar in downtown Chester, the Gold Room should survive for a while, so Misfit's job is probably safe, but like many people these days, she must be willing to switch jobs at a moment's notice, do something entirely different to survive. The word "career" has become nearly mean-ingless. We have all become career improvisers.

At someone else's mercy, we can fit in momentarily, but from their careful, cost-cutting calculation or sudden, inexplicable whim, we become misfits again, for that is what we are. We're not misfits as fashion statement, but essentially. Try as we might, we cannot adjust ourselves dexterously enough to our rapidly shifting surroundings, which we have no role in shaping. In Flannery O'Connor's "A Good Man Is Hard to Find," there's a misfit who says, "I was a gospel singer for a while . . . I been most everything. Been in the arm service, both land and sea, at home and abroad, been twict married, been an undertaker, been with the railroads, plowed Mother Earth, been in a tornado, seen a man burnt alive oncet." He has also killed, robbed and been jailed, and though everything has happened to him, nothing matters, because nothing makes sense. Sound familiar?

You think you're a housepainter? Wrong! A secretary? Wrong! A nurse? Wrong! A professor? Wrong! A pipe fitter? Wrong! A dock worker? Wrong! Though nothing adds up, one still has to eat daily, so one solution is to become a mass murderer, if only in an auxiliary capacity. At Concord and 7th, I saw a flyer in a torn plastic sleeve, stapled to a light pole:

US MARINES

- WE HAVE EDUCATION OPPORTUNITIES
- NON COMBAT JOBS AVAILABLE
- FULL TIME (ACTIVE DUTY) OR PART TIME (RESERVE PROGRAM)
- FULL BENEFITS TO START / FAMILY COVERAGE
- DO THINGS THAT OTHERS ONLY DREAM ABOUT DOING

BETTER YOUR FUTURE, CALL OR TEXT
SERGEANT WILLIAMS

To kill or be killed is here presented as improving oneself and one's family, as sheer survival, for in trading in one's freedom, humanity and conscience, one will get adequate health care and nutrition, maybe even a home in a safe environment. To attain these basics, however, one must first become a berserker. Kill! Kill! Kill! In Harrisburg, I had encountered a National Guard poster:

> There are all kinds of moments you'll experience where you serve the people of your community in the National Guard. If you've got it inside you, this is your time to act.

The accompanying image showed soldiers standing outside a suburban home during some kind of rescue mission. This is very reassuring, for they are not threatened in any way, nor are they menacing anybody. They're not kicking down some foreigner's door and terrorizing his family, and most importantly, they're not getting their nuts blown off seven or eight time zones away. As a National Guardsman, you'll only be rescuing your neighbor's Siamese from some midget tree, this poster was implying, and you'll be home in time to watch your dreadful Phillies.

I wanted to get away from downtown Chester, drink in a neighborhood dive and hear, or overhear, what those folks have to say, so I decided to go to the Love People Lounge on Highland Avenue. I had no idea what that neighborhood was like, but I had seen this bar from the train, many times, and had always wanted to walk in because of its irresistible name. When I got there, though, I found out that it had been closed, with even its sign removed. Oh well, I thought, let's find another place to drink, so I started walking.

In many distressed cities, as in Detroit, Gary, East St. Louis or Camden, to walk into the unknown is to be a reconnaissance scout or a suicide, not so much a tourist, and Chester has a violent crime rate more than four times the national average, and it was sunny that day, meaning perfect for a mugging, but also ideal for a pleasant walk, and I was getting very thirsty for a Colt 45 or a Yuengling, so I kept walking. In truth, it wasn't half bad. I passed Give Me Suga, an inviting Caribbean joint serving jerk chicken and oxtail. I saw people sitting on their porches or steps, and two pudgy middle-aged men, one black, one white, sprawled on folding lawn chairs beneath a bouffant tree. Every so often I'd see a desperate sign offering a home for less than $20,000, cash, and presently I came to another house that looked abandoned, with no glass in its windows and its door boarded up, but there was a newish Direct TV dish attached to its wall. Is it possible that someone was watching a movie on demand, say, *Titanic* or *The 40 Year Old Virgin*, while lying on a bare mattress, with a half-finished bag of Cheetos next to him? In winter, snow drifts into the gaping windows as he cheers our hapless Flyers. Since it is dark, and nobody's outside, no one who's up to any good anyway, he can comfortably piss from the second floor, his dick en plein air, as they say. With tall grass and weeds besieging, and no air-conditioning or heat, this home is a rough-and-tumble, back-to-nature dwelling, a cabin in the woods, except no bears will attack you here, only men down to their last quarter or fix.

There were no lit beer signs at the front, so Sporty's West End Cocktail Lounge didn't even appear open, but I could hear the hum of the air-conditioning, so I opened the door and walked in. Sporty and his bartender seemed a bit startled to see me, but everything was cool as I sat down and ordered a bottle. It was just after 1 p.m., and I was the only customer. For the next two hours, the few other patrons only sneaked in to buy a six-pack or can to go. As she left, a woman in her late forties shouted to Sporty, "Make some money now!"

"I'm with you on that!" Sporty then returned to his video game, with its thin, whistle-like gunshots constantly discharging. Video blood splattered as he charged through his enemy, shedding corpses by the wayside. There was a pool table and five televisions, all left on, with the biggest one showing an episode of *Have Gun—Will Travel*. A sneaky Chinaman was caught reading other people's mail, then later, some mustachioed crank snarled, "Who cares what any woman wants." During a firefight, a bullet merely grazed a man's elbow, causing him to rub it.

In most working class bars at this hour, you'd find old men, at least, and perhaps contractors who have finished their work early, but here, like I said, I was the only drinker. Dangling from the drop ceiling were stars, astroids and a round cornered piece of cardboard urging me to "CELEBRATE." I noticed the young bartender had on a snug tank top, and a pair of black and white shorts, showing some sort of African design. There were signs all over the walls:

FOUR THINGS YOU CAN NOT RECOVER
1- The stone after the throw . . .
2- The word after it's said . . .
3- The occasion after it's missed . . .
4- The Time after it's passed . . .

A BIG LATINO NITE
Featuring A Ethnic Diversity
For A Rollicking Good Time

A ATLANTIC CITY BUS TRIP $25

NO LOITERING PERMITTED
In This Establishment
If You Don't Have A Drink
Or If You're Not In Line
To Play Pool.

FEDERAL PRISON
CONVICTED FELONS & DRUG DEALERS BEWARE
1 GUN — 5, 10, 15 YEARS OR MORE
NO PAROLE
OPERATION CEASE FIRE
REPORT ILLEGAL GUNS 1-800-ATF-GUNS

On the last was an illustration of a prison cell, with the silhouette of a man sitting on a cot, his head down. Across from him, an open toilet and toilet paper. A large handgun hovered outside the prison bars.

There was also a group portrait of movie gangsters, with Al Pacino's Scarface in the middle, hoisting his badass M16A1, then, high up on the wall, an image of Martin Luther King and Obama, their heads merging, with "I HAVE A DREAM" on top, and "I AM THE DREAM" on the bottom. In almost every black bar, you'll find images of Obama. At Scotty's, near my South Philly apartment, there's an Obama shrine complete with red tinsel, foil flags and a string of tiny lights resembling condomed pricks or aerodynamic milk bottles, all surrounding a sacred likeness of our Chief War Lord and Patron Saint of All Banksters.

Hardly loquacious, Sporty finally grunted that the bar was empty because it was the end of the month, "Come back in a couple days, there'll be people here." Running out of beer money is hardly the poor's biggest concern these days, for towards the 28th and 29th, the fridge may have long been empty, not to mention that pile of ignored bills, some still in their envelopes, unopened. Soon, the cable may be shut down, then gas, electricity and water, in that order. Chester is already half shut-down.

Martin Luther King spent three years in Chester, and graduated from Crozer Theological Seminary in 1951, and outside the Crozer Library, there's a large bronze bust of King. On another visit to the Gold Room, I met a woman who said she was born on King's birthday, "And that's very special to my family, because King was such a special man, you know."

"I'd say he's more important than any American in the last fifty years."

"I'm very glad you think so," she smiled.

I could feel myself getting a bit worked up, "Obama ain't shit compared to King! King threatened them, and that's why they had to kill him. King wanted to change this society. Obama doesn't want to change shit!" I stared hard into her eyes. "If they're propping up Obama now, that can only mean Obama is serving them! He serves them!"

"I agree with you," she said, "I've always felt the same way. I've always known they had to kill him. Oh Lord, I think I'm going to cry. I'm going to cry!"

A TRENTON EDUCATION

8-29-13—I had been in Trenton, I dunno, maybe two hundred times before I decided to know it a little. For years, I would stop there on the way to NYC from Philly, or vice versa, but I was never compelled to wander from the Trenton Transit Center. This lack of curiosity is inexcusable, for "there is no place that isn't worth visiting at least once," as Evelyn Waugh wrote somewhere, and which I'd amend to "a bunch of times," for each subsequent encounter can only deepen one's understanding, for people are always infinitely fascinating, no matter where they may dwell, and how they cope with their environment cannot but be instructive. Shoot, man, even Northern Virginia is worth visiting more than once, I'd concede, though that would severely test any sensate being's taste, hope, faith in humanity, tolerance, self-respect and sense of humor.

Having owned a car for less than two years in my life, and I'm two months shy of fifty, I've always been a walker, but I never really developed a passion for aimless walking until I lived in Italy in 2003–4. Europe is a compact continent with an extensive rail system, so any of its cities, towns or villages can be reached by train, and from the station you're free to wander as much as you want, without fear of missing your last train back, for there's always one coming, it seems. The towns there are also much more accommodating towards walkers, and even the countryside is walkable, with public paths through fields and orchards.

Then in 2005, I had the luck to be in East Anglia for nearly a year, thanks to a T.K. Wong Fellowship, so I was able to meander through many of the villages mentioned in W.G. Sebald's dirge-like masterpiece, *The Rings of Saturn*, which begins, "In August 1992, when the dog days were drawing to an end, I set off to walk the county of Suffolk, in the hope of dispelling the emptiness that takes hold of me whenever I have completed a long stint of work." All the places described by Sebald had seen much better days, with some, Great Yarmouth, for example, considered laughable, when noticed at all. Sebald's home city, Norwich, had also become the butt of jokes although it had been England's second-greatest city, but such is life, for everything will become (bad) jokes in due time, if not obliterated completely from this unfunny earth. Everything will become New Jersey, in short, if not, horror of horrors, Trenton, friggin' New Jersey.

OK, OK, so listen up, y'all, I was on State Street, just minding my own business, you know, slow-sipping a Colt 45 on the steps of the Trenton Saving Fund Society, founded in 1901 and deader than your sex life, when this dude hollered, "You're from Southeast Asia?"

"Yeah. What?"

"Ever heard of Angkor Wat?"

"Yeah, that's in Southeast Asia."

"Ever heard of Nagasaki?"

"Yeah," I grinned, "but that's not in Southeast Asia. That's in Japan, man. That's where they dropped the second atomic bomb!"

Ignoring my irrelevant information, this man, about thirty, continued to quiz and educate me, "Do you know where the word 'nigger' comes from?"

"Negro? As in a mispronunciation of negro?"

"No, man. Negro comes from Naga, and Naga is a sacred snake. If you're a Southeast Asian, you must know how sacred the snake is, for you guys have turned the snake into a dragon, like Bruce Lee, enter the dragon! So the black race is sacred. We are the original and most powerful race, but the white man can't stand this, so they have corrupted our name from Na-ga to nig-ger. Are you following me?"

"Yeah."

"The white man would have you believe black people are only from Africa, but that's nonsense! We were everywhere. We built Angkor Wat and the Egyptian pyramids. To keep us down, the white man has rewritten our history. He wants the world to think we're just savages but we're the original man, the true man and the greatest man. The Buddha was a black man. You ever noticed his full lips and kinky hair? King Solomon was black, and Jesus, of course, was black. From us, everything has come. We're not just black, we're all colors! See those people right there? What do you see?"

"I don't know. Three people?"

"What kind of people?"

"Black people?"

"No, no, no! One is blue-black, one is reddish, and one is kind of yellow, like you. You see, black people can be all colors, because all colors come from black, but black itself is not a color. You got that?"

By this time, I had taken out pen and paper to jot down this copious lecture. Across the street was the handsome First Presbyterian Church. Built in the Greek Revival style, it hides what's left of Colonel Johann Rall, commander of German mercenaries during the pivotal Battle of Trenton in 1776. George Washington, his conqueror, now stands atop a fluted column lording over this city. When the monument was unveiled in 1893, *The New York Times* deemed it "the greatest day in the history of New Jersey."

Satisfied at having an eager student, the dude presented me with his profile, to appear more melodramatic against the slanting sunlight, then continued, "The pyramids are also a lot older than what the white man says. They're more than 150,000 years old, and so is Angkor Wat! Do you know that lightbulbs were found inside the pyramids? And batteries too, but all these facts have to be suppressed by the white man, because the white man can never admit that the Naga race, the so-called nigger race, reached a higher level of civilization thousands of years ago, when the white man was still living in caves!"

As he was talking, a passerby saluted him, "Peace! God!" So he asked me, "Did you hear that?"

"What?"

"What he said."

"Peace? God?"

"Yes. Peace! God! He called me a God, because I am a God. Every black man is a God, and you, as a colored person, is also a God, but the white man is a corruption. He is in fact the devil, you heard me, and his days are numbered. A black scientist created the white man 6,600 years ago, but it's time for the black race to reassert his superiority. Look, look," and he pointed to his arm, leg, leg, arm and head in turns, "what do you have?"

"What do you mean?"

"What does that spell? The first letter of each!"

"Allah?"

"Yes, Allah!"

"But what does it mean? It's just a linguistic accident, man! If we were talking another language, you wouldn't have Allah at all!"

"But we are speaking English, and English is the universal language. This is no accident. The time for Allah has come, and it will happen here, in America."

Many will have recognized by now that this man was spouting from the Nation of Islam's teachings, and much has already been written about the Black Muslims' problematic views on race, so I will only add that any man who thinks of an entire race as evil in origin and purpose is undoubtedly a racist, so this black man lecturing me was clearly a racist, and I cringe whenever anyone insists that black people cannot be racist since blacks are not structurally in power. To condemn, despise or demonize anyone for the color of their skin alone is the very definition of racism, and this is a moral, individual failing that can befall anyone, of any color, and at any time too, I should add, from moment to moment. To deny blacks this moral agency, to posit that they cannot lapse or sink into racism, or rise above it, is to deny their very humanity, so what would that make you but the ultimate racist?

Done with my education, for now, my lecturer left me his name, Melchezidek, meaning "my righteous king," and his phone number, then he hopped on this beat-up bike and rode away. One can't help but wonder how can a man with such a worldview function in the larger society, populated as it is with so many devils? In Trenton, though, as in most of our cities and towns, he may not have to, since blacks and whites are still mostly segregated in a society billed as post-racial when it elected a president who's only half demonic in genetics, even if almost entirely evil in actions, it has turned out, with yet another bloodbath coming in Syria.

The government that harassed, then murdered Martin Luther King now commemorates him, in the most superficial manner, each year. Flatulent speeches are given, but no sanctioned maven ever asks why he was gunned down, or points out that the syndicate that squashed King continues to kill, torture or lock up anyone who can seriously shine a light on its sinister workings. Witness the recent murder of Michael Hastings, for example, or the humiliation and breaking down of Bradley Manning. In any case, Trenton never recovered from the rioting that followed King's assassination, though it was already in decline, with the erosion of its industrial base, and white flight, occurring well before 1968. Note that nearby Levittown, a prototypical suburb built from scratch, was completed by 1958.

With its compact layout, Trenton is very walkable, though one must watch out for bullets, knives and cars careening out of control after their drivers have been shot dead. With four more months to go, Trenton has already tied its all-time record of thirty-one murders for an entire year, and the homicide figure only indicates a portion of the bloodshed, of course. On August 15th, for example, a twenty-four-year-old ex-convict kicked and punched his girlfriend, stabbed her dog to death, then shot two cops, sending both to the hospital, with one still in critical condition as of this writing, fourteen days later. The shooter was himself killed by police bullets. So practice extra caution when wandering through North or East Trenton, and don't you even think that the South or West Ward is entirely free of lacerating or puncturing surprises. Oh shoot, am I shot?! In short, it's wisest not to trek through Trenton, but what the hell, let's just go, and so I was putzing around Clinton Avenue when it started to rain hard, so, soaking wet, I decided to duck into La Guira. Opening the door, I entered a tiny vestibule to espy an apparition behind bulletproof plexiglass, so I asked, "Bar?" After my grim ghost nodded towards a second door, I entered a darkened purgatory, hitched myself onto a stool, then inquired, "What kind of beer do you have?"

"Every kind."

"Tecate?"

"No, sorry."

"Rolling Rock."

"No, sorry."

"Uh, Yuengling?"

"Yes!"

I was the only customer. On TV, a swooning hostess asked some toothsome chica, *"¿Como le gustan los hombres?"* Grinning, she chirped, *"Muy románticos! Buenos trabajadores! Altos!"* She was about to choose between two well-inked beefcakes, half-naked, with "Leo" and "Tauro" signs dangling on their toned chests, but suddenly there was kicking, punching and hair pulling, for we had switched to *The Steve Wilkos Show*, as the bartender didn't want me to be flummoxed by Spanish. I found out he was Dominican and had been in the US all of five months. Though his English comprehension was bare-bones, we did try to converse, and all was friendly and pleasant until some middle-aged guy arrived and got all weirded out by my camera. He was the bar owner. To calm down this excitable crank, I explained that I was visiting Trenton from Philly, and only took photos to share the countless virtues of his lovely establishment with the rest of the world, and I was having a great time until I encountered his hectoring, irritated mug, but since he was being so rude now, I would never return, so he barked, "Don't come back!" I didn't appreciate this pissy mofo ruining my hopped-up sense of well-being and equilibrium, a glancing nirvana that had cost me a dear $8, including tip, so I called him an asshole before I left.

It turns out, though, that Mr. Martin Rodriguez has ample reasons to be touchy, for his dismal bar has become a ground zero for mayhem and police misconduct. A look at the recent history of La Guira, then, becomes a window into Trenton itself. In February of 2012, cops were called to deal with an unruly customer, Darrell Griffin, whom they roughly arrested, along with a second suspect, Michelle Roberts, for reasons unclear, though a surveillance camera does show a policewoman grabbing Roberts's hair, screaming at her and slamming her head against the wall, all after Roberts has already been handcuffed and not resisting. Roberts claims she has only gone there to drop off a dish of lasagna for a private party, but the cops thought she was filming them with her cell phone, so they went berserk. In any case, no charges were ever filed against Roberts or Griffin, though both are suing the Trenton police for excessive force used in their (illegal) arrests.

Though not one of Jacob's cursed creation, and hence not inherently and irreversibly evil, Griffin is hardly a placid Buddha, however, or a turn-the-other-cheek Jesus. Hell, he might not be any kind of God at all. In 2005, a twenty-year-old Griffin was charged with shooting Omar Hightower in the head. With such a slug stuck in his brain, Hightower suffered seizures for years until he finally died in 2013. Charges against Griffin were dismissed, however, because the state could not gather enough evidence against him. Peace! God!

In April of 2013, La Guira again made the news when a surveillance camera caught officers of the New Jersey State Police strip-searching a man down to his briefs, as other patrons looked on. Caught twice now by La Guira's annoying cameras, the cops have decided the remedy is to go after Martinez himself, by visiting his business often and citing him for petty or imaginary violations. They're trying to shut La Guira down in retaliation, Martinez has protested to the press, for it is certainly no nuisance spot in this half-boarded-up neighborhood. Well, it is a crappy bar, but within its concrete, asphalt, garbage and broken glass context, it is a heavenly oasis where Gods and Goddesses can drain Coors Light, Bud, Cîroc and Grey Goose as they bump, grind, shake and twerk. (See, see, Mr. Martinez, I am talking up your blasé shithole, so you should give me a shot of Jameson the next time I walk in!)

The *güira* is a Dominican percussive instrument, by the way, and a nice chunk of Clinton Avenue, where La Guira is located, could have gone kaboom! this last April, when scavengers removed a stove from an abandoned home, thus releasing gas from broken pipes. It's not clear why gas was still kept on there, but not much works the way it's supposed to in Trenton. Indicted for corruption, its mayor, Tony Mack, has refused to step down, though his continued presence has blocked state funds to this strapped city. "Napoleon" or "the Little Guy," as Mack is known, claims he has been entrapped by the FBI.

As its mayor tries to avoid prison, Trenton goes on falling apart. Leaving La Guira, I walked for miles through desolation and neglect, but it wasn't just that, for people still had to live here. Each day they had to walk past these empty, boarded-up or overgrown homes. Some were trying to ward off the degradation and violence with positive messages. On Martin Luther King Boulevard, a home owner had hung up a pink banner with a white cross over a purple heart, "Love One Another. John 3:34." Not far away, I saw another banner on the wire fence of a garage. With two painted daisies, and lettering in four colors, it pleaded, "Can't we do something different for OUR FUTURE?"

Presently I came upon Olden Avenue, with its many Polish businesses, still thriving after many decades. Employing my standard salutation, I asked a man, "Hey, where can you get a drink around here?"

"Let me see. You can go to Stevie Teez. It's just down the street. It's a strip bar!"

"Oh, man, I don't need no extra! I just want a beer!" In fact, I didn't even care for a beer, but one often talks just to talk, and in a strange neighborhood, sometimes one talks just to see how one is received. In any case, onward I marched, past Stevie Teez, and finally out of Trenton altogether, into Ewing, where I saw an "ARMED FORCES CAREER CENTER" at a strip mall. A uniformed soldier was getting into his SUV, so I waited for him to drive away before taking out my camera. Post 9/11, soldiers are often found in public, so it's no longer a surprise to find yourself in the International House of Pancakes, for example, next to a crowded table of soldiers, and they won't be in dress uniforms but battle fatigues. On TV, soldiers are also often inserted into commercials, newscasts, political events or sporting contests. This is done to remind us that we're in an endless war and, more importantly, to condition citizens into accepting the presence of soldiers in civilian settings. The relentless erosion of the Posse Comitatus Act is mostly done on a visual and psychological level, for now, but already one sees soldiers with live weapons where they have no right to be; the Constitution is but a quaint myth in contemporary America. Hardly anyone cares about it, not the Obama apologists, and certainly not our mesmerized youths with their eyes glued to Miley Cyrus's ass. Children reared on Hannah Montana can now follow their sexually deranged, hair-horned and tongue-wagging idol into a psychotic adulthood. Peace! God!

I took my photos in full view of the recruiting office's plate glass windows, with who knows how many eyes behind them, so within seconds, a uniformed soldier appeared to say that that was not allowed, so I smiled, apologized, then walked away. He also smiled. After I had gone about twenty yards, however, and was already past the back of this building, two more soldiers came running out, with one asking me to stop, which I did. When he asked me my name, I readily gave it to him, though I really didn't have to, as he had no jurisdiction over anyone in this civilian setting. I knew I had done nothing illegal, as taking photos in public is never against the law, though it may sometimes be rude. A second soldier then demanded I delete my photos of the recruiting office, which I did, as he watched. (I knew I could still retrieve these images later, as long as I didn't shoot over them.) By this time, a third, older soldier had appeared, so four well-trained, gung-ho combatants had so far been dispatched to handle one dumbass middle-aged retard with his beat-up, often repaired camera with a dusty lens and missing eyepiece. If they could get so excited over a harmless American at some stupid Jersey strip mall, imagine their possibly lethal overreaction to anything remotely suspicious in, say, Afghanistan or Iraq? There, even a munchkin raising a lollipop to his mouth might make one of our brave heroes jump, holler and discharge.

Faced with this farcical situation, I laughed, shook my head and told the soldiers, "This is ridiculous. You will go to bed tonight thinking how absurd this is." That's when they gave me the predictable line about the heightened alert needed against the threat of terrorism, but I said a terrorist would not need to take a photo of their office, especially with a huge camera and standing in full view of their plate glass windows. As I've pointed out before, you can bomb a place just fine without snapping photos of it beforehand, but if you must scope out a public target, you can just stroll by and look at it, or you can go on Google Maps and get all the information you need about its exterior.

Back and forth we went, with a soldier telling me that "it is illegal to take photos of a federal building," which is not correct, or all those thousands of tourists snapping photos daily of the Capitol, White House and countless other buildings should be arrested immediately. One of the grunts wanted to walk back in, but the other was becoming quite heated, maybe because I had said, "You guys are being brainwashed into becoming so paranoid. Don't you see how ridiculous this is?" When the pissed one snapped, "I'm defending our country," I responded, "You're not defending anything! You've been standing out here harassing me!"

"Call the cops," he said to his more composed partner.

"Call the cops for what?!" I smirked. "What am I doing that's illegal?"

To intimidate me, the other guy did pretend to use his cell phone, but he ended up not calling anyone, and they finally walked back inside.

If this was Iraq, Afghanistan or, hell, Southeast Asia a generation ago, a smart mouth like me might be laid to rest in several chunks, then pissed on, but since this was only New Jersey in 2013, I have lived to relate this tiresome tale. Soon enough, though, these jumpy fellows will be well armed and blazing within your earshot, right here, in the Homeland.

The War on Terror has been incoherent and nonsensical from the beginning. On the pretext of going after Bin Laden, a known former CIA asset, the US invaded Afghanistan, then it attacked Saddam Hussein, whom it had propped up for decades, and now Washington is openly supporting terrorists in its war against Syria. On the home front, every terror plot going back to 9/11 has been abetted by Washington, at the very least, if not entirely schemed by it. In Portland and Cherry Hill, such plots were used to entrap innocents, while in Boston, it was to frame its own assets while terrorizing the entire country, all for propaganda purposes. In short, the US can't be fighting terror when it is the world's most prolific and relentless generator of terror. Without terror, America would be out of business, literally. As the US is about to ratchet up considerably the terror it has been unleashing on Syria, all Americans should feel sick to their stomachs, but most of us will simply sit back and watch, in boredom or great excitement, and when tired of this extra bloody entertainment, we'll yawn and switch back to our regular programming.

CLOSE CALL IN NORRISTOWN

10-6-13—Wandering around so much, I'm constantly among strangers, in completely unfamiliar neighborhoods. Though these novel situations have opened my eyes much, it would take but a single unfortunate encounter to blacken or close them, even for good, and in Norristown this week, I had to call 911 as I quickly ducked into a store to wait for the cops to save my ass.

Having prowled around Gary, Camden, Newark, Detroit, Oakland and North Philly, all on foot, I still don't think of Norristown as all that menacing, though, all over town, there are unmistakable signs of a drawn out economic depression that's only getting worse. Its industries trickled away decades ago, and its Main Street has become mostly irrelevant thanks to two nearby shopping malls, one of which, King of Prussia, happens to be the largest in the US (as far as leasable retail space). Norristown's major employers are two hospitals and the county government, and that's it. People loiter downtown. They slump on curbs and sometimes sprawl on sidewalks. Last month, John Pergolese was given a citation for sleeping in front of the entrance to Church's Chicken. Outside the McDonald's/gas station, I saw a gent lying faceup, with one hand shielding his face from the sun, the other outstretched. Next to him was a rotund woman in a "Jazzy" power wheelchair, with a black umbrella over her head, and two backup umbrellas tucked into vertical pouches behind her seat. On a large, flat rock, a man hunched over, while another had flopped himself on the mulch.

Outside Dunkin' Donuts before noon, there's usually a small crowd of young moms with their tots, some in strollers. Having bought a Boston Kreme and watery coffee, I sat inside and observed. Through the plate glass, I could see a woman in a black V-neck T-shirt with "BEATLES" over silhouettes of the Fab Four; another in a turquoise hoodie with "LOVE" in glittery red, yellow and blue; and yet another in a pink "ROCK & LOVE" T-shirt. Like millions of poor white women everywhere, the ones here tend to wear their hair straight back, pulled taut, in a style known in the UK as the "council house facelift," and since this is 2013, they're not in dresses or skirts, but sweatpants, tights or no-name jeans. Though it was warm, a young man had on a knit cap with tasseled earflaps, topped by a red pom-pom. His brown shirt was fronted with "AERO" in Marine camouflage, which at first I mistook for "ZERO."

Mercy! Marching into view, here came a middle-aged platinum blonde in glittery black and silver. Her orange face had often been seared by a tanning lamp, it was clear. Uncomfortably puffed up from being carved up and stitched, it resembled a much abused pincushion that should be retired soon, I think. She was followed by a Hispanic woman with a rose and a crown of thorns tattooed on her wide biceps, and a crucifix nestling in her cleavage. After this Christian had entered and gotten her glazed communion, a white woman shouted across the room, "I can't get over how beautiful that purse is!"

"Thank you! Thank you!"

"You know, when I see a purse that I just love? I become obsessed! I just can't get over it!"

"Thank you! Thank you!"

When in a strange town, I often try to find a dirt cheap bar, not only because it suits my budget but because that's where I can most likely chat with regular people. On my first visit here, however, I walked for several blocks on Main Street without seeing a tavern. There were gold-for-cash businesses, bail bondsmen, ambulance chasers and a Harley dealer, but no bars, and so I asked a peculiar-looking older woman who was limping along with a cane and wearing two bandannas, one on top of another. Her eyes were barely visible. After she pointed to a beer store nearby, I explained that I'd prefer a place to sit down, so she said, "They have tables and chairs there," then, after a sigh, "Ah, you're such good company."

It was thus I met Clare, who would be my guide for that afternoon in exchange for a tallboy of Colt 45, three bags of "red hot flavored" potato chips and a pack of Carnival cigarettes, at $5.65 the cheapest available. Born near Norristown, Clare spent her early childhood in Kansas City before returning here, where she's been ever since. Paying $500 a month, she has a room in a house shared with "five or six" other people.

"Are they all clean?"

"Yes."

"You're lucky. It only takes one dirty person to make your life miserable."

"I know."

In Philly, I once met a black man in his mid-sixties who had shared a house with "seven other knuckleheads. Most of them were cool, though, but one guy would never flush the toilet, and never close the shower curtain, so water would be all over. Man, it was gross. He said he was germaphobic, so he wouldn't touch the toilet, any part of it." Having to endure such living conditions, he was now quite cheerful to be living outside, "It's like camping!" In college, he had wanted to study business, but his ma said, "Business ain't nothing but a way for white people to rip off black people," so he switched to music.

Another man, white and fifty-threeish, was paying only $280 for a room, but he also had a housemate who wasn't quite toilet-trained, "One of these guys shits on the toilet seat."

Sixty-seven years old, Clare's been married twice, to a man named Don for three years, then to a Dan for six, "Dan kept me lonely. I had no one to share my life with, no one to talk to. I was in nursing school, and I couldn't talk about it," so she walked out, leaving her engagement ring on the dresser. Clare would mutter these fragments about her life, but mostly she was silent, with her eyes often hidden. Sometimes her mouth moved silently, as if she were underwater and behind glass.

"I don't pay attention to time, I'm retired. I'm in a time-free zone." Then, "No, I'm in a time-freeze zone." Pleased at her own joke, her thin lips blossomed.

She said, "significant other," then changed it to "culpable other," and smiled. Several times she even smiled at my humor, but then she would fade out.

On her left arm, she had tied a red T-shirt into a sort of tourniquet, though she wasn't bleeding, at least not obviously. Noticing an Eye of Horus ring on her bony finger, I asked if she liked Sun Ra, but she had never heard of him. Suddenly she blurted, "Five hundred rapes!"

"Huh, what?"

"500 rapes."

"What are you talking about? What does that mean?"

"That's the only way in."

"Into what?"

"Everything!"

By this time, we were sitting in this stark joint, Pub Deli. Run by a Chinese lady, its first rule is, "Please do not stay in store more than 1 hour." Over the glass counter, there was a large cardboard sign, "Yuengling Cerveza. Historia y Tradición desde 1829." Tucked in a corner, Latino men drank Bud Ice beneath a life-size image of a Tecate babe in boxing gloves. Hispanics make up 30 percent of Norristown's population.

Clare was a nurse "for about fifteen years," then took care of horses, which she liked best. She had also been homeless, and once, was "forced to take a bath in a creek."

"By whom?"

"I don't know. I don't remember. It doesn't matter. I don't care," with "care" barely audible. Then, "Don't speak English to me, I don't even speak English."

I laughed, "But we've been speaking English."

"If you mumble, I'll understand. I don't speak English anymore. I don't like the accent."

"What accent? Whose accent?"

"Everybody's. I don't like the anger. It makes me feel ugly in my head. Vile. I can't even think any more because of this accent. This is not how I was taught."

"What?"

"The accent."

She explained her name meant "blue moon in French," which is incorrect, of course. She said she wanted to get back to "Missoura," but it was clear she had no means to do so, and the Missoura she's longing for won't be waiting for her. In a restless and speed-obsessed culture, nothing is even seen properly, much less preserved, so the next whatever is always best, though only for a second. I have never bought into the cult of progress, but only care for what's right, balanced and sane, so if it takes looking backward to move forward, so to speak, I'm all for it. In the name of progress, so much horror and degradation have been set in motion, and if you don't know this, you don't know history. Of course, mindless nostalgia is just as idiotic. In downtown Norristown, there's a large mural that depicts the city as it looked nearly a century ago, with this caption, "Rebirth of the Past."

There won't be any rebirth in Clare's future, that's for sure, for she is worn out, isolated and near the end, with her eyes practically closed to spare her from looking at present-day Norristown. I asked about the streaks of caked blood on her face and arms.

"A friend of mine did that. That's all right. If it makes you happy to scratch me, you can scratch me."

As my guide, Clare wanted to show me where George Washington had been "during the Civil War," but she led me in the wrong direction, away from Valley Forge, so after a ten-minute hike, we ended up in a wooded area next to the train track. Sitting on a railroad tie, we were dappled by the late afternoon sun while being bitten by a swarm of huge mosquitoes. Behind us, a gaggle of schoolchildren straggled home. Going without adequate shelter, food and clothing, and courting much pain or death, people everywhere have banded together to fight against what they found insufferable, and Americans will undoubtedly have to do so again. We can't simply consent to having our blood sucked and sucked, so unless we lie down, blanch out and pitifully beg for the mercy that's not coming, there will be many Valley Forges in our future.

Indifferent to reconstructed or staged history, I had never visited Valley Forge, but on my next trip to Norristown, I was vaguely planning on seeing it, but only after I had located a dive bar. Though Norris Beer Deli barely qualified as a bar of any kind, I walked in anyway, since I saw a bunch of people drinking. It was truly bare-bones boozing. After paying $2.50 for a tall can of Rolling Rock, I found myself sitting at a beat-up Formica table, next to a trash can. Though it wasn't yet 1 p.m., there were about ten people in this tiny joint, and I thought I was the only non-Spanish speaker until I heard some old guy behind me mutter, "Piano, piano," to no one in particular. I turned around to ask, *"Tu sei italiano?"* He didn't respond at first, since, let's face it, the likelihood of being addressed in such manner by an East Asian in Norristown is, well, near zero. But then he said, "It means take it easy," so I nudged, *"Lentamente?"* thinking he'd blurt, "Hey, where did you learn that?" But the man said nothing, and his face was blank. In his mid-sixties, he appeared fatigued, or maybe just drunk, as in nonstop drunk. Though he wasn't interested in conversing, he did ask to borrow my cell phone to call his daughter, so I heard him shout, "You know I love you but, listen, if you don't want me to come over tomorrow, I won't!"

The factories attracted immigrants. First, the Irish came in large numbers, then the Italians, and from this community rose Norristown's two most famous sons, Tommy Lasorda and Mike Piazza. Norristown is also known for a boxer, the lanky "Joltin'" Jeff Chandler, ex-bantam king. There are no boxing gyms left in Norristown, and in trying to start a new one, a sweet science promoter is quoted as saying, "I want to utilize boxing as an outlet for anger. Instead of picking up knives and guns these kids can pick up gloves."

Leaving Norris Beer Deli, I'd find Johnnie's several blocks away, and its worn, dingy exterior told me immediately that it was the perfect place to park my ass for a couple of hours. Johnnie's looked old and cheap enough to be a popular neighborhood tavern in this struggling town, and I was not wrong in my assumption, but since it was only 1:30 p.m. when I poked in, there was only one other customer. A pint of Yuengling set me back but $2.50, so that was very nice. Two loud televisions bookended the long bar. There was a grill to make cheesesteaks and burgers, a scrawled sign advertising boiled eggs, and a murky jar containing macerated phalli in some red solution. Maybe they were the remains of those who had violated some hidden rules of this establishment. I'd hate to relocate to Norristown in such a manner.

Feeling at ease, I then introduced myself to the barkeep and customer by saying I was a writer just looking around. I told them I lived in nearby Philly but had traveled across the country to see how the economy was.

"Oh, it's bad all right. It's bad here," the black man declared. "The only people who are doing well in Norristown are the Mexicans and the Chinese. They're opening up businesses. Everybody else is shooting at each other!"

"Oh, come on, man, it's not that bad!"

"Yes it is," the white barkeep chimed in. "Just last Friday, there was a shooting right on the corner, half a block from here, and it hit the car of one of our bartenders coming to work."

"Right on the corner," the forty-fiveish black man confirmed. His name was Chaz, as I'd find out soon enough, and the barkeep was called Margit. She was about twenty-five.

"And about five hours later, there was another shooting, not three blocks from here!" Margit continued.

"So two shootings within three blocks in five hours?"

"Yes, man, this is Norristown," Chaz smirked.

"And it didn't make the news because no one got hurt?"

"No, no news, but we know about it. Everybody knows about it. You just have to watch your ass around here, that's all. It's Norristown!"

"Why do you think there is so much violence here? Has it always been this bad?"

"No, it hasn't always been this bad. It's the people from Philly coming up to cause trouble!"

"Oh, come on, man, it's not just people from Philly who are shooting, and Philly has always been there, so why now? Is it the economy?"

"Maybe, and people are just getting crazier and crazier, that's all."

"Do you have work?" I asked Chaz. "What do you do, man?"

"I paint houses."

"Oh yeah? I used to do that, I did that for ten years, but I was the worst motherfuckin' housepainter. I mean, I could sand and scrape and all that, but I wasn't all there. I mean, I worked hard and everything, but I didn't really know what I was doing."

I could see that Chaz wasn't sure how to respond to such a cheerful confession of incompetence, but after a few seconds, he said, "I know what I'm doing."

If you ask an idle rich dude what kind of business he's in, he might say, "I'm an investor," and a poor man with little to do might claim to be a housepainter, carpenter or contractor, so Chaz may actually be worse at holding a beveled brush than yours truly. In fact, he may never have stood for hours on a forty-foot ladder, in 100°F heat (while hungover).

Wanting to hear about Margit, I opened, "I know a lot of bartenders, and they all tell me business has gone down quite a bit. Is that true here?"

"I don't make as much, that's for sure."

"People tip less?"

"Yeah, and they drink less, but this isn't my only job."

"What else do you do?"

"Inventory."

"What's that?"

"I go into stores and take inventory. I work for this company called RGIS. It's across the river, in King of Prussia. They've sent me to three other states, New Jersey, Delaware and Maryland."

"You get paid OK?"

"Yeah, it's all right. They're always hiring. They don't have enough people."

"In this economy? Are you serious?!"

"Well, sometimes you have to get up at three, so you can get to where you need to be by six. The stores are all over, you know, and if you have children, it can be a problem."

"You have kids?"

"Yeah, two. They're five and seven."

"And they're at home when you leave at three in the morning?"

"Yes, but their father is home."

"You know, I'm so glad to meet you two. I knew right away this was the right place to walk in."

"Nice to meet you too," Chaz said, and he and Margit smiled.

"You know, I've traveled all over the country, and people are always so cool. Just this year, I was in Oakland, St. Louis and Los Angeles, and if you don't show an attitude, you're not going to get any."

I know I was simplifying quite a bit, but forgive me, I had been drinking on an empty stomach. Chaz and Margit just grinned at my raving. "Hey," I continued, "what are those in the reddish jar?"

"Sausages," Margit answered. "Pickled sausages. Want to try one?"

"Maybe later."

"Here, here, just try it," and she fished one out and cut it in half so Chaz and I could each have a piece.

"Wait," I said, "I want to take a photo of this first," and I took out my Canon for the first time. Done, I left it on the bar as I bit into this long brown treat, and though it tasted like ammonia, to tell you the truth, I was very touched by Margit's sweetness.

"Hey, why don't you take a picture of us!" Chaz shouted, and I readily obliged as he kissed her cheek.

Showing them this image, I said, "If you give me an email address, I'll send it to you when I get home."

Soon, Johnnie's would start to fill up, and I would meet two more people: Kenny, a black man in his late fifties, and Don, a fifty-three-year-old white man. Since Don was only two barstools away, I quickly struck up a conversation. I told him I was very glad to discover this bar, for the people here were so friendly, "Is this the best bar in Norristown?"

"There are a couple more like it. The one across the street from my house is not bad, but I can't go there anymore."

"You've been flagged?"

"Yeah."

I laughed, "For what?"

"For arguing with my wife. It was nothing. It was stupid! She was an alcoholic, you know. That's how she died."

"How old was she when she died?"

"Just forty-eight. She had problems with her liver, kidney and heart. Here, check this out," and he stood up. With both hands, he pulled down his shirt to show me an elaborate tattoo over his heart: above a Grateful Dead skull were crisscrossed skis and ski poles, and above everything was his wife's name, Maureen, with her birth and death dates. On each side of the skull, three large roses completed this inky shrine.

I asked Don if I could take a photo of his tattoo, so he stood very still for ten seconds. I noticed that he had huge knuckles, and sported a large turquoise ring that would bust up a face really good with a straight left. On another finger was the Iron Cross. Done, I showed Don his own image on my viewfinder, to which he said, "Delete that face." Since he didn't say, "Delete the photo," I did nothing, and that may have been my first mistake. Don said his wife would drink all day long, but that's hardly unusual in Norristown, to which I replied, "When I painted houses, I'd try to drink no more than three shots after work, for if I did, I'd feel like shit the next day."

"Three shots ain't nothing. I know many people who must do a fifth before work, then drink two 12-ounce bottles of beer for lunch, then drink and drink after work. Three shots ain't shit!" Then Chaz added, rather oddly, "You buy me a shot? I'll show you how to do a shot."

I ignored that last bit, and it was then Kenny entered the picture. A black man in his early sixties, he declared that he could down six shots without feeling hardly anything, and to further show that I hardly knew how to drink, he leaned closer to me and said, "You shouldn't leave your money on the bar like that, man. You're showing off!"

I've drunk in Missoula, St. Paul, Madison, New Orleans and El Paso, etc., and I've always left my bills out, so I said, "I've always done it like this, man. If I don't leave my money out, the bartender might think I won't tip her."

"You don't even have to tip her, and people might take your money, and you're showing off, too! Do you see anybody else leaving their money out? When in Rome, do like the Romans."

"Twelve bucks fifty is showing off?!"

"It's the end of the month, man. Many people here don't have five bucks in their pockets! Here you are with your big camera, and your money out," and Kenny just shook his head.

"I'm just a writer," I explained to Kenny. "I travel around to hear stories and to take photos, but I'm not a journalist. No one is paying me to do this. I'm a poet. I've published eight books."

"I write poems, too!"

"Oh yeah? Hmm. Do you have one in your head? One that you can recite to me?"

"Sure, but let me remember it," and here I possibly made my second mistake, for as Kenny closed his eyes to dredge up his poem, I took out my mini recorder and asked him, "Hey, can I record this? Otherwise, there's no way I will be able to remember it."

"No!"

"No?"

"Have you heard of the music industry?"

"What do you mean?"

"What do you have when you put a poem to music?"

"You have a song?"

"Yes, and a song can make a lot of money!"

"OK then," and I put my recorder away, but not before Don, that cheerless dude with the Iron Cross and eye-socket-collapsing turquoise ring, had seen it. Now, most poems are instantly forgettable, so you must forgive me for not recalling a single word of Don's rhyming and philosophical composition, and he was into it, too, as he recited. After he finished, I said, "See, man, now I won't remember any of that tomorrow morning, because you didn't let me record it!"

"Hey, why are you raising your voice?!" It was Don.

"Huh, what?"

"Stop shouting! You've been shouting!"

"No, I haven't been shouting. I'm just talking to this guy."

"You're annoying everybody by shouting, so stop shouting!"

I looked at Kenny, "What's up with him?" But Kenny said nothing. Keep in mind that Johnnie's is no foofoo lounge at a five-star hotel, but a loud and smoky dive with a jukebox often blasting heavy metal or grunge. As Kenny and I resumed our conversation, Don interrupted again, "Stop cutting him off! Why don't you listen!"

We have a psycho here, I was starting to think, but it was also odd that Kenny made no attempt to calm his friend down. As Don glowered at me, I glared right back, and I was so annoyed by this man's irrational behavior that I could hardly pay attention to Kenny, and the place was also very loud, as I've already pointed out. Suddenly, though, Don extended a hand towards me, but I didn't shake it.

"Shake it!" Kenny urged. "Shake it!"

"I'm sitting here having a good time, bothering nobody, and this guy is giving me shit for no reason," I said to Kenny, but after Don had withdrawn his hand, I actually got off my stool, walked over to him and said, "Listen, man, we're cool, right? I'm just having a good time, and everybody has been so nice to me, so I don't want to leave here with any negative energy, so we're friends, right?" By this time, I had my left arm around Don's shoulder, and my right hand out for him to shake, and as we gripped hands, he said, "Yeah, we're cool."

All writing is self-vindication, and all talking, too, for that matter. Further, how we see ourselves is always radically different from how others perceive us. Still, a writer can strive to minimize these distortions by treating himself as just another subject, as simply another vain and bumbling fool, in short, who's always trying to prove, with sad results, that's he's not a vain and bumbling fool. In any case, I fully thought I had dissolved my tension with Don, and so I returned to my stool feeling much lighter.

"Hey, I want you to meet my family!" Kenny shouted. "I'll show you the real Norristown. We'll go just around the corner, so put your money away. Let's go!"

"How long will we be gone?"

"Just a few minutes. Let's go!"

My third possible mistake that night was not in going with Kenny, though you may think that's foolish enough, but in leaving my scrawled notes on the bar. I didn't want the barkeep to think I had left without tipping her, and I wasn't done drinking. If I had been born more cautious, I'd not routinely find myself in these uninsurable situations, but shoot me, man, my curiosity is often stronger than my sense of prudence, and in this instance, it was only 4:30 p.m., OK, and we were on Main Street, so it wasn't like I was roaming around Ciudad Juárez in the dark, which I've also done. Further, I intuitively felt that I could trust Kenny, and in this, I was almost right.

Across from Johnnie's, there was a fire station with this sign, "REMEMBER WHO FOUGHT O OUR FREEDOM," and we only walked four hundred feet or so before turning left on Chain, where there were plenty of people on the sidewalk, including children.

"I never take strangers to meet my family," Kenny declared, "so you'll buy me a beer later, OK?"

First, Kenny introduced me to a niece of his, a gorgeous girl about eight years old. I shook her hand. Next I met a pleasant old couple on a porch, then, before I knew it, I found myself in a living room, with four lovely women in front of me, relaxing on a couch. I shook their hands. Kenny then led me into the kitchen, but on the way, he picked up a shot glass from the dining room table and downed it. "Hey, whose shot was that?!" I asked.

"Mine!"

"But how come it was sitting there on the dining room table?"

"Because they knew I was coming, that's why."

After shaking hands with several more folks, and even chatting briefly with a Puerto Rican woman living next door, we walked back to the bar.

"Hey, Kenny, the women in your family are very beautiful."

"Yes, but the men, they are dangerous."

Thinking it sounded like a bad sitcom line, I actually chuckled as I replied, "They can't all be dangerous, Kenny. In each family, there are a few pussies!"

"They're all dangerous!"

"Me, Kenny, I can't fight worth shit. I wouldn't know how to beat up that trash can!"

"I would never say that if I were you."

"I've only fired a gun once in my life, at a shooting range. I mean, I fired a bunch of shots, but it was only inside a shooting range. How about you?"

"I know how to use guns."

"On the streets, too?"

"Wherever."

"Hey, have you ever shot anyone? Killed anyone?"

He paused, then, "Yes, but that was a long time ago. That's why some people drink, so they don't have to think too much about what they've done."

"How many people have you shot?"

Kenny didn't answer, but only said, "Hey, remember to buy me that beer," as we reentered Johnnie's.

I would never get a chance to. Though my stool was unoccupied, my notes were gone, and I pointed this out to Kenny as I reclaimed my seat. Wanting his beer, he was right next to me, but then he disappeared for a few seconds. When he came back, Kenny whispered, "We've got to get out of here!"

"But I have to find out what happened to my notes," I smiled, "and get you your beer too!"

"No, they think you're a cop. We've got to go!"

I picked up my bag and slowly walked out, but not before I had said goodbye to Chaz, though he seemed terribly uncomfortable shaking my hand, "Let go of my hand!" I also paused to look Don in the eyes, smile and shake his hand, "I don't know what's happening, man, but it was good talking to you."

It seemed like the perfect time to go home, but Kenny suggested we go to another bar, since he still wanted that beer I owed him. The issue became moot, however, because Don had barged outside to confront me, "Hey, are you a cop?"

"What?!" Seeing that Chaz had come out, too, I looked at him and said, "Didn't I tell you I was a writer, right from the beginning?"

Chaz said nothing, and Kenny said nothing, and I was left to confront the enraged Don, "That picture that you took of me. Erase it!"

"Man, you don't have to be like this, but I will," and I erased the photos in front of him. Showing his true self, Kenny then shouted, "Take the card! Take his card!"

This has turned into a robbery, pure and simple, and a potential physical assault. First off, a Lexar 16GB 300X card costs $150, and it was not blank but filled with photos, so there was no way in hell I was going to let him take it. As I put my camera into its bag, Don grabbed my left forearm, but I immediately yanked his hand away, then I took out my phone as I stepped backward and opened a door, right behind me.

I had no idea there was a door there until I opened it, and it could easily have been locked, but there I was, suddenly, inside Berks Insurance, and it was my first time in an insurance office, by the way. Mr. Berks, bless his soul, quickly instructed a male employee to not let my harassers in. When Kenny tried to enter, this employee chased him out and locked the door. Within two minutes, two of Norristown's finest showed up, and one asked me, "What do you want to do?"

"I just want to walk to the train station and get the hell out of Norristown! If you have questions, just ask the people in this store. They saw everything from beginning to end." As I walked away, the cops watched my back, and so ended my pleasant day trip to Norristown. Its motto, *"Fervet Opus,"* and it's boiling all right, though not from industry.

STAGNANT RIVERSIDE

10-28-13—Though Riverside has successfully reinvented itself before, it is now stuck. During the middle of the nineteenth century, it was a resort town, a place for the well-to-do of Philadelphia to mellow during the sultry months. They chugged up the Delaware by steamboat. Some steamed into town on rails. There were summer homes here, and a grand hotel with a ballroom. When the train reached the New Jersey Shore, however, Riverside couldn't compete with the Atlantic Ocean, and so it slumped into irrelevance, a forgotten fork in the river, but then it picked itself up and morphed into an industrial center. For a tiny town that never had more than 9,000 souls, it became a leading manufacturer of watch cases, worsted fabric and hosiery.

These industries lasted for decades, but with the invention of wristwatches and cheap synthetic fabrics that could be churned out in countless other places, they petered out. Once more, Riverside lay on the canvas, with its mouthpiece knocked into the fifth row, and it was snoring loudly (in a darkened arena) when the housing bubble arrived, affording a decade-long reprieve. Coinciding with this, there was also the opening of the River Line. For only $1.50, one could go all the way from idyllic Camden to picturesque Trenton, thus throngs of shoppers and diners would get off at the Riverside stop, so went the local daydream, but of course this conveyance has also been whisking money away. In any case, outsiders who do detrain all seem to head for the Madison, a rather upscale pub in a brand-new building. They don't go anywhere else.

On a recent Friday afternoon, I strolled down Scott Street, Riverside's main drag, and pretty much had the sidewalk to myself. I passed a closed Golden River Restaurant (despite its Chinese-sounding name, it advertised classic diner fare), then a kaput Beadscape, "Beads and a bit of déjà vu," then a tits-up American Clothes, "AMERICAN STYLES FOR ALL WOMEN AND CHILDREN." In its display windows, there were trophies and a potted plant where clothing should be, and painted on a wall was an ecstatic cartoon face surrounded by musical notes and a G clef, all to disguise, sort of, that the business was dead. In front of its door, a trash can had been placed to prevent anyone from lying there. Franco's Taqueria, however, was open.

Continuing, I encountered a storefront sign offering walk-in zumba and yoga instruction on Mondays for only $5 per class. I'm assuming these lessons are conducted separately, for it would be difficult to hold, say, a Pincha Mayurasana "feathered peacock" pose, with one's arms jackknifed on the floor and one's feet straight up in the air, while rhythmically thrusting one's hips to salsa or samba. With persistence or prayer, however, all things are possible, I've been told. The tropical pink and green of this display led me to think it was a South American operation, but no, the proprietor of Pizzazz, "Fitness with Flair," was a discernibly blond and pale Karen Lightfoot, and she would turn up again, just two doors down, as co-pastor of the Riverlution Church.

Lightfoot's bio declares that she is a "prophetic minister" who has been "trained by the Holy Spirit with a special anointing in ministering with flags." With her husband, Ken, a mailman by day, Karen is semaphorically steering lost souls into the Kingdom of God, provided it's not too foggy. The 3,000 square feet of the Riverlution Church was, not that long ago, occupied by Barbara Shropshire, Riverside's last bookseller. In neighboring towns, there are Christian bookstores and one that purveys African American literature.

Though I had seen few signs of commerce on my walk, downtown seemed neat, dignified and pleasant, and the kids leaving school were all calm and cheerful. Seeing a crossing guard, I chirped, "This is a pretty town."

"What?!" She broke into a huge smile at the apparent absurdity of my assertion.

"This is a pretty town."

"I've never heard that before." She could barely refrain from laughing. "This town has really gone downhill, though it's picking up a little."

"From what I've seen, I can tell that it was once really beautiful, but it's still nice. Are you from here?"

"Been here my whole life, either in Riverside or Delanco, across the creek." She was about forty years old. "Where are you from?"

"I live in Philly. I just took the train up to look around. I've read about this place."

"You have?!"

"You said this place is picking up, but how?"

"Immigrants. They're bringing some life to Riverside. Most of them are Brazilians."

"But what brought them here?"

"Construction. You see these white trucks all over? They belong to contractors. There are a lot of contractors here."

Elsewhere, white contractors employ Mexicans, but since many of the Riverside builders are Portuguese, they hire Brazilians, most of them undocumented. The tension over this influx boiled over when Riverside passed laws penalizing employers for hiring illegal immigrants, and landlords for renting to them. Though these laws were challenged in court and never applied, they did chase many of the Brazilians away.

Leaving downtown, I strayed into the residential neighborhoods, and notwithstanding a handful of boarded-up houses and many For Sale signs, all was, again, tidy and dignified. Hinting at Riverside's former wealth, there were a number of huge homes. Flags fluttered on poles or were furled over porches. With the country fighting war after war, one is bombarded with an infinity of patriotic symbols, signs and declarations.

Every couple of blocks, there was a flyer taped to a pole advertising a yard sale, for as our military contractors gorge on billion-dollar contracts, we are reduced to selling whatever we have left to make ends meet, be it silverware, DVDs of movies no one has ever heard of, or broken toys. We take our gold bracelets from dealer to dealer, hoping for a slightly better price. Some even sell wedding rings.

Making its partial withdrawal from Afghanistan, the United States is leaving behind seven billion dollars' worth of equipment. To take these home would be too expensive, and since anything that's left intact may possibly be weaponized, Uncle Sam is destroying everything before selling it for scrap. Suddenly filled with foresight, Sammy doesn't want a Special Forces grunt or CIA dick blown up, two years hence, by some ingenious Taliban contraption made up of a microwave timer, a high-tech ice cream scoop, an SUV fan belt and a Katy Perry standee.

Doubling back to downtown, I saw, in a window, a baseball trophy with an American flag stuck on it, so I took out my camera, tried to find the proper angle and adjusted the ISO, aperture and shutter speed. With its scratched sensor and erratic software, this beat-up machine is just about ready for a Kabul junk dealer. Oh Lord, will you buy me a new Canon or Nikon?

"Taking photos, eh?"

I turned and saw some beefy guy with a beard, in his mid-fifties, so I said, "Yeah, I'm taking a picture of this flag."

"Right on!"

Since he seemed a friendly sort, I asked, "Hey, I've walked a couple of miles and haven't seen a single bar. Where can I get a drink around here?"

"See that flag down the street? There's a bar right there. In fact, that's where I'm going!"

So that's how I met Steve. The RaceTrack 75 Sports Bar appeared newish, with all its barstools shiningly upholstered in checkered flag pattern. There were seven televisions, but only four were beaming and babbling. The two up front showed American sports, while those at the rear had on Portuguese programs. Behind the bar, a sign touted, "RIS-

SOIS. CAMARAO E CARNE. PASTEIS DE BACALHAU." Another, "FRANCESINHAS A MODA DO PORTO." Four dapper men at the back conversed in Portuguese. Ragged by comparison, I sat at the front near Steve and a white-bearded gent in a tan baseball cap, blue flannel shirt and gray sweatpants. He seemed cheerful enough, but worn out. A bottle of Bud was only $2.50, but I didn't know this, so ordered Yuengling, which set me back four bucks. This space was too open and bright for my taste, but thankfully there was no music to disrupt conversation. I said to the tired man, "I was told Riverside is filled with bars, but I walked all over town today and couldn't find any."

"There used to be lots. There was one across the street."

"Why are they gone?"

"I don't know . . . Money."

"How many bars are left now?"

"Let's see, there's the Beer Factory, the White Eagle, JD's, McCrossen's, this place and Towne Tavern, which is more upscale. I can't afford to drink there. There's also Casa Brazil. So that's, what, seven bars? There used to be at least twenty."

"How long have you lived here?"

"I was born here, and never left until I joined the service. I was in Vietnam for two tours. When I got out, I moved to Florida and stayed for nearly forty years. 9/11 brought me back."

"What do you mean?"

"I had a business doing laundry for these big hotels, but the tourists stopped coming after 9/11. I'm old anyway, so it was time to come back. I live off my Social Security now. Each day, I come here and take it easy."

"They pick him up each day at noon," Steve chimed in. "Each day! Then take him home in the evening."

"Who do?"

"Her husband." Steve nodded to the bartender.

"I come, drink my twenty bucks, then go home." The tired but cheerful man chuckled.

"Wow, these people are really nice if they pick you up at your house each day."

"They are, and I don't even tip most of the time. I'd start out thinking I'd tip, but between having one more beer or tipping, I'd choose the beer. They don't mind, though. Do you, Teresa?"

"Do what?" She was at the cash register, with her back turned.

"Do you mind that I'm so cheap?"

"No, I love you, Joe!"

"They're the nicest people. Some of my friends say, 'Why do you drink at that Portuguese bar? You should be at the White Eagle!' But they treat me very well here."

Leaning closer, Steve confided, "Many people here don't like the Portuguese or the Brazilians. They come and take our jobs, you know. A few years ago, we passed a law to get rid of illegal immigrants."

"Yes, I've heard about that."

"There was this Brazilian café owner, he got mad, so he put a sign in his window, 'No Americans allowed.'"

"That guy's not Brazilian, he's Portuguese," Joe corrected Steve.

"Yeah, you're right, but after he put this sign up, the sheriff came and told him to take it down."

"Wow, that's pretty weird, that sign," I cringed.

"That guy owns a few apartments," Joe added, "so he was also mad because these new laws were chasing his tenants away. Hey, you're not Portuguese, are you?"

I laughed out loud, "No, I'm Vietnamese."

"If you turn your head this way, Joe, his eyes become rounder and he does look sorta Portuguese," Steve joked.

We all just sat there for a moment. I then asked Joe, "When were you in Vietnam?"

"Sixty-seven and sixty-eight. I was just eighteen years old. Just got out of high school. I fought in the Tet Offensive," and Joe just stared at me, his cloudy blue eyes clearly seeing what wasn't in Riverside, New Jersey, that day or ever. After the weightiness of it all had settled again, Joe continued, "My father fought in World War I and World War II, and four of my brothers were in the service. I was a baseball prospect, you know. After high school, I had sixty scholarship offers—"

"Six?!" I interrupted him.

"No, sixty."

"Sixty! You must have been great!"

"I was. I was a catcher, and I hit .400 in high school. I could probably have made it as a professional, but my father said, 'We have a war now,' so I enlisted. I didn't know what I was doing. I had a small life. We were into bebop and Elvis, and next thing I knew, I was killing people. Your people!" Joe started to tear up. I put a hand on his shoulder and moved it back and forth. The red-eyed vet continued, "The government put us into this terrible situation. All of a sudden, we were there. Our first day, we saw two American corpses, and they had their genitals cut off and stuffed into their mouths."

"What?! I've never heard of anything like that."

"But that's what we saw. And now, I'm thinking I'm not sure who did this. I'm thinking maybe it's our own government that did this, to get us riled up. They did it so we would hate the Vietnamese."

Steve hadn't really paid attention to what Joe was saying, for he had probably heard it before, but suddenly he interjected, "I spent twenty years in the Army, and I was in Desert Storm, but now I'm not sure what it was all about. The politicians don't care about us, man! They've sold this country to China! Look at this," and Steve took off his watch to show me its back side. "What does it say?"

"The spirit of America."

"And you know where it was made?"

"China?"

"Bingo! Of course, China, and I bought this watch from the *VFW* magazine!"

"This used to be an industrial town," Joe jumped in. "Half the clothes in the world was made here. Now we don't make nothing. What we need is a tariff on all this made-in-China stuff. That's how we level the playing field."

Higher tariffs mean higher prices here, plus a cut in profits for all the US firms who have moved their manufacturing to China, not to mention a hurting for America's real first family, the Waltons of Walmart. Since our bought politicians lick these fat cats' asses, it ain't gonna happen, OK? So we sat there and shot the cow pies (to dust, until dusk). Joe asked my age, then kidded, "You know who your daddy is?"

"Dad!" I shouted.

"You two look exactly alike," Steve opined with a straight face. To prove this to all and sundry, I asked Steve to snap a photo of me with my head clumped against Joe's. Steve then showed me his dented nose, a result of a punch in mean-ass Tennessee, "And I wasn't even screwing his wife!"

Speaking of wife, Steve's own showed up, but within twenty minutes, they argued and she stormed out, only to return forty-five minutes later to ask him, sweetly, to come home. They left with this weasel-like character with a cane. After they were gone, Joe explained that the weasel had been jailed for about thirteen years for murder, and was now stealing pills from Steve's wife to get high. "Four or five of them killed somebody, but this guy got the longest sentence."

Joe had reached his brew allotment, so I bought him two more Buds, but then he paid one last round with a credit card. "You know, I'm supposed to be dead," Joe grinned. "I have liver cancer. Seven years ago, a doctor said I had six months to live."

"So that's your last beer, Joe!" Per nurse Teresa. "After you finish that, my husband will take you home!"

Cheating on death, or maybe just one doctor's erroneous betting line, Joe will chug and chatter until his own factory shuts down, for good. During the height of the housing bubble, there were plans to turn the Taubel Hosiery Mill and the imposing Keystone Watch Case building into condominiums. Needless to say, these schemes have been scrapped.

Before I left the bar, I met one more gentleman who filled me in on Riverside. Born in Portugal in 1962, Harold was two years old when his parents brought him to the States. They first settled in Newark.

"Why are there so many Portuguese in Riverside?" I asked. "What's the attraction?"

"I don't know. It's like somebody moved here first, then the rest followed. The river may have something to do with it, and the hills. It reminds them of home, maybe? Most Portuguese are fishermen."

"You know, my sister-in-law is Portuguese, and her family is from Stockton, California. They're farmers."

"Hmm, I don't know any Portuguese farmers, but there must be farmers, I suppose. Most of us are fishermen. The codfish is huge in our culture. The codfish is ninety percent of our culture!"

Later in the conversation, Harold gave me his take on Riverside's immigration quandary. "First, the Brazilian men came, and they were living ten or twelve to an apartment. Each morning, you'd see hundreds of Brazilians coming out of these buildings. Then some of them brought their wives and children over, so suddenly there were all these Brazilian kids in the schools. The locals really didn't like that. They were saying, 'These people are here illegally, they don't pay taxes, and now we have to educate their kids too?' And since these kids didn't speak English, they had to be put in ESL classes. Even as a Portuguese, I can see why people were upset."

"But you also hire Brazilians for your business?"

"How can I not? How can I compete if I don't hire Brazilians? Everybody everywhere is hiring illegals!"

Eventually, the solution is for Americans to become illegal immigrants elsewhere. Living twelve to a room in Shanghai or Dubai, we can eat, speak and do everything very badly in a culture not our own. Still, it beats chewing air in Barefoot, Kentucky, or Zigzag, Oregon. Each month, we'll wire some renminbi home. "Where are you from?" we'll be asked repeatedly by the locals, and each time it will sting us anew because that's another way of saying, "What are you doing here?" Even our foreign-born children or grandchildren will be similarly interrogated. "No place special," they will answer. "My grandparents came from the United States of America. Ever heard of it?"

On our way to such banishment, we'll pass through wars, riots, oppression and madness, though many of us are loony enough as is. Taking the River Line away from Riverside, I happened to sit in front of a raving man who, at first, I thought was on a cell phone discussing business matters. Sounding self-important, he spoke loudly enough so that the entire train car could hear. Most riders ignored his monologue, but some couldn't help but smile at the inspired madness, "Yes, the Heifer Foundation does excellent work, but so does the Lactation Institute, with its bovine specialists.

"No, there is no coordination between the tongs and the yakuza, but I'll have to check with my Chinatown contacts before I get back to you. You have to keep in mind, though, that a tong is not necessarily criminal. The Duck Soup Tong, for example, is perfectly legitimate.

"Yes, Schwarzenegger has gotten back into the news. He just cracked some joke about Iowa. I know that state well, and just this year I was in Cialis, Iowa, and Viagra, Iowa, and I can tell you that it is an invigorating state, and also very upright. You really should visit Cialis and Viagra, Iowa."

And this man was still delirious as I stepped off the train in Camden. Into the night, I walked, and into the dark he rode away. Good night, everyone. Good night.

CHEAP ROOMS IN KENSINGTON, PHILADELPHIA

11-7-13—The elevated train rumbles above Kensington Avenue, so riding on it, you can see all of these desolate windows on the upper floors, many of which are boarded up, bricked over or hollow. Ruins of factories loom nearby. Until recently, there was an open coffin in the yard of The Last Stop recovery center. Lying inside it, a wide-eyed, pink-faced dummy stared up. At ground level, you can shuffle pass these cheap hoagie joints, Chinese takeouts (with bulletproof order windows), pawnshops, bodegas, discount clothing stores, used appliance dealers and a church of the Black Israelites, who believe that only blacks, Latinos and Native Americans can enter heaven. Many storefronts are empty, many lots trash-strewn and weed-infested. Here, most of the barbershops are owned by Vietnamese immigrants, and with competition so fierce, they all advertise a five-buck haircut. Revealing their primary clientele, American and Puerto Rican flags grace their signs. On side streets, there are all these "abandominiums," which serve as shooting galleries, but the biggest one of all are the wooded flanks of the railroad tracks running along Tusculum Street. Shootings follow illegal drugs, so here, there and everywhere are death shrines with their candles and stuffed animals. At Ella and Cambria, there's one housed in an old TV cabinet, of the type made fifty years ago. "R.I.P. BUM," it mourns. In Camden, I have seen one that said, "R.I.P. CUNT."

When I first strayed into this neighborhood twenty-five years ago, I thought the people rather misshapen, their faces dull, but between the poor diet, cheap alcohol and abundant drugs, it's hard to appear otherwise. (To be fair, they'd probably deem me a gargoyle also.) Much has been written about the illegal drugs and sex that plague Kensington, and hardly a week goes by without a shooting or two, but normal families also live here, and beneath the bloody headlines, there is also resilience, dignity and beauty. Three years ago, for example, I was invited by Emily Diefendorf to address her sixth-grade class at the Visitation School. Before my talk, we met at the Thang Long ("Rising Dragon," Hanoi's old name) Noodle Restaurant, and had pho. Most of the kids were Dominicans or Puerto Ricans, and though many had never had this dish, with one or two never having even used chopsticks, they all behaved exceptionally well at the meal, then afterwards in the classroom. Respectful and attentive, they were a tribute to their school and teacher, a transplant from Indiana who had majored in journalism and history. Kids being kids, though, they did ask me some goofy questions. My favorite, "You told us you can't sing and you can't dance, and you weren't any good at sports, so, ah, what are you good at?"

On that occasion, I also met Tung Nguyen, the school's handyman. In 1981, he survived a boat escape from Vietnam to wash up in Indonesia, where he stayed for a year in a refugee camp. Finally admitted to the US, Tung first found work on an oil rig in the Gulf of Mexico. Three weeks on the rig, then one at home, so he saved much, though the pay wasn't all that great. The twenty-seven men on the rig ate really well, though, but they weren't allowed to drink. When idle, they fished. After this company went bankrupt, Tung tried to find work in Spokane, Seattle and Kansas City, before arriving in Philadelphia, where he was hired by a steel processing plant. He remained there for thirteen years before it shut down. All four of Tung's kids had attended or were at the Visitation School, with the oldest ready for college. She was being offered a full eight-year scholarship to four different schools, including Temple and Penn. I asked Tung what it was like to have kids in Kensington, and he just shrugged,

"You don't let them out after dark, that's all. They basically just go to school, then come home."

So an exceptional student can escape Kensington via the Ivy League, but what of the mediocre kids? In a healthy and functioning society, which we no longer are, even the stragglers and dim-witted have productive roles to fill, and can contribute. This is a terrible time to be young in America, frankly, except that it will get even worse, much worse. There are few jobs, and most college degrees should be double-ply, so you won't stink up your hand using it once, and we're not just talking about a bachelor's in printmaking here, but also a law certificate from a first-tier school, etc.

At the other end of the arc, it's not so great to be gray, either, for there's little money, with less coming all the time. Having paid taxes all your working life, you're now shortchanged in your old age, for they have looted Social Security to fund wars and bank bailouts. They have also swindled away your retirement investments, should you have any. Having been fleeced for decades, you're now treated like a parasite by the real parasites. Recently, a Detroit columnist challenged himself by trimming a grand from his monthly budget, as in reducing his cable subscription to two thousand channels, for example, but many of us don't even have $1,000 to spend each month. Take Tom "Whitey" Kopeski, whom I met the other day at Jack's, a Kensington dive. Whitey gets $792 in Social Security, plus $71 of food stamps. "So how much do you spend for rent?" I asked.

"$300."

"Wow, that's pretty good! But you have to share a kitchen and a bathroom, right?"

"Yeah."

"How many people are in the house altogether?"

"Five, but some of them bring in a woman every now and then."

"You're not married?"

"No, I've never been married."

"Why not?"

"Most women just want to be your mother. After the first few months, every girlfriend you have will turn into your mother! Do this, do that, you're not doing that right! They want to control every little thing that you do. It's wired into them!"

"What's the longest you've been with a woman?"

"Continuously? Six or seven months."

"You're not lonely when you go home?"

"No! When I go home, I have peace, and I like it that way." Then, "When I was twenty, I fell in love with this girl, and I treated her the right way. I was considerate and listened to her, but guess what she did? She left me for an asshole! You see, all they want is someone like their dad, and since she had an asshole for a dad, she needed an asshole for a husband!"

"But don't some people want the opposite from their dad or mom? I mean, shouldn't she have wanted a nice guy for a husband?"

"I was that nice guy, and she didn't want me! They may think they want a nice guy, but subconsciously, they really need an asshole!"

"Is your mom still around?"

"No, she died a long time ago. She was only forty-one."

"Wow, that's pretty young! That's ridiculous! What did she die of?"

"Kidney problems. It runs in my family."

"And from drinking, too?"

"Yeah, probably."

"What was your mom like?"

"She raised five kids all by herself, since my dad was never around, and whenever he showed up, all he wanted was money, and he hit all of us. He'd sucker-punch us. At fifteen, though, I hit him back, and I was kicking him too as he lay on the ground. He never hit me again. My older brother also beat him up once, with a baseball bat."

"What did your father do for a living?"

"He was a writer."

"A writer?! That's interesting. What did he write?"

"He wrote for newspapers. He worked for the *Courier-Post* in Camden, then the *Philadelphia Bulletin*. Later he worked for the *Trenton Times*."

"And how old was he when he died?"

"I don't know, and I don't even care. I don't even know where he's buried."

"Boy, you really hate your dad!"

"No, it's not hate. If you hit a dog, he'll bite you back. He has to. When I beat him that one time, I didn't feel any hate, just satisfaction."

"How old were you when your mom died?"

"Nineteen. I was right there. Whenever she got sick, she would just lay there and be real quiet, and she had been laying in bed for about a week, and it was around two o'clock when I stepped out to get a hoagie, and when I came back, I tried to talk to her but she wouldn't say nothing. Suddenly I realized she was dead. It was about 2:30 a.m."

As we were talking, an old woman walked in and went to the far end of the bar. Though she didn't say hi to Whitey, he let on, "I used to date her, forty-three years ago. We went back and forth for about a year and a half. Sometimes, when I have money, I still buy her a drink."

"Man, you've been around here a long time!"

"I have only lived in three places: Camden, Fishtown and Kensington, but I've traveled some, you know. Had a few adventures. I used to hitch-hike. It was so easy then. People weren't paranoid. Now, everybody's looking over their shoulder. It used to be, you'd walk into a bar, any bar, and people would talk. Now, some of them don't even want to talk to you. There's so much mistrust, and unfriendliness, and anger too. People are pissed!"

"Did you hear about the blind guy who was beaten up?"

"Yeah, yeah, and there's a video of it."

"What was most incredible was all these people walked right by and did nothing. Here was a young guy beating up a blind guy, and kicking him while he was on the ground."

"And they didn't even know each other, from what I heard."

"No, they didn't. Dude just felt like beating up someone blind, an easy target. Anyway, anyway, where did you go when you traveled?"

"I've been to Los Angeles, Toronto and Montreal, and when I was twenty-one, I went down to Miami and stayed for a few months."

"Who did you know down there?"

"Nobody. I just took a bus, and went down. I wanted to see Florida. When I got there, I found a job right away, so I stayed for a while."

"What did you do?"

"I was a waiter. I've done that a lot, and I've bused tables. Mostly, though, I worked in factories. There was so much work, then, you could always find something to do. You could quit one factory job and find another one that same day!"

"The kids don't have any idea how easy it was to get work, because there are no jobs now. I feel sorry for them."

"We've sent all our jobs overseas! To China! Kensington used to have these factories, but they're all gone, every single one of them. I used to work at ITE, we made circuit breakers, and there were so many garment factories in this area."

"In 1988, I worked for this guy in Logan who made sweat shirts and sweat pants. Even in the late eighties, there were garment factories here."

"Not anymore!"

Whitey never served in the Army, for he had an extensive juvenile record, "We used to break into houses and steal cars."

"What did you take?"

"Whatever that was there! But the cars, we only took them for joy-rides. We really didn't keep them."

"Were you locked up for all this shit?"

"Yeah, a couple years, in a juvenile facility. It wasn't that bad, but it was bad enough. It straightened me out. I haven't been in trouble since."

Whitey had been drinking, very slowly, a $1.50 can of Schaefer. The beer is dirt cheap in Jack's, at only two bucks for a pint of Yuengling. A hot dog is $1. A grilled cheese sandwich is $2.25, plus 25 cents for a slice of tomato. A cheesesteak is $3. A life-size cardboard of John Wayne guards the front. At the back, Marilyn Monroe teases. A photo from 1993 shows twelve faces, all white, but an image dated 2005 has five black patrons out of the twenty-three shown.

"You come here every day, Whitey?"

"When I have the money, yes, but I always run out by the end of the month. That's when I have to sit home for about a week."

"What do you do at home?"

"Nothing. I don't even have a television."

"And even if you did, you'd need cable."

"I can't afford that! By the end of the month, I can't even afford to eat. That's when I go down to St. Francis."

"How many times do you eat there each month?"

"About ten. They're very nice down there, and the food is pretty good. Today, they gave us macaroni and beef, plus a bologna sandwich. Sometimes, they even have roast beef!"

"Wow, that's pretty good!"

"But the line is getting longer all the time, though. More people need help these days."

"Who goes there?"

"Everybody. Men, women, young people, kids. You see moms pushing strollers. Everybody goes there. You should try it sometime."

"Today is the 2nd, so you really didn't need to go down there, right?"

"Yeah, but I went anyway. Saved a few bucks. Plus, I like it down there. I can't really cook at home, you know. When I buy my own food, I usually just get a hoagie, or I go to this salad bar. I don't really eat much."

"How much do you drink a day, when you have the money?"

"I don't know. Fifteen bucks? I drink until the money runs out by the end of the month. Sometimes I borrow from people. My landlord, he's Chinese, he lends me money sometimes."

"How much does he lend you?"

"Twenty, sometimes forty bucks, but I always pay my rent on time. He's a nice guy, my landlord."

Behind the bar, there were all these lottery tickets cascading down, like festive streamers. They ranged from $1 to $20, and nearly always, you could see one or several people scratching away as they drank. Handing over a ticket, Pat the bartender would say, "Good luck, sweetie!" Or, "I've got a good feeling about this one, hon!"

Broke as he is, Whitey sometimes goes to Sugarhouse and diddles with the penny slots. Pat had just been to Parx Casino, where she lost a chunk, but this same week, she snagged a winning number, plus aced a trifecta at the horse race. Having inherited her row home, she doesn't have to worry about rent, and only serves drinks at Jack's once a week. A big seller here is the 40-ounce Hurricane bottle, to go. Malt lick'er. Working, Pat sang along to the jukebox, "Everybody plays the fool, sometimes! No exception to the rules. No, no!" Then, "It's jew, babe! I got jew, babe!"

The poor's worst habits are magnified and roundly condemned, but these same vices become glamorized in the rich. A cloudy-eyed chick in sweat pants who's strung out on drugs is nothing but trash, but if she came from money, she'd be a socialite, like Britney Spears. A slumping man at the bar scratching away his last buck is a fool, but if he had an office in Lower Manhattan, he'd still be respectable as he gambled away everyone's money. A small-time killer is a monster who deserves to be beaten, then shot, but our most prolific mass murderers, of foreigners and Americans, are (s)elected to the highest offices in the land.

St. Francis feeds nearly four hundred people a day in Kensington. There's also Rock Ministries, where neighborhood kids can learn how to box, for free. Speaking of right crosses and left hooks, Rocky Balboa was placed in Kensington, for South Philly, the real Italian neighborhood, was not crummy enough. The bar scene in *Rocky V* was filmed using the interior of One and One Half Bar and the outside of Bentley's Place, across the street from it. Only Bentley's Place is still around. Before it shut down, a can of Bud at One and One Half was down to $1.25 during happy hour. McCarthy's, at the same intersection, is also gone.

Recently, I found myself sitting in a near empty Bentley's Place. It wasn't quite three o'clock. A young black man came in trying to sell men's socks, but got no taker, then a Puerto Rican guy walked around with a shoe box with a photo of some smiling middle-aged dude taped to it. There was also a slit to insert money, "My uncle died last night, and I'm trying to raise money for his funeral."

After he left, I stared at a sign advertising a tin of sardine for only two bucks, knocked down from $2.50. "What do you get with that?" I asked the bartender.

"Nothing."

"No piece of bread, no cracker?"

"Nothing, just a plastic spoon. My husband bought all these cans at the Dollar Store. We must have food to open on Sundays. See that sign for the hot dogs? There ain't no hot dogs."

In Kensington, serving cans of sardines qualifies an establishment as a restaurant, and you can be an instant hotelier by renting any spot to sleep by the night, week or month. No bed is necessary, just a piece of plywood would do. Flophouses dot this neighborhood. If you're a prissy mofo who's leery of sharing a room with four or five other bodies, you can come to Charles Rickard. Charles has a building at Kensington and Tusculum. For just $300 a month, you can have your own suite of bedroom, kitchen and bathroom. If you talk nice, or are pleasant to look at, Charles may knock it down to $200, however, so do bargain. A garbageman is currently occupying the front part of the third floor. "He's my best tenant ever. He's about the only one who has never stolen from me. The rest would take whatever, even my utensils."

The other sections of this spacious wreck of a house is available. A bedroom on the second floor even has two TVs, although only one is working. In the adjacent kitchen, there is an image of the Last Supper, and one of Christ praying on the Mount of Olives. In the yellow light, you'll nod, watched over by these reproduced Jesuses, and should you OD, God forbid, it won't be that big of a deal, at least not to Charles, your final earthly landlord, "I've had people die in every single room of this house. See that chair there? A woman died sitting right on it!"

Charles himself sleeps on a bare mattress littered with receipts, bills, medical prescriptions and pill bottles. On the floor are clothing, tissues and more miscellaneous pieces of paper. When I asked Charles why he had the television on, he said, "I just turned it on for you! To show that I watch television, to show that I'm not an animal, you know what I mean?" He complained that sometimes when he jerked off, a family of squirrels looked at him from outside the window, as if to laugh at him.

Fifty-six years old, Charles has served in the Army, and has worked as a plumber, roofer, electrician, car mechanic, bug exterminator and embalmer of corpses, but when his meth-dealing brother tried to run him over with a truck, he became disabled, so now collects $700 a month in Social Security. When not in a wheelchair, he hobbles around with two canes. Smiling, he admitted to having an encyclopedic criminal record, "I've done a lot of bad things."

One set of crimes Charles has never been charged for, however, is robbing from corpses, "We'd strip them of their jewelry, and lots of time, we'd switch them from their coffins, to a cheaper version, you know. Some of them, we'd bury in Styrofoam coffins."

"You're shitting me?!"

"No, I'm not. This was twenty, thirty years ago, but I'm sure it's still happening today. When the family leaves, that pit is still open, and that mound of dirt is still there, so we'd jump right in and do what we have to do, you know what I mean? We got it down to a science. We're fast!"

With his Social Security and rent from his tenants, Charles makes out OK, and he still does an occasional odd job, using his many skills. For $35, he'll rid your house of roaches, mice, rats and even bedbugs. A faded sign outside his house also advertises, "CAR WASH $1."

"How many cars do you wash a month?"

"None. Maybe a car a year."

There is also a well-perforated portrait of Martin Luther King over his door. "What's up with that? Are those bullet holes?"

"Yeah, yeah."

"Your shots?"

"No, I love the man! I got it from this guy I was working for. He had three portraits of Martin Luther King he was using for target practice, and I asked him if I could have them all, so he gave them to me."

"It's pretty weird to see it like that."

"I just put it up as a conversation piece, to get people talking, you know. There are a lot of prejudiced people in this neighborhood, but I ain't one of them. The Puerto Ricans, they're prejudiced too. They don't even like themselves! I love Martin Luther King, and I voted for Obama, twice! I'm half Italian and half Jewish. My parents met in Africa. I'm not prejudiced at all. One of my tenants was this Thai woman. She lived with me forever."

Leaving Charles's house at dusk, I was tempted to duck into Bentley's Place again. At that hour, I would probably run into Ralph. Done with hanging dry walls, this fifty-seven-year-old man would treat himself to two beers, no more, for that's all he can afford now. Once he easily made $200–$300 a day. At thirteen, he got his girlfriend pregnant. At seventeen, he came to the US from Puerto Rico. Ralph has three kids altogether, from two different women. His younger son, thirty-four, is living with him, and he's in touch with the others. Thirteen years ago, the mother of his last child got shot six times, but miraculously survived, "I saw her in the hospital, and they got her cut up from her pussy to her neck, and her thigh also. They had all these clamps on her. She stayed in the hospital for nearly a year, and when she got out, she was walking like this," and he dipped a shoulder and contorted his body, "but now she's all fine, like nothing ever happened!" She never told him who had tried to kill her, or even why she was shot.

At this hour, the whores were becoming more visible on Kensington Avenue. The economy is so bad, Ralph had told me, you can now get a blow job for only three bucks. Out of cash, Whitey was likely in bed already. Meanwhile, Charles could pop in a video rented from the Woodshed XXX Store. Glancing at each other knowingly, the squirrels clicked their tongues and cackled. One floor above, the garbageman lifted weights. He is saving to buy a house, but with two kids to support on $23,000 a year, gross, the same as working at Taco Bell, it won't happen for a while, if ever. As the stores closed, zombies straggled about, to be shadowed by those who would profit or take brief pleasure from them.

Kensington has a few nicknames, none too flattering, but I'd like to nominate one more, The CIA's Asshole, which I got from my longtime friend Jason as we were BSing that one time in Bentley's Place, "All that heroin the CIA sucks up in Afghanistan, where do you think it ends up?

It ends up in places like this, so Kensington's really the CIA's asshole."
Leaving the CIA's asshole, I got on the El at Kensington and Somerset,
and on my way home, I could see, etched against a purple sky, the twin
spires of the Visitation Church. The next day, Emily would instruct,
coach, coax and inspire her class anew. On her classroom's wall, there is a
quotation: "Whatever you can do or dream you can. Boldness has genius,
power and magic in it. Begin it now. —Goethe." Just across the street,
however, there would likely be, as not, a nodding junkie or two.

SALUTING THE TROOPS IN MARCUS HOOK

12-26-13—First settled by Europeans in 1640, Marcus Hook was once called Chammassungh, Finland then Marrites Hoeck, from which the present name derives. The Hook, however, does serendipitously evoke its pirate past, when Blackbeard plied the Delaware, and one of his mistresses, Margaret, lived here, in a plank house still preserved.

This town's peak posterity came much later, however, in the legitimate business of oil refining, plus there was a steel mill just down the road. Though its population never surpassed 5,000, Marcus Hook had thirty-six taverns at one point, including three openly gay bars. This, in a heavily Catholic region with many Irish, Italians and Poles. Though Market Street is only a mile long, it had twelve bars.

The steel mill and an oil refinery have shut down, with the surviving one operating at much reduced capacity. Only 2,397 people live here now, and there are only six bars left, with only Keyote's kind of gayish. The town is still clean and orderly, though, and on a recent visit, I saw that many residents had, as usual, arrayed Christmas decorations on their tiny lawns. Many of these wooden, plastic, nylon or cement figurines were rather beaten up, however, with one Santa Claus a deflated mess with his face smudgy and featureless, and his legs severed, as if blown away by an improvised explosive device. Next to him, two faded and chipped deer nestled in a dirt-filled bathtub. At 11th and Washington, though, I saw an extravaganza of inflated nylon and many-colored lights, with even a green and red "HOLLY COPTER" on the roof. (Just wondering, but shouldn't it be "HOLY COPTER"?) Through a brilliantly lit door, I glimpsed an old woman carrying a casserole dish as she walked from kitchen to living room, but it's probably time to scoot, I thought, for earlier I had seen this sign, on a different house, "THIS PROPERTY PROTECTED BY THE SECOND AMENDMENT." Next morning, the headline in the *Delco Times* could read, "Prowling Victor Charlie Shot by Vigilant Mrs. Claus."

Real military hardware can be found elsewhere in Marcus Hook. Just to the side of the elementary school, there are two pieces of artillery, and by the river, there is another big gun next to the Delaware County Vietnam Memorial. Beneath 183 names, there is a curious inscription, "THIS MEMORIAL IS ALSO DEDICATED TO THOSE VIETNAM VETERANS THAT WERE KILLED IN VIETNAM, BUT WHO DIED AT HOME." I'm assuming that this is a reference to Agent Orange and suicides, but what else? There are so many ways to die years later from a war. As for Agent Orange, it was manufactured primarily by Monsanto and DuPont, with the latter headquartered in Wilmington, Delaware, a ten-minute drive from Marcus Hook. Your brother could work for DuPont, as DuPont killed you.

Altogether, there are nine war memorials in Marcus Hook, and this is hardly unusual in small-town America. Across the river, the center of Gloucester, New Jersey, is dominated by a cluster of war memorials, with a large slab commemorating the death of just one soldier, Corporal Marc T. Ryan, who died in Iraq at the age of twenty-five. On the polished granite are three images of him: as a football player, then soldier in full combat gear, plus a smiling head shot. Ryan's father and grandfather were Marines, and Ryan was only killed on his second deployment to Iraq. He had also spent a year in Afghanistan. Before his last mission, Ryan had applied to be a state trooper, but was not hired.

For much of 2013, dozens of banners hung from utility poles on Gloucester's Broadway Street. On each is an image of a native son lost in a war, going to back to World War I. The portraits are large and mostly in colors. William Bernard Hamacher was only eighteen when he was killed in Quang Tri, South Vietnam. Daniel Gilbert Booth was buried at sea in World War II. On and on it went. Next to Gloucester, tiny Brooklawn, with fewer than 2,000 souls, has three pieces of artillery in its center. In many towns, you may even find a tank or two. Such a militarization of the landscape is so common in America, many may even assume that it is a universal tendency.

With our citizens being told endlessly that America is constantly threatened, our flag now appears everywhere as a kind of talisman against attack or national disintegration. In Gloucester, the Venezuelan-owned Citgo gas station flaunts three large stars and stripes, and across the street, the Coastal station has a small flag, plus a sign, "GOD BLESS AMERICA." Flags drape in private yards and porches, and in the window of Twisted Delights, a pretzel bakery, there is an elaborate patriotic display with images of the Statue of Liberty, an eagle and the Lincoln Memorial, all over a flag background, with "GOD BLESS AMERICA" on top. Such an insistent, even strident manifestation of patriotism betrays a siege mentality, but this is encouraged and orchestrated from the top down.

Troops are now routinely inserted into ball games, and news broadcasts often feature footage of a returning soldier surprising his or her family in a variety of settings. In Minnesota, a soldier came back to his wife and four kids as a scuba-diving Santa Claus at a shopping mall aquarium, and at a hockey game in Detroit, another greeted his parents and girlfriend on the Jumbotron, before suddenly appearing in person, behind them, and as the crowd wildly cheered, he got on one knee to propose to his sweetheart while Bruno Mars's "Marry You" played over the sound system. On YouTube, most of the comments gush sentimentality and patriotism, as expected, but there was one user with an Arabic name who merely left, "This video failed," to which another responded, "sorry it didn't blow up, you muslim." At a Devil Rays game, a soldier's young daughter was invited to throw out the first pitch, except that she didn't know the catcher was actually her dad, who she thought was still in Afghanistan. With mask thrown off, they had a tearful reunion in front of cameras and crowd. With so many well-staged scenes as these, one has to assume there is a Pentagon unit dedicated to such theatrical propaganda. Notice that the troops featured in these touching reunions are never visibly damaged, as in missing one or several limbs, an eyeball or part of a brain, etc., for that would scare off future recruits. At the last Eagles game, the honored soldier was a sexy ex-cheerleader of the team itself. In photos released to the press, Rachel Washburn is positively glamorous even as she totes an M4 carbine. Born into a military family, Washburn now has two Afghan tours behind her, yet she will reenlist, then study to become a human rights lawyer, so all the bases are covered, for she's attractive, smart, selfless, brave and, most importantly, conscientious. After honorably participating in Enduring Freedom, Washburn will nobly defend human rights, so America's open-ended war must not, cannot, be immoral. Plus, if even a hot cheerleader is willing to charge into battle to engage terrorists over there, what does that make of all the lame-assed doofuses lounging about over here, with their Xbox, fantasy football and porn addictions? So get off your fat asses already and enlist to kill, and be killed, for your elite's access to oil, natural gas and opium!

Many Americans oppose not just any war, but even the concept of violent resistance against attack or oppression. In short, they don't even believe in using force to survive. A much larger percentage, however, support just about any of their nation's wars. Since one's forefathers had their battle experiences, one must fight in the war(s) of one's generation. In various disguises, organized violence is an American rite of passage, so any boy who shuns the football team, gang or Army is considered a hollowed-out, pussified geek with a moist handshake who won't even defend himself, much less his country.

The water tower in Gloucester has the familiar POW/MIA flag painted on it, and in Marcus Hook, this image flutters outside the post office, the idle Sunoco refinery and at some private homes, among other places. Inside a circle, a large Caucasian head is seen in profile, with a watchtower in the distance. To indicate captivity, there is a strand of barbwire, and beneath everything is this caption: "YOU ARE NOT FORGOTTEN." To make sure his neighbors don't forget about America's many wars, Mark Lane has even set up a military museum inside his wife's thrift store, Andrea's Attic. I had called ahead to make sure it was open, and before I walked in, I noticed a sign in the window, "I SUPPORT HELPING THE NEEDY. I OPPOSE FUNDING THE LAZY," then in the vestibule, I was greeted by the photocopied faces of about forty local criminals, with transgressions ranging from child sexual molestation to burglary, to assault. As far as crimes go, Marcus Hook is a very tame place now, a Mister Rogers' neighborhood or petting zoo, as compared to when it was dominated by the Pagans, a 1 percent motorcycle gang that cooked meth, warred with the Mafia and chased the Hell's Angels out of Philly. They also provided other useful social services such as making sure pharmaceuticals were available to penned-in and pent-up Amish kids, and babysitting teen-aged girls rounded up from the MacDade Mall in Ridley Township. After school activities included bareback buckling, mattress swimming and (sort of) synchronized gymnastics. In honor of Shakespeare, perhaps, there was also the two-backed beast relay "drill" team, which broke out at frequent intervals in between beer runs. Seeing a middle-aged woman at the cash register, I assumed that it was Andrea, but she introduced herself as Lesley, then warmly said that her husband, Mark, would show me the museum.

In a space no bigger than a reasonably large bathroom were crammed military uniforms, helmets, bayonets, swords, newspaper clippings and, most interestingly, panoramas featuring toy soldiers, with some housed in small aquariums. There were no tags, so the viewer had to decipher each scene by himself, although Mark was right there to answer questions. A depiction of the Cu Chi Tunnel showed a GI, tiger and snake above ground in a jungle setting, then below the earth's surface, here made of cardboard, I saw a Viet Cong and an American "tunnel rat." Suffering frightfully high casualties, tunnel rats were small, slim men who had volunteered to go underground to flush out the VC. Their motto was *Non Gratum Anus Rodentum,* Not Worth a Rat's Ass.

"Were you in the service?" Mark asked me.

"No, no," I smiled. "How about you?"

"Actually, no. I registered, but never enlisted, and then the draft was over."

"There are lots of Vietnam vets in this town. Do they ever come in here?"

"No."

"How about kids? Do you have classes in here?"

"Well, sometimes a kid or two would come in, but this space is really too small for a class. I can't keep an eye on them all, and these little kids might just break everything."

"This museum is fascinating. This is, like, the highlight of Marcus Hook! Do you want more people to come in?"

"Well, I'm not sure, because I have to be here to show anyone around. I work a regular job, you know, in Chester."

"What do you do over there?"

"I work for a paper company. We make cardboard stuff."

Mark never rushed me as I looked around, and I took my time examining everything. Inside a bombed church, a wounded Nazi clutched a wine bottle. Above him, pigeons nestled in the destroyed ceiling. Wearing a keffiyeh, bandolier, rope belt and armed with made-in-China plastic M16 and scimitar, an Arab soldier had been plopped in front of an American Hummer with a bullet hole in its windshield. Barely hidden lampshades kept parachutes abloom as paratroopers dangled. Sporting a mohawk, a member of the 101st Airborne spied on a Nazi and a Japanese soldier. When Mark asked if I was Japanese, I said, "No, Vietnamese," so he brought out a Vietnam-era ammo belt, "I've been meaning to ask someone about this. Can you read this for me?"

"This is Chinese, Mark. It's not Vietnamese."

"Are you sure?"

"Yeah, Vietnamese use the alphabet, with these accent marks on them. This is definitely Chinese."

"This is from the Vietnam War, so I thought maybe it was used by the South Vietnamese."

"The South Vietnamese would use American gear, and since this is Chinese-made, I'm pretty certain that it was used by the Viet Cong, so this is a Chinese belt used by either the Viet Cong or the North Vietnamese."

Marcus Hook doesn't even have a Chinese restaurant, much less a Vietnamese one, so there's no Vietnamese writing on any local menu for Mark to detect should he want to try a bowl of rice vermicelli with grilled lemongrass beef, etc., and in many Hollywood Vietnam movies, Vietnamese writing has been erased from the landscape. I'll get to that later, so hang tight! Meanwhile, Mark responded, "Hmm, I think you're right! Boy, am I glad you came in today. You taught me something, so thank you!"

"No, thank you for taking the time to show me your museum. This place is wonderful!"

And I really meant that. I'm a sucker for any eccentric project. After a while, Lesley came in to say hello, and she was just as open as her husband. From Lesley, I found out that Andrea in the store's name refers to her daughter from another marriage, "We are a nonprofit organization. We give out free books, furniture and clothes. We also have a food bank. And I'm doing all this in honor of my daughter, who was killed."

"Wow, this is amazing! And I thought it was just a regular thrift store. How did your daughter die?"

"Her boyfriend killed her. Andrea was a senior at San Diego State. She was the director of the Women's Resource Center. She also did ceramics and fashion design. She taught martial art and volunteered as a conditioning trainer for the football team. My daughter did so much in her twenty-seven years, and this asshole just killed her! He stabbed her! And you know how I found out? Four days after he had killed her, he had the balls to call me collect, and I had no idea why he was calling me. He said, 'Andrea and I got into a fight,' so I said, 'What do you want me to do about it? You want me to take your side?! You work it out with her.'"

"So what did he say?"

"He didn't really say anything, then he said, 'I didn't really mean to hurt her,' and that's when I thought something serious may have happened. Before he hung up, he managed to say, 'I think I may have broken Andrea's neck,' so I called Andrea to leave her a message, then I called her landlord, and that's when I finally found out."

"So the boyfriend lied about the broken neck, because he had actually stabbed her?"

"No, first he broke her neck by strangling her, then he stabbed her, then he tied a cord around her neck, then he put a plastic bag around her head. When they found my daughter, she was unrecognizable! And you know something else? He wasn't even supposed to be there! After dating for eighteen months, they had broken up for two weeks, but Andrea let him stay while he looked for another apartment, and during this time, he even ran up her credit card."

"Wow, what a total asshole! So is this guy locked up for good?"

"No. We did get him convicted for murder one, but before the sentencing, he hanged himself in prison. That's the best possible outcome, because now I don't have to worry about going to California every few years for his parole hearing. Everything I do now, though, is in honor of my daughter. I want to continue Andrea's legacy, because she was such a giving person. If a person can buy a pair of jeans for $2 at my store, instead of paying $25 somewhere else, then I'm doing it in the spirit of my daughter. As for the food bank, I don't just give everyone the same box. I figure out what each person needs, so nothing is going to waste. You don't want to give people something that they don't even like, or don't know how to prepare. Everyone is different. I also make sure I give it to people who really need it, because if you're sitting in a bar all day, and can afford another tattoo on your damn neck, then you shouldn't be coming to me. The other day, this guy came in and said he had just had open heart surgery, so I asked him, 'Which hospital was it at?' and he was like, 'Uh, uh, uh,' so I just told him to get the hell out of here! I know him, too. He's a child molester. I have his picture up there on the wall as you walk in."

Before I left Andrea's Attic, Lesley wanted to give me a loaf of bread to take home, but I had to decline, since I didn't want to take from someone who really needed it. Moments later, I didn't turn down several pints of beer sent my way by complete strangers at Connolly's Pub, however, for that would be very bad manners. "Why is everyone so nice here?" I asked the bartender, Jenny.

"That's just how we roll," she cheerfully said.

Granted, it was Christmas Eve, but the friendliness here was exceptional, and I was included in it all even as an outsider. Presently, a man offered me a stick of beef jerky, and Santa Claus came barging through the door to hand me, and everyone else, a candy cane. This was only my second time here. Neither too dark nor too loud, this cheap bar is a very pleasant place to pass the hours. On my first visit a few days earlier, I had met Jim. After four years in the Army, spent in Texas, Virginia and North Carolina, he has worked thirty-five years for FedEx, and plans to retired in two years at age fifty. He'll move to the country to be left alone, he said, and to hunt and to fish. Divorced, he has three daughters aged eighteen, nineteen and twenty, with one in college and one in nursing school, "And just think, I never even finished high school!"

I exchanged a few words with a man named Cowboy, so called because he had owned a horse as a teen. Now an electrician, Cowboy made $12 an hour at his first job forty years ago, when he was seventeen. "That would be a good wage for any age nowadays," I said.

"I agree. It's not as easy as it used to be. Now you can't even bend the facts on your resume. They'll find out on the computer!"

Wearing a camouflaged hat, a man showed off a wooden carving that had "LIVE FREE OR DIE. DON'T TREAD ON ME" over a gun that doubled as a pipe. Another man wore a hat that said, "Bite Me."

The bartender had quite an emphatic figure so one of the guys asked her to turn to the side a bit, "Boy, you do have one heck of a profile!"

"It's the padded bra," she laughed.

"It pushes you up," the man shouted to general merriment.

Some middle-aged cat named Gatto walked in to buy a tall can of Ice to go. "This keeps me young," he grinned at the bartender, who didn't laugh. I did, though, which cheered him up, and Gatto told me he had a date that night. Taking out his Samsung tab, he showed me a sitting woman in a dreamy pose, "That's my lady. Ain't she hot?"

"Yes, she is," and she really was, at least from my angle and in that dim light.

Showing me another lady, Gatto continued, "I'm dating this one too, and I'm going to get her," meaning the bartender who was only about half his age. Oh, the desperate optimism of so many middle-aged men! We'll have our first stroke or even a triple bypass thinking we still have it, though many of us barely had any at any point in our lives. (Mind you, whenever I mention a medical term or procedure, it's strictly from hearsay, as I've never had health insurance in my life, Obamacare be damned!)

I chatted longest with John, a sixty-seven-year-old Vietnam vet, "I was there for two and a half years. My brother also served. He got hit by a mine. My youngest brother also wanted to go, but by then the war was over."

"Your brother didn't die?"

"No, he came back and worked in the post office for thirty-five years."

"That's miraculous! He didn't lose anything?"

"No, they patched him up good. He was fine."

"Why did you sign up again? You were only supposed to be there for one year, right?"

"The money! They paid you good if you went over again, so I went back twice."

"How much extra money did you make?"

"I sent some of it home for my mom to keep, but she gave it to my sister for her wedding, so I only ended up with $6,500 when I got out. Still, that was a lot of money then, enough for me to buy a Corvette. What I always wanted!"

Since John served on a Swift boat, I mentioned Kerry, but he said, "What are you talking about?"

"John Kerry. Didn't he serve on a Swift boat also?"

"I don't know, but I wouldn't trust anything these politicians say!"

Changing the subject, John declared, "I may be retired, but I still work a little, just to do something. Every day, I spend two hours cleaning up this bar."

"You do look in excellent shape!"

"That's because I'm active. I don't just sit around."

"Why don't you travel? Take a trip somewhere?"

"Nah, nah."

"If I had the money, I would travel all the time."

"It's not that I can't afford it, but I'm just not into that. Plus, they don't like us Americans overseas."

"Where?"

"In Europe. A couple of my friends came back and said they hated us over there."

"Oh, c'mon!"

"They can't stand us in France."

"That's not true! That's way exaggerated! Ethnically, what are you, John?"

"I'm Irish."

"Then why don't you go to Ireland? Drink some good beer! I've been to England and Scotland but never Ireland. I'd love to go to Ireland."

"You go. I stay here!"

During his Navy days, John visited Tokyo, Singapore, Bangkok and Sydney, so it's not like he hasn't been anywhere. The ladies Down Under were the most expensive, but they were also the most disease-free, according to John, so it was worth it, "You get what you pay for." Discharged, he spent a week in San Francisco before going home, where he's been ever since.

"Did you like San Francisco?"

"Not at all!"

"You didn't find it beautiful? I think San Francisco is very beautiful."

"All I know is I went into a bar, and there were nothing but men there, and one said to me," and here John switched to a swishy voice, complete with a queer hand motion, "'How are you doing?'"

"Well, did you go to another bar?"

"I went to two more, and they were all the same!"

"So you were in a gay neighborhood, then."

"The entire city was a gay neighborhood! I couldn't wait to get out of there! Then at the airport, some Hare Krishna called me a baby killer!"

I don't know if people with an unhappy upbringing wander more, but my dismal childhood has left me with no fond memory of home, negates its very concept, although, paradoxically, I try to make each alien pit stop my instant casa, if only in my mind. In Marcus Hook, a car slowed down to ask me for directions, which pleased me enormously, and I could barely refrain from giving the lady (wrong) directions. With deep regrets, remorse and infinite self-pity, I painfully informed her that I was not from there. Though permanently homeless in the figurative sense, perhaps I emit some at-home signals with my gait or posture, for I have been asked for directions even in foreign cities like Florence and Seoul.

Unlike in beer commercials, American bars tend to be almost exclusively black or white, but Connolly's was well-integrated, with the regulars greeting their white and black friends equally warmly as they came in. At one point, though, all the black patrons sat at one end, and whites at the other, while I, yellow as ever, was the odd one there, not that it mattered. On television, however, there was a horde of yellow guys doing some frightful shit to their own kind, as in bayoneting children, crushing a boy's head with a boot and mowing down hundreds of unarmed villagers with machine guns. As these Mongoloid monsters committed gleeful carnage, a Caucasian man could be seen trying to save two Asiatic tots. No movie buff, I had no idea what I was watching until I saw Sylvester Stallone, which cued me in that it was one of the *Rambo* flicks.

It's only incidental that Burma is the context of *Rambo IV*, for what's shown is a Barbaric Other that should be killed en masse as well as, paradoxically, saved from itself. For more than a decade now, this plot has been applied most feverishly to Muslims, but it can suddenly be shifted to any other group, or a subgroup, within this country. The empire's media mesmerize, stultify and brainwash through a fairly transparent magic, but if it works, why change? Take *Apocalypse Now*, considered by many to be not just a great Vietnam War film, but one of the greatest films ever. No one here cringed when Coppola pompously declared that his baby "is

not about Vietnam—it is Vietnam." Imagine a foreigner making a film
about the US without speaking parts for Americans, and where written
English is glimpsed but for a few seconds, yet declaring, "My film is not
about the United States. It is the United States." Reviewing the redux
version in 2001, I wrote:

> In *Apocalypse Now*, Vietnam is more or less one continuous jungle,
> with corpses casually dangling from trees, and arrows and spears
> flying out of the foliage. The arrow attack scene is lifted straight
> from *Heart of Darkness*, where a black riverboat pilot is impaled
> by a spear. The phoniness of this is breathtaking. The NVA and
> Viet Cong did not win a modern war with arrows and spears.
> But a scene from a 1901 book has to be shoehorned into a 1979
> movie because of Coppola's fascination with savages. As Wil-
> lard's boat travels up the Nung River, the only signs of civilization
> are two US army bases and a French plantation. This has nothing
> to do with the Vietnam of reality. As anyone who has been there
> will tell you, Vietnam is (and was during the war) grossly over-
> populated. Rivers and roads are lined with settlements. The US,
> by comparison, is more wild. Another thing a visitor to Vietnam
> can readily see is the ubiquity of the written language— that is,
> of civilization. Signs and banners are everywhere. None of this is
> apparent in any of the panoramic shots of *Apocalypse Now*. Cop-
> pola hasn't just withheld speech from the Vietnamese, he has also
> banned them from writing.

Similarly, in *The Deer Hunter*, another Hollywood Vietnam War
"classic," the realism is strictly reserved for the white characters, especially
on their home turf, in a Pennsylvania town not too unlike Marcus Hook.
The Vietnamese, on the other hand, are deranged, cartoonish screamers
who get a great thrill out of gambling with other people's lives. Jun-
gle-dwelling Commies or living in Saigon, they're all the same. Though
there is no record of Vietnamese playing Russian roulette with anybody,

much less Americans, it is this movie's central metaphor. Factual error aside, *The Deer Hunter* fits neatly within the racism and war-justifying mythology that's pushed constantly by this empire's media: that only Americans are real, fleshed-out people with a psychology and range of emotions, unlike these shadowy, hateful, subhuman and funny-looking foreigners who deserve to be shot, over and over.

Sorry about the little detour through Hollywood, perhaps my least favorite (crime) precinct on this earth, but it does help to explain, I think, how someone as good, generous and sober as Lesley Lane can be so indiscriminating when it comes to supporting our military, how she cannot see that, conditioned to unleash great violence with sanctimony, these armed men and women have destroyed many families worldwide.

OK, so before we leave Marcus Hook, let's just say hello to its just-deposed mayor, James Schiliro. Jay, as he is commonly known, used to strut about town with a stogie jutting from his maw, for it's good to be a puffed up fish in this wee puddle. Granted, the pay wasn't all that, but life isn't just about cash, but respect and stature. As mayor, Jay was looked at differently, and the shouted greetings became much heartier whenever he stepped into the Star Hotel, Lefty's or Connolly's. Though Republican, Jay went to Obama's second inauguration, and why not? It was a fine party. Jay's stance for gun control was somewhat unpopular, but he didn't want slugs to bounce around Marcus Hook, as they routinely did in adjacent Chester or Wilmington. All was well until February, when Jay could no longer suppress a certain sensation surging up from below. Divorced, Jay was free sexually, except that the object of his desire was male, and underage, too, though only by a year. OK, OK, I'll cut to the chase. As his teenage daughter slept upstairs, thirty-eight-year-old Jay Schiliro plied a twenty-year-old man with wine, then asked his young buddy, between twenty and thirty times, if he would consent to be sucked. To show that his passion was true, Jay waved his gun around, then pointed it at his own head when he was firmly rebuffed, before discharging (the 9mm handgun) into the wall.

Now, you can't live more than a few days without racking up a few ghastly sets of bones in your closet, so I'm not retelling Jay's lapsed moment to shame but to applaud him, for here, finally, is a model politician. While others will suck you dry through unfunded wars, bad laws and Wall Street, Jay is actually willing to back up his (covert) actions with his (open) mouth. No hypocrite, Jay Schiliro should be the next president of the United States, for if we can't have a leader who looks out for our interests, we should at least have a representative one. With, say, Monica Lewinsky as veep, it should be an unbeatable ticket. For Schiliro's campaign slogan, I suggest, simply, "JAY SUCKS!" Just like our government, though only one is even half amusing.

CANNED BEER AND SLIM JIM IN VINELAND

1-6-14—On a drowsy, sputtering bus into Vineland, I glimpsed a 9/11 memorial by the side of the road. Next to a flagpole, there was the Twin Towers at the height of a middling crotch. Fleetingly I thought of getting off at the next stop to scrutinize, but decided no, for it was clear I was only on the outskirts of town, and Vineland is vast, despite its modest population of only 60,000 souls.

Vineland was founded by Charles Landis in 1862 as a utopia. He banned alcohol and stipulated that all inhabitants must farm. To prevent the spread of diseases, houses were kept apart from each other. Flowers and shade trees were planted on each road. Concluding that the local soil was suitable for growing grapes, Landis lured Italian immigrants and named his new town "Vineland." A tireless developer, Landis also tried to recreate Venice in America, but the result is merely Sea Isles, New Jersey. With his ambitions, Landis was mocked as King Landis, but his surest place in history is as the first man to successfully plead temporary insanity at a murder trial. A journalist had questioned Landis's wife's mental equilibrium, so Landis promptly shot the insolent hack. It doesn't take too much gray matter, though, to suspect that Landis's deep pockets had something to do with his acquittal. Now as then, the powerful can openly exercise their insanity while the rest of us will be beaten down for the slightest tic.

From habitually frivolous Yahoo! News, this yahoo, yours truly, did manage to glean recently that dolphins munch on blowfish to get high, and moose booze on fermented apples. It's good that no dolphin or moose was to be found in Vineland, for these tipsy critters would have had to pay gouging fines or spend many a lonesome weekend in the lockup. All utopias start with the best intentions, but to be told to do anything against one's will is a sure, incremental step towards hell, no? Now, multiply that by ten thousand times and you get, well, fill in your zip code here! You must not paint your house a wrong color, collect rainwater or hand out sandwiches to the homeless, but a uniformed pervert is free to diddle your pudenda before you board that jet plane, ma'am. Just be glad you ain't on that no-fly list. Though we can't afford real cheese or butter, we must donate half of our shriveling paychecks to the health extortionist company. An army of goons are also overhearing our phone conversations and reading our emails, and the top thug of all can even have any of us snagged, medievally tortured or shot, without charge and in secret, and if we rebel, we're only doing it in the prescribed manner, by abusing or mutilating ourselves, lashing out at other hapless sinkers or, best yet, waving cute signs for an hour or two. Meanwhile, those who have herded us all into this quicksand are glorified and worshipped. Too often, our hatred of suffering is transformed into a contempt for sufferers and, as programmed, we marvel at the undeservingly or criminally powerful. Over and over again, we vote for our own doom, and the more serious our predicament, the more trivial the news that's jammed down our throats. Today's urgent headline, "LeBron leaves skid marks on court. Watch how it happened!"

Rolling past a few strip malls, we were still nowhere near downtown, as I could detect no taller buildings in the distance. Two rows in front of me, an older lady moaned to the driver, "Are we almost there yet? I have to use the bathroom real bad!" As we kept going and going, I had visions of a natural disaster erupting at any moment, complete with mop and bucket. Even without individualized defects, the body is a drag that takes constant upkeep just to make it halfway presentable. Still, it is an awe-inspiring presence, each one of us, as I certainly learned from the nude drawing classes I took during my brief stay in college.

Attentive looking and listening are the prerequisite for reverence, but in a speed culture, these approaches have been conditioned out of existence. Here and now, even standing still is suspect, is loitering. In a speed culture, meaning itself becomes instantaneously obsolete, moment by moment, to make room for the next bang or flash, signifying whatever. But who wants it this way? The same people who are raping you blind!

Lost in the uproar over the bogus sign-language interpreter for Obama was the fact that what was said was also nonsense, although so pious, sonorous and stately, and if that gesturing clown has a rap sheet, it's nothing compared to the staggering historical crimes of the lying psychopath he was mistranslating.

Finally, we were allowed to get off, and without knowing where I was heading exactly, I started walking. Across the street from the Transportation Center, I spotted a large sign at a gas station, with "UNITED WE STAND" beneath the stars and stripes. Attached to it was a mini-mart offering bottled corn syrups, chemical snacks and lottery tickets. Continuing, I ran into US Petroleum, a shuttered gas station with six flags painted onto the sides of its flat roof over the gassed pumps.

I passed a storefront with "JOHN 3:16" in its window. No Bible worm, I had to ask the nodding angel perched on my right shoulder, which made him shout in indignation, "You dumb shit! Here goes, 'For God so loved the world that he gave his one and only Son, that whoever believes in him shall not perish but have eternal life.' Got that?!" More interesting was a faded poster with "PRAY HARD for the Nation" coupled with a photo of a man's lower limbs in holey jeans and beat-up sneakers. Here, the nation was presented as materially destitute, not spiritually eroded, although it is that, too.

Soon the buildings got older, so I knew I had reached Vineland's historical core. I passed Lean On Me Agape Ministry, which aimed at "Producing Communities of no Need," as announced on its blue sign. Taming or sating desire is one thing, but this sounds like a proposal for cemeteries . . . In quick succession, I ran into a torpedo, a 40mm naval gun and a Civil War memorial, with its eagle-topped column flanked by a Union soldier and a sailor. I saw a flag sticker on a car window, "September 11, 2001. We Will Remember," but what do we recall, exactly? You're liable to get into a fistfight if you merely point out the absurdity of a skyscraper collapsing at free-fall speed without being hit by anything, or the intact passport of an accused terrorist conveniently located among the dust of a pulverized building, or the five-story Pentagon being hit *on the side* by an airliner shaving the ground, and when the purported architect of this disaster is finally shot, his never-seen corpse is immediately dumped into the ocean without leaving any trace behind, not even a hair or a pixel, all in the name of being sensitive to Muslims, a people our government has demonized for decades?! These questions are not the feverish hallucinations of any tinfoil-hatted brigade, but sane skepticism towards the endless preposterous lies from a government that routinely dishes up bullshit.

Like many others, I have raised these questions over the years, and for this, I have been branded a freak by one of the left's most disdainful gatekeepers. After *CounterPunch* canceled my Postcard series on its site, which is its prerogative, of course, its editor, Jeffrey St. Clair, responded to readers' complaints by questioning my sanity, "Perhaps Linh has simply joined the conspiratorialists and *Dissident Voice* is a more comfortable venue for him. We've chased most of the people who question the moon landing, whether JFK is really dead and the circularity of the earth off of *CounterPunch*." So to point out the obvious lies of a criminal government is to believe that this earth is flat? Good Lord, with such a rebel, who needs sheep?

The lies of 9/11 have replaced the Constitution to become the foundation and compass of this country. Everything that's done now is pivoted around this central deceit, this fiction, so if we refuse to see through these outrageous lies, we won't quite understand that we're being lorded over by psychopathic criminals. Again, we're not being ruled by bumbling and bickering fools, but evil-to-the-bone, habitually lying criminals.

Continuing, I chanced upon the world's tiniest park, perhaps, for it was only the grassy base of one street lamp. Among the mostly brown leaves was this plaque: "City of Vineland Operation Desert Storm Victory Mini-Park. Honoring the bravery & skill of the U.S. Armed Forces during the Persian Gulf War of 1990–91, which helped to free the Middle East country of Kuwait from its hostile invaders." Below, the names of local politicians took up nearly half of the bronze surface. Irish, Italian, Welsh, Polish, Puerto Rican and Jewish, they also give you a good clue as to who dwells in Vineland.

In spite of whatever progress that's been made in racial relations, Americans still tend to vote by race or ethnic group, and there's no telling if this narrow tribal instinct will abate or become more vehement as we become more desperate. Fighting over scraps, will we fragment into roving bands to rob, rape and kill each other? Should that happen, it would only cheer up our ruling class, locked in their gated enclaves and guarded by our cousins, the selected few who still have jobs. In a recent email, my good friend Chuck Orloski wrote, "The elite learned plenty from trying to occupy divided-Baghdad, and knowing how millions of Americans are DIVIDED but armed-to-teeth, their CONTROL-method will take the shape of instituting mass-deprivation. Citizens will be more prone to shoot one another, and consequently, they will not have to absolutely rely on American soldiers shooting Americans. They study history and have solid population-demoralization plans in effect, and to date, it's working on schedule & according to their psychotic-favor."

Though Vineland's Landis Avenue is not nearly as depressing as many small towns' Main Street nowadays, it has its share of shut-down businesses, including a food market with a window broken and taped up, and an employment agency, "JOBS NOW / TRABAJO AHORA," with its plate glass frontage struck twice by some blunt instrument. The military undercurrent also resurfaces in the form of Armageddon, a store selling paintball equipment. Before we splatter each other for real, we must practice with red, green and blue paints. I gotcha, sucka, right in da head! How fun. Oh shoot, I'm hit! Nothing was scheduled at the forlorn Landis Theater, and on its marquee was this sad appeal, "PLEASE SHOP DOWNTOWN."

Having walked nearly a mile without seeing a single bar or liquor store, it dawned on me that Vineland might still be a dry town, like many in Jersey, but then I spotted "MOTEL / PUB / WINES & SPIRITS TO GO." The same sign also informed me that a night here would cost but $30, plus tax, and a week stay would set me back only $122. There was also a curious announcement for judo classes in the evening. Fingering the change in my pocket, I briefly entertained the lovely notion of getting shit-faced on, say, Pabst Blue Ribbon for hours, then crawling upstairs to my very own room, to be feasted on by mutant bedbugs and other devilish Jersey creatures, with what's left of me tossed into the dumpster the next morning. Opening the door, I didn't hesitate before stepping into this gloomy, subterranean tavern.

Settling down, I noticed there was only one other customer, not counting a huge stuffed animal with a beer can and shot slug in front of him. Two televisions were on, beaming ESPN sports and a History Channel's show on torture devices. As expected, the emphasis was on distant regimes, and not our own fearsome DC Gang, with its many black sites, School for the Americas, Abu Ghraib and Guantanamo gulag. Though torture was disavowed as an effective means for extracting intelligence, bin Laden was shown shooting a machine gun, as well as the Twin Towers being hit, so revenge as justification for torture was deftly tucked into this program. There was nothing on tap, just canned beer, so I ordered a Bud. Behind the bar sat a fake hand grenade with "COMPLAINT DEPART-MENT. TAKE A NUMBER" attached to its pull ring. A sign read, "WE DON'T CALL 911. WE'LL BEAT YOU UP GOOD, THEN CALL 911." A dive bar beneath a shady hotel must attract more than a few dealers, whores, deadbeat dads and others who have skipped bail or are fleeing from a warrant, so I was not surprised to see graffiti in the bathroom threatening undercover cops.

"Hey, where's everybody?" I asked the burly bartender.

"I dunno."

"Is it always like this?"

"Yeah. Usually."

"But there's, like, no other bar around here!"

"I dunno. No one has money around here."

The place did have customers, but they only came in to buy, say, a $1 can of Colt 45 or a pack of Cheyenne cigarillos. Very unusual for a bar, there was a clear price tag before each item on the shelves, but since its clientele counted each penny, this was a sensible arrangement. On the floor, there was a $4 fan for sale. In a loose-fitting sweat ensemble, a groggy woman would appear occasionally, but it wasn't clear if she was a customer or an employee. Though she had access behind the bar, she did nothing that I could decipher. In her haze, she would look at this and that, then lurch out. Her eyes were so unseeing, I wouldn't be surprised if she navigated by sonar. Mindful of the bar's leeriness of undercover cops, I didn't want to ask too many questions.

After learning all about the various techniques to shred, pierce, penetrate, burn, break, stretch, crush, cook or electrocute a person in the most painful, drawn-out and humiliating ways possible, the other sitting patron split, and so I was left with the rather taciturn bartender. After some prodding, however, he did reveal to me quite a bit of his life story. Born in North Carolina, he has a brother who used to rake in the bucks supplying night crawlers to stores in three states, "I'd help him out, and we'd deliver all over North Carolina, into Tennessee, a bit of Georgia and even Alabama. My brother used to make $300,000 a year, and it wasn't even a year-round business!"

"$300,000 a year for selling worms?!"

"You betcha! He'd buy them for next to nothing and sell them for a bundle."

"If it was such easy money, why didn't everyone get into it?"

"Everyone did, finally, and that's why my brother is no longer doing it."

"If you all made that much, you must have saved some."

"No, we didn't. We blew it all."

"On what?"

"You know, just living, drinking. When you work so hard and drive all night, you treat yourselves well, and I didn't make that much, really, since I was only working for my brother."

"Why did you come up here?"

"I came with my parents. They had jobs at the glass factory."

"Is that still around?"

"No, it shut down. Look at these bottles," and the bartender pointed to the rows of hard liquor behind him. "Do you see much glass here?"

"Well, it's hard to tell from this distance."

"Most of these are plastic. There are hardly any glass bottles here!"

It was now past four o'clock, and I hadn't eaten anything since 7 in the morning, so I asked the bartender for a 35-cent bag of Wise potato chips, a 15-cent pretzel stick and a 30-cent Slim Jim, with its geriatric beef, mechanically separated chicken, corn syrup, sodium nitrite and dextrose, etc. Matched with a $2.15 can of Bud, my lunch came to $2.95, before tax. I didn't order the most deluxe item available, Crackers 'n Cheez, with its tiny plastic scraper, for I needed to stretch my travel budget, you know what I mean? In any case, I surely got my five food groups in, starch, sodium, lactic acid, fructose and yeast.

"You can't beat that!" The bartender smiled.

I dug in. As I ate, a second man appeared behind the bar. Smiling, he appeared awfully amused, not just at me but at everything. His assured manners tipped me off that this was perhaps the boss, but it wasn't until I talked to him that I realized he owned not just this bar, but the hotel above, and what's more, he was the sensei of the judo dojo advertised on the sign outside.

I should have recognized this confident and relaxed older man from an ensemble of photographs on the wall. Surrounding a woman who was tagged as "BOSS," he appeared four times, as "DAY MANAGER" (wearing shades), "NIGHT MANAGER" (in a white fool's cap, complete with bells), "FINANCIER" (sporting a leprechaun hat while raising a glass) and "ADVISOR" (brandishing a brass-knuckled fist). Among these was also a black-and-white photo of a shack, with this caption, "Ray's home 1945. Eminent Domain Abuse [crossed out]. Blighted. Underperforming. Illegal."

"This is a very strange town," I said to Ray. "Yours is the only bar around, and yet I'm the only one sitting here."

"Ha, ha! They've all closed down!"

I extended my left arm towards his empty bar. "So how do you survive like this?"

"You see all these people walking in and out!"

"And that's enough?"

"Sure! Many of these people come in five or six times a day. One lady, she'd show up maybe a dozen times every day, and you know something else? It'd be much cheaper for them to buy one six-pack instead of six cans, but they don't think like that!"

"Maybe they don't start out thinking they'd drink six or seven cans, then they just keep going and going."

Ray tried not to laugh. "That's a charitable way to look at it. They know, because that's what they do every day!" He briefly showed his teeth.

A man in his late fifties walked in, saw Ray and shouted, "Hey, Ray! How long have I been coming here?"

"I don't know. Thirty, thirty-five years?" Ray smiled.

"No, no. Forty years! I came in the day you opened!" Laughing, the man walked out with his tall can of Colt 45.

Changing the subject, I asked, "So, Ray, how come you only charge $30 a night for a hotel room?"

"Because I'm a nice guy! What can I say? And you only have to pay $25 a month to join my judo club."

"Is your room OK, though? Is it clean?"

"Of course it's clean. Have you seen the men's room here? How often you see a bar bathroom like that? It's perfectly clean!"

"Yeah, it's pretty clean."

"No, it's not pretty clean. It's perfectly clean! I don't put up with any nonsense whatsoever. I don't even allow cursing in my bar. Do you see all of these 'NO PROFANITY' signs? I enforce it!"

"But when people talk, they talk, and they will say shit when they're drunk." I wasn't trying to test Ray. It just came out. He let it go.

"My rooms are clean and safe," Ray continued. "I don't allow unregistered guests to come in, so you won't get a knock on your door after dark. I'm not like those guys across the street. All kinds of problems happen over there."

"How much do they charge, by the way?"

"They don't have a fixed price. They charge whatever they want, depending on what you look like. They're Indians, I think. They may charge you sixty or sixty-five bucks."

"If they charge so much more than you, why aren't you getting all their business?"

"If you want to come in and out all night, and have five people partying in your room, then you go over there. I don't allow any of that. I also don't allow children."

"Do people stay with you long-term?"

"Yeah, we have about six people like that."

"How much do you charge a month?"

"You're interested?" Ray smiled. "I only charge $550. You can't beat that!"

"And what do you get for that?"

"You get your own bathroom, and you get a little TV."

"Can you cook in there?"

"No, I don't allow anything that will generate heat. I can't risk having this entire place burn down."

"But a microwave is OK?"

"Yeah, a microwave is fine. Just no heat!"

"But it must get expensive if people can't cook in their own rooms."

"Hey, I can't solve every problem! And besides, many of these people don't buy much food anyway. Many of them eat for free, at these different churches."

"Every night?"

"Yeah, every night, if you know where to go, and these people do know, believe me! So they don't have to worry about food, really."

"They can save their money to buy beer!"

"Yeah, because everybody drinks! Even during the Great Depression, people drank. That's why I'm in business. Even if they have no money, they'll find money to buy drinks."

"But if they really go broke, won't they cut back?"

"No."

"Oh, c'mon!"

"Listen, the people I sell to are already broke. I cater to losers and bottom-feeders! That's just how it is. Only 5 percent of the population are supposed to make it. The rest just survive from day to day, if that."

"Hey, Ray, what's up with that shack in the photo?"

"That's my childhood home! Seven people lived in it, my parents and us kids. Do you see any electrical wire running from it? No! That's because we had no electricity."

"Did you have running water? A bathroom?"

"Yeah, the woods!"

"So you went from that to this!"

"I worked my tail off! I raised six kids, and they all went to college. Two of them are now lawyers, and one's a doctor. I didn't even finish the tenth grade. My wife doesn't have to do anything but count money. The other day, she told me she needed one of those money-counting machines, but those things are expensive! I told her, 'Just keep using your fingers,' so she said, 'But I'm getting older. What if I have arthritis?' And you know what I said?" Ray laughed. "I said, 'If you get arthritis, I'll get me a new wife who doesn't have arthritis,' so that was that."

"How old are you, Ray?"

"Seventy-five."

"Wow, man, you look about twenty years younger!"

Ray grinned, "I was a judo champion, I watch what I eat and I don't drink."

"That's funny as shit. You sell all this beer and you don't drink at all?"

"Never."

"When did you stop?"

"I never started. I've never cared for alcohol."

"But you've tried it."

"Yeah, I've tried it, but I didn't like it at all."

"You must do something else! Pot?"

"No, I'm just a clean guy. I don't even like my vegetables cooked. If you look in my refrigerator, you'll see sticks of carrot and celery."

"What does your wife make for you each night?"

"Anything I ask her to," Ray smiled. "Anyway, when I first moved here, the cops were suspicious. They thought I was a front for the Mafia, but I run three legitimate businesses. I have a judo team. We compete. I cause no trouble whatsoever."

"The cops have never been called to your hotel?"

"Not for anything serious. Just late payments for child support and stuff like that."

"No shootings, stabbings, drug dealings?"

"Never! That's because I strictly control who's allowed in. I have cameras all over. If there's a fight outside my bar, I'll know immediately, and I'll tell them, 'Keep that up and I'll never sell to you again,' and they scatter. They need to come back the next day for beer, you see."

Having risen from nothing, Ray is understandably self-satisfied. In fact, I've met many men of his generation who are exactly like that. In Marcus Hook, a sixty-seven-year-old told me he was planning on kicking his youngest son out on the kid's twenty-first birthday, job or no job, "Hey, I worked myself up. Why can't he?" Seeing the kids as spoiled, these tough, leathery old farts don't want to hear about diminished opportunities, or that most prospects now point downward. On the way to Vineland, I had seen several tents as the bus passed through Camden. In fact, hundreds of folks live in makeshift dwellings or abandoned homes in Camden. For these destitutes, Ray's childhood shack would be a huge improvement. In Tom's River, an hour away from Vineland, there's also a large tent city. Increasingly pessimistic, most of us don't dream of any bright future, but are planning for the worst. How many of us are squatting in foreclosed homes? How many are scraping by on just a fraction of what we used to earn just a few years ago? How many are quickly exhausting their scant savings? How many will be fired next week? Meanwhile, this criminal government continues its systematic impoverishment and suppression of us all. Fragmented and confused, we have no plan to combat any of this, but are looking to be saved by the very architects of our ruination.

LOSING IT IN JOLIET

3-3-14—The story of Joliet is familiar enough. With its industries gone, a city turns to the casino as a last-ditch salvation, but cannot reverse its decline. The details of this disintegration, though, can be interesting. Take two recent crimes. In one, four people, two men and two women, invited two male friends over for some partying, which in America nearly always involves alcohol and/or drugs and the promise of sex, but the two guests ended up being strangled to death, with their corpses serving as an uneven mattress for some macabre screwing. Yes, you read that right, two of their killers ended up fornicating on top of the cadavers, though, to be fair, the revelers were sensitive enough to place a dirty sheet between the live and dead bodies. Done, they tried to saw up their victims, but without the right tools, the process turned tiresome and messy, so one of the women went out to get a chainsaw or two, and that's how the story leaked, oozed and splattered. When cops came, they discovered the dead dudes in one room, while in the adjacent one, three ensouled and sentient beings, fastidiously and exactly made in the image of God, no less, were playing video games.

The perpetrators are all white, and the victims black, but they had also been friends before the incident. One of the white women had a child with a black man, and a black victim had a white fiancée. It's not clear, then, to what degree race was a factor. Another question to ask is why didn't this bizarre double murder and abuse of corpse case make more of a splash nationally? Granted, we live in a culture where the media can suppress (or inflate) anything, where a Honey Boo Boo's fart resonates much more loudly than the bomb that killed Michael Hastings, and information flow rests in the hands of a remarkably homogeneous group that also dominates our feeble protest zone, but one would think more people would know about such an iconic crime that illustrates all too perfectly our remarkable degeneracy and blood-splattered ennui. Mentally and spiritually voided, let's kill even our buddies, not to rob them, but just for the hell of it, then why not, let's fuck for a while on top of Eric and Terrance, then dismember them, and when that doesn't quite work, let's play some cool video games for an eternity. Also, when a crime is committed by a group, be it four, ten or an army, it is even more of an indictment of the culture.

Extremely violent, always farcical but draped in a thin coat of kitsch, that's who we have become in 2014. The other day, John Kerry, liberal darling and antiwar activist, delivered this straight-faced howler, "You just don't in the twenty-first century behave in nineteenth-century fashion by invading another country on completely trumped up pretext," and Kerry wasn't talking about the vicious American attacks on Iraq, Afghanistan or Libya, but Russia's bloodless entry into the Crimea.

The second recent Joliet crime of note also involves a corpse, but no murder. A homeless couple checked into a Joliet motel to stay warm and to, well, party. They gulped so much vodka, she died, but that didn't stop the boyfriend from continuing. Why stop, he reasoned, when there was still money left on her debit card, so he whooped it up for two more days lying next to his serene and, finally, easygoing girlfriend, and only called an ambulance when there was no more cash left to withdraw. To avoid any penalty or unpleasantness from management, he did beat the noon checkout time by over an hour, and though the putrefaction had admittedly befouled the sheet a bit, it wasn't like it had been that clean anyway. Hell, he wouldn't be surprised if they kept it as is for the next guest. Now, the theme of living next to a deceased loved one is as old as the earth, and turns up in folklore, literature and the movies. Just think of Faulkner's "A Rose for Emily" or Hitchcock's *Psycho*, for example. The judge was not impressed by Derek Tanke's cultural awareness or performance art skills, however, and so slapped him with a one-and-a-half-year prison sentence.

Already in Chicago for two college readings, I decided to visit Joliet also. I had thought about staying at the Bel-Air, since it was likely super cheap, but there was no information about it online. Further, the logistics for my weeklong trip were already complicated and taxing enough, what with four nights of sleeping on a Greyhound bus, so I decided to play it safe and book a room at the Harrah's Casino Hotel. At check-in, I wouldn't yield my debit card since I knew it had less money on it than a corpse's, so the unsmiling clerk said a cash deposit would do, but I firmly refused this also, "Don't worry, I won't order any room service or porn!" Stiffly, he gave me my key. All other Harrah's employees were as chirpy as could be, however, for each had apparently been well instructed to shout out greetings to every guest. At only $53, my room turned out to be quite palatial, at least by my gutter standards. There was even an upholstered couch. Smiling, I peeled the layers of clothes from my filthy carcass. Such a deal, but Joliet in the dead of winter is hardly a vacation destination.

I've written a story about haunted hotel rooms, and before I fell asleep that night, I also thought about the corpse in the Bel-Air, across the Des Plaines River. Composed primarily of a bed and bathroom, each hotel room is so intimate yet so public, and in each, so many tragedies and farces have occurred. Opening an eye, I half expected to see a drunken ghost standing by the bed. Come, you can lie down next to me, and though I have nothing for you to drink tonight, I'll buy you a beer first thing in the morning.

In any small American city or town, the most beautiful and dignified buildings are invariably the oldest, built before World War II, at least, before car culture and the growth of the suburbs gutted every small downtown. The ugliest buildings are from the seventies, when modernism's worst concepts have been disseminated to even the most provincial of outposts. Postmodernism is a jokey attempt to reverse this blunder, but its very mixed success doesn't reach small and depressed, post-industrial places like Joliet, for which the Rialto Square Theatre, built in 1926, remains the undisputed architectural gem. It's appalling to think that it was almost torn down in the seventies.

Done with ogling the ornate façade of the Rialto, I ducked into the Route 66 Diner, nearby. Inside I saw a black cop sitting at a table, and two other people who appeared to be office workers. Settling down at the counter, I noticed a large poster of badass Johnny Cash, with "I walk the line" beneath his name. Built in 1926, Route 66 was one of this country's very first highways, and the song "Get Your Kicks on Route 66," first recorded by Nat King Cole in 1946, is another romance of the open road, that most American of traditions. Like Cash's hit, "I've Been Everywhere," it ticks off places along the way, not so much to be seen as to be counted.

"I've been everywhere, man." I've been to Dull Knife, Big Hole, Milk Creek, Tampico, Matamoros, Manila, Okinawa, Mogadishu, Baghdad, Kandahar, Tripoli and Kiev. "I'm a killer!"

The Joliet sex-on-corpses crew are Juggalos, by the way. That is, they're fans of the Insane Clown Posse, a group whose music veers from revenge fantasies to kitsch, and whose stage tactics employ elements of the carnival. Your average Juggalo is white and of the lowest class. Working for minimum wage at, say, Jack in the Box, he must grin and sweat for more than four hours to pay for a single ICP baseball cap, and a full day's work won't even bag him an ICP hoodie, and yet he is impassioned about this music, and will spend his scarce cash to declare his allegiance to it, to show that he is indeed a Juggalo, for the ICP expresses not just his anger and frustration, but also his softer side, that is, his sodium citrate-, whey- and annatto-infused American cheesiness.

Dark tendencies have long existed in American music, with Mamie Smith already belting in 1920, "I'm gonna do like a Chinaman, go and get some hop / Get myself a gun, and shoot myself a cop," and Cash himself kicked open a mental door with his "But I shot a man in Reno just to watch him die." Now, though, with the Insane Clown Posse, M.O.P.,

Gravediggaz, Natural Born Killaz and so many more, we're entering a new psychotic territory, and gleefully too, even as the corpses pile up.

My breakfast consisted of two eggs, over easy, plus two link sausages, home fries and wheat toast. The waitress, a Mexican lady, kept my coffee cup full with frequent refills. "More, hon?" she would ask. Soon, a man sat next to me, so I struck up a conversation. After I told him I was visiting from Philly, he filled me in on Joliet, "Yes, the steel mills are long gone, and Caterpillar has cut back too. It's all these free trade agreements, you see, starting with NAFTA. We do have a new trucking hub that keeps some people employed, but overall, it's not looking too good."

"So there's no recovery?"

"Of course there's no recovery," he laughed.

"Everywhere I go, I hear the same story, and yet the media keep telling us we're well into a recovery."

"It's their job to lie. There's no recovery. I used to have five employees working for me. I had to let them all go."

"What kind of business are you in?"

"I make these rip saw machines. They cut up lumber real fast," and he took out his cell phone to show me a photo of a large, box-like contraption.

"So now it's just you working?"

"Yes, I'm a one-man factory. I'm trying to build my business back up. Hopefully, I can sell it in three years to a young person."

"Then retire?"

"No, I'll just go work for my brother. He has a machine shop."

"You haven't thought about moving away?"

"No, I'm too much of a Joliet person. I was born here. Even in college, I stayed at home. And my wife's also from Joliet. She's not doing too well. She's in a nursing home."

"Hmm. Do you have kids?"

"I have no kids, and you know something, that's a good thing, too, because I wouldn't want to be a young person in this economy."

"I agree."

"Isn't that right, Anna?" he shouted to the waitress. "It's not easy to be young nowadays, right?"

"What are you talking about?" She smiled. "I'm not young."

Returning to me, he continued, "Anna is a great person. She has a good kid. He likes to box."

"There's a boxing gym here?"

"Yes, we have a really good boxing gym. It's run by this fellow from Ghana."

"This town must have changed so much from when you were a kid."

"Yes, it used to be mostly farmland around here. Most of my relatives were farmers. Some of them still are."

"How are they doing?"

"They're doing OK, I guess. It's not easy, though."

"What do you mean?"

"OK, how do I explain this. In the past, farming required a lot of labor, but with the improved mechanized processes, you don't need as much manpower. With these new machines, you don't have to go over a piece of land as many times," and here he paused to give me time to digest, and I did appreciate his effort at making his explanation as simple as possible. "With these new machines and techniques, they only need a fraction of the people they used to, and they also save on fuel."

"Maybe soon," I exclaimed, "they'll have all of these machines run by themselves. Then they can fire all the workers!"

"I'm sure they're working on it."

All this time, my new friend had managed to talk and chew at the same time, unlike my monomaniac and uncoordinated self. Seeing that my food had barely been touched, he said, "I should let you eat. That food is going cold!"

We each turned to our portion. Every now and then, though, he would say something to the cashier or the waitress, who both knew him well. When he recounted that he had recently gotten a speeding ticket, only the second in his lifetime, with the first going back to 1974, Anna blurted, "Nineteen seventy-four! I don't born yet!" Interesting, I thought, since up to this point, her English had been very convincing, but nearly all her phrases had been lifted directly from the common diner catechism.

Catechism?! WTF! Did I just make a mistake there? You decide. In any case, as also a foreign-born mofo, I know all too well that a linguistic trap, pothole, sinkhole or wrong turn can sabotage my social carriage at any moment.

Before I left the diner, something curious happened. A rather shabbily dressed old man said to the cashier as he was paying for his coffee, "Can I have an application?"

"What?"

"An application."

"For what?"

"For a job, just in case you're hiring."

"No, no, we're not hiring."

"I just figured I'd ask," and he meekly walked out.

Turning to me, the still baffled cashier said, "He lives in the Plaza Hotel right next door. He comes in here all the time."

Leaving the diner, I decided to get away from downtown, so I crossed the river, but my progress was slow, thanks to the abundant snow on the sidewalks. After trudging for nearly a mile, I found O'Charley's and marched right in for an open-ended pit stop. It was still morning, so I half expected to find a few old men nursing cheap beers, but instead encountered a handful of neatly dressed customers, including a businessman on an early lunch break. There was a clock with the map of Ireland, but the time was neither local nor Irish. I pointed this out to the bartender, Marianne.

"Yeah, I know. There's something wrong with the battery."

After stating that I was only visiting, I asked Marianne if there is a large Irish community in Joliet. "No, not really," she answered. "We're, like, the only Irish bar here, and I'm not even Irish. I just work here."

"It seems like a very pleasant place," and from what I had seen, it was.

"Yeah, but we're getting more crimes, though. We have gangs here. There are black and Mexican gangs. They mostly just shoot their own kinds, but sometimes we get hit in the cross fire, and sometimes they also rob us."

"In this neighborhood, too?"

"Yeah, in this neighborhood! It's not safe to walk around here after dark."

O'Charley's was pleasant enough, but a little later, I would really get comfortable in a place called Vela's. A cheap bar and Mexican restaurant, it's run by a native son, Dan Gutierrez. Rotund, bespectacled, with a salt-and-pepper mustache and in a gray, long-sleeved sweatshirt, Dan appeared as a Santa Claus chillaxing at home, during the off season. Also born in Joliet, Dan's dad opened a market there in 1953, "We used to go to the Haymarket in Chicago to pick up stuff to sell. Some of the farmers would bring their produce to the market in horse and buggies!"

From his dad, Dan learned how to run a business, but his work experience has extended way beyond that. He's been employed as an electrical inspector of natural gas pipelines, and in factories making shingles, caustic soda, sucrose and aspartame. "Hey, isn't that that evil shit that will give you cancer?"

"Not unless you drink a million gallons of it!"

"But many people do!"

"I wouldn't worry about it. When I was working, that aspartame dust was always in the air, and we all breathed it in."

Currently, Dan's day job is as a senior pipe designer and project manager for AMS Mechanical Systems.

"Isn't it enough just to run this bar?" I asked.

"No way," Dan laughed. "It's almost four, right, and you see how empty it is."

"But it will fill up soon with the after-work crowd?"

"Yes, people will trickle in, but it's not enough. Plus, I need my day job for the health insurance. They like me there. I keep my own hours."

"I walked all over town today and didn't see too many bars. I would think a cheap neighborhood joint like this would pack them in."

"Yes, but people are drinking less. I've noticed it. And you know what else? More of them are paying with credit cards instead of cash."

"So they're out drinking even when they can't afford to drink?"

"Yes, I think so. Like my ma said, 'People will always find a way to drink.' Some of them come in here and try to sell me their Link cards."

"That's the food stamps?"

"Yes, that's the food stamps. They would try to sell me their Link cards for half price, but I won't buy it, since I don't want them to drink away the money they should spend on their kids for food!"

"You know, Dan, I've talked to many bartenders and they all tell me that people are drinking less, and even putting less money into the jukebox," and Vela's had been silent for a while, with the last song being "Pistoleros Famosos," Los Cadetes de Linares's celebration of Mexican outlaws, *En los pueblitos de norte / Siempre ha corrido la sangre . . .* Yes, Mexicans also often sing of blood and shootings, but these ballads are so sweetly sung, they don't quite incite.

OK, OK, back to Joliet. Dan also refuses to sell lottery tickets, but there are two gambling machines in Vela's, Mega Winner and Hot New Game. When a woman of at least fifty marched in, Dan greeted her, "Good evening, young lady!"

"You know what I want."

"Miller?"

"That's right!"

After he gave her the tall yellow can, she asked, "How much is it?"

"$2.50."

"Thank you, darling!"

"Thank you, baby."

She then went over to one of the gambling machines and grimly got down to business. I said to Dan, "It's funny that she expects you to remember what she wants, but then pretends to not know how much it costs."

"She always does that."

"How often does she come in here?"

"Not that often, maybe only twice a month. She always comes around this time, and she always sits at the machine. She'll spend about a hundred bucks before she leaves."

"Wow, that's ridiculous! And she doesn't look like she can afford it. What does she do, do you know?"

"She cleans houses."

I laughed, shook my head, "If she doesn't waste that money, she can drink and eat better."

"Or buy clothes for her kids, take them out to dinner, but if she wants to throw her money away, that's her choice! You can't win with those machines." Dan smiled. "It involves no skill whatsoever. It takes your money, but once in a while, it will give you back a little, but when someone does win, it makes these loud noises. At night, I have to turn up the volume on these machines so everyone can hear the winning sounds!"

"These gamblers are like kids, man. They like cartoon figures and happy noises!"

"But they're very serious about it." Dan smiled. "If you go to the casino and see one of these old people at a slot machine, you better not sit next to him, because he might be playing three machines at the same time. Grandpa will get pissed off if you sit next to him!"

Dan is likely a grandpa himself, I thought, but one never sees oneself as old, or at least nowhere nearly as old as how one is seen by everyone else. "I stayed in the casino hotel last night," I said. "I don't think it's doing too well."

"No, it's not, and it's not doing much for the city either. Before it opened, they said that it would bring business to the city, but the people who go there, stay there. They don't come out to the bars and restaurants in the rest of Joliet."

"There was nothing in my room about Joliet, no guidebook, no restaurant guide. Nothing!"

"Yes, of course, they want you to keep your money inside Harrah's."

"So this casino hires a few people, but it also rips off a bunch of locals who lose their money gambling!"

"Yeah, well, the city also gets tax revenues, but I know of people here who've lost their houses gambling."

"That's incredible!"

"You know, they'll give you credit if you run out of cash, so you may have to sell your house to pay off your debts."

By this time, more people have arrived, mostly for the pool tournament that night. As should be clear by now, Dan is very resourceful, and though he certainly knows how to make money, he also cares enough to give back some. Once a year, Dan stages an eating contest. For thirty-five bucks, each contestant gets a five-pound burrito, and from the photo he showed me, it looks like a murdered homunculus wrapped in an old sheet. The first pig who can stuff all this into his maw wins $100, and once, a young man managed to do so in an astounding sixteen minutes. Dan sells around forty of these a year, with $15 from each going to a charity. Of course, Dan also makes a bundle from all those who crowd in to gawk at this messy spectacle.

Leaving Vela's, I walked to the train station, and on the way, passed a mural of Bill Sudakis. Playing eight years in the majors, Sudakis managed to bat just .234, but did hit 14, 14 and 15 home runs in three separate seasons. If he's remembered at all these days by anybody, it's for a hotel brawl with a Yankees teammate. Early in his career, Sudakis was switched from third base to catcher, a decision which may have wrecked his knees, so he was probably misused and ruined, but that's just life, kid. Suck it!

Not every town can produce a Hall of Famer, so Joliet's baseball hero is merely Bill Sudakis, but even there he's barely seen, for his likeness is shoved under an overpass, behind some columns and, to make matters worse, someone has drawn a huge phallus jutting from his crotch, so there Bill stands, erect yet forgotten, showing cracks and peeling, like Joliet itself, like so many other wrecked and neglected places in this insane clown posse nation.

HUNGRY IN CHICAGO?

3-10-14—I've been coming to Chicago forever, but always just for a day or two. The first time was when I was only a teenager and visiting an aunt in St. Louis. Another time, it was to take a physical exam for now-defunct Midway Airlines. I was trying to get a job as a baggage handler. The day before, though, I had been at a Philly party where someone handed me a joint. Never one to refuse heartfelt hospitality, I inhaled, but somehow this didn't prevent me from being hired by Midway. Perhaps they used the same urinanalyst, piss parser or golden shower technician as Major League Baseball, you know, the one that kept clearing Sammy Sosa even as he hit, like, 600 home runs in one season. In any case, I never took that Midway job, for I had found another while waiting for their decision. Back in the late eighties, it was that easy to find work, so even a no-skill, no-degree, beer-swilling and, occasionally, very occasionally, actually, pot-smoking, coke-inhaling or acid-dropping bum like me could pick and choose. If you could lift stuff, no matter how awkwardly, you were hired.

In recent years, I had mostly come to Chicago to do poetry readings. Though my fifteen minutes as a fringe poet is rapidly flaming out, there's still a bit of kerosene left in the guttering lamp. Gone are the days when I could be paid nicely to squeak, squawk and bloviate to a full Santa Fe theater as a guest of the Lannan Foundation, or be flown to Paris, Berlin or Reykjavik to make people wish they had stayed at home instead, but invitations to read still trickle in. Shoot straight, though, and doors will slam in your face, buddy, if not worse, much worse. When I could hardly think and write, I was being published in *The Guardian*, *The New York Times*, and being interviewed on the BBC, but now, I can barely give my seasoned blathering away.

So an invitation to read at Roosevelt University brought me to Chicago this time, and since I wanted to linger awhile, I wiggled my way into an additional reading at Wilbur Wright, a community college. Through an informal arrangement with a poet friend, Daniel Borzutzky, I ended up talking to his students after they had discussed Ariel Dorfman's *Death and the Maiden*, a play about political torture. To give this work more context, Borzutzky's also showed us a YouTube video of an escrache demonstration in Buenos Aires.

Started in Argentina, escrache has spread to other Latin American countries as a popular movement to oust, shame and ostracize retired generals, politicians and other powerful figures who have committed unpunished crimes. After locating the criminal in question, the organizers would inform his neighbors that here lives a state-sanctioned mass murderer or torturer, or a looter of public funds. Later, thousands of people would converge on this man's house to publicly indict the blood-drenched fat cat. Though this Latin American version of a Cheney, Rumsfeld, Bush or Obama is never physically attacked, the monster will be shunned by many of his neighbors, with local businesses even refusing to sell him a meal or a newspaper.

Critics of escrache have denounced it as a form of vigilante justice and, as the outburst of an angry mob, something that should be declared illegal, but the protesters are only reacting to acts that are themselves clearly illegal, not to mention outrageously immoral. The protesters' public harassment does not compare to their targets' torturing and/or raping, then throwing their victims from airplanes into the ocean, or kidnapping their children and erasing their identities.

Too often, the state will use the legality argument to bind its opponents, while doing whatever it pleases, legal or not. Not satisfied with a monopoly on violence, the state also wants to be the sole interpreter of what's right and wrong, as implied by the often-bandied-about legality question, and the more criminal this state is, the more illegal, the more it will shriek about the need for everyone else to walk the straight and narrow, according it its own power-drunk markings. Talking to Borzutsky's class, I asked the students to consider escrache in the North American context. Who are our criminals in high places and what should we do about them? Unlike our southern neighbors, we have neither the clarity to identify our enemies from within, nor the courage or unity to confront them. To be fair, though, our top criminals don't move among us, with many never even mentioned by our obfuscating media, as great a killer of brain cells as any, and worse than any glue. Even when not anonymous, however, the most malignant Americans are hidden behind guarded gates, bulletproof glass or acres of real estate, so that it would take considerable enterprise to target them.

When faced with an illegal and ultraviolent enemy, we must resort to any and all tricks, be extra clever and strike hard, for real, but most of us are too tightly bound to our bifurcated harness to do more than jiggle, every once in a while, an electronic voting machine. Geez, I wonder who they'll let us pretend to vote for the next time, if there's a next time?

On one of my three days in Chicago, I wandered around West Town. I began in Wicker Park, a Polish neighborhood and Nelson Algren's old haunt turned barrio Boricua turned hipster haven turned, finally, into the yuppie bastion it is today, but not before considerable acrimony and even vandalism from the retreating hepcats. Lawdy, I know it's awfully silly to regurgitate black slang from nearly a century ago, but hepcats are no more hooey than the hipster tag. On snowy, icy or slushy sidewalks, I then trudged into Humboldt Park, Chicago's current San Juan. There, I spotted New Life Covenant, with its large banners announcing that it is a "CHURCH FOR THE HURTING." Aren't we all, my fellow collateral damages or direct hits? Finally, I found myself in what's left of the Ukrainian Village. At the corner of Western and Chicago, there was a man about forty years old walking with a cardboard sign in the middle of the street, between cars. Increasingly common across America, this sight will be ubiquitous soon enough. I got close enough to read, "PLEASE SPARE SOME CHANGE?!? HOMELESS, HUNGRY, BROKE & COLD."

Chris was his name, and he told me he had been homeless for fourteen months, and usually made about $20 a day, panhandling. Wanting to hear more, I offered to buy Chris lunch. Bacci was nearby, but Chris said, "I can't eat pizza. I have no front teeth." To prove it, Chris flashed his nude gums. Across from Bacci, there was Village Pizza, and since it also served submarines, we went there instead. Needing something hot, I ordered a modest heap of ravioli that turned out god-awful, while Chris went for Italian beef with french fries. They looked much tastier than my red slop, that's for sure.

"So, man, what did you use to do?"

"I was a bike courier. That's how I lost my front teeth. Someone rear-ended me!"

"Holy shit! So did you get, ah, compensation from your employer?"

"No way, man!"

"But you were at work. You were working!"

"No, no, that's not how they saw it. This is how it works. If I had a package on me, then they would count it as me being on the job, but I was between deliveries, so I wasn't technically working for them."

"But you were only out on the streets to do deliveries. You weren't just riding your bike around!"

"I know, but that's not how they saw it."

"OK, OK, so they hired you as a contractor, and not as a regular employee on the clock?"

"Yeah, that's basically it."

"Man, that's ridiculous!"

"Yeah, so one second I'm on the bike, then suddenly I'm in an ambulance, and since I had no health insurance, I still owe the hospital all this money."

"So what did you do when you got out?"

"I didn't feel like being a bike courier anymore, so I got a job with Allied, the moving company. That lasted for a few years. Then I got a job at another moving company, but business was so slow, they had to let me go eventually. That was my last job. The accident, though, wasn't the only reason I quit being a bike courier. I really got out because the money wasn't as good anymore."

"What do you mean?"

"I used to make about 750 a week, for only four days of work, but then it got down to only 225, and I had to work all five days. Everything changed after 9/11."

"Hmm, how did that affect your job?"

"The security, man! Before 9/11, I could go into an elevator and take my package directly to the office, so I would be out of there in two minutes, but after 9/11, I had to go through all these people, from the front desk to the mailroom, just to deliver my stupid package, and I had to fill out all of these forms, too, so what used to take me two minutes to do now took me fifteen or even twenty, so at the end of the day, I couldn't deliver as many packages, and I was being paid by the package."

"And it's not like terrorists are itching to send package bombs!"

"Yeah, but people were so scared then. Plus, you have the internet now, and that has hurt also. Before, companies had to hire bike couriers to deliver everything, but now, they can send all these images and documents through the internet."

"So what's the plan now? What are you going to do?"

"I'm on three waiting lists to get into these recovery houses. I'm hoping it won't be more than another month."

"Are you an addict?"

"I'm in AA, but I haven't drank in a while."

"So the recovery house is just a way to go inside."

"Yeah, and to have an address, because you can't even get a job without an address."

"Are you from Chicago originally?"

"Yeah, born and raised here, in McHenry, and I have never left except for when I was a roadie for these bands."

"Oh yeah? Which bands?"

"You ever heard of Alkaline Trio? No? Well, that's the most famous one, but I've also worked for Sidekick Kato and Apocalypse Hoboken."

As this civilization goes into serious decline, even its band names get really uninspired and stupid. We can't even do nihilism right. Around 1990, I was the road manager for indie-folk Baby Flameheads, but I only lasted for half a tour. Night after night, we'd hit another bar, and there was nothing for me to do but get juiced up, through two or three sets, but then I was expected to safely drive the van away after last call. Yes, curse me, all of you who are blame-free! As a young man, I made many sapling mistakes, but now that I'm older, I'm blundering as a middle-aged fool.

"Chris, don't you have family that can help you out? Where are your parents?"

"My mom's still alive, but she's remarried, and my stepfather hates my guts. He gets really pissed off if he thinks she's giving me money, so I don't want to bother her."

"What does he do?"

"He was laying concrete until he was laid off about five years ago, but he's about to retire anyway, so it doesn't really matter. He's saved a lot of money."

"How much money did this guy make?"

"A lot, man! He was making $38 an hour at the end."

"Wow!"

"Yeah, and he'd put half of each paycheck into the bank, but with what's left, he still bought whatever he wanted. He's not hurting. He's loaded!"

"$38 an hour! You're lucky to make 10 these days."

"I know."

"And how about your mom? What does she do?"

"She works in a bar in McHenry." Immediately cheered by this thought, Chris beamed his pink smile. "If I was still drinking, I could get drunk for free each time I go see my mom!"

"Hey, it's very good you don't miss drinking. How much did you drink?"

"Oh, man, I can't even tell you. I'm half Slovak and half Bulgarian. Both sides of my family are drinkers. You ever heard of rakia? It's a Bulgarian brandy. Try it sometime. It will knock you out!"

By this time, I had managed to ingest my ravioli, plus the equally bad accompanying salad. Chris, however, had only eaten half of his sandwich and fries. If I had less manners, I would have grabbed at least a few of his fries to chase away the bad taste in my mouth. Chris ended up throwing half of his lunch away.

Unlike what his sign said, Chris wasn't that hungry after all, but this penchant for wasting food and everything else is very indicative of our culture. Coming from Vietnam to the States as an eleven-year-old, I was immediately struck by how much food was wasted each day in the school cafeteria. Quite casually, my classmates would toss away even unopened cartons of orange juice or milk. Later, a girlfriend would laugh when she saw me struggling to finish my dinner, "You don't have to eat it all, you know!" She thought it was cute. To this day, I won't throw away anything that may have a milligram of nutrient on it, and that includes fast-food ketchup packets. It's not just that I will eat absolutely everything I've paid for, but that a bunch of people have gone through a tremendous amount of trouble and coordination to make and deliver, for example, this roll of bread, red onion, string bean or slice of (sorta) cheese to (sorta) nourish me, so I won't insult them by throwing even a speck of it into the trash can, though those ravioli surely deserved to be flung from the top of the Sears Tower.

Among the minor quirks of an empire in decline is its gross celebration of gluttony, hence our huge restaurant portions and thousands of eating contests, with some of these revolting spectacles even shown on television. We also have celebrity chefs, just like the Romans in decadence, but before this American Century, however, before this epoch of oil-fueled prosperity and endless war, people were also fascinated by the spectacle of not eating. They would pay to see Starving Artists and Living Skeletons.

Soon enough, though, these types will reappear in ballooning numbers among us, and we won't even need tickets to gawk. Too feeble to mount even an escrache, we deserve nothing less.

All over Chicago, there are these posters that plead for donations to food banks, with "1 in 5 kids faces hunger," and I've seen enough homeless Americans rummaging through dumpsters for bits of meat and limp french fries to know that hunger has become a serious issue in this greatest of nations, the indispensable one and global beacon, but too many of us will keep squandering all resources as if the worst is not coming, for even as we sink into Third World status, we can't or won't shake imperial habits.

Perhaps we're only mirroring our obscene leaders, for they routinely issue pompous pronouncements and threats as the rest of the world laugh in incredulity or contempt. Even as we support Neo-Nazis in Ukraine, for example, Hillary Clinton sees fit to compare Vladimir Putin to Hitler, and Chris Murphy, a Democratic senator from Connecticut, huffs that "Europe is not where they need to be right now. I think they are willing to give Putin a much longer leash than we are." Nice word choice, eh? I wonder how "leash" translates back in Moscow. Personally, I think we should apply the tightest of leashes to Obama, Kerry, Hagel, Holder, Pelosi, McCain and the rest of our psychotic leadership, for only after we've roped them all in, then away, very far away, can this increasingly sad country be rediscovered and rebuilt.

COLUMBUS'S BOTTOMS

4-3-14—I was in Columbus all of ten hours. Even downtown, some of the sidewalks were clogged by snow, and as I crossed the Sciotto into Franklinton, my trudging became even more laborious. Mostly I walked on the side of the street, and on side streets, right in the middle. From an attic window, a torn American flag hung, and on a garage, there was a crudely drawn handgun, accompanied by "BEWARE I WILL SHOOT." I passed a house that was for sale for $15,000, cash, and saw portraits of Lincoln and Washington in the windows of Dr. Edward A. Cutler's office. The peeled paint and exposed wood of the second floor made me think his business was no more. Online, there's this 2007 testimony about Dr. Cutler, "He is the 'Mother Teresa' of Columbus, serving the poorest population with kindness and love. Dr. Cutler is passionate about the practice of medicine. He provides the highest quality of service, going beyond what anyone would expect."

Most of Franklinton is in fairly good shape, though forlorn, a series of Charles Burchfield watercolors come to life. The first white settlement in Columbus, it was founded in 1797 by Lucas Sullivant, and thanks to its low status topographically and economically, Franklinton is also known as the Bottoms. In the beginning, no one wanted to come, so Sullivant had to give lots away, on a street he called Gift. There is also a Sullivant Street, naturally.

Like George Washington, Sullivant was a land surveyor, that is, his job was to map out territories that had been claimed and parceled by the United States government, vast tracts of land long inhabited by natives who would have to be chased out, or killed. For his service, Sullivant was awarded 6,000 acres, roughly 6,000 football fields that were, naturally, teeming with Injuns. In Columbus's Genoa Park, there is a statue of Sullivant as pioneer, with his left hand holding an American flag that's tilted forward. His right shades his surveying eyes.

In the same park, there's also a bronze of Sullivant's wife, Sarah, holding up an infant. Done in a sort of jivey essentialism that's modernism many years and miles removed from its original blossoming, it's a celebration of Sarah's adoption and rearing of Arthur Boke, a son of one of her slaves. Boke spent his entire life with the Sullivants and is even buried in their family plot, so his inclusion in that household is indeed remarkable, but there's a dark side to this that has gone strangely unexamined, for why ruin the feel good story? First off, Arthur Boke is named, exactly, after a close friend of Lucas Sullivant, and this white man just happened to be a house guest of the Sullivants when Boke's mom got pregnant, so if she gave him up right after birth, it can only mean she wanted nothing to do with a child born of rape. What else do you think happened? History is replete with whitewashing, so this is just another example. In some accounts of Boke, his birth mother's inhumane status has also been lifted to "servant," and since there are huge differences between servants and slaves, this ain't similar to, say, calling a fast-food worker a "sandwich artist." In Columbus, there is also a two-lane bridge named after Boke.

Of course, this city's namesake is an endless source of debate, with radically different verdicts from opposite camps. Had Columbus been sunk at sea, however, or eaten as tapas by Caribs, so that we would have a different history, one without Columbus, Ohio or Washington, DC, bane of the world, though boasting of lovely landscaping, fine museums and two poppin' jazz clubs, it's fair to assume that other European ships would have arrived soon enough, to begin a similar scramble for conquests, with their attendant decimation of Native Americans.

As Americans now, we are the beneficiaries of each American state crime past and present, though depending on how low on the totem pole we are, we can also be America's victims, though the biggest victims, by far, are the ones on the receiving end of America's serial destruction of nations and peoples. Dodging American bombs, depleted uranium tank munitions, drone missiles and/or economic dismantling of their societies, many have decided it's best to flee to the belly of the beast. Ending up in places like Columbus, Ohio, they sell Slurpees or drive cabs, etc. For years, Americans have already been going to Ukraine for sex vacations, so with its further impoverishment through Yankee meddling, our paunchy creeps can expect an even better value while in Kiev.

It was getting cold wandering like that, so I was ready to duck into the nearest beer pit. I had to pass on the charmingly named Rehab Tavern, however, since it simply looked too bright, cheery and spacious for my svelte wallet. On the edge of Franklinton, it's spearheading a gentrification push from downtown, I asked a man on the street and was pointed to Charley's Place, but after a ten-minute walk, I discovered that it was closed. A nearby bar was also lightless, and it was already late afternoon. Holy Sheela-na-gig, if bars are shuttered left and right in an Irish neighborhood, the sky must be falling! A Kafka line voiced itself, "Slowly, like old men, we crawled through the snowy wastes," but there was no we, just me, and against terrible odds, I managed to crawl to the door of The Patio, where inside, new friends were waiting to save me.

"What would you have?"

"What do you have?"

"Bud, Miller, Schlitz, Pabst."

"Schlitz, I guess."

It was clearly a neighborhood hangout, for almost every stool was taken, and folks were chattering, bantering and laughing with each other. The two guys to my right were merely muttering, however.

"You ever been charged with a felony?"

"Well, not really, but yeah! It was Stephany. She told the cops I had hit her, but I only swung at her once! I'm not even a fighter, man. I hate fighting. I don't even know how to fight."

"How long were you two together?"

"Twelve years, man, and I only swung at her once!"

On the wall, there was a large picture of the Fightin' Irish, the Notre Dame logo, and next to it, a framed photo of some bald dude wearing a T-shirt that said, "I'm too sexy for this T-shirt." Behind the bar, a large banner announced, "THE PATIO. THE BOTTOMS." I was getting hungry, too, so seeing a sign advertising hoagies for $5.50, I asked the man next to me, the swinging nonfighter, "Is the food here any good?"

"Yeah, it's good, very good!"

"Thanks, man," and so I ordered the Italian hoagie. The other choice was ham and cheese. My sandwich did turn out excellent. Wider than a Philly hoagie, it was also heated, and came with slices of hot Italian peppers. I was still working on my first can of beer when a middle-aged man named Sandy bought a round for the whole bar, and so I had another one coming. In Irish dives across this country, such generosity is hardly unusual, I've come to learn. That evening, I also bought beers for others, but not for the entire bar, unfortunately, since I simply couldn't afford it.

After the two dudes to my right left, an old man showed up. Over seventy, he wore an OSU jacket and seemed quite delighted to listen to the jukebox while sipping, very slowly, his can of Bud. When the Eagles growled, "Witchy woman, she got the moon in her eye," grandpa ad-libbed, "She got crabs, ha ha," and with "Mr. Sandman," he would scat along to the "bung bung bung bung" refrain. "Mr. Sandman, bring me a dream. Bung, bung, bung, bung!"

When I told him I had just gotten off the bus from Philly, Bob said he had lived in Lancaster and Harrisburg, Pennsylvania. He had also spent time in Germany and France while in the military, "I didn't like the Army at all, but I'm glad I did it. It's just something you have to do, you know what I mean? We had a captain who was a real asshole. He would make us do all kinds of stupid things, just for the hell of it. One time he made us polish rocks."

"Why?"

"Just for the hell of it! Because he was an asshole! You've never been in the Army, have you? I got back at this guy, though, I trashed his living quarters, and though I was punished for it, he never bothered me again."

Retired, Bob no longer had to take crap from anyone, except, of course, the iron dictates of his increasingly capricious, cruel and worn-out body. For the moment, though, all was well as he sang along to yet another oldie.

"A man who looks forward to spring is looking forward to his own death," Leonardo wrote in a notebook, but in the US today, there are millions who can't wait until they're close enough to death, literally, so as to collect Social Security, because that's the only lifeline they have left. If you're laid off in middle age, you're practically unemployable in this economy, so you must scrounge whatever together to get by day to day, for we have morphed from a nation of tradesmen and professionals to a ragged society of temps, desperate improvisers, odd-jobbers and hustlers.

In The Patio, I met one such jack-of-all-trades. Forty-three years old, Monroe was a carpenter, housepainter, bartender and valet, "I work at Colombini. You know where that is?"

"Yeah, I saw it on the way here. It looks nice."

"It is nice, and pretty cheap too."

Monroe wore his salt-and-pepper hair and beard long and unkempt, and wouldn't look out of place in a raccoon hat, but instead, he had on a baseball cap that advertised WinTicket.com, the horse race betting outfit. Two front teeth were missing and his speech was slurry when not whiny, so I had to strain just to comprehend him. Though extremely personable, he wouldn't make an ideal bartender in any establishment with pretensions to class, and so it's no surprise he's only an emergency beer slinger.

"You say you also paint houses," I said. "That's not bad money. How come you're not doing that?"

"No one's hiring. For four years I worked for the guy who owns the Hollywood Casino. You know about that?"

"Yeah, I saw a billboard."

"He paid us good, man. Me and this guy, we were paid $200,000 for five years' worth of work."

"Holy shit!"

"Yeah, man, it was great."

"I've made that kind of money for maybe two years in my life, and I'm fifty."

"I'm counting on this guy to hire me again. It beats parking cars. Hey, have you heard of Dave Kingman?"

"Who?"

"Dave Kingman, baseball player."

"Cubs?"

"Yeah. When I was a kid, I caught a Dave Kingman baseball, then he signed it. It's worth about $200,000."

"No fuckin' way!"

"Yes fuckin' way! It's worth $200,000, easy."

"For a Dave Kingman baseball?!"

"Yeah, man. I've done the research. The only problem is, I don't have it right now. My aunt has that baseball."

"Why did you give it to her?"

"I didn't. She just has it, but I'm thinking I'll get it back when she dies, you know. I did catch it, and it even changed the shape of my palm," and to prove it, Monroe held up his hand.

"I don't see anything."

To give me some basis for comparison, Monroe then raised both of his hands, palms out, so that he looked like a surrendering soldier.

"Seriously, man, I don't see any difference."

He let it drop, brooded briefly, then, "Hey, you want to see my girlfriend?"

"Sure."

He took out his cell phone, flipped it open, and on the tiny screen, I could see a thin woman in a black tank top making some kind of a face.

"Hey, she's hot!" I blurted.

Glad that I had come round to seeing life his way, Monroe smiled.

By this point, I was feeling pretty fine in The Patio, and would have stayed longer if I didn't have to head back to the Greyhound to continue my journey. That night, I would sleep on the bus, as I had the previous night. Before I left, though, the two dudes who had discussed felonies returned, and Trevor, the one who claimed to hate fighting, got into an altercation with a man named Henry, and though older, Henry promptly knocked Trevor to the ground. As he got up, half of the bar surrounded him and told him to beat it, and though smartened by Henry's right hook, Trevor pretended he still wanted to rumble. The bar owner, though, was right there, and with a hand on Trevor's shoulder, said to him in an avuncular tone, "Just go home and come back tomorrow, OK?"

Before he finally left, though, Trevor even asked the bar owner for a $20 loan, and without hesitation, the older man gave it to him. It's all family here.

"He's on something," a woman said as people laughed, then Sandy patted me on the back as he walked by, "You didn't expect this much excitement, did you!"

Hey, people will occasionally fight in bars, but it's good that they are socializing face-to-face, for without this direct mixing, what you find in this culture is not meditative solitude but a noise-, chat- and porn-filled solipsism. The benefit of being left alone is that you can hear yourself and your conscience more clearly, but this is not possible if Gwar is blasting in the background, the television is never off, and on the computer screen, a torrent of upskirt photos shares space with the Dow Jones index ticker. Mingling is good, is all I'm saying, and I'm certainly not advocating mass, compulsory or compulsive alcoholism, for we're not that spiritually distilled yet. We're not that Southern Comforted.

Now that I've brought up solipsism, I would be remiss if I didn't remind you that Columbus is James Thurber's hometown. Before our current age of militant illiteracy, Thurber's "The Secret Life of Walter Mitty" was known to every American by tenth grade or so, and in this 1939 story, a henpecked wuss imagines himself to be an ace pilot war hero, famed surgeon, then cool, gangsterish killer who's also a lady magnet. Mitty is basically Don Quixote removed to small-city America, and though there are dark and violent strains to his fantasies, he's viewed as charming and harmless. America's priapic dreams, however, are nothing to be chuckled at. Increasingly vehement and bloody, they're on course to blow up this Columbus experiment, if not the rest of the world also.

ABANDONED IN BENSALEM

4-20-14—When I told my friend Anwar of my plan to traverse Bensalem by foot, he laughed, "You can't even walk there. There are no sidewalks!" Though this is not quite true, I did find myself mostly schlepping on edges of roads or people's lawns. To not get splattered by SUVs, sometimes I had to hop puddles or even step in mud. Covering twenty miles over two days, the only other pedestrians I encountered was a Mexican immigrant, a few derelict types, perhaps homeless, and a well-tattooed teen couple with bad skin wearing black T-shirts. Since I didn't chatter with them, I can't tell you if they were going to their meth dealer, the Wawa or a Bible study group.

Half a century ago, there were still farms in Bensalem, then the strip malls and shopping centers took over. Now this township is mostly an asphalt quilt of parking lots, freeways and highways, with a golf course and three cemeteries to provide large green spaces. The biggest land hog, however, is the Parx Casino and Racetracks. In a TV commercial, some dork in an irregular dress shirt and remaindered jacket goes on a blind date with a mature goth chick. Opening the door, she greets him with, "So, are you ready to get lucky?" "OK," he meekly answers. They end up at Parx. After he wins big, her crimson mouth tells him, "You were great."

A huge bronze horse head, muzzle down, greets visitors to Parx, and this is rather perverse, since a decapitated, nose-diving stallion head not only suggests horrible luck, but also evokes the Mafia, but since Parx is Bensalem's biggest tax teat by far, and also gives quite a bit to charities, let's not quibble over how that money is earned. Making next to nothing, we're trapped in a stacked-deck, cartoon and ringing-bell economy dominated by shadowy crooks.

Living in a "bedroom community," Bensalem's inhabitants are expected to make their money elsewhere anyway. Most commute into Philly during the day. One person, though, who almost never leaves Bensalem is Anwar's wife, Momna, but then she can hardly be said to ever be in Bensalem itself, for Momna spends her days locked inside her rented home, with the windows closed, curtains drawn and AC turned up. Plopped on her couch, she watches Indian dramas on television or chats with her mom on the phone. All Americans flee to the suburbs to escape other people and be left alone, but Momna has taken this to a whole other level. She won't even go to the supermarket, much less a restaurant. Since she landed at Philadelphia International Airport in 1999 from Pakistan fifteen years ago, Momna's knowledge of the USA has hardly improved.

After a long day of trying to sell knockoff purses at a dying mall, Anwar spends nearly an hour on the train, then drives away from a parking lot so vast, it has its own shuttle service. Before arriving home, however, Anwar often has to stop at Walmart, Sam's Club, Bottom Dollars, Acme or Patel Brothers, the Indian supermarket, to pick up something on Momna's order, for, as I've already said, she won't leave the house, much less drive. Momna lies around so much, bleeding cracks have appeared on her skin and her weight is scaling up to dangerous levels, but whatever health problems there are will remain undetermined, for she won't go to the doctor.

Anwar and Momna have two children, fourteen-year-old Farah and twelve-year-old Saaed. Not allowed by their mom to participate in extracurricular activities or even go to parties, not that they're often invited, the kids have few friends. One white boy, however, did try his damnedest to get into Farah's ridiculously frumpy pants, and for about three months, called her at least once a day, sometimes as late as 10 p.m. The social stigma of being with the often-mocked Muslim girl would be worth it if only, if only, but then he gave up. At home, the kids watch Indian shows with their mom, and thus know next to nothing about the Phillies, Eagles, Flyers, Beyoncé, Lady Gaga or Miley, though Farah did get Anwar to buy her a Justin Bieber watch, and each kid also has an iPhone 5, to be in sync, sort of, with their classmates. Anwar indulges his children since he feels guilty about losing the family's life savings and home during the stock market crash of 2008. Farah orders ugly shoes online that she barely wears.

Anwar works seven days a week and spends almost nothing on himself, but this does not mean he has sworn off all fun. Two or three times a week he meets his mistress who's also a married immigrant from Pakistan. To save money on motel rooms, Anwar has rented a storage compartment at just over a hundred bucks a month. Roll up the steel door, you'll see a queen-size mattress and nothing else. Eminently practical and focused, Anwar just wants to provide for his and his family's needs. Oblivious to world events and politics, he does not care that the US demonizes and routinely attacks people very much like him. In the most literal sense, Anwar believes in America, for even as his daily intake shrivels to nothing, he insists that the economic recovery is on track, simply because all the major news outlets say so. In Anwar's mind, America does not lie. If you ask him about his business, Anwar will say, "So far, so good," as if that means anything, as if he has not sold his good car and is not driving a piece of junk whose heater doesn't even work in winter. Pinching pennies, Anwar never buys from the mall food court anymore, not even when he's desperate for a break from his wife's sloppily made and monotonous wrap sandwiches. A Mexican worker at a pizzeria sometimes gives Anwar unsold food, so that these unpopular slices, of, say, chicken and broccoli, can be nuked the next day for lunch. With whatever money he can scrape together, Anwar is investing again, however, for he wants to regain that $146,000 he lost during the last stock market unraveling, and it's no good to warn him against the upcoming crash, when he and millions of others will be fleeced and laughed at by the big-boy insiders.

Marrying Anwar, Momna got to move to the United States, although she's hardly in it. In fact, she does not even associate with the Pakistanis or Indians who are her immediate neighbors. In a small park near her home, they can be seen each evening, but she doesn't join them. Though Momna's alienation is extreme, there is an antisocial and anticommunity component to any immigrant, I will insist, for to head to another country is to repudiate your own home and personal history. It is always a selfish escape, though many times a necessary one, as in getting away from bombs, drones or car bombs, or from the lack of beans, rice or potatoes to fill your stomach, in the place you were born. Many are political refugees, a rank that already includes many Americans who have the means, mettle and/or luck to resettle in another country.

Living in Belize, Joe Bageant escaped from an America of "self-referential illusions. Like a holographic simulation, each part refers exclusively back to the whole, and the whole refers exclusively back to the parts. All else is excluded by this simulated reality . . . The corporate simulacrum of life has penetrated us so deeply it now dominates the mind's interior landscape with its celebrities and commercial images." Sprung from the hologram, Bageant achieved amazing clarity about his native land, for his mind and heart remained here, mostly, even as he dreaded each return. Ensconced in Mexico, Fred Reed muses endlessly about a self-destructive, cornered and belligerent America that's no longer capable of logic. Hearing little and understanding less, it constantly snarls, threatens and shoots. Also dwelling in Mexico, Morris Berman does not hide his contempt for the "stupid and nasty" population he left behind. Though still living in the States, Dmitry Orlov has concluded that "getting the hell out" is the only solution, for a coordinated resistance is not possible when you have a drugged-up, incoherent, deranged and fragmented populace pitted against a Big Brother government that can't win any war outright but is entirely uninhibited about killing civilians, for it has had many decades of practice.

That there is no consequence to massacring foreigners, our criminal rulers have long known, but they also know that when Pentagon guns are turned on Americans, a good portion of the world will break out in cheers, just as we've whooped and hollered as our tax-paid munitions splattered their loved ones. When blood darkens our streets, our victims will dance in theirs, no doubt, so why are our transfat asses still parked at this sad cul-de-sac as that day of reckoning looms? When you're broke, though, it's hard to move a mile, much less out of the country, so many of us will simply escape into our private universe, inside our various screens, and ignore, as best we can, an increasingly ugly reality. Moreover, some still believe there is no serious decline, while others that a unified fight is possible.

For the most hopeless, there is always suicide. This month, a thirty-year-old Bensalem man and his fifty-nine-year-old mother attempted, it appears, a suicide pact by breathing toxic fumes from a borrowed generator. Only she died, however, so now he's charged with her murder. Neighbors said they had fallen on hard times and "had nothing left." Not that long ago, it was highly unusual to have young adults living with their parents, but not anymore. As this trend continues, many Americans will know exactly one house their whole lives, but at least they'll still have a home.

Should you be homeless in greater Philadelphia, there is one place you can have a private bed and bathroom for a few hours, at minimal cost. Keep this information in mind, for you might need it. At Bensalem's Neshaminy Inn, you'll only have to cough up $34, including tax, if you check in after 7 a.m. and leave by 4 p.m. This will give you plenty of time to refresh yourself or even have sex, with or without a (paid) partner, many of whom routinely patrol the hallways. Dozing before dark will also spare you from the worst of the bedbugs, and don't even think of complaining about heroin addicts' bloodstains on the walls, no sheet on your bed or used condoms beneath it. You didn't pay much, OK?

In 2010, Jamil "Smooth" Murray was arrested for running a prostitution and drug ring from this motel. In 2012, an eight-month-old boy died in a Neshaminy Inn room after ingesting his mom and dad's heroin. In 2013, Enoch "Drees" Smith was convicted of being a pimp, drug dealer and rapist. He operated from several Bensalem motels, including, of course, the Neshaminy. An emotional, at times tearful Drees explained to the jury that his heroin- and crack-addicted women were certainly victimized by "sick" people, but he wasn't one of them. He was a protector, not a monster, and the hundreds of condoms found in one of his blingy pimpmobiles were for his personal use alone, "I'm a man, I have sex and I strap up." Cops routinely come here to sniff for fugitives, and two weeks ago, they snagged an accused murderer.

A genuine social asset of the Neshaminy Inn, however, is its Bottle Caps Bar, located to the right of the reception area, with its bulletproof plexiglass. I had been told that a mug of Yuengling was only a buck during happy hour, but I couldn't quite believe such excellent tidings, not until I was relieved of but a single bill by Rob, the bartender.

"Good Lord! This must be the cheapest bar anywhere!" I exclaimed at this liver-tickling and heartwarming development.

"And it's not even five! I gave you a break."

"Hey, thanks! If this place is so cheap, where's everybody?" Unbelievably, I was the only customer.

"Don't worry, they'll show up soon," and sure enough, people started to stream in right after five. A couple immediately started a game of pool. Everyone seemed to know everyone else, and the buzz that day was about some asshole who had cracked his head the night before. Much blood was spilled. Derrick had been a regular at Bottle Caps, but then he disappeared, leading to rumors that he had died, for Derrick had always been a prime candidate to get killed, thanks to his endless series of arguments and altercations. It turned out he had merely gone away to prison. Released, Dereck promptly showed up at Bottle Caps, but then his foot got caught in a barstool rung, and he was taken away in an ambulance.

Rob, "One time he put some date rape drug into this woman's drink. I couldn't prove it, but it sure looked like it, because she had never acted like that before."

"And he was hitting on me before he cracked his head," the woman next to me added. "He wouldn't take no for an answer. He got all pissed off because

I wouldn't give him my phone number. 'Can't we just talk?' he kept saying. 'No,' I said. 'What do we have to talk about?' Plus, it'd be irresponsible for me to take someone into my life at this point. I'm sick! I was married for twenty-eight years. I don't need to be with another immature man!"

"You say you're sick," I responded, "but you don't look sick to me. You look fine."

"Why, thank you!" Pattie smiled. "But I'm in pain. I have cancer, four kinds of cancer."

"Four?!"

"Yes, I was diagnosed with breast cancer sixteen years ago. It's my left breast. Now I also have brain, spinal and lung cancer."

"That is ridiculous! I didn't even know you could get four different kinds of cancer. How did you become so unlucky?"

"I don't know, and it's not like I abuse myself, you know. I don't smoke, don't take drugs and I only have two drinks when I come out. This is my regular seat. I always sit here."

"How often do you come out?"

"Ah, maybe four times a week. I live with my parents now, so I need to step out every once in a while. Otherwise I'll go crazy! My parents are in their mid-seventies, and old people have different habits. We eat dinner at 3:30 or 4, and they're in bed by 9."

"You moved back in after your divorce?"

"Yes, I had no choice. My husband left me."

"Your marriage, what happened?"

"I don't know what happened. I thought we had a great marriage. We got along perfectly and never argued. We had grown up together. In fact, we played with each other while still in diapers! He did leave me right after the death of our daughter, so I thought maybe he had a nervous breakdown. I was so embarrassed, I couldn't tell anybody. I thought my husband would return, but he never did."

"So he had shown no sign there was a problem?"

"None! He was always telling everybody how great I was, and how much he loved me, then he was gone!"

"That is incredible! But how did he break the news to you? What did he say?"

"Each Saturday, he would hang out with his buddies. It was the boys' night out, and I was already in bed when he called from the bar. It must have been 2:15, 2:30. He said, 'Pattie, I thought it over. I've been thinking about this. I'm not coming home,' and it was so ridiculous, I just said, 'We'll talk about it in the morning.' I thought he was just drunk, but he never came home again."

"Wow, what an asshole!"

"Yes, he is an asshole, but I still love him. I just don't understand it. He left everything behind, including all photos of his children. We have two. Besides my daughter, who's gone, I also have a son."

"So he's not talking to his son at all?"

"No, and Ryan doesn't want to talk to him either."

"I can understand why, but this whole situation is incredible!"

"Isn't it? Like I said, I was too embarrassed to tell anybody, but my mother caught on, so she called me and said, 'Jack is gone, isn't he?' That's when I came home. I'm back in the same room I grew up in, and you want to know something else? My husband didn't even pay for our daughter's funeral!"

I just shook my head, then, "You said your husband may have freaked out because of your daughter's death. How did she die?"

"Her kidney failed her."

"Good Lord! You have four kinds of cancer, and your daughter died of kidney failure!"

"And she was only twenty-one years old! She had a future, too. Jill was studying to be a medical assistant at Lincoln Tech Institute. She left me two grandsons, though, and her fiancé treats me like his own mom. He calls me all the time."

"Every other day?"

"No, four or five times a day!"

"Isn't that too much? I think that's too much."

"No, it makes me very happy. My grandson, who's only five, also calls me all the time."

"What about your other grandson?"

"Oh, that's by a different man. It was a date rape. Her boyfriend thought if he could get my daughter pregnant, we would make her marry him, since we're Catholics, you know. Jill was only five two and weighed 90 pounds, so she couldn't fight him off. After Jill died, the judge gave this boy to his father, but he never wanted his kid, really. Still, my grandson is very upset because he thinks I abandoned him. In any case, I'm in no condition to take care of anyone anymore. The doctor said I only have one or one and a half years to live."

"I bet you'll be around a lot longer than that!"

Pattie smiled wanly, "If God wants me to go home, I'll go home, that's all. I'm at peace. Hey, I want to show you something." She took out her smart phone, got online and, with the help of a magnifying glass, was trying to find something on Facebook. "I'm legally blind, you know. It's the chemotherapy."

"Can you see me at all?" I grinned.

"All I can tell is that you're darker than me, and that you're a very happy person."

"I'm usually pretty cheerful . . ." Maybe I looked like LeBron James to her, I thought, but I'm glad I didn't attempt such a dumb joke. It's the Yuengling.

Finding what she was looking for, Pattie pointed to a woman on Facebook. "Who's that?" she asked.

I leaned closer, "Ah, I don't know. Is that you?"

"No, it's my husband's new girlfriend!"

"Well, she looks kind of like you."

"Exactly! That's what my mom said also."

"So he left you to be with someone who looks sort of like you."

"They have a history, though. I think they have a son together, but this happened before we got married even."

"So they've stayed in touch all this time."

"I don't really know. I don't know anything anymore."

"It's funny that you have to go on Facebook to find out who he's with. Did you have to friend him?"

"No, I didn't friend him. The jackass! In Facebook, there's a public area that anyone can have access to."

Pattie also showed me photos of her son, who's living in Phoenixville, forty miles away. Working between eighty and ninety hours a week, he's employed as a manager at Wawa, the convenience store, and as a medical assistant at a hospital, "Ryan is a workaholic, and a miser too. He saves every penny and hasn't even bought his first car yet."

"He sounds like a great kid!"

"Yes, he is. Ryan's very responsible, doesn't get in trouble, calls me all the time and never asks for help, although I give him a little bit here and there. I also buy him clothes."

"You actually know his taste?!"

"Yes, I know exactly what he wants."

"Is that his girlfriend?" I asked when shown a photo of Ryan with a gorgeous young lady.

"No, I don't think so, my son is gay. He was born that way. I'm sorry, but no one chooses to be gay. It's not worth it. My son has gone through so much as a gay person. When he was in school, kids beat him up and stepped on his privates. A boy even urinated on him. Ryan was born gay, that's all. Even when he was tiny, I knew Ryan was gay."

"How?!"

"Oh, I could tell. From the time he was four years old, I knew. Ryan was always talking with his hands, and we're not Italians!"

A man who leaves his wife is also a kind of immigrant. He rejects the home he's always known for another. Is it a surprise that Americans have the highest divorce rate in the world? If ditched lovers are also counted, then our rate of betrayal becomes truly stratospheric. To start over and advance or save ourselves, if only in our minds, we're willing to destroy everything. Soaked in a depthless, sampling culture, we're also expert at forgetting. Not only do we have no historical memory, but our personal past can be willfully and instantly erased, with hardly a ripple in its wake, and there's no one around, no community, to remind us of our shames. Extreme narcissists, we cling to bizarre narratives that allow us to make the most preposterous statements without flinching, or indulge in the most perverse and damaging behaviors.

Oh, shut the frack up! What are you, a preacherman?! Enough with the shale oil! OK, OK, I'll end my Bensalem travelogue by recounting Joseph Galloway, for he's a very interesting dude whose quandary is certainly instructive. (But then all predicaments are lessons. I know.) Born in 1731, Galloway married into the extremely wealthy family that founded Bensalem. From 1766 to 1775, he was the Speaker of the Pennsylvania Assembly, but when talks of independence from Britain broke out, he argued against it, and advocated, instead, only parliamentary representation under the Crown. The colonies needed military assistance from their mother country, he argued, and they were also too divided to form a separate nation. Galloway was a reformer, in short, not a radical, so during the Revolutionary War, he sided with Britain, a decision that cost him his vast estates and even his wife, for she stayed behind when he fled to England.

As tiny men of a vast yet dying empire, we're no historical actors like a Joseph Galloway, yet our reading of events will also determine whether we, too, will lose everything, and like him, we might also have to hightail it out of here. After Pattie left, I watched the news at the Bottle Caps Bar, and the huge, capsized ferry on the wide screen reminded me of the very last American movie I saw before coming to the States. There was no way I could have known that, someday, I would be cast, like you, you and you, as a collateral damage extra in a new, drawn-out *Poseidon Adventure*.

LOWER-CLASS UPPER MANHATTAN

5-6-14—Getting off the Greyhound bus at the Port Authority Terminal, I immediately saw a man his mid-fifties digging through a garbage can. With his right hand, he held a plastic tray on which were placed whatever edible scraps he could find. Lickable flecks clung to his ample brown beard. Chewing while scavenging, he was quite leisurely with his task, and no one among the many people sitting or standing nearby paid him any attention. Done with one trash can, he moved to the next, and since there were so many in this huge building, I imagined his daily buffet to be quite ample and varied.

Like central libraries, bus stations are daytime havens for America's homeless, but the man described above is a throwback of a sort, for his number has dwindled considerably ever since Giuliani decided to hose most of them away. Los Angeles has its Skid Row, San Francisco the Tenderloin, and you can find hundreds of roofless Americans sprawling all over Northwest DC, the showcase quarter, but much of Manhattan has become quite sanitized, purged of not just the homeless but any other kind of poorer Americans, as well as the artsy, bohemian types, who have mostly migrated to Brooklyn. Pumped up by Wall Street, much of Manhattan has become off limits to all but the super-affluent. You can work there, sure, after taking two trains and a bus, but don't think of moving in, not even into a closet, or curtained-off corner of a roach-motel-sized, shared apartment. As the rest of the country sinks, this island is buoyed by bailouts and quantitative easing directly deposited into its too-big-to-fail swindling houses, but hey, the Bangladeshi cabdrivers and CUNY-graduated waiters and bellhops also get their short stacks of nickels and dimes, so don't bitch, OK? Dwelling in this Green Zone, it would be easy to think that this country's near collapse is but a ridiculous rumor.

Speaking of Gotham cabbies, only 8 percent are native-born these days, and pointing to this fact, Pat Buchanan blames the liberal welfare state for the decline of the American work ethic. What he ignores is that the terms for driving a cab in New York are so bad, even many Pakistani immigrants have stopped driving. Instead of pocketing a share of each fare, most drivers must rent their vehicle at a fixed rate, so that they may even lose money at the end of a twelve-hour shift. Thanks to an increasingly superfluous supply of labor, however, you can always get someone to do anything, and this is the direct result of having a porous border in a sinking economy. Globalism is not just about exporting decent jobs, but also importing cheap labor until everyone everywhere makes just about nothing. That's the master plan, dude, so although *ningún ser humano es ilegal* is self-evidently true, it's also a smoke screen to make slaves out of us all.

In *Taxi Driver*, Travis complained, "All the animals come out at night—whores, skunk pussies, buggers, queens, fairies, dopers, junkies, sick, venal. Someday a real rain will come and wash all this scum off the streets." Well, 42nd Street is certainly spic-and-span now, with Travis's beloved Lyric Theater, where he took Betsy to see some starkly instructive coupling, long gone, as is the pen with half a dozen naked women. Standing in an individual booth, you deposited quarters to lift up a window, then after tucking dollars into the G-string of your chosen date, you're allowed to knead her for a bit. Many greasy spoons and mom-and-pops have also been shooed from Manhattan, to be replaced by chain stores and restaurants. In Manhattan alone, there are now 200 Subways, 74 McDonald's, many of them open 24/7, and 194 Starbucks. Dunkin' Donuts has 500 locations citywide. The biggest corporations shall roll over all!

The lamer Manhattan becomes, the more popular it is with the tourists who come to ride a double-decker bus and gorge at a Midtown Applebee's, TGI Fridays, Olive Garden, Outback Steakhouse or Red Lobster. They travel to Babylon to experience all the comforts of Annandale, Virginia. Not long ago on 42nd Street, however, I did find another throwback, a guy who French-kissed a mouse for tips, but before I could deconstruct his amorous technique, stratagem, fudged aims and secret meanings, six cops, no less, appeared to tell our ratty Casanova to beat it. Hey, there are still enough weirdos here. When Occupy was still happening in Zuccotti Park, I ran into a guy who was trying to enlist people into his "Fart Smeller Movement." To show what he was talking about, this dough-faced gent displayed a photo of himself squatting down, with his nose wedged into a woman's ass as she was, presumably, liberally exhaling. Listen, man, I don't want to come off as nostalgic for the New York of gutter punks and a nightly, Boschian bacchanal in Tompkins Square, with its in-house cannibal, but the *Lawrence Welk* version of the city just ain't cutting it.

Leaving Port Authority, I trekked north, and just past Lincoln Center, I encountered a young male beggar in a New Jersey Devils cap and dirty jeans. With his small, beat-up backpack and nearly empty cup, he sat in front of the cheery window of a clothing boutique. Head down, his face was obscured by this sign, "HOMELESS. Too honest to steal . . . Humble enough to Beg. JUST Trying to SURVIVE. ANYTHING HELPS! GOD BLESS." Two blocks from him, I then spotted a young blond woman in a bouffant ponytail, also begging. It was brisk, so her legs were wrapped in a thin, gray blanket, of the austere kind not found in any normal home, but to be handed out after an earthquake, hurricane, false-flag terrorist attack or Second Coming of Jesus. At least it's not the packing stuff I've seen wrapped around the street pariahs of our nation's capital. On her bulky, hooded jacket, there was a small patch of the American flag. Reading a large book, she was also looking down, and so I couldn't immediately tell that I had met her before, in Philadelphia.

Born in Russia, Liza is twenty-two years old. When she was seven, Liza was adopted, along with a younger sister, and brought to Cambridge, Massachusetts, but she never got along with her new mom, and so was put on lithium at eleven, then sent to a boarding school at fourteen. Liza's drinking problem began around this time, and she was stuck in ninth grade for three years. Liza quit school, drifted around the country and drained half a gallon of whiskey a day, to the point of passing out, but she has pretty much cut out this suicidal habit. With her, um, all-American good looks, Liza can always count on making more than enough to survive, just by sitting behind a sign that says, "A LITTLE KINDNESS GOES A LONG WAY. GOD BLESS." For Liza's twenty-first birthday, her adoptive mother, a very rich woman, sent her $20.

In 2011, Liza met her boyfriend, Harvey, at a Rainbow camp in Washington State. The Rainbow Family holds one large gathering each year in a national forest. While there, they shun money and alcohol while saying yes to universal love, world peace, hallucinatory drugs, food sharing, bartering, cotton, skin, mud, strumming, drumming and singing, as well as shitting in the woods in a green, hygienic and inoffensive manner. Assholes, though, do show up and sometimes ruin the good vibes, but that's just life on this sick and unmoored planet. To the Rainbow Family, the world at large is considered Babylon. Done with ommmming while standing in a circle, Liza and Harvey went down to San Francisco and chilled at the Occupy camp for a while, and for cash they begged in nearby Daly City, making over $200 a day. It was mostly her bringing in the dough, for Harvey is no retinal lollipop.

Born in small-town South Carolina, Harvey inherited a dilapidated house and crappy car when his parents suddenly died in an accident. A year later, he sold this house to a friend for $70,000, or $500 a month, then hit the road. There is an army of young, jobless Americans drifting from city to city. To survive, they beg, dumpster-dive and use soup kitchens. Many sing or play music for change. In Berkeley, they swarm all over the university area, their scruffy presence contrasting sharply with the yuppieish or Gap-fashioned students, though I have been told that some of the homeless neo-primitives are actually alumni of UC Berkeley.

In this economy, it's all too easy to move from an overpriced dormitory to totally free off-campus accommodations that include sidewalks, church verandas, condemned homes, store entrances and landscaped knolls off freeway exit ramps. In Berkeley, you can also sleep unmolested at People's Park, where you will have plenty of company.

Universities have colluded with banks and government to fleece students and shackle them to a lifetime of debt servitude, but as long as you're still enrolled and your payments deferred, life will seem good and promising, for the university's primary job is no longer to teach, but to maintain this rosy illusion. In these United States of universal debt bondage, universities have become a marketing branch of the criminal banks. It's all good, children, so just sign here to get your very own academic(ish) casket!

So Liza and Harvey are basically professional beggars, but before you scream, "Get a job, losers," consider that less than 59 percent of working-age Americans are actually employed, and 47 percent of the population are on some form of government assistance, a record high, so nearly half of us are already de facto beggars, although most are not sitting on concrete in heat or cold, looking sorry, at least not yet. Simply put, many Americans have become redundant in an economy rigged to serve the biggest banks and corporations. With no one hiring us and our small businesses bankrupted by the behemoths, many of us are forced to beg, peddle, push or steal, though on a scale that's minuscule compared to what's practiced by our ruling thugs. As we shove dented cans of irradiated sardines into our Dollar Store underwear, they rob us of our past, present and future.

In this sick order, even the best among us are reduced to being outcasts, if not criminals to be locked up, tortured or killed. In this sinister arrangement, you're lucky if you're merely ignored, like the fiercely astute Paul Craig Roberts. Although countless Americans depend on him to understand more clearly the dangers and rot afflicting their unraveling society, he's not paid for his articles, but must depend on readers' contributions to keep writing. In this evil madhouse, even Paul Craig Roberts is a beggar. Meanwhile, morons are paid handsomely to waterboard the masses with septic sludge.

Past Columbia University, I crossed into Harlem, then Washington Heights. In the upper reaches of Manhattan, there are signs of the black market everywhere, for people must do what they can to get by, and since the residents here are mostly nonwhite, City Hall has pretty much left them alone. Like Jews a century ago, Latinos and blacks are selling just about everything on sidewalks. One guy was offering four old pairs of sneakers, which he left in a heap. Another had four pressure cookers displayed on a cloth-covered ironing board. At 168th and Broadway, a man was selling tamales from a shopping cart. It was only $1.25 per, and you could choose from chicken, pork, cheese, beans, Oaxaca-styled or sweet. Like most conversations on the street, his sign was strictly in Spanish. Within sight of this, however, there was a huge McDonald's packed with locals, including a grimy man with his head on a table, soundly sleeping. A guy in his mid-twenties asked one customer after another if he could have some change "for something to eat." He even approached people at the counter as they were paying. With his palm out and eyes like a basset hound's, he leaned towards a pretty young lady and muttered at her platinum-plated hoop earring. She gave him nothing.

To be fair, the panhandlers hounding this Mickey D's are a direct result of having two homeless shelters half a block away, and they don't usually come inside. In any case, step outside this corporate fortress and Washington Heights is still a wonderful mess of small stores and eateries. Isn't it telling that the liveliest streets and neighborhoods in America are filled with recent immigrants? They haven't been here long enough to become zombies, and don't think I'm talking racially, now, for European cities are also much more exuberant and life-affirming than their American sisters, many of which have become desolate and menacing. Strapped to automobiles and conditioned to stare at one screen after another, bona fide Americans dread eye contact and the human breath. Alienated from all those nearest to us, we expect to be saved and led by our distant brainwashers and slave masters.

For any community to be healthy, local initiatives must be encouraged, nurtured and protected, so let's reclaim our home turf, reestablish the common and, in the process, regain our collective sanity and dignity. With this in mind, let's check out Word Up, a volunteer-run bookstore and mini art center in Washington Heights. Just over a year old, it is filled with people by day and hopping at night with either a concert, literary reading, play, film showing or lecture. Kids can even show up in the afternoon to get help with their homework. Sounds too good to be true, and in this culture of Lil Wayne and Justin Bieber flanking a wife-beating boxer named "Money," this nourishing oasis is barely hanging on, sustained only by donations from a recent crowd-funding campaign. Already working for free, the fifty-plus people who keep Word Up going are also beggars, but that's just how it is now, and if not for the tireless efforts of its head beggar, Veronica Liu, Word Up would never have come into being in the first place.

Born in Toronto to Hakka and Filipino parents, Liu came to NYC sixteen years ago. Before Word Up, she started Washington Heights Free Radio, which is operated out of her apartment. Liu is also a cofounder of Fractious Press and helps to organize the yearly book fair at the Ding Dong Lounge in Morningside Heights. Liu has a day job, and makes no money from her various community-building efforts, which she does because, I don't know, maybe Liu's insane? According to the norms of Babylon, she is certainly batshit, but to gain, no matter how fleetingly, a bit of light and grace with one's words or actions is a reward in itself. Some may even claim it is a necessity. Since every evil act is accompanied by a lie, a disguise or suppression of meaning, a society that traffics in practically nothing but lies or distracting nonsense is also one that's drowning in serial and habitual evilness. Meaning is not just calling everything by its proper name, but grasping their relationship and having a sense of proportion, but these have all been banished from our public discourse. Bushed and Baracked, we seethe, scream, take our medication, then joyfully jerk, with pomposity and authority, the voting lever.

Two thousand and five hundred words already and still no lager? So how is this a damn Postcard?! I hear you, I hear you, but at six to eight bucks a pop further south, I had to walk seven miles before I even dared to mumble in my humblest voice, and with my eyes filled with shame and mortification, "A bottle of your cheapest, please."

Yah, yah! I feel so much better already! Don't you? I'm so hopped up, I can run a marathon! OK, OK, I must calm down before I get flagged. We're in Reynold's, a musty Irish grotto in the middle of Nuevo Santo Domingo. There was a stuffed animal over the bar, but no one could tell me what it was, not even the Wisconsin-born bartender, Brian. Although there were less than a dozen souls there, I couldn't imagine too many rooms in Washington Heights that contained more white people. I asked Brian, "Do Dominicans drink here?"

"Yeah, sometimes. Not really."

"So where do they drink?"

"On the streets. If you come here in the summer, you'll see them all over the sidewalks with their bottles of Presidente! They like to drink outside, play dominoes outside. It's a different culture. Besides, it's too expensive inside a bar, and most of them don't have that much money."

In his mid-forties, Brian wore his beard long and bushy in a style that's now associated with Duck Dynasty. It evokes a down-home America that hunts, fishes and salutes the flag. Brian's thoroughly at home in Washington Heights, however, and is in fact married to a Dominican woman. In NYC for twenty-five years, he can't imagine returning to DePere, Madison or Milwaukee, where he has all lived, "It was very boring in Wisconsin. There was nothing to do." This summer, he'll take his wife to his home state for the first time.

"Hey, maybe she'll love it there!" I said.

"I doubt it." Then, "There is a Latino guy who comes in here every now and then, and each time he does, he'd buy beer for the whole bar."

"That's pretty generous! How can he afford it?"

"No kids!" Brian smiled, "and I don't think he's married either. He's an older gentleman, retired. He used to work as a police detective."

"The last time he was here, he gave me $10 for cab fare," Peggy interjected, "and I was just going to take the bus. What a nice man!" Sitting in a corner, she had been playing one crossword puzzle after another. She was bundled in a sweatshirt, hoodie and a padded nylon jacket. Like the rest of us, she was certainly not dressed to kill, as is common further down the island. She did wear blue eye shadow, however, and her squarely trimmed fingernails were perked up by white nail polish.

Born in Brooklyn Heights in 1941, Peggy moved to Washington Heights as a child and has remained there ever since. The only other place she's been is Wildwood, New Jersey, where her family used to go during the summer, for its beach. "I've never been anywhere, and I'm proud of it!"

Peggy worked forty years as a school crossing guard, and now comes to Reynold's every day at 8 a.m., as it opens, "I get up at 5:30 or 6, then I come here. I come here to watch television because I don't have one at home." She runs errands for the bar, does its laundry at a laundromat down the street, and they pay her with bottles of Coors Light, "People also buy me drinks. I never go without." Peggy entered Reynold's for the first time forty-four years ago, six years after it opened. "They built this bar around Peggy," Brian joked.

Peggy's husband died in 2003. Nearly daily, she orders a pastrami submarine from the same deli, and though she only pays them once a week, she does remember to tip the bicycle delivery man two bucks each time. Presently, two Dominican couples walked in, but only for the women to use the bathroom, it turned out, and soon after they left, a shouting match erupted over a clogged toilet.

"It's your fuckin' fault, you asshole!" a patron in his early fifties hollered at an older man.

"Hey, calm down! I'm not allowed to show someone where the bathroom is?"

"Fuck no! Not when you know they're not going to order anything!"

"How was I supposed to know? Unbelievable. You're just a crank, man, and a racist!"

"I'm no fuckin' racist! You saw some Dominican pussy and lost your fuckin' mind."

"Listen, I'm sixty-two years old. I don't need to take your bullshit."

"God bless you, but why don't you shove your fuckin' head down the toilet. Maybe that'll fix it!"

The seething crank turned out to be Pat, a unionized building manager. Born in Ireland, he returns there often with his wife. When I told Pat I had been to England and Scotland, but never Ireland, he replied, "There's nothing there. You're not missing anything." The people who live in Harlem are "animals," Pat also informed me, and he spoke of how dirty it is compared to Washington Heights. During my three hours in Reynold's, Pat never relaxed or smiled. Just about anything anyone said, he contested, and even when he agreed with you about something, he sounded argumentative. Maybe he'll burst a blood vessel soon. Maybe someone will kill him. Pat did play Hendrix's "All Along the Watchtower," then Tony Bennett's "Rags to Riches," however.

"Now, it's the other way around," a woman said in a throat cancery voice.

"You got that right!" Pat sneeringly concurred.

It was late afternoon by now. Swiveling on my stool, I turned to survey the glary, sun-splashed scenery through the open door. A guy on a cheap scooter rolled by, then two smartly dressed kids with their mom appeared. It couldn't have been a babysitter, I don't think, for she was also fashionably attired. Her boots were certainly not remaindered-bin quality. Across the street, a store was for rent, and there was a jeweler with "WE BUY OLD GOLD" in the window. The ubiquity of these signs is yet another indication of our destitution. Have you sold your heirloom, keepsake or wedding ring? I too have learned how to eBay.

I was very much at peace in that fine low-life establishment, but like the Buddha, Jesus and George Harrison said, "All things must pass," and so I had to extricate myself from Reynold's. In any case, I don't want to go from lower class to rags. My clothes are already torn and tattered. With the Fed right there, I'll stay a beggar. So don't blow or kiss me, blow up Goldman Sachs!

ADRIFT IN LEVITTOWN

5-17-14—In 1947, the first Levittown was built in New York State, then in 1952, an even bigger one was erected in Pennsylvania. Marketed as "THE MOST PERFECTLY PLANNED COMMUNITY IN AMERICA," Levittown was the prototypical American suburb. For only $10,990, or $100 down, then $67 a month, you could own three bedrooms, two bathrooms, front lawn, backyard and garage, plus access to five Olympic-sized pools, with free swimming and diving lessons thrown in. Most soothingly, you no longer had to deal with strangers above, below or abutting you, or dark-skinned neighbors who may alarm or irk you as you went about your white routines. Government, banks and developers all agreed that suburban living was a white proposition, so if you weren't pale enough, it didn't matter if you had risked life and limb for Uncle Sam, for he wouldn't back your mortgage should you want to move into a mixed neighborhood, not that anyone would sell a wholesome, *Leave It to Beaver* house to your Ma Rainey ass anyway.

The American Dream was understood to be white, and in Levittown, white living precluded even selling and buying nearby, for all businesses were banished from the residential enclaves. To get a cup of joe, it was necessary to drive a few miles, and to down a handful of beers, you might end up flying through the windshield, but it was definitely worth it, for no Negroes were in sight. That's just how it was, and in more subtle ways, still is, but to what degree? You tell me. Abraham Levitt explained, "As a Jew, I have no room in my heart for racial prejudice. But the plain fact is that most whites prefer not to live in mixed communities. This attitude may be wrong morally, and someday it may change. I hope it will."

Just over half a century ago, most Americans were convinced the races should be kept apart. In my teens, I spent three years in suburban Virginia, and there, I was told by a friend, schoolmate and neighbor, W. Salo, that blacks had been kept out of the neighborhood until the early seventies, "Realtors just wouldn't sell to them, and even now, many people don't like to see them around."

Salo and I were among a group that played basketball regularly. There was Kelvin, a black kid and son of a lawyer. Kelvin would go on to graduate from the University of Virginia, become a real estate broker and move to Dallas. He made a bundle during the housing boom.

Since Salo was a fan of the Washington Bullets, I said to him, "What if Wes Unseld moves in?"

"Get that nigger out of here!" Salo laughed.

In 1957, a Jewish Levittowner alerted a friend, World War II vet and aspiring electrical engineer William Myers, that a Levittown home was for sale, but when Myers moved in with his wife and three children, an American hell opened up, for the Myerses were black. For more than a week, up to a thousand people protested nightly in front of their new home. An ice cream man serviced this enraged mob, and reporters and photographers also showed up. Sticks of dynamites landed in the Myerses' driveway and rocks were thrown, with one hitting a white policeman, knocking him out. Windows shattered. A Confederate flag was unfurled from an unfinished house nearby, and racially charged music was blasted day and night. "Gone are the days when my heart was young and gay / Gone are my friends from the cotton fields away." Mrs. Daisy Myers heard footsteps in the dark outside her children's bedrooms, and picked up the phone to receive threats, such as "Do you want to die in that house?" A woman sneered, "I'll never let my children drink chocolate milk again!" A nearby neighbor bought a black dog and named him "Nigger."

The Myerses also had many supporters, white and black, who brought flowers and food. A white woman showed up and offered to clean their house. These allies were also threatened, naturally, with some having crosses burned in front of their own homes. Finally, state troopers were brought in to snuff out this dangerous and embarrassing situation, and the Myerses were left alone to live in Levittown for four years. Many of their neighbors did apologize and Mrs. Myers was even made president of the Dogwood Hollow Neighborhood Association. Contrary to rumors, the Myerses had not been brought in by Communists or Jews to stir up trouble, but simply wanted a decent place to live, and when a job opportunity for Bill Myers opened up elsewhere, they moved away.

Levittown also made international news when a gas riot, this nation's first, erupted in 1979. When OPEC pushed gas prices to $1 a gallon ($3.25 in today's money), sixty truckers decided to block a Levittown intersection, Five Points, to protest, and there, they were cheered on by thousands of locals. "More gas! More gas!" they chanted. Soon, though, the mood turned ugly, with gas station windows smashed, gas pumps broken and cars and car tires set on fire. A rig plowed into a line of cops, injuring several. Cops beat up protesters, sending a hundred to the hospital. Two hundred people were arrested.

Americans have come to accept high gas prices, but as their incomes continue to shrink while inflation rises, they will wish they weren't marooned in a place like Levittown. Without the car, this place would be dead. Walking twenty-five miles through Levittown this week, I often felt like an intruder, as well as a rat trapped in a maze. There, most streets are curved to slow down traffic, and many arc and loop in loony ways, making orientation difficult. Further, many sections are without sidewalks. Bewildered and even edgy, I became acutely aware that Levittown had been built for the automobile and not pedestrians. Levittown hates the human body, frankly. Denuded of a 4,000-pound steel carapace, one feels silly and obscene just wandering around. I crossed the street to avoid disturbing a flower-pruning housewife, ignored the stare of a man in a muscle T, drinking a beer on his porch, while four girls in their early teens eyed me curiously. As dogs barked at me from behind wire mesh or picket fences, I looked at my shadow on the asphalt and did my best to keep going east and north, but those serpentine roads were seriously messing with my head. This layout is designed to deter through traffic of all kinds, for Levittown does not want outsiders. It chases visitors and their money away. Waiting for their kids to be released, a long line of cars idled outside an elementary school.

To encourage neighborliness, fences were originally banned in Levittown, but they went up almost immediately, and the Levitts had to relent. Folks move out of the city primarily to distance themselves from other people. Though many Levittowners loved the public swimming pools, others set up tiny ones in their fenced-in backyards. In 2002, four of the Olympic-sized pools were finally closed. In Levittown, you often see portable basketball hoops set up side by side on the curbs, so kids from adjacent houses can shoot in solitude. If moats and drawbridges were more affordable, I'm sure there would be thousands in Levittown.

Irrationally walking, I ended up at a spot I thought I had left behind permanently, just like Jonah after he had been spat out by the whale, but unlike him, I needed not preach, for there were churches all over Levittown. Among their signs, "JESUS SAID YOU MUST BE BORN AGAIN. DELIVERY ROOM OPEN." Another, "PRACTICE MAKES PERFECT. BE CAREFUL WHAT YOU PRACTICE." At St. Michael the Archangel, I saw a sign for an upcoming flea market. A spot could be rented for $15, and a table for $5 if you didn't have your own. The day itself would likely be festive, and it is exactly this kind of small-time selling that's missing from so much of America, not just Levittown, so why not make it all the time, all over, and not just in a church parking lot once a year? By eliminating zoning laws that ban commerce, Americans can earn cash in these difficult times, and keep money in their communities besides. With people selling on their front lawns, porches and stoops, and others wandering around offering potato chips, iced tea, beer, cigarettes, socks, hats and pirated DVDs, etc., each neighborhood will be enlivened, and neighbors will finally get to know each other as they haggle over a ratty couch, beat-up hair dryer or set of baseball cards of the 2010 Seattle Mariners. They can discuss the dada farce of electoral politics after swapping Xanax for oxycodone, for example, or perhaps a shoplifted bottle of cough syrup. A pop-up restaurant can appear in any kitchen or beneath any tree. Instead of pushing rancid tacos with brown shreds of lettuce for a monster conglomerate, you can be your own boss by offering chili and corn bread on a sidewalk table behind a hand-scrawled sign, "TEXAS CHOW." It better be great, though, because not ten feet away, there's a guy dishing up some mind-blowing squirrel po' boys.

Since small time selling also develops business skills, it would be an excellent alternative to a bankrupting college miseducation, since we don't need more majors in ambulance chasing, speaking-in-tongues economics or tattoo-art appreciation, etc., but simply people who know how to survive by squeezing a dollar out of 50 cents. Ah, but we're living under a government that sucks all money upward, towards the biggest banks and corporations, so if they don't even allow the mom-and-pops to survive, how are they going to tolerate this kind of freewheeling commerce? Further, Americans have been well-conditioned to despise the busy sidewalk. Sure, they might go to New Orleans to drink, holler and vomit in the French Quarter, but when they get home, they want everything to be placid outside their bay window. Destitution, though, will change behavior for sure, and I'm sure Americans will come out of their isolation to not just sell or barter, but also to establish common cause so they can fight back, at last.

In the here and now, though, all is superficially pacified, with many citizens still eagerly displaying their allegiance towards one or another of our bank-jerked marionettes, Obama, Clinton or Romney, etc. Walking around Levittown, I also encountered many flags, including POW/MIA and Marine Corps ones. The US must lead the world in patriotic flag display per capita, and I can't imagine too many other countries where countless citizens erect flagpoles in front of their homes. God, country and racial purity were the concrete foundations of Levittown, except that it's 2014 now, so I did see a few black children getting off school buses. I also ran into a Turkish-American Muslim Cultural Association, a Turkish-American Social Club and a Liberian restaurant, the last two side by side at a strip mall.

Originally, there were only six different types of houses in Levittown, but after half a century, each has been modified enough to appear reasonably unique, with a different landscaping in the front yard. Here, there's a miniature windmill, and there, yet another fake well. Cutesy flags with birds, ladybugs, sunsets and such abound. On a little pole, a cartoon frog rides a rainbow-colored bicycle. Maybe he's a queer amphibian, but to each his own, man. It's none of my business. At some homes, though, overgrown grass, weeds and dandelions have taken over, even if there's still an old car in the driveway. A handful of large apartment complexes have also sprung up, but hey, when you have no taxes from manufacturing, and not that much from local commerce, you can't say no to more tax-paying residents, even if they're just low-income renters. At Five Points, I saw four check-cashing joints, with one that's also a pawnshop, then I passed American Dream Realty, with its flashing sign that promised to save you from your life-sinking mortgage. Unattended, two used lawn mowers and a lawn tractor were for sale, with the last priced at $450. That can easily buy a month's groceries for a family of four, and you can't eat grass.

Levittown was born during a time of unprecedented confidence and hope among average Americans. This country was on top of the world. Eager to move up, thousands of Joe Six-Packs lined up to buy Levittown homes. There were no For Sale signs baking in the sun day after day among the dandelions. To observe, and hopefully meet, a few contemporary Levittowners, I decided to duck into a bar, as usual, but the first one I chanced upon, Cazz's Bar & Grill, didn't quite do the trick, since I could only overhear, and not talk, to anybody. Still, it was very instructive, for at one point people were discussing their lunch breaks.

First dude, "I don't even have a lunch break. I work right through, seven hours straight, and I don't mind it, since they wouldn't pay if I stopped to eat anyway. I'd rather go home early."

Second dude, "You should feel lucky to have a job."

Third dude, "But that's the wrong attitude, man! Everyone should have a lunch break, a paid lunch break, and a couple of smoke breaks too."

Second dude, "Good luck with that."

Woman, "I use my lunch break to run errands. I'd go to the bank or something. I get an hour."

They also mentioned a young man who had died of a drug overdose, another who had hanged himself, and a recently deceased old fart who was a pack rat. Though the jukebox was quiet, three televisions stared at me from the opposite wall, and as I was seated at some distance from the conversing group, I couldn't catch everything. It was clear, though, that several of the men were Army veterans, for they started to talk about Okinawa, sake, Vietnam, "Me love you a long time" and getting coochie coochie in the Far East. With so many overseas "commitments," it was practically an American male's rite of passage to catch syphilis or gonorrhea from a foreign whore and/or leaving his likeness behind in the forlorn face of a bastard child.

At the same strip mall, however, there were two other bars, including My Brothers Pub, and I'm very glad I discovered it, for here I was able to make the acquaintance of Brian, Dave, Rob and Joy. Soon as I walked in, I could tell it was my kind of dump. Rob explained, "Cazz's is like a family bar, while Rio attracts a younger crowd. You'll find some nice chicks in there. Here, you'll hardly ever see a woman. This place is like, I don't know, maybe this place is a gay bar."

"Hey, speak for yourself!" another patron piped up.

Picking up my pint, I noticed the beer mat said, "The only lasting peace between a man and his wife is a separation. —Lord Chesterfield." Beneath a large TV on the opposite wall, there was an image of a flag, with "HONORING THOSE WHO SERVED," and another of Uncle Sam pointing, with "This finger wasn't made to press 'One' for English."

Fifty-three years old, Rob wore a faded tank top and an old polyester cap. Stubble invaded his lined face. For eighteen years he owned a print shop, with the last eight in Manhattan, in the West Village. Now he clips hedges, cuts grass and sells earnestly kitschy paintings of landscapes, one of which was propped on the floor at the bar, "It takes me four hours and a half, on average, to do a painting, and I can sell it for sixty-five to seventy-five bucks, but then you have to subtract the cost of the materials, which comes to about $13 a painting."

"Hey, maybe you can cut your cost by using cheaper paints? Paints are expensive!"

"I know, I know, but I only use the best! I only use Winsor Newton."

"That is the best, but most people won't know the difference if you use something cheaper. A tube of Winsor Newton can run you $20!"

"Cheaper paints have a different consistency, and I can tell when I mix them or slap them onto the canvas."

"Man, you're really picky."

"Well."

"And the colors are different, too, I know, but you're not making that much from these paintings in the first place."

"If I charged more, no one would buy them. I know what people are willing to pay, and also what they want. I can't use too much blue, for example."

"Hmm, I never thought of that . . . Who buys your paintings, by the way?"

"Mostly the people from this bar. Dave, the cook at Hurricane Jack's, told me his boss wanted a large painting of palm trees in a hurricane, so I made a hundred and fifty bucks from that deal! It took me seven hours, man, wore me out! Palm trees always sell well. Hawaii scenes."

"You ever been there?"

"No, of course not! But I can picture palm trees without seeing them. I have them in my head."

"You never paint from life?"

"I don't need to!"

"Well, you're lucky to sell anything, because most people won't touch any painting, period. Tell me more about your print shop. How did you lose it?"

"Simple. The landlord sold the building in 2009, so I lost my business, but it was partly my fault for not paying attention. If I had found another place before that happened, I wouldn't have lost all of my clients, and I was raking in the bucks too, man. After all the expenses, I was making $6,000 a month! I was eating well, drinking well and I took vacations when I wanted too."

"You can't start it up again?"

"No way! My clients are gone. At this point, I'd be happy with anything. It used to be, you could always get a job that paid $10 an hour, but you can't even do that anymore. You see Brian there?"

"Yeah?"

"He bartends here three or four nights a week, but Brian also has a day job. Brian is a drummer so he works at a music store, and you know how much he's getting paid? $8.50 an hour. After tax, that ain't shit!"

"I know people who are making less than the minimum wage."

"Is that legal?"

"It is if you can't find another job. I mean, you're not going to sue your boss."

"True."

"About the printing business, you said you weren't paying attention, but what do you mean?"

"Personal shit, man. My girlfriend was leaving me, so I was very distracted."

"Hmm. How long were you two together?"

"Eleven years! And we had a kid together! I also treated her son like my own. We were a family."

Before this girlfriend, Rob was married for sixteen years, so he has three kids altogether. With his business gone, Rob couldn't keep up with the mortgage, so he took in renters. Even though he only charged $550 a month, none would stay long. The place has become rather run-down, Rob intimated, and the cable TV has long been shut off, "I was paying $95 a month for television, but now I just watch the same DVDs over and over."

"*The Sound of Music*?" I joked.

"Yeah, *The Sound of Music!*"

Rob figures he has four or five months before he's kicked out. Before that happens, though, the electricity will have been turned off, for he hasn't paid those bills either. Sitting in the dark, Rob will have to sing these lines to himself, "Doe, a deer, a female deer . . . Far, a long, long way to run."

"What will happen then?" I asked. "Where will you go?"

"I guess I'll have to move in with Joy," his current girlfriend.

"Does she have kids?"

"Four, but only two are living with her."

"How old?"

"Twenty-six and seventeen. The older one is a manager at Home Depot."

"Will they like you moving in?"

"Probably not, but what can I do? I'm not going to lie on the street."

Though going broke, Rob goes to the bar every day, where he spends $20 for beer. If you tip properly, that's only five pints. Rob also smokes two packs of L&M daily, so that's another $10.50, "But I can't just sit home and brood, man. I've got to come out and talk to people. What do you want me to do?"

To make matters worse, Rob hasn't managed to finish a painting in a year, though the urge to depict snowcapped mountains and tropical beaches may just resurface tomorrow, or at least Rob hopes so. In any case, the Hawaiian sunset has been sitting on the floor for a while, so maybe Rob has stopped because he's tapped out his small roster of Medicis.

Suddenly, some orchestral music erupted. I had no idea what it was, but was later told that it came from the soundtrack of *Gods and Generals*, a film about Stonewall Jackson. Rob's reaction, though, was immediate, "Hey, what is this shit! Don't you know how to put a good song on the jukebox?!" The guilty party was also a regular and, to spite Rob even further, played Los Tigres del Norte afterwards.

"Oh, great, now we get to hear some Italian shit!"

"It's Mexican, Rob," a couple of people shouted in near unison.

To purge these insufferable sounds from memory, Rob then played some John Lennon. By this time, his girlfriend, Joy, had shown up to become the only female in My Brothers Pub. About Rob's age, she was cheerful enough yet worn out. When I told her I liked to walk around and hear people's stories, Joy said, "I've got a story for you! You should hear my story!" And she leaned over Rob, who was between us, so I could hear her better, "You know I raised two kids by myself because my husband died three days after our wedding!"

"Jesus, that's like the worst luck ever! How did that happen?"

"He had health issues, he was a crack addict, but I had no idea he was going to die like that! I had to write thank-you notes to the guests for having come to both the wedding and funeral."

"That's ridiculous."

"People did give me money, though. I'd get, like, fifty bucks per person."

If Rob dies, Joy can pocket another round of bereavement contributions, after deducting the minimal burial cost. A cardboard coffin will do. Unemployed and still awaiting to be certified as disabled, in body and mind, Joy can certainly use the cash. As for Rob, he can still frequent My Brothers Pub postmortem, just like George, a deli owner when alive. Brian has seen this ghost, and Dave will swear that a stool got knocked over without anyone touching it. This happened just before I walked in.

"So you raised two kids by yourself?" I continued.

"Yeah, we already had two kids. I have four altogether, but my oldest two are not talking to me. I haven't seen them in seventeen years. I can't do anything about it. It's a long story."

"So now you have this guy!" And I patted Rob on the shoulder.

"Yeah, so I guess it's working out in the end, because this is true love," and Joy looked at Rob with tenderness.

Rolling his eyes, Rob said to me, "Look at who I'm stuck with."

"Ah, he loves me!" Joy said.

"It's not like I have a choice," Rob smiled.

"You know, I didn't even like Rob in the beginning, but he kept following me around. He kept saying, 'You want to party? You want to party?' And I don't even do drugs, but after a year, I finally went with him."

"That's not how I remember it." Rob grinned.

Rob's parents moved to Levittown in the early sixties, then he himself bought a house here. Joy, however, can't be counted as a true American-Dreaming Levittowner since she's only living in an apartment complex, and perhaps the worst in this frayed, perplexing and faux arcadia. Online, I found several comments along this line, "This apartment complex is filled with reasons why you should not live here! I can't wait until my lease is up. The neighbors are loud and disrespectful at all hours and the facilities are dirty and dangerous (ex: broken glass pieces, rusty metal, roaches). I cannot get rid of the roaches, ants and centipedes in my studio! My bathtub and toilet actually have filled up, from the drain, with sewage . . . Over a month ago someone broke into all four buildings' laundry facilities and ruined the machines to steal the quarters, the machines haven't been repaired yet. They haven't even cleaned up the broken glass from the windows and the sharp metal from the broken machines."

So that's where Rob is moving in four months, and where a Home Depot manager must live with his mom and kid sister. Rob said that many locals have come to refer to Levittown as "Leave It Town," but where does one go now to find a decent job and home in a national landscape that's increasingly leeched of possibilities? At Five Points, I saw an armed forces recruiting station, but Rob is too old to be shot at by Russians, Chinese, Iranians, Syrians or whoever our masters decide we must fight next. In the meantime, all he can do is drink away his worries, and his last pennies also, for old habits die hard. When the Founding Fathers wrote "the pursuit of happiness," perhaps all they meant was having regular access to bad beer, but this simple, working-class pleasure has become out of reach to many Americans.

Not long ago, nearby Trenton, Camden and Philadelphia were world-class industrial centers, adjacent Bristol had factories, and even tiny Fairless Hills, next door, had a steel mill. Now there is nothing. Without high-paying manufacturing jobs, Levittowners are reduced to serving beer and cheese fries to each other, or mowing each other's lawn. If this continues, soon there won't be just a ghost or two at the local bar, this entire town will turn ghostly.

It is dark and I'm alone on the train platform, waiting for my Philly-bound. Hearing sounds of bottles and cans clacking, I turn to see, in the dim orange light, an apparition pushing a shopping cart. Leaving this at the station, he carries several plastic bags of what he's managed to scavenge this day and enters a tunnel. Less than a minute later, he appears on the other side, then quickly vanishes into the inky dark. I wonder how much he will get for his trouble?

FRACKING WILLISTON

7-15-14—Oil made this America-dominated, futuristic world, and with its increasing scarcity, will unravel it. Most pampered yet most disappointed, we're living in the age of peak oil, water, gold, copper, wheat, rice, cabbage, porn, greed and banking shenanigans, etc., for with more mouths than ever going after a shrinking donut hole, the ugliness is just getting started, and let us not forget, this age of oil has also been an era of mass carnage, a century of resource wars that have wiped out hundreds of millions, but for the survivors, us grubby schmucks, what a cool ride, eh?

But wait, wait, here comes the game changer, a fracking revolution that will make the USA energy-independent, and extend this gaseous joyride for a few more decades, at least. If you believe the hucksters, North Dakota and Texas as deus ex machina will lead this sagging nation to a new epoch of prosperity.

Each well can be fracked up to 18 times, and for each fracking, you must pump millions of gallons of water, twenty-five railcars of sand and more than five hundred chemicals into the ground, less than half of which is sucked out, meaning much of the toxic cocktail stays in the earth to poison the soil and water until Jesus returns, pigskin in hand and singing "God Bless America," but let's not be tree-hugging terrorists here. If not for this, we'd be forced to invade innumerable countries to steal their oil, God forbid. To not rape their lands there, we must violate our own foundation, but just to be on the safe side, we're doing both, of course.

This empire will be defended at all costs, even if the entire world is blown up and this nation itself destroyed, for nation and empire are not one. A nation is the total fabric, the water and soil that nourish, the all-consuming anthill, while the empire is the violent wet dream of a few sneering egotists. It's the fist-fuck that kills. The Amtrak route that goes from Chicago to Portland, Oregon, is called Empire Builder, and it was on this train that I saw Williston, North Dakota, for the first time. With so much freight traffic coming in and out of Williston, the Amtrak train is always delayed, from several hours to half a day, and so the conversations on board often focused on fracking as we approached the Bakken Shale Play. The conductor said, "Yes, this is a hassle, but I also look at it as our country's future!"

Having sold drilling rights to an oil company, a tall, beefy man in golf shirt and khaki shorts intoned, "Of course the money is nice, but more importantly, our family has become a part of history."

Wearing a blue Abbey Road T-shirt, a boy of about eight boasted to the portly woman from outside Spokane, "My grandpa is, like, the president of Exxon. He keeps a notecard on everyone he's met. Me and my mom, we flew from New Jersey to Boston, where we stayed a few days, then we flew to Chicago, where we got on this train. We will get off in White Fish, Montana. In Montana, we have a house like a castle. It has a deck overlooking the river. Sometimes I go swimming in that river."

A man was pointing out the different crops, wheat, hay, soybeans and oats. He said, "My family has always been in farming, but I now work for the Klondike Cheese Factory, in Wisconsin."

"And where're you going?"

"Stanley. To see my girlfriend."

"She works there?"

"Yes, she's a project manager for a new shopping center, but she's about done. Soon she'll move in with me."

"Sounds good."

"Yes! We first met twenty years ago, then I got married. That didn't last. A couple years ago, I looked up my girlfriend on Facebook, and there she was!"

"That's incredible."

"Well, not really. Everybody's on Facebook."

"I mean, it's incredible that you're hooking up again."

"We've always been meant for each other, but stupid me, I married the wrong woman. I have three houses: one I rent out, one I live in and one I use as a fishing lodge. It's just a cabin, really, on my sister's property. All of my brothers and sisters live within a five-mile radius. My new house is really nice, man, but it needs a woman's touch, you know what I mean?"

"It sounds like you're doing OK at the cheese factory."

"Yeah, I make $17 an hour, but I'm the sanitation supervisor. A new guy would make 11 an hour. It's not bad, but many of them can't take it. One dude quit just after a day! I don't even bother learning their names until they've been there awhile. For the first couple of weeks, I just call them, 'Hey, new guy!'"

"Your girlfriend's OK with moving to Wisconsin?"

"Yeah, she's made her money. They've been paying her $125,000 a year, but she's worked her tail off! She won't make half of that in Wisconsin, but a meal won't cost her $25 either."

"She may not even find a job in Wisconsin!" I laughed.

"Yes, that's true too!" He then fumbled with his cell phone for a minute before showing me a photo of his girlfriend in a business suit. She's surrounded by a dozen men, also in suits. Smiling, they're all wearing hard hats and holding shovels.

Looking out the window, I saw a distant red barn, an abandoned church and, episodically, car and appliance cemeteries rusting in the failing sun. Smoothing out the baserunning path of a spiffy diamond, a white-haired gent waved from his small tractor. To not disappoint the old fart, someone must have waved back, I hope. Inside this long steel tube, our bodies shook nonstop, as if sobbing. A man in his fifties observed, "I've taken this train many times. Fifteen, twenty years ago, you could see so many buffaloes, elks and pronghorns, but now, there's almost nothing left. It's very sad."

To service hundreds of oil rigs, many roads have been carved out of the landscape, and fences have gone up, so there's a "fragmentation of habitat due to energy development," to quote a Fish and Wildlife official, and even without accidents, fracking is inherently toxic, but we also have more than a thousand spills of oil- and chemical-laced fluids a year, in North Dakota alone, so it's no wonder that the only wildlife thriving these days in the Northern Plains is the sexually hard-up and hard-drinking roughnecks.

Approaching Williston, we could see with increasing frequency trucks and tankers on nearby roads, and long trains carrying oil, chemicals and sand. Here and there a rig, and we passed an austere man camp, then another. This time, I would not stay, but only get off on my way back from Portland. When I told the conductor of my intention to spend time in Williston, however, he let loose this alarm, "I wouldn't do that if I were you. It's the most dangerous place!"

"Oh, c'mon! How bad can it be?!"

"You have male-on-male rapes there. They'll spike your drink, then rape you, they're so desperate. People are killed and robbed, and the cops won't even come, since they're overwhelmed."

"But I already made my hotel reservation!"

"I'd rather lose the money. It's not worth it. You may get killed and dumped in a field, and no one will ever hear from you again."

"You're making it sound like the most dangerous place on earth. I've been to Detroit and Camden. Surely I can deal with Williston."

"It'll be worse, I guarantee you. One time the crew ordered a pizza delivery, and we just locked the doors until it came. I don't even dare to step outside in Williston."

"You must be joking, right?"

"No, I'm not. If there's a shooting or stabbing in Williston, the cops will ask, 'Is he dead yet?' If the person's already dead, the cops will just let the body lie there, and only get to it when they can. It's out of control. It's hell on earth."

"How can people function if it's so dangerous? What about the locals, the people who've always been there?"

"They keep off the streets, especially women. If you're stuck there, you're stuck there, but the only women who go to Williston anymore are the working girls."

A man in his early fifties, the conductor had said all this without even a gleam in his gray eyes, so he was excellent at keeping a straight face, but then he stated, "Last year, there were 3,700 murders in Williston," which would average out to over ten a day, and though I roared in laughter, he still would not smile.

Besides the ridiculous body count, much of what the conductor said isn't out of line with current Williston lore, with incidents of male-on-male rapes sworn to by countless people in spite of repeated police denial and the complete absence of news accounts. On the train away from Williston, I talked to a man whose wife worked as a nurse in its hospital for thirteen months, "Did she hear of male-on-male rapes?"

"No, but it was crazy enough. Lots of fights. Beatings, stabbings, sometimes shootings. One time a guy came in who had been slashed by a prostitute," and he laughed at this amusing memory. "He was this big black dude, and he had hired two prostitutes, and as he was busy with one, the other went through his stuff. When he started bitching about it, the one he was with took out a knife and slashed him across the belly. After they stole from him and took off, he had to drive himself to the hospital, and that's how he showed up at the emergency room, all bloody, with one hand holding in his entrails."

"It's not a good idea to hire two prostitutes. Even if they don't steal from you, it's too confusing."

"You're right!" And the cheerful man, Anton, laughed again. Though Russian, he was born in Brazil, came to the US as an infant and now lives in Woodburn, Oregon. Though he owns ten acres of farmland, it's not enough to pay the bills, so he must work as a painting contractor. In fracking country, Anton has a crew of five, and they all live in a rented farmhouse thirty-five miles from Williston, "I pay them $20 an hour, and we work six days a week. I brought them from Oregon, because it's cheaper that way. The ones who are already in Williston would want to be paid 30."

When Anton arrived in Williston three years ago, eating choices were limited yet expensive, but now, with new restaurants opening, he can get a reasonably price meal at Rice & Spice, for example, and the line at McDonald's isn't nearly as long. Rents are still preposterous, with a two-bedroom going for $2,500, higher than Chicago or Seattle, but Anton is only paying $1,250 for his out-of-the-way farmhouse. Exhausted drivers are what worries him most, not violent criminals, "There are a lot of accidents there. I was rear-ended recently, so my back and neck are hurting again. The guy didn't even have insurance. This really pisses me off! I'll have to see a doctor when I get back to Oregon."

A week after seeing Williston for the first time, I finally pounded its sidewalks, and the experience was, well, anti-climactic, for here was a pleasant and still tranquil Midwestern town. I was neither mugged nor raped on sight, but then again, I'm no catch, admittedly. Yes, there were two strip bars right by the train station, Whispers and Heartbreakers, but there were also the Lord's Ten Commandments painted on a nearby building. A few thoroughfares, 2nd Street and 2nd Avenue among them, were busy with truck traffic, but the rest were quiet, even sleepy. Moms, kids and ordinary women strolled downtown streets. Teenagers wandered. Outside the Salvation Army Store, three bikes were left unattended, and on a store poster, grandma licked an ice cream cone, "ICE CREAM / OLD FASHIONED / IT'S GOOD!" It was near the Fourth of July, so flags were everywhere, and outside a home with a miniature plastic castle, I spotted a sign that pleaded, "COMBAT VETERAN LIVES HERE / PLEASE BE COURTEOUS WITH FIREWORKS." I ran into a handsome polyresin buffalo in front of a modest home, then a bronze moose outside the Moose Lodge. Seeing me snapping it, a man shouted out, "Hey, I just sculpted that!" I passed an Asian bistro, Basil, and its price for pho, $14.50, did make me jump, but later I'd pay just $8.95 for an acceptable lunch buffet at China Sun, one and a half miles from downtown.

I entered through a bowling alley. As I sat down, the cashier said to the only other customer, a lanky black man standing at the counter, "You're not working today?"

Ignoring her question, he replied in an African accent, "I need a Chinese girl."

After a long moment, she said without emotion, "Go to China."

"I went to China. There were no Chinese girls there. I need a Chinese girl here."

After another drawn-out minute, she monotoned, "I'm no Chinese girl."

In this flat manner, they ping ponged back and forth until his to-go order was ready. After lunch, I went to my hotel, a Super 8, which cost me $108.87 per night, a great bargain in this steep town. On the way, I'd see several help wanted signs. In the window of Conlin's Furniture, a Help Wanted sign promised a salary of $50,000+, with health and dental benefits, 401K, paid vacation and "a beautiful work environment." "You owe it to yourself to stop in and fill out an application," it pleaded. The unemployment rate for Williston is less than 1 percent. From the parking lot of Super 8, I could see the sign for DK's Lounge & Casino, so that's exactly where I headed after a quick shower. Country music greeted me as I opened the door. After easing onto a stool, I asked the barkeep what she had on tap and ordered a Beaver Creek, based on its charming name alone. A fine IPA at five bucks for a 20-ounce mug, it was not nearly as expensive as I had feared. Settled, I surveyed my environment to find the ratio of men to women to be about 6 to 1, which is about average for most bars anywhere, especially in the late afternoon. The two loveliest women, young and slim, turned out to be waitresses, however. A man to my left explained, "The prettiest women in this town all come from elsewhere. The local chicks are like Yetis."

"What?!"

"You know, the Abominable Snowman, or, in this case, Snowwomen!"

"Oh, c'mon, man, I'd never call a woman that."

"You might not say it, but you would think it!"

"Well, since the men are beefier here, the women have to be beefy."

"That's one way to look at it. It's their insulation, their winter packing. It does get cold here."

"Hey, maybe these nice-looking women aren't even real! They're just holograms! I bet you can put your hands right through them," and I stuck my arms straight out.

"Ha ha! I'll call Erica over so you can try."

"No, man, don't do that. I just got here. I don't want to get beat up! Do they have a bouncer here?"

"Not today. Only on weekends."

"So it's really not that bad. What will happen, though, if I do something really stupid?"

"The clientele will take care of you."

"I've heard so much about this place. I was expecting more chaos, but look at this," I waved at the bar, "it's pretty mellow right now. I'd even say it's melancholic."

"It won't be if you return on Friday. There will be three hundred guys in here and you'll be lucky to get a seat at the bar. Have you seen the movie *300*?"

"No. What's it about?"

"The Persians are invading Greece, so you have this army of three hundred fighting them, and it's the same kind of rampage here. You have so many different states, so many different attitudes all converging on one small town that's just not ready to deal with such a rampant onslaught. There's too much testosterone here, so you even have males raping males, and that's why I'm getting out of here!"

"What about the prostitutes? I imagine there must be hundreds of them here. Shouldn't that relieve some of the pressure?"

"Surprisingly, no!"

"How much are they charging, by the way?"

"Oh, I have no idea! I have no idea."

"But listen, listen, if I was a prostitute, I would run right here and make some quick bucks, no?"

"But it's not safe here! If you're a woman, and you're by yourself, you run the risk of having the shit beat out of you if you come to a hotel room."

He then pulled up some Backpage ads on his cell phone, "Look at these! 'My first time in Williston.' Then there's 'I just got to town, and I'm ready to play.' Check this out: 'I want it in my mouth.' 'Smoothy Skin, Luscious Lips, Extreme Water Flow.' What the hell?! This one, 'PETITE EXOTiC

ASiAN DOLL,' has 'NO BLACK MEN THNKS.' So a bunch of them are here, like you say, but there are risks, because there is so much violence here. You have bar fights, stabbings. The men are beating each other up!"

"But you haven't seen any violence yourself?"

"No, not yet, but I've had enough."

"How long have you been here?"

"Just since November, so eight months, but I also worked for a year on an oil pad in Killdeer."

"Maybe you're just burnt-out."

"That too. They have me cleaning these pipes all day long, and I work eighty hours a week. The tips of my left fingers are numb and my right hand tingles. All day long I must hold this machine and sometimes I must lift these heavy pipes that are covered in oil and muck. It doesn't matter how good your gloves are, they're very hard to hold on to, so I'm done, man."

"What about the chemicals? Do you worry about all the shit you've been exposed to?"

"Well, I don't know. When I was on the rig, I heard all these warnings about the H_2S gas, about how it can destroy your sense of smell, then kill you without you even knowing, but there's also this crap that must be sucked from the ground and hauled away, and we're talking water, chemicals and all the natural, you know, whatever that's deep down in the earth, but the combination of it all is something no human should ever smell. The nauseation, oh God! I mean, you must check the level. You must bend over and look into the hole. It's not exactly like an outhouse, which we've both experienced, but over time, the continual smell of it, honestly, hell, there were times I was ready to drop to my knees! It's like your body knows. No human being should ever have to smell that."

"So it's probably best you're getting out of here, before it really kills you!"

"Well, I'm done. Soon enough, I'll go back to Grand Forks, five hours east of here."

After AC/DC's "Hell's Bells," Johnny Cash came on, and it's remarkable how soothing yet invigorating was his music. Jaunty, smirking, it exuded endurance and defiance, but with a touch of melancholy. For the men and women who're toughing it in Williston, the Man in Black is as good a patron saint as any.

"On the train, I met this stripper who was going to Grand Forks to work," I continued.

"She can't be, because there's no strip joint in Grand Forks. Maybe she meant Fargo?"

"No, Grand Forks. When I asked her what she was going to do in Grand Forks, she just smiled and said, 'I give people pleasure.' She said she could work anywhere."

"So she's a prostitute!"

"Yes, but she also said she was a stripper, but maybe she just wanted to sound classier. She did have the Space Needle tattooed on her left forearm. That's pretty classy."

"That's classy?!"

"Yeah, man, the Space Needle has a lot of details. It's not like the St. Louis Arch or the Washington Monument. To do a proper tattoo of the Space Needle, you must include the elevator and the rotating restaurant at the top."

"I see what you mean."

"So this chick said she started stripping in Seattle, but they charge a girl $120 a night to dance there, so she moved to Portland, where it's only thirty bucks. Now she's going to Grand Forks."

"What do you mean charge a girl?"

"These clubs don't pay but charge a girl to dance."

"$120 a week?"

"No, a night! So they must make at least that in tips to break even."

"Holy shit!"

"I've heard they're charging the same in Williston."

"No way!"

"That's what I've heard. Have you been down there?"

"I've only been to Whispers once. I saw this forty-eight-year-old dancing."

"A forty-eight-year-old?!"

"You know, different men have different tastes. Some like them old."

"If she told you she was forty-eight, she was probably fifty-five or sixty!"

"I felt kinda bad for her, so I did tip her a dollar."

Since coming to Williston, my new friend, David, has only touched or been touched by a woman one other time, when he went to a beauty salon to have his back hair removed. In his early forties, he does have a girlfriend, a woman in California. Born in the Philippines, she married an American, then divorced him. Though David said they had been dating for fourteen years, how strong can this long-distance relationship be? Maybe she's just a hologram! Or an emoticon.

Before leaving, David asked a waitress a few questions for my benefit, "Miss, this is your first night, right?"

"Yeah."

"What brought you up here?"

"To North Dakota? My husband."

"What state are you from?" I chimed in.

"Colorado."

"What city?"

"Boulder."

"I used to teach in Boulder!"

"Oh yeah? What did you teach?"

"Creative writing."

"Great!"

"I live in Philadelphia. I just got here. I thought Williston would be a lot crazier."

"Yeah, everyone makes it out to be so awful, like oh my God, and that you can't even go out at night, but it's not so bad. It's fine here, really."

"So what does your husband do?" David continued. "Is he working in a shop or on a rig?"

"A rig."

"Oh, nice, so he must be making decent money. Just out of curiosity, though, can we ask you why you're working here?"

"'Cause I don't want to sit home all day to watch TV and eat. That's no fun! I actually have two jobs. In the daytime, I work for Stallion."

"Stallion! What do you do for them?"

"I'm just cleaning for them now, but they're training me to drive a truck. I should get my permit soon. Then I'll really be a productive person."

"Hey, you're becoming more North Dakota!" I stupidly added. Not only had I slept sitting up on a train the night before, I was well sloshed by this point.

"More North Dakota? You mean I should add fifty pounds and put on more makeup?" She laughed.

"At least fifty pounds. Winter is coming! When in Rome, ah, you must eat more fried chicken!"

"That's not what they eat here, dude," David corrected me.

"Whatever. When in Rome, eat more chicken fried steak!"

"I feel fine now, but maybe I'll take your advice." Laughing, she walked away, and soon David also left.

DK's was still buzzing, but since the jukebox was mute, I could hear someone telling jokes from behind the black curtain that split this huge bar. Unlike me, he was no drunk fool but a real comedian, one Mike Brody from the Twin Cities, and though I have no doubt his lines could disarm and undress, and his delivery was ruthless yet nuanced, I could hear no laughter or applause whatsoever, so it's quite possible he was performing for himself alone.

Soon, though, my attention was drawn to a woman sitting to my right. In her early fifties and rather exhausted-looking, she was having trouble getting the attention of the barkeep, Erica. Talking to her, I found out her name was Verna, and that she was working as an administrator at a man camp, "Our company is considered a leader in this field. We only work with companies. We don't take individuals. Halliburton is one of our main clients."

"How much do you charge for a person per night?"

"You know, I don't even know! They don't tell me, but it's around $150."

"But they get three meals a day, right?"

"Yes, they eat very well."

"And they can't bring guests or alcohol in, right?"

"Absolutely not! But it's not a prison," she laughed. "They can always leave. They can come here."

Arriving from Polk County, Wisconsin, Verna has been in Williston for a year and four months. She's originally from St. Paul. In Wisconsin, she worked for Spooner Train, an outfit that offers dinner on a moving train, at $50 per person, or dinner, drinks, then an overnight stay on a parked train, at $299 per couple. They sell nostalgia, basically.

"I came here thinking I'll get a job at the airport. It has turned out well, but I'm tired. Everybody's tired here. That's why there are so many accidents. I was just rear-ended."

"How many hours do you work a week?"

"Eighty-four."

"Wow, that's so many! Why won't they hire two people and give each $40 a week?"

"No one will come then. You get paid more because you work more. It's not so much they're paying you more per hour, it's the fact they're giving you more hours. Every six weeks, though, I get two weeks off."

"Do you go home?"

"Yes, but that's another story. My home has been trashed!"

"What do you mean?!"

"Squatters! The last time I went home, I discovered that it had been broken into. My white carpet is now red and purple, and there were beer cans and liquor bottles all over."

"What about your electronics? Did they take your TV?"

"No, they didn't take anything. I'm sure they were planning on coming back. There was no hurry. They're probably there right now, partying."

"Oh, man . . . So did you call the police?"

"Yes, I called, but the police are useless. They haven't done anything. They didn't even bother to take fingerprints."

"What about your neighbors? Did they see anything?"

"I have no neighbors. There are no other houses around."

"It sounds like a teenaged thing. Maybe a bunch of teenagers broke into your house and use it for parties."

"Whoever they are, they know that I've left to work in another state."

"You know, maybe the cops are not investigating because the kids who broke in are related to them."

"I wouldn't be surprised."

"Maybe the cops themselves broke into your house! So, anyway, there's nothing you can do about this?"

"Nothing."

"No security system?"

"They can always cut the wire. They're not stupid!"

"Maybe you can plant land mines in your yard!"

"That's an idea. At this point, I've given up on that house. After I bought it, it went up in value, so I put it on the market at $240,000, but it didn't sell, so I lowered it to 169, finally, but at this point, I won't even get that. It will take a lot to fix. You know, they even broke some of my windows, so that my pipes burst from the cold. At this point, I don't care if a tornado hits it!"

"I think you should go back and lob hand grenades at the house, get even with these motherfuckers!"

"You know, I can't even get worked up over it. I'm tired. For years, people have been messing with me."

"What do you mean?"

"Have you heard of crowd stalking?"

"Yes, but who are stalking you?"

"I don't know, but that's the whole point."

"I don't understand. I mean, what do they want from you?"

"I don't know either."

"Maybe I'm stalking you!"

"Maybe you are."

"Maybe I'm one of them!"

"Even in Williston, strange things have happened. My car has been broken into several times. Someone slashed my armrest. Why would they do that? Another time, someone cut some of the wiring under my hood."

"So someone's really messing with you, but why?"

"I don't know. I wish I was actually crazy, so I could be cured, but it's worse this way, because I have no idea what's going on."

"How long has this been happening?"

"For years! Once, someone scrawled 'HI' into the dirt on my TV. I'm wondering why God is allowing this to happen."

"To test you?"

"Test me for what?! I already believe in Him! I used to really believe in Him, but since I got here, I've only been to church twice."

"Which church?"

"Oh, two different churches. I don't believe in religion, only in God, so any church will do."

"Now that you've made some money, maybe you can run away, very far away!"

"I'm sure they'll find me."

The lights had gone up, so it was about time to leave. Around twenty-nine-year-old Erica, a small crowd of supplicants had gathered, but each would walk out of here as needy as ever. Erica works nine and a half hours a day and makes a pretty penny, but it's also time for her to move on. Soon, she'll be a field operation assistant for Oasis, another oil services company. With an eleven-year-old at home, she wants weekends and all holidays off. One hundred percent Williston, native Erica is as lovely as they come, not that she needs any endorsement from a dirty old creep. "Thank you, ma'am," I muttered as I staggered into the night.

Approaching Williston from the north, you'll see an indigo sign with white lettering, "WELCOME TO WILLISTON / BOOMTOWN, USA." On the back, there's a black and red tableau of fourteen men in hard hats, all busy carrying planks, pushing a wheelbarrow, climbing up a ladder, painting or standing on a scaffold, etc. The caption, "Will!ston / It's getting better together." Around town, you can also find posters that blare, "Excuse our mess!" but with "mess" crossed out, to be replaced by "progress." A shopping center is being built, and east of downtown, luxury condos have gone up. Beneath this triumphant optimism, however, there is a toxic current that is poisoning not just bodies and souls, but also the fractured foundation of this still beautiful town, for when the rigs are hauled away, sooner rather than later, all that will be left will be an unholy mess.

In the window of Skinful Pleasures, a downtown tattoo parlor, there's a sign, "Walk-ins Welcome!" Next to it, however, there's a "Fuck You" black T-shirt. Although this juxtaposition is merely coincidental, it also sums up Williston's ambivalence towards its lucrative rape. Fracked ten thousand times, North Dakota will never be the same.

With few industries, North Dakota has long been reliant on the military to feed its coffers. Hence, its nuclear base in Minot, drone bases in Fargo and Grand Forks, and drone research facilities in Grand Forks, Grand Sky and elsewhere. The University of North Dakota even awards a bachelor's degree in Unmanned Aircraft Systems Operations, the first of its kind worldwide, needless to say. ("Mom, I think I want to major in drones!") Fracking, however, may turn out to be this state's worst pact with the devil.

On the day I left Williston, there was a bazaar downtown, with stalls set up right in the middle of Main Street. In the mild sunshine, I saw no roughnecks or fracking whores, only ordinary families leisurely perusing knickknacks and clothing racks. Smiling, two girls sat to have their caricatures done. On a table, there was a donation jar to help kids from Rickard Elementary go to Washington, DC, this April. There, they will visit the Air and Space Museum, among other attractions. Wearing a "Home of the Brave" T-shirt, a blond "God Bless America" on his flute. He was excellent, too.

TRASHED IN WOLF POINT

7-22-14—It always amazes me how many people get on a train just to play cards, for outside their windows, a most amazing world is constantly unfurling. It doesn't matter if it's the Southwest Desert, Northern Plains, Cascades or Rocky Mountains, they don't look up from their miserably dealt hands to notice that Eden is just a glass barrier away, but that's how it is with the über-domesticated. They prefer a shrunken, airless civilization, as contained in fifty-two puny pieces of laminated carton, to the unscripted richness they're entitled to at all times. Although it's free, they don't take it. O heaven, often it becomes so beautiful, I just want to kick open that emergency window so I can jump outside, tear off my Ross, brand-names-for-less, sale-rack clothes, and run a hundred miles, just so I can see everything a bit better through my cheap bifocals. I want to rub tumbleweed on my privates and feast on anything that crawls or sleeps out there. I want to eat pebbles! OK, Saint Jerome, now I give the microphone back to you!

Sitting on the train a while, you do get weird, for this mode of transportation, like all mechanical conveyances, is a derangement machine. From submarine to bike, to roller coaster, each teases and jerks the mind, and transports it to some place entirely unnatural. We're only meant to walk, shuffle or hop on our own two feet, grasshoppers. As Kafka writes in "The Wish to Be a Red Indian," one does not need spurs, reins or even a horse, but before we get off this damn train, let's eavesdrop on this conversation between mother and son.

"We were here. Now we're about here. Soon we will be here." With her lavender nail, she pointed at three spots on a map.

Responding, a boy no older than five jabbed at a random place on this nonsensical piece of paper, "And right here is a waterfalls, Mom, and if you fall into it, you die!" To show that he was serious, he contorted his face and made a loud farting sound with his mouth.

It was already dusk when I rolled into Wolf Point, for my train was seven hours late. In this town of 2,700, downtown is just three blocks and visible from the station. Flanked by modest two-story buildings, Main Street was mostly empty, and I encountered no other pedestrians as I passed Missouri Breaks Brewing, a movie theater, then the Elks Lodge. That's two bars already within one block, but after crossing 3rd Avenue, I quickly spotted three more, Dad's Bar, Stockmans 220 Club and Arlo's. Though these seemed more promising than the first two, I couldn't decide, so I asked the only other person in sight, a short, squinting man who was smoking a cig on the sidewalk, "Which one should I go in, man?"

"This one!"

Stockmans had two spoked wagon wheels stuck to its marquee-like false front parapet, and inside, it was spacious, with about a dozen gambling machines at the front, and two pool tables at the back. There were only five other customers. "I just got off the train," I confessed to the man who had steered me in. "I've never been here."

Mervin Running Bear is his name, he said. Though born in Wolf Point, he has worked in Alaska, on crab and halibut boats, and in Washington State as a construction worker.

"So what do you do now?"

"Oh, everything: construction, housepainting, roofing, plumbing, whatever."

"Can you do brickwork?"

"I've done that too! I'm not a real professional at anything, but I can do everything."

"That's good! You're good! I used to be a housepainter, but I was like the worst housepainter."

"If they pay you, you're good!"

Though Mervin's words are lucidly presented on this screen, and move along snappily, without stumbling, they were actually huffed up raspily, eyes squinting, with quite a bit of strain in real life, as if his tongue was too hungover to move. His brain fluid must have been 100 proof. "I also worked for the Chinese restaurant next door," he continued. "I did prep work," and he made chopping motions with his right hand. "Richard Chan, I know him. He died."

Merv introduced me to Ray, whom he called "the nutty professor," and Monk, a fat, oafish man with clear menace in his eyes. When I asked Monk if he was married, he roared, "Why get married when you can get it for free! Putang! Suck this helmet off my shaft, bitch!" Over the next two days, each time I mentioned Monk to anybody, the response was invariably, "Oh, that guy's an asshole!"

As for Ray, he teaches sixth grade at North Side, Wolf Point's lone middle school. A decade ago, this school system got unwanted attention when it was revealed they had padded rooms to confine children, almost always Indian, and that teachers and counselors were prescribing Ritalin, without authority, to countless kids. A white teacher was fired after molesting three Indian girls, and an Indian wrestling star committed suicide after being kicked off the high school team, just before the state tournament, for having chewing tobacco. Though Wolf Point is on a reservation, the tribes have no say over the schools, which are run by a board that is almost always exclusively white.

Scouring several school rating sites, I could find only one review of a Wolf Point school: "There are 4 teachers that actually teach, care about education of students and enjoy and work hard at teaching their field. This school has daily fights in the halls, is a FEDERALLY failing school for eight years, only looks out for their 'favorite' students. These are those from the 'right' family, or family owns a business in town, or are personal friends . . . The Senior year is a year of crafts, PE, multiple shop classes—a joke. There is no preparation for a trade/skills for future, college prep classes are a joke—subject to mood of tired teachers waiting for retirement. Counselors spend time with their favorite students and ignore rest of student population. If students make bad choice there is no due process, just expelled for the year and told, "see you next year." . . . Shop class is sit in your seat and you get a C—if you glue something together you get an A. Literally. The district is out of money and can't make payroll next year 2013. Staff morale is terribly low. I have put 7 kids thru this school, there are more examples, just out of space."

An indication of the poverty in Wolf Point is that 98 percent of the public school children qualify for free or reduced priced breakfast and lunch, compared to 40 percent statewide. For many parents here, this is about the only benefit of sending their kids to school. With Wolf Point being so poor and remote, it's hard to attract any qualified professionals, so at the local clinic, doctors routinely work on five-month contracts. Barely here, they're already looking forward to escaping.

Soon a woman nicknamed Chickadee came in. In her sixties, she also appeared groggy. Seconds after we'd been introduced, she leaned her forehead onto mine, "I'm in mourning. My nephew committed suicide two days ago."

"How old was he?" I asked, our foreheads still attached.

"Twenty-two. Oh, he was a beautiful kid! My son died of exposure in Denver, and my other son was stabbed to death by his girlfriend. Come," and she led me by the hand to a plastic-wrapped Styrofoam board hung over the door. On it were six dim photos of Andrew "Gator" Robinson, alone and with family. The largest image, however, was the logo of the Denver Broncos, a blue and white horse head in profile with red, flowing mane and a red, sinister eye.

After serving in the Army for two years, where he was a tank crewman during Desert Storm, Gator returned to Wolf Point and worked in construction, road maintenance and as a part-time firefighter. He had a turbulent, intermittent nine-year relationship with Doran Flynn, but by November 26, 2008, they were living in the same house with their two sons. That Friday, payday, Gator came home early to take Doran out to celebrate their nine-year anniversary. At Stockmans, their second bar that night, Gator finally fell asleep, however, so Doran drove him home, thinking she would return to whoop it up some more. What happened next is unclear, but Gator ended up with abrasions on his hands and face, bruises on his scalp, contusions on his arms and legs, and a single stab wound to the heart. Charged with involuntary manslaughter, Doran was jailed for two years and now lives on the opposite side of the state. Gator was only thirty-seven when he died.

After half an hour in town, I had become aware of three premature deaths already, but it was just the beginning of a long list of tragedies. "And your other son," I asked, "how did he die again?"

"On the street, in Denver. He died of exposure after drinking Jack Daniel's and cough medicine. He wanted me to come see him, but I never did. Now I feel so bad. Had I shown up, maybe he wouldn't have died!"

"It's not your fault, you couldn't have known." I clutched her hand a little harder.

Suddenly looking shifty, Chickadee whispered, "Mervin is getting jealous because we've become friends!" Walking hand in hand, we returned to our stools. After I bought her a Coors Light, however, she demanded a Jägermeister. I said sure.

"Now that you know about me, what about you? What are you doing here? What do you do?"

I could have said "PayPal-buttoned, reader-supported blogger," but I opted for the short answer, "I'm a poet. A writer."

It took two seconds for Chickadee's face to become flint-hard, "I don't believe you!"

"OK, then," I laughed. "What do you think I am?"

Seeing Chickadee leaning forward, I obliged, so with our foreheads clumped together, she positively seethed, "You are a nothing!"

Poet, nothing, same difference, but it was strange to see it turned into an accusation, so I laughingly retorted, "What's wrong with being a nothing? Everybody's a nothing!"

Coming to my defense, Mervin leaned over Chickadee's shoulder, "I'm a nothing too!"

"See, we're all nothings!"

Not content to settle with this, Chickadee had to squeeze in a final verdict, "But you're really a nothing!"

I had not slept in a bed in three nights, so I should have gone straight to my hotel after Stockmans, but I decided to check out Elks. Like Moose International, Elks was founded as a white-men-only organization, but both have since allowed women and nonwhites, excluding only atheists. When not used for meetings and, I don't know, bizarre or goofy rituals, the Elks Bar/Casino in Wolf Point is open to the public, so in I barged to discover an all-white clientele. It had a much better beer selection than Stockmans, and the atmosphere was also more subdued, with no clumping of heads, suicide shrines or tales of death. I tried to strike up a conversation with the man to my right, but it didn't go very far. No one was unfriendly, though, and I stayed awhile. After learning I had just gotten off the train, a woman gave me detailed directions to my hotel, and the barkeep even offered to call the Homestead Inn to ask if there was a shuttle.

"Don't worry! It's only, what, a mile away? I can walk. It's no problem."

"It's after dark now, and the bad types come out."

"It's OK, really. I'll walk!"

Wolf Point is 50.5 percent American Indians and 42.5 percent whites, yet its mayor is white, and this is because the Indian population has a higher number of minors, who cannot vote, and also because many Indians live just outside the town's boundaries, so even though they work, shop and drink in Wolf Point daily, and send their kids to school there, they have no say over its leadership. What you have, then, is a white-ruled town in the heart of an Indian reservation, and to show that this matters, consider that two years ago, the Tribal Council voted unanimously to request that Custer Street be changed to Crazy Horse Street. Addressing the City Council, a tribal leader, Stoney Anketell, explained, "Custer was an Indian fighter and he massacred a lot of innocent women and children.

It seems grossly inappropriate to have his name on the Assiniboine and Sioux reservation." A month later, this was casually rejected, with Councilman Craig Rodenberg announcing, "We decided not to go forward with any change." Councilman Lee Redekopp affirmed, "The name stays the same." Mayor DeWayne Jager concluded, "That takes care of that."

I'll give you another illustration of who's in charge. For the nation's bicentennial celebration, a small equestrian statue was commissioned by Wolf Point. Sculpted by Floyd Tennison DeWitt, a Wolf Point native then living in Amsterdam, it was placed in the middle of Main Street and became the town's focal point. A plaque states that "Homage to the Pioneer," is the work's title. Since pioneers were settlers, this means the whites who swarmed in to displace the Indians that were massacred, starved or corralled into reservations. Above the first plaque, however, there is a smaller one with a revised title, "Homage," and on the town's website, there is an explanation that this bronze is an all-inclusive "homage to the American Indians and the community's pioneers and founders." For this to make sense, there would have to be both Indian and Cowboy, sitting side by side, sideways, on one horse, but as is, the lone rider is unmistakably white, holding a cowboy hat and wearing chaps and spurs, so no matter how cute the dancing around, it's clear that this is an homage to the annihilation of the Indian, and not his presence, then or now. If Indians were deciding, this would be a sculpture of Sitting Bull, but save for a clumsy bust over his grave, there's no public effigy of the great Indian leader anywhere in the US, period. You will have to go to Denmark to find one, and it's only in Legoland, a novelty theme park.

Although there is no bronze of an Indian in Wolf Point, you can find two wooden Indians inside its hangar-like museum. It's a matching lamp set, with a stylized eagle on the loincloth of the muscular brave, and a circular, target like design over the crotch of the sexy squaw.

Next morning, I got up just before dawn to explore. After passing McDonald's, with its American flag flashing on an electronic sign, Old Town Grill and Lucky Lil's Casino, I was surprised to hear Cat Stevens singing. At first, I thought it came from a car radio, then I realized there was a speaker mounted outside Albertson's, the supermarket. All day long, there would be plaintive rock emanating from it. "And if I ever lose my hands, lose my plough, lose my land . . ."

Trailing his Labrador Retriever, a white man had on a black T-shirt, "TEENAGED DAUGHTER SURVIVOR." Draped in old military jackets, three middle-aged Indian guys straggled by. The one with a camouflage hunting hat made eye contact and nodded his head. I grinned, "How're you doing?" A cop car slowed, rounded the corner, then slowed again as it reappeared a minute later, coming from the opposite direction.

Since the bars were still closed, I was forced to enter an eatery. There were three Indian warriors, Duck, Bob Tail Bear and Cloud Man, on the menu's cover of Old Town Grill, and at each table, there was a red phone.

"What is this for?" I asked the lone waitress.

"Oh, it's to call me if you need something!"

"Well, shouldn't I, like, just talk to you?"

"Yes, of course! The owner installed them when this place opened thirty-five years ago. Can you imagine how exciting it must have been then? I wasn't there. I've only been working here thirty-two years."

I had me some boffo chicken fried steak, my first decent meal in a day and a half. At the next table, two kids played, drew and occasionally threw a rubber ball around. Once it landed under my table so the boy had to crawl under it. From the kitchen came the music of Eminem.

"What is that noise?" Chuckling, a patron asked the waitress, and no, he didn't use the red phone either.

"What noise?"

"The noise coming from the kitchen."

"Oh, you mean the music? It's the cook's music."

"That's music?! It sounds like a rig with a flat tire!"

Eminem ain't all that, but all across America, you see rural kids dressing and acting like urban gangstas and ho's, but such is a result of the deliberate program to make us as depraved, and hence as helpless, as possible. Stripped of self-control and -respect, we're being hypnotized by our masters into worshipping death, destruction, gross consumption, bright vomit and bestial sex, and we're even being charged to have these foul and funky effluvia dumped on us. Of course, the ones who don't pay will still get splattered on. A raging and infantile solipsism has become our national posture.

Speaking of posture, mine would be somewhat altered by a black Doberman pinscher a day later. We'll get to it. Meanwhile, I left Old Town Grill in great spirits. After walking ten minutes, I hit the Silverwolf Casino, which also doubles as a funeral chapel, I kid you not, with open or closed casket wakes. Among the slot stuffing zombies, occasionally you'll find a dressed-up cadaver, such as that of Dakota's, Chickadee's unfortunate nephew. Since every Montana bar is already a mini casino, a place like Silverwolf faces a lot of competition. Here, many convenience stores are also casinos.

Attention, all of you with the shakes! Each day, the first Wolf Point bar to open is Arlo's, so under its bucking bronco and cowboy sign I entered, to find two grizzled dudes at the bar talking about fishing, with side remarks about being broke yet not eating just Spam, thanks to what God has tossed into creeks, rivers and lakes. They discussed how this or that fish was jumping, or not, from this or that fishing spot, but as a city fool, I can't tell a ling fish from a humpback whale, so much of this discussion lapped right over me. The electronic beeps, burps, rings, fanfares, cymbal rides and phony cachinks of the gambling machines provided background noises, as did the clashes of pool balls from the half-dark back.

In Arlo's, it's either Bud or Bud Light if you want to go draft. On the wall, there's a large drawing of an ass kicking a man in the ass and knocking his glasses and beer pitcher from him. Its caption, "WELCOME TO ARLO'S / HAVE A 'KICK ASS' TIME!" After one dude left, I talked to the other, Darrel, who's better known as Cheeseburger, or simply Cheese. Half-white, half-Chippewa, fifty-seven-year-old Cheese has lived in Wolf Point his whole life, save for the seventeen years he worked for Union Pacific, when he mostly slept next to the tracks from North Dakota on through Glacier National Park.

"I built those tracks you'll be riding on when you head up those mountains."

"You slept outside all those years?"

"Pretty much. For living in a tent, I was paid an extra $700 a month."

"How much is that altogether?"

"$3,000, after tax."

"You did well!"

"Yeah, I did great. Fact is, I liked it anyway. One time, my wife and kids came out to see me, and they also had to sleep in a tent. My boys liked it so much, they didn't want to go back to Wolf Point."

"How many kids do you have?"

"Six, but only three naturals. The others, I adopted."

"Relatives?"

"Two of them are relatives. Nieces. The other one, his dad died in a car crash in Canada. I got along with his mother quite well, so I put him in school."

"You're a pretty nice guy!"

"But he's an asshole!" Cheese laughed. "Little asshole, he tried to beat me up when he was fourteen, but couldn't. I was thirty-five. He tried again when he was sixteen, eighteen, twenty, twenty-two . . . The fucker, I made him play sports, made him play football. I made him enlist in the Army. He wanted to go overseas, but I put an end to that. You little asshole, you still can't kick dad's ass!"

"Are your kids still around?"

"They don't live around here no more. They're in Billings, Wyoming, Minnesota, California, Canada . . . They're all over the world. They want concrete!"

After a sip of Bud Light, Cheese continued, "I taught my kids how to survive, how to fight, how to kill, how to be good. I showed them how to care for children. Elders. How to care for the animals." With a pause after each exclamation, Cheese then barked, "Put up your own tent!

Haul your own wood!

Start your own fire!

Dig your own shithole!

Your own fire pit!

You must watch your surroundings."

Cheese then mellowed, "I'm down by the bend. Sucking on a Bud

Light, I roll me a big doobie. I watch the sun comes up, the sun goes down. The moon comes up, the moon goes down. I listen to the deer playing behind me, rabbits running beside me, but these kids, living on concrete, surrounded by garbage, these kids are fuckin' spoiled!"

"When you say you've taught them how to kill, what do you mean? Who do you kill around here?"

"The enemy!"

"What enemy? I don't see any enemy around here!"

"There are always enemies around!" Then, "You have to be careful around here. You come in here, and everyone's laughing and smiling, but the second you turn your back, they can become the biggest assholes in the world! Someone may be watching you, then follow you as you leave this bar, so you've gotta be careful around this shithole. I was born and raised on the rez. I know."

Cheese said his sister was pissed off because she didn't see him in church the previous Sunday, "I did go, but I left early, before mass started. I wasn't there, but I was there in spirit."

When I mentioned Chickadee and her nephew, Cheese said, "That's also my nephew. He hanged himself." Then, "See that cane over the bar? The woman who carved that hanged herself too."

In Arlo's, I also met Jack, a transplant from New York, and Darryl, a white farmer who grows wheat and raises cattle. I overheard Jenn, the bar manager, jokingly speak of a plan to round up five Wolf Point ho's and bring them to a Williston man camp, "Make some quick bucks, you know! It's all about looks, right? She's got to be worth pokin'!" Fracking country is only eighty-six miles away.

Without knowing the context, I also heard Cheeseburger shout, "It's all my parents' fault, goddamnit! I want to be white! I want to be German!" The sarcasm was particularly biting considering "INDIAN PRIDE" was on the back of Cheese's baseball cap. Also, on his fleece vest was a green button with a marijuana leaf and "It's 4:20 somewhere." The Ann McNamee song came on: "Bring me a ritual, a tribal game / Moonlight on the water, shadows on my mind."

When Ervin, a man with mutilated hands, declared, "I'm a Sioux!" Cheeseburger retorted, "Well, you're a short Sioux!"

"Fuck you too, fag boy!"

And so it went, with much bantering and laughter, but occasionally also melodramatic accusations, drunkenly delivered. Here, people are remarkably open, but they will also turn skeptical suddenly, as in, "That's what you say," accompanied by a sharp look.

When a tallish young man walked in, many of the patrons rushed to the door to give him a hug. While others beamed at his presence, he himself showed no emotion and said next to nothing. His eyes were scarcely more alive than a dead fish's. A soldier, he would be home for a month before being sent back to Afghanistan. Nineteen, he wasn't even old enough to drink, so after a minute, he disappeared.

The next morning, I got up way too early, so decided to turn on the TV. Looking for the local news, I stumbled onto a live cam of some bird nest over an orange-lit parking lot, with a road and darkened hills in the background. Every now and then, I could hear a distant car, but mostly there were just cricket sounds. Strange, I thought, why would an entire channel be devoted to this? When the bird finally stirred, however, I realized it was an eagle, and so I watched it shift back and forth for a while. It was pretty silly, I agree, and I wondered how many others doofuses were doing the same. Suddenly, though, the channel went blank without warning, and there was no more eagle!

On my last morning in Wolf Point, I walked south from downtown, and the further I went, the shabbier the houses became, until I was staring at a couple of decrepit trailers. Though no one was in sight, I could hear an old man talking to someone. Suddenly, a barking dog came charging and bit me, hard, on my right thigh. This left a bloody gash and bruise that would only heal a month later. Luckily, though, his teeth didn't make contact with my skin, as he didn't bite through my jeans. From the shadows, the old man raised his voice and the dog backed off, and that's how I met Alfred Comes Last.

"That's strange, he usually doesn't do that. You OK?"

"Yeah, I guess so. Is that your dog?"

"No, but I know the woman. She's inside."

"I'm just visiting. I'm just walking around to check out this town."

"There isn't much to see."

"And where are you going so early?"

"To the senior center. I volunteer there. You want to come? They have free coffee."

The pain was bad enough, I felt like pulling my pants down to see how my damn thigh was doing, but I sucked it up and followed Al to his destination nearly two miles away. Along the way, Mr. Comes Last told me his life story.

Born in 1942, Comes Last is a pioneer in his tribe, for he was the first to become a welder. After the tribal authorities sent him all the way to San Jose to learn his trade, he stayed in California to work, before moving to Arizona, Colorado and Washington, where he welded ships, railcars and farm equipment, etc. In Wyoming, he taught other Indians to weld, then did the same after moving back to Wolf Point. With three women, Al has six children, and he's been with his current wife for thirty-six years.

"When I was a kid, there was only one frame house in Wolf Point. The rest were made of logs."

"Each family has just one log house?"

"Yes."

"Didn't the richer people have more?"

"We were all the same. No one had any money."

"How big was a log house? How many rooms?"

"Two, a kitchen and dining area, and a bedroom. At night, though, we'd sleep in both rooms."

"How many brothers and sisters did you have?"

"There were eight of us."

"Eight?! So ten people slept in two rooms?!"

"That's just how it was." Then, "A lot has changed here. The kids today only know how to drink and smoke." He let out a grunting laugh. "If the grids go down tomorrow, how will they survive?"

By now, we had reached the senior center. Each day, it serves over a hundred hot lunches for free. With increasing poverty, there are fewer resources available in Wolf Point, with Basket of Hope Food Bank and several thrift stores shutting down recently, and The Lord's Table, a soup kitchen, inoperative because of a break-in. After Al had introduced me to Sue, the senior center's director and cook, we got coffee and sat on the narrow porch to look at the traffic zoom by. A hundred yards away, freight cars were parked on the tracks.

Smoking an American Legend, Al lamented, "When I left the house this morning, I had nearly a full pack, but people kept bumming cigarettes off me, so now I only have a half-pack. They always say, 'I'll pay you back! I'll pay you back!' but they never do." Tersely and without emotion, Al then let on that one of his sons had died in a house fire just two weeks before, and a daughter was in a Billings hospital. Having fallen down the stairs the previous day, she had a blood clot in her brain. "My wife is with her. I should hear from her soon."

"Is your daughter conscious?"

"I don't know. She wasn't."

"I'm surprised at how calm you are. This is pretty serious!"

"I'm praying inside." Then, "Us Indians have a saying, 'Deaths come in threes,' so since my son died two weeks ago . . ."

"You're waiting for two more deaths?!"

"I hope my daughter doesn't die. My wife should call soon."

"I've been here a couple of days, and I've heard of several deaths already. I talked to this woman, Chickadee. She said her nephew just killed himself."

"Yeah, he hanged himself in a closet. His mom had just taken a shower. She was getting ready to go to work, you know, and when she opened the closet to get her clothes, she saw him. A lot of people die around here. Everybody's dying. Most of my friends are dead. They destroy their liver or die in a car crash. It's the alcohol. Some weren't even forty years old."

A small, dark man, Al wore dark glasses and a weathered hunting cap. On his gray hoodie, there was an irregular black stain near his heart. The steel door opened and Sue came out to hand Al a phone. Without turning away, he spoke briefly to his wife in a small, flat voice, then informed me after he'd hung up, "She's OK. My daughter's OK."

"That's great news! They did a good job, the doctors."

"Yes." Then, "You know, most of the medicine men these days are fakes. They'll take the people's money, but they can't heal them."

"You're talking about the Indian medicine men?"

"Yes, the Indian ones. Most of them are fake. When I was a kid, we had a great medicine man. He healed my grandfather. After he had been struck by lightning, they brought him to the hospital in Poplar. My grandfather was all burnt, he had no skin left, but at the hospital, he said he wanted to be taken back here, and so the medicine man covered my grandfather's body in herbs and oil, then buried him for three days, with just his head sticking out. For three days he just drank water and ate nothing. People didn't know what was going on, they thought the medicine man was going to kill him!" Al chuckled. "But the ground took the electricity out, and so my grandfather was healed. He lived to be ninety-two, and it was me who dug his grave and buried him. In the old days, the medicine man didn't even ask for money. People paid what they could, or they would just give him some food or a blanket, whatever."

Before I left Wolf Point, I'd see Mervin and Cheese again, and Al and I had a few beers at three bars altogether. On the street, we'd run into Kerri, his youngest daughter, and their interaction was rather curious, for it was filled with melodrama. Slurring, she'd fling vague accusations at him. It was not yet noon, yet she was totally clobbered, and when she laughed, I could see that her upper front teeth had been knocked out. In March, Kerri had been at a meth and alcohol party where a man was stomped on the face repeatedly and kicked in the stomach. He died two days later of a ruptured liver.

Anyplace I go, I gravitate towards the bars, so of course I'd see drunken people, but nowhere else have I seen so many folks so shit-faced from morning until last call. As I mused over these thoughts at the train station, a tall and smiling gentleman approached me and asked if I liked Wolf Point. I said yes, and meant it.

His name was Thomas, he said, and he was grateful for his wonderful life, "After high school, I enlisted in the Navy, and thanks to that, I've seen the world. I've been to Japan, Philippines, Thailand, Singapore and Australia. I'm very blessed. I have a great wife and two great children. My son is in college, and my daughter was a contestant for Miss Montana. I'm very blessed. I've had a good life."

"Since I've been here, I've seen so many drunken people, but then I thought, The sober people are working and not on the streets!"

"Yes, alcoholism is a huge problem here. My dad was an alcoholic, but I haven't had a drink in twenty-one years! A year after I got married, I told myself I didn't want to drink again, and I haven't."

"That's amazing!"

"I didn't want to turn out like my dad. I'm a businessman. I have work to do."

"What do you do?"

"I had a convenience store and gas station in Frazer. The tribes lent me $25,000 to open this business, but I worked long hours and made almost no money. It hasn't worked out. I asked the tribes for another $25,000, but they refused. Before this, I was an assistant manager at the Walmart in Williston. I also opened a bank in Wolf Point, but that didn't work out either. I've worked in various offices. I've taught."

"So what are you going to do now?"

"I'll figure out something. I have a degree in business administration from the University of Montana. I'm very good at managing people."

Frankly, it was weird to have such a sober conversation with this perfectly composed man, and one who was cheerful, grateful and optimistic in spite of his own derailments. After the train arrived, Thomas introduced me to his neatly dressed, calm and confident son, then I got on to go farther west.

Though much longer than usual, this Postcard is incomplete and would even be misleading had I not met a final Wolf Point character, Candy, and it was entirely by chance that I found myself sitting across from this lady, nearly a week later, as we were heading east from Portland.

Seeing the WPT tag over her seat, I could tell where Candy was heading. As I had learnt by now, everyone knows just about everyone else in Wolf Point, and so Candy cheered up when I mentioned Merv, Chickadee and Cheese, etc. "I was Cheeseburger's girlfriend for a day!" she laughed. Of Mervin, she remarked, "He had a lot of potential, but it has all gone to waste." Also, his last name is Garfield, and not Running Bear.

"Twice, I saw him drinking in the morning, before 11, and each time, he said he had already worked that day."

"He works in the bar! I like that guy, but he has his mean streak. He used to beat up his girlfriends."

"I'd never guess. He seemed so mellow."

"He is, usually."

"I also met Alfred, an old man."

"Alfred?!"

"Yes, a short guy in his early seventies."

"I thought Alfred was still in jail. He violated his daughter!"

"You're kidding me?! Are we talking about the same Alfred?"

"If it's an old man, then it's Alfred Comes Last."

Pulling out my camera, I found a photo of Al and showed it to Candy on the viewfinder. "Yes, that's him!"

"Had I not talked to you, I'd go home thinking he was just this sweet old man. I met his daughter, too. She would curse him, then hug him. It was very weird to watch."

"Yes, it's a pretty messed-up place," Candy sighed, "but it's home."

"How often do you return?"

"About once a year, a year and a half. A friend of mine just got his left leg sawed off, right up to his buttocks, so I'm going home to take care of him."

"Wow, you're a great friend!"

"I've known him since I was fifteen. He messed up his leg because he was trying to clean it with bleach."

"Clean it with bleach?!"

"I'm sure he was drunk. He has diabetes. It's a huge problem in Wolf Point. Before she died, my mom also got one of her legs sawed off."

And so on and on it went, a litany of horrors. Her daughter, Sky, is a meth and heroin junkie who for years endured an abusive boyfriend who beat and spat on her face, almost daily, "and big, globby spits too." One of Sky's four children is in a foster home, while another has been adopted by an aunt. Candy's own boyfriend jumped onto the back of her truck. Enraged, he banged on her rear window as she sped away, but suddenly, the banging stopped, and Candy thought the man had merely exhausted himself and not fallen off, his spinal cord snapped. "I haven't been with a man since he died in 2009. I moved to Oregon. I used to cry all the time, I was a crybaby, so they finally had to put me on medications, but now I don't feel anything. At my mom's funeral last year, I didn't even cry, and that's not right."

So what does this all mean, and how has it gotten to this? In the nineteen century, the Sioux could amass hundreds, sometimes even thousands, of warriors to fight the US Army, and they kicked Uncle Sam's treacherous ass several times, with the most humiliating the butchering of vain and foolhardy Custer and over three hundred of his troops. Led by Red Cloud, Crazy Horse and Sitting Bull, the Sioux was a tribe to be feared, but now, on reservations from Pine Ridge to Fort Peck, where Wolf Point is located, they are a travesty of what they used to be, mired as they are in misery and aimlessness.

After the Indian has been killed, only an addicted and defeated American has emerged, but this is hardly the final chapter, for as the US itself becomes broken, the red man's resilience, resourcefulness, probity, simplicity and toughness will resurface to help lead us all out of this glammed-up farce. That is, if they don't decide to settle some old scores.

Writing in 1782, Ben Franklin observed, "The Indian Men when young are Hunters and Warriors; when old, Counsellors; for all their Government is by Counsel of the Sages; there is no Force, there are no Prisons, no Officers to compel Obedience, or inflict Punishment.— Hence they generally study Oratory; the best Speaker having the most Influence ... Having few artificial Wants, they have abundance of Leisure for Improvement by Conversation. Our laborious Manner of Life compar'd with theirs, they esteem slavish & base; and the Learning on which we value ourselves, they regard as frivolous & useless."

I don't know about you, but it sounds infinitely saner than what we have now, and it's not like we aren't heading in that direction anyway as we power down. Of course, many will shake, scream and leak from all orifices as they withdraw from the all-American buffet of Rush Limbaugh, Jon Stewart, Robin Thicke, Miley Cyrus and R. Kelly, a man who once filmed himself pissing into an underage girl's mouth.

TRI-CITIES' DIRT

7-31-14—Though this may sound like a joke, it's certainly no joke, for I'm not a joking type: When I came to the US in 1975, the very first American song I learned was "Old MacDonald Had a Farm." Though I could not properly pronounce any of the words, and understood only half of them, at most, I sang along with all the other kids in Miss Dogen's class at McKinley Elementary in Tacoma, Washington. To this day, I remember one kid cracking up at me, and if I should ever see his laughing face again, I'm sure I'll recognize it even after many decades. I'll confront my adversary, "Hey, man, it wasn't very cool of you to laugh at me, like, a century ago!" Anyway, as I was swaying back and forth and mouthing along, "And on that farm he had a cow, E-I-E-I-O," I was thinking in Vietnamese, "Cute, the natives here are peasants at heart, for they love to sing stupid songs about cows," but I was wrong, wrong, wrong, of course. It's remarkable, and risky too, that only 2 percent of this nation's people produce food for the rest, and doing any sort of farmwork is about the last thing most Americans want to do.

With more reliance on machines, fewer farmhands are needed, but the remaining ones are paid like raw fertilizer. According to the 2002 National Agricultural Workers Survey, the latest available, a farm worker makes just $6.84 an hour, if paid by the hour, or $8.27 an hour, if paid by the piece (and converted to hourly). Since most Americans won't bend over and sweat bullets under a hellish sun for such chump change, 78 percent of our crop workers are foreign-born, with over half of them illegal immigrants. A solution seems obvious. We can stanch our influx of foreigners, since this will force wages to be raised high enough to attract fat-assed Americans, like me, you and our in-laws, into picking strawberries, apples and melons . . . "No way, Jose," sayeth Old MacDonald, "for this will jack up my prices and make me so uncompetitive, I won't be able to export my crops or even sell domestically, for Americans will prefer to buy imported veggies and fruits, E-I-E-I-O!"

True-blue Americans are also averse to farmwork since it's seen as a step backward. For destitute immigrants, however, just making it into this country is progress, and even if they can't stand toiling in the fields, at least they can view it as a stepping-stone to something better. In any case, the ideal trajectory is to move from the farm to suburb or city, not the other way around, and since this is a worldwide phenomenon, there's a global disdain of rural people, for they're called hicks and bumpkins in every language. We feel a twisted pride at being totally amputated from nature, and, worshipping the city, we're even conditioned to rank ourselves according to its size. "My city is way bigger than yours!" Ah, but which will last longer, city or country?

Ruminating over these thoughts, I arrived in Pasco, Washington, and it was comforting to return to this state, for though I only stayed there a year, it was my first American home. Before I got off the train, though, I was able to corner an actual farmer, a man in his late forties. Sitting in the lounge car, I asked him some basic questions as we hurled past Ritzville, then Connell, "Is there a bias against white laborers? I mean, if a white guy and a Mexican guy shows up, who would you hire?"

"You can't really put it like that, because I work with labor contractors. I don't hire individual laborers."

"What I mean is, Is there a general perception that Mexican guys just work harder?"

"It doesn't matter because white guys don't show up! You don't have to turn down people who don't show up!"

"Oh, c'mon, man, there must be some white guys who show up. In your estimation, what is the percentage of whites among farm laborers."

"One percent!"

"Oh, no way! Only one percent?!"

"Well, maybe a little bit more, but not much more. I see Mexicans and other Latinos, but also some Asians. Japanese, Chinese, I really can't tell the difference."

"Filipinos?"

"Yeah, some Filipinos." Then, "Nowadays, a farmer's profit margin is so slim, with fuel cost going up, plus fertilizers and pesticides, everything going up, so if I don't plan very carefully, I may even lose money! It's hard to find good workers, so the labor contractors have us by the balls. If he's fast, a worker can easily make $100 a day."

"Very fast?"

"Yes, very fast, but on the other hand, you have people who are paid by the hour who are very slow! Getting back to what you were saying about white workers, I think it would be a good idea to allow kids to work, like in the old days, so they can be introduced to this kind of labor."

"When I was thirteen, I picked strawberries. This was in Salem, Oregon." An old school bus picked us up. It was mostly a kid thing and entirely legal. Among the teens and even preteens were a few Asian adults.

"Did you like it?"

"I didn't do it for long, but I actually did. I only made, like, seven bucks a day, but I was very proud of it. Back then, a bar of chocolate was only 20 cents, I think."

"When I was eight, I already knew how to drive a tractor. My legs were so short that each time I had to shift gears, my entire body would slip down and I couldn't even see above the steering wheel." He laughed. "When you let kids work, they mature quicker, but the state has to get into everything. They like to stick their nose into everyone's business!"

When I was thirteen, I also tried to sell made-to-order song compilations, as recorded off a cheap radio onto a cheapo cassette. If you gave me a list of, say, "Love Will Keep Us Together," "Disco Duck" and "Why

Can't We Be Friends," etc., I would wait until those exact songs came on the radio, at which point I would have to push Play and Record immediately, for if too much of a song is cut off, you wouldn't pay me, would you? Though I only charged 5 cents per tune, I only managed to sell a single cassette, for the kid's dad promptly told him to stop patronizing this copyright-violating criminal. I don't think he would have, anyway, since my sound quality was clearly felonious. I'm recalling this episode primarily to show that poor immigrants and other destitute people often come up with the weirdest ideas to make money, from the ingenious to the farcical. In an overly regulated society, however, this natural drive is often stamped out, and at a very early age at that. We're bred to be cogs.

I got off the train, entered the station and walked past a couple of Mexican cowboys. Sitting by their sparse luggage, they were waiting for the Nueva Estrella bus to Los Angeles. After a ten-minute walk, I saw the first sign of downtown, the Templo Ejército de Salvación, with some guy sitting under a nearby tree. Hunched over, a large and slovenly woman was patiently picking up a bunch of something from the sidewalk. I doubt they were cigarette butts, for there couldn't have been that many to harvest. Against a slatted chain-link fence, a handful of ragged men rested on the sidewalk.

Things spruced up in downtown proper, and I walked past Manualidades Carlitos, Carniceria La Barata, La Princesa Family Clothing/Ropa Familiar, La Estrella Muebleria, Mi Casa Muebleria, Viera's Bakery and Joyería Esmeralda, etc. On many stores, about the only English was the "OPEN" sign. Since even the worst beer on Amtrak was $5.25, I had been a teetotaler for a day and a half, so I had no need for any *carnicería* or *agencia de viajes*, but in looking for a cheap beer oasis, I somehow managed to miss the charmingly named Library Tavern, which I'd only spot on my way out. I did stumble onto a very festive farmer's market, with kids running around and folk music from a guitar-strumming duo called Winters & Skalstad.

Needing a cheap hotel, I had booked an out-of-the-way one in Kennewick, across the Columbia River. I asked a Hispanic man to point me to a bridge, but he said he had just gotten into town the day before, so had no idea. A second Hispanic man gave me directions in Spanish. The handsome suspension bridge was bookended by three homeless people, with a couple sleeping on the grass next to a shopping cart on the Pasco side. In Kennewick, a white-bearded man in a dirty denim jacket slumbered on a rustic lumber bench outside the Veterans Memorial. Next to him was a raw and irregular wooden cane.

Stepping onto the bridge, I encountered a frank warning, "NO JUMPING OFF BRIDGE / $250 FINE." Since it's only forty-eight feet above water, I'm not sure if you'd meet the devil by leaping from it, but just to be on the safe side, I'd counsel that you securely attach to one of your big toes a Ziploc-bagged money order for $250, exact, just so you can square your account with the government post mortem.

I've crossed from Juarez, Mexico into El Paso, Texas, but the shift from Pasco to Kennewick may be even more abrupt, for only in the second case does Spanish disappear almost entirely.

With its endless strip malls, much of Kennewick is rather nondescript, but it does have a dignified historic downtown. After an excellent lunch in Andy's, a diner where older folks can cheerfully annoy the Mexican waitresses with long winded tales about their grandkids or great-grandkids, I decided to walk into Parkade, and it was there that I met Jack.

Behind the bar, colorful gambling tickets were as prominently displayed as liquor bottles, and I noticed a couple with sexually suggestive names, Lick It and Booty Call. To pick your pocket, they must appeal to the playful infant inside you. Hence, the bright colors and cartoon figures. It's all a game, you see. Sex also fits into this lure since it is, at bottom, nakedly infantile, especially in its fantasy form. Let's play! Bare, even a senior citizen is just a child, and will even act like one. Will you be a good girl?

The "Game of the Day" was Ale House Rock, and Katie, the bartender, would shake the plexiglass box vigorously, convulsing her own small frame, before pulling out a ticket. Though this couldn't have improved the odds one whit, it showed that Katie was trying hard to land you a winning combination. Handing her a stiff Lincoln, a man in a cutoff plaid shirt got five bright tickets to scratch.

Ah, it's great to be back in Washington State, for everywhere I looked, I could see the colors and logos of my favorite corporate-owned teams: Mariners, Seahawks and the carpetbagged Sonics! Before first pitch, soldiers marched onto the diamond and stood stiffly as the singer belted, "Rockets' red glare, the bombs bursting in air." Then followed a well-staged reunion of a small boy with his soldier father, returning from his imperial posting in Afghanistan. "That's just great," the TV announcer gushed. The Mariners Moose did his little jig.

OK, let's just meet Jack already! With his golf shirt, slacks, easy manner and gray, thinning hair, Jack came off as a well-situated man near retirement, "I've been in this area my whole life. I haven't even traveled. My wife doesn't like it. I went to a friend's funeral this morning, though, and it got me thinking. This fellow, I knew him for over forty years. He was always in great shape, played golf, played tennis, didn't even have a beer belly, then suddenly, he dropped dead! It got me thinking. Maybe I should enjoy myself a little."

"What are you waiting for, then? You should take a little trip! Just go!"

"Maybe I should. I've worked my whole life. Five years ago, I retired, but that didn't even last a year. I got so bored, I went right back to work!"

"What do you do?"

"I'm an inspector. I inspect construction sites."

"Well, I'm a writer. This is my first time in Kennewick. I just got off the train this afternoon."

"I can't say there's a whole lot to see around here. Pasco, where the train station is, has a lot of Mexicans, so that's a bit different, but Kennewick and Richland are just houses, with a few bars like this."

"Has Pasco always been Mexican?"

"Ever since I was a kid, there were Mexicans there, but now there are more. Way back then, there were many Asian farmers, you know."

"Japanese?"

"Yeah, mostly Japanese, but also Filipinos. The Japanese were truck farmers. The Fujimotos had a lot of kids. I went to school with a couple of them."

Truck farming is a single family cultivating a modest plot of land and selling what they produce locally. Though this practice has been pushed to nearly extinction by agribusiness, its idyllic image is often used by agribusiness itself to pimp everything from gooey, pseudo-health-food concoctions to reconstituted chicken. The decline of truck farming has resulted in the loss of financial autonomy for countless American families. It's hard to imagine what a few acres used to mean. From the 1908 Yearbook of the Department of Agriculture, "Where markets are good, the income is so large that a family can make a living on a very small area of land. In fact, 10 acres would be a large truck farm, and 2 or 3 acres properly managed, with good markets, will bring a fair living to an ordinary family." With his truck farm a dim memory, Old MacDonald has become super efficient at cranking out preternatural chalupas for Taco Bell, E-I-E-I-O!

With a new interest in healthy eating, truck farming is staging a comeback, and though we have a long way to go, it is the wave of the future, as globalism unravels thanks to higher fuel costs due to increasing scarcity and, most alarmingly, a rash of wars over remaining resources. Those who insist we're going through an energy revival must be passing methane between their ears each time they fill up. Five years ago, gas was just $2.45 a gallon, more than a buck less than today, and, ten years ago, $1.84.

On its last leg, globalism will continue to seek out the cheapest labor. Jack revealed, "Around here, they're now importing workers from Thailand."

"I've never heard of that! How many are they bringing in?"

"Hundreds!"

"So even the Mexican workers are not cheap enough!"

"Apparently not."

"How long do they stay?"

"That, I don't know, but I know there's a bunch in Yakima, picking apples."

Later, I'd discovered news stories about six hundred Thai workers being brought here in a human trafficking scheme concocted out of Beverly Hills by one Mordechai Orian, an Israeli citizen. In Thailand, peasants went into debt to pay recruiters up to $21,000, but once here, they weren't making $2,000 a month as promised, but much less, and sometimes nothing. Instead of three years of regular work, they were often furloughed without pay. Some lived in a shipping container. Some were beaten. Workers spoke of eating just bananas and even hunting birds with rubber band slings because they were so hungry.

Though the Department of Justice was notified of this case in 2003, they didn't prosecute until 2009, only to drop all criminal charges in 2012. Unbelievably, even guilty pleas were dismissed. (Though American justice is certainly not blind, Eric Holder should be dubbed Eric the Blind!) In the end, Orian, along with several guilty farms, were only slapped with fines, but let's not lose sight of the core problem here, which is your government's own human trafficking scheme, for why bring in foreign workers when so many Americans are out of work, underemployed or seriously underpaid? And please, don't feed me the cow patty about ruddy unemployment statistics, for those figures are as bogus as, say, anything that's barfed up daily by Washington, DC. If adequately paid, Americans will work on farms, so one solution is to supplement their wages, and this won't just yield economic but social benefits as well, for a people should know how to grow their own food.

Besides agriculture, the other big employer in the Tri-Cities area is the Hanford Nuclear Plant. For decades, it was the main provider of plutonium for America's nuclear bombs. Though mostly decommissioned, it still employs 11,000 people to monitor and somehow clean up the irradiated mess. I asked Jack if the locals were worried about living next to one of the most toxic sites ever.

"People don't really want to talk about it much. Too many of them must go there every day. There is a higher incidence of anencephaly around here, though, and everyone's aware of that."

"What is that?"

"That's when a baby is born with only half a brain, or no brain at all!"

"So it's just a risk of living here!"

"The odds are still pretty low!"

To put bacon on the table, you must play Russian roulette with your newborn's brain, so to speak. Moving from such grimness, Jack and I talked about Lewis and Clark, Jack's love of buying old books, Armstrong Custer's virtue as a writer and, finally, the Kennewick Man, which is a 9,300-plus-year-old skeleton found in the shallows of the Columbia. Though local Indian tribes want him back for burial, some scientists are contending that this man was possibly Caucasian, and thus not one of their ancestors, and it is imperative that his remains be made available for further studies. If he is indeed Caucasian, then his people did not walk across the Bering Strait from Asia.

When talking about any spot on earth, the word "native" is always relative, for no one has sprung from the ground anywhere. Innumerable tribes have washed over this grassy carpet, and most have disappeared without a trace. We've fought and slaughtered each other unendingly to claim this or that knoll, if only for a moment. Though only a fool would think of any place name as final, it's positively goofy to place quotation marks around, say, "Canada" or "British Columbia," for, using that logic, you'd need to do that with each place on earth, and even for the earth itself, for who's to say that the realm we inhabit, in its totality, shouldn't be called "heaven," "mother of mothers," "eternal battleground," "sometimes shaking," "convenient footrest" or "great big ball of shit"? Even a concept like "country" can be interpreted differently, for the Vietnamese, for example, don't say "I come from this country," but "I come from this water." Water is country in Vietnamese. Though born in Vietnam water, I now live in a water called America. Oh my, how rapidly has this water gone downhill! The water has gone berserk. Seriously, though, is our water up the septic creek without an Aqua-Bound paddle? Like you, I fear where this water is going.

My most enjoyable conversation with Jack at the bar was continuously tinted, mocked, challenged or perverted by an unending stream of background music. As we discussed the mysterious Kennewick Man, Rage Against the Machine repeatedly screamed in our ears, "Fuck you, I won't do what you tell me!" In moments like this, I sincerely wish I had lived 9,000 years ago. It was about time to go, in any case, for neither one of us was too sharp by this point. Out of the blue, Jack asked, "What do you think of lesbians?"

I wasn't sure what he meant, but I answered, "I don't know. I like them."

"That's good because there's one standing right next to you!" Jack gave me a conspiratorial smile. "And she's pretty too!" Jack then jumped off his stool to go to the bathroom. It really was time to go.

Walking two miles to my hotel, I spotted a garage and driveway turned into an old-timey gas station. It was most lovingly erected, this nostalgic shrine to gasoline! Then at a print shop, there were two cartoon soldiers with "Bring Them Home Safe" painted onto its plate glass window. Stripped of weapons, they were presented as chubby toddlers with button noses, huge eyes and smiling, lipless mouths. In the eyes of the home folks, our expensively trained killers are just helpless babes. Downtown, there's also a small ceramic elf with a sign, "SUPPORT OUR TROOPS."

The next day, I returned to Parkade hoping to see Jack again, but there was no one there but an aloof barkeep, so after an uncomfortable pint, I crossed the street and entered Players, which from a distance I had mis-read as Prayers. What is this, a born-again bar? It was Sunday. Inside, I quickly made the acquaintance of Pablo, a natural ham, "I have the smallest dick in the world, but women love me, because I know how to listen."

And to prove it, he showed me three beat-up cell phones, "Each phone is for a different girlfriend." I still don't get it. He also had two lollipops in his pants pocket, so the man must suck.

Born in Mexico, Pablo has been in the Tri-Cities area since he was three, so he's basically a native. In 1966, Pablo was sent to Vietnam, and though he signed up for an extra tour, he insisted to me he never shot anybody, "Everyone has a mother. I love human life! I don't want anyone's mother to cry. I'd rather be shot at than to shoot anyone! I didn't kill nobody."

"Where were you stationed in Vietnam?"

"I don't remember. I don't want to remember! When I came home, my father asked me about Vietnam, and I said, 'It has become a part of me!' Every place you go becomes a part of you, so Vietnam has become a part of me. It's inside me!"

A Kennewick man, Pablo avoids the Mexican taverns in Pasco, "My own people don't like me! I'm comfortable here, in this bar and across the street. Players used to be off-limits to nonwhites, though. If you came in here ten years ago, they'd have killed you!"

Sitting one stool over, a white patron corrected him, "Fifteen years ago."

"OK, so fifteen years ago, they would have killed you!"

Ah, the crudities of ethnic affiliations! Kennewick and Richland were historically sundown towns, which means that all blacks and browns had to get out by dusk, and even in Pasco, blacks were mostly confined to East Pasco, across the railroad tracks. Pasco's status as the Tri-Cities' enclave for all lower-tiered residents continues to this day, for the area's two homeless shelters are in Pasco.

Pablo also told me he was an oil painter, and that he could conjure up, from memory alone, the perfect likeness of my unstable mug. Beat it, Jean-Auguste-Dominique Ingres and all the rest! Lest you think Pablo is all arts and humanities, he also showed me his crude side when he went after the bartender, "Hey, Lisa, when are you going to take me home?"

"You'll never get me drunk enough."

"She's thinking about it," he winked at me. "It will happen sooner or later."

"You better stop thinking about it," Lisa said, "because it will never happen."

"Hey, I'm not into red-headed women!"

"My hair is not red."

I thought it was odd, Pablo's sudden nastiness, but he went even further, "I'm not into bowlegged women!"

"Hey, I ride horses," Lisa said matter-of-factly.

"I don't care! I'm not into bowlegged women!"

Trying to shift the mood, I interjected, "Pablo's infatuated!"

"He'll get over it," Lisa calmly said.

Before Pablo left, he ticked off for me a list that's all too common among men, "I've been with a German, a Bosnian, a Russian, many white women, one Mexican but never an Oriental woman, a Vietnamese woman."

Sixty-two-year-old Pablo's trophy-hunting expedition can't last much longer, for it doesn't matter if his mind will age or not, his carcass will be stricken down before he knows it. Already, every other front teeth is missing, with the remaining barely anchored in his eroding gums. No orange juice guzzler, this pirate look-alike, although with a black cowboy hat instead of a tricorne. Scurvy or no, Pablo will continue to forge ahead for there's no time to lose!

Though I spent two nights in the Tri-Cities area, I only booked a hotel room for a single night. As my train was scheduled to leave very early in the morning, I decided to save a hundred bucks and sleep at the station, and if this wasn't possible, I could easily curl up outside somewhere. I had scoped out a few likely spots and it was warm. I've slept behind a bush, outside a school gym, under a truck and, in El Cerrito, California, on someone's porch swing. Yes, the last one is very bad, and I sincerely apologize, but it was irresistible, that super comfortable porch swing, with a cute canopy, even, so thank you, sir or ma'am, for your involuntary hospitality! Again, I apologize. Once I slept under the veranda of a San Antonio restaurant. Thanks to an hours-long thunderstorm, the temperature plummeted, so I had to wrap several undershirts around my head to keep it warm. That obviously sucked.

This time, though, there would be no discomfort whatsoever, for the Amtrak employee was kind enough to let me stay inside as he locked up for the night. He even warned me against locking myself out should I decide to step outside. Also, sleeping at the station allowed me to hit downtown Pasco at the crack of dawn, and so I was in Viera's Bakery before 5 a.m., to find the place already hopping with farm laborers coming in to grab donuts the size of a baby's head, and other enormous pastries. Since everyone's in a hurry, there was no need for any tong etiquette. People loaded up their sugary kickstarters on plastic trays, paid, then marched out.

Since my train was way late, I had extra time to wander, and thus I ran into a sixty-five-year-old man, waiting alone at a bus stop. With his deeply wrinkled face and missing teeth, he looked at least a decade older than sixty-three-year-old Jack. He had on a blue hoodie and his denim jacket looked hard, it was so new. Born in Pasco, he went into the Army "to see the world" and got as far as New York. "I passed through Philadelphia, but I didn't see much of it. I've also been to Denver and I worked in Phoenix for ten years. Five years ago, I moved to Boise, Idaho. I'm in town to see my nieces and nephews. My wife died three years ago. Like many people in my family, she died of diabetes. All of my brothers and sisters are also dead. I'm the only one left. I have a brother who died of diabetes when he was only thirty-five."

As he was talking, I could see a chubby fellow waddling by with a gallon bottle of orange soda. He was headed for the Thunderbird, a motel with a cheap weekly rate. As Pasco's most troublesome spot, it's visited daily by the cops. Grinning, I actually blurted, "It looks like that guy is going to die of diabetes too!"

Turning around to look, the old fellow chuckled ever so briefly, "You're probably right."

When I asked about jobs in Pasco, he said, "It's potato packing season, so you shouldn't have a problem getting a job here. You can sort potatoes or cut them into french fries. They'll pay you nine or ten bucks an hour. That's more than Boise, where they only pay about seven an hour. The cost of living is much cheaper there, though."

Rudely terminating our chat, the 65 bus came, so there went another person I'd never see again, though his visage will stay with me forever thanks to photography. In fact, he's closer to me now than much of my family. Promiscuous, the photograph is cheap, but these fading, badly shot, often kitschy and disposable images are all that will remain of us when our bones are tucked into the ground, to be dug up by whomever, whenever. No matter how dastardly or noble, words and deeds won't hold in flitting minds that are often addled by bullshit, but calcium approaches immortality. Sort of. When the Kennewick Man closed his eyes nearly 10,000 years ago, he couldn't have known his frame would one day fascinate, inspire and disrupt. For many whites, the idea that whites have thrived on this continent millennia before Columbus establishes that whites are also "Natives" here, which means that American Indians have no intrinsic claim to this vast territory, and later-arriving whites were just coming over to join their long-lost relatives, so to speak, and were not genocidal invaders.

Again, this native argument is inherently flawed, since no one is intrinsic to any place. This entire earth, mother of mothers, provisional heaven or absolute hell, has been irrigated with blood from continual dispute, and if you've been granted a reprieve from such stark violence, don't forget that it's all too pedestrian to be bombed or burned from your cozy hovel, and to witness the map of your nation go up in flames. Just ask the Libyans, Iraqis or Ukrainians, or the so-called Americans not too long from now, if events continue on their current trajectory. A tireless sower of mayhem and always looking for a fight, the butcher will be butchered, and to save our own skin, each of us will have to settle on a cleaner identity.

SQUIRRELLY PORTLAND

8-7-14—Our train was hugging the Columbia River. Sitting in the lounge car, a father looked at that huge, snaking ribbon of silvery water and said to his young son, "I'm just jonesing to go fishing. That's the first thing we're going to do when we get home!" Then, "That Colts shirt really looks great on you, Jack!"

Later, he explained to a stranger, "We're originally from Portland, but it just got too squirrelly for me. I'm a traditional guy, I like to keep things simple, so I just had to get out of there."

Speaking about his wife, the man said, "My wife is a people person, but I'm a bit on the crunchy side."

About seven years old, Jack had been silent all this time as his dad chattered, but now he interjected, "You mean crusty! You're crusty, Dad, not crunchy."

Everyone who was within earshot cracked up, and of course the kid was right, for the opposite of being gregarious is being crusty or cranky, and not a granola bar-munching, tree-hugging pot smoker who dwells in the Hawthorne District of squirrelly Portland. Crunchy, the man certainly wasn't, and not crusty either, for he was positively bubbly sitting across from his son as Oregon and Washington sped by outside the windows.

East of Davenport, Iowa, you might be slapped with a fine if you dare to use "squirrelly" in any sentence, and "crunchy" is too self-consciously cute and misleading to be of much use to anyone who's not squirrelly. No regional idiom, it's just a subcultural burp that, hopefully, won't linger too much longer. In any case, how crunchy is Portland really?

All over this country, there are places of refuge, towns and cities where people go to escape prevailing mores and tastes. Some of these oases are merely regional. If you're a Montana free jazz musician, poet, vegan activist blogger, transsexual hipster flaneur, nude yogic speller of inappropriate portmanteaus or just a plain, generic weirdo, you might gravitate towards Missoula. If you're in eastern North Carolina, Carrboro offers kindred spirits. Nationally, San Francisco and Lower Manhattan were for many decades magnets for American misfits of all types, but their exorbitant rents have sealed them off to the vast majority of us, provided we don't care to sleep on cardboard.

Though hardly cheap, lesser cities like Austin and Portland have therefore emerged to welcome artistic, political and, most lucratively, lifestyle refugees from the rest of America. "KEEP AUSTIN WEIRD" is the unofficial civic slogan for one, and, what else, "KEEP PORTLAND WEIRD" for the other. Who said that crunchy and squirrelly types are more original than middle America? Just because they're into, say, biodegradable earplug piercings or butt plugs made from recycled F-16 tires does not mean they're not, essentially, copycats and clones.

In a consumerist culture, people rebel by buying a different brand, and instead of staging a real rebellion, which requires secret planning and stealthy strikes, American pseudo-radicals are constantly fingering themselves as soon as they hit the sidewalk. It's a fashion thing. In this illusionistic and narcissistic society, it's imperative that you look a certain way if you want be slotted into one of the socially acceptable subgroups. It's all cosplay, all the time, for even the nerd look has been commodified and imbued with irony.

Before my recent trip to Portland, I hadn't been there in over five years. In late 2008, I came up from California, and between Klamath Falls and Eugene, I chatted with an older man, Bob, who had worked for thirty-one years in a sawmill in Florence, on the Oregon Coast.

"The spotted owl fuss put me out of work," he lamented. "These environmentalists live on the East Coast, never been out here, so they don't know how much forest we have. Just look for yourself," he indicated with a nod. Sitting in the lounge car, we stared at the blond fields, viridian evergreens and snow-tipped mountains. Canada geese flecked a small patch of sky. The winding lake seemed short of water. Even at 4,000 feet in November, there was no snow.

"You can cut them responsibly, and they'll grow back," he continued. "Many old-growth trees are already rotted in the center, so a storm would knock them all down anyway. Wasted." To illustrate, Bob drilled his index finger vigorously into his left palm. "Since our logging industry is mostly dead, we have to buy lumber from overseas, from people who really don't give a hoot about the environment."

With the sawmill silent by the river, Bob got hired by Safeway, the supermarket, but business was slowing, the town depressed, and what's worse, many people would rather drive sixty miles to shop at Walmart. The fishing industry was also dead. Without logging and fishing, Florence had opened a retirement home, a golf course and a casino in Hail Mary bids to revive its economy.

At sixty, Bob had two years of mortgage to deal with. "I just hope Safeway doesn't go bankrupt. At my age, it will be hard to get hired again. I don't want to move to the city to find another job. They might just turn me into a wafer, you know, a cracker," Bob chuckled. "Do you know that Charlton Heston film, *Soylent Green*?"

"No. What is it about?"

"It's a sci-fi where old people are turned into a cracker. They become food."

"That's pretty funny!"

"Yes, it is, and that'll be me in a few years."

"Jonathan Swift suggested that Irish babies at the age of one should be eaten," I countered. "Beyond one year old it's not cost-efficient to raise them. Also, that's the best age for the most tender meat, according to Swift."

"What's his name?"

"Jonathan Swift, Irish guy."

"And he was joking?"

"I think so."

Not to be outdone, Bob related, "During the Siege of Leningrad, some people ate their children."

"After they were dead?"

"No, they killed them and ate them. Some also sliced chunks from their own buttocks."

"But," I protested, "the lost blood! There's no net gain!"

"Maybe not, but when you're desperate, you'll eat your own ass!"

Rolling into Union Station this time, I was wondering if the donut hole I was munching on was actually Bob, or maybe he had lucked into a winning Classic Gold scratch ticket, and was just kicking it back in his paid-off home.

With numerous small parks, several with man-made waterfalls, Portland has a greener and more attractive downtown than most American cities, and with its many upscale shops and eateries, it also looks pretty affluent. It has extensive bike lanes, walking paths removed from motorized traffic and an excellent light rail system, so it's easy to get around. Moreover, the streets aren't overly wide, so they aren't stressful to cross and car noises don't aggravate.

From 1990 to 2010, Portland's population grew by 33 percent, and it's still spiking up, so clearly, this city's allures are recognized by plenty of people, including an army of homeless. Ubiquitous downtown, they lie in a row on Burnside Street in Chinatown, sprawl under the Steel Bridge, sleep in and around Chapman Square. On many blocks, they sit and beg, and in every park, they hang out. Each dawn, mountain-bike-riding cops rouse the homeless from hundreds of commercial doorways, so the day's commerce can commence. By the airport, a tent city called Dignity Village has existed since late 2000.

Many of the homeless here are younger than thirty-five, and whether they're gutter punks, deadheads, juggalos, Rainbow Family members or nothing specific, many have come to view being homeless as a lifestyle in itself, and not a temporary predicament. Though they welcome a couch or hotel room every now and then, their long-term aim is not to gain employment and permanent shelter, but to keep from doing so for as long as possible. Many of them were in the Occupy camps and this is hardly a surprise since their non-goals, if you will, echo the non-demands of that failed movement. Instead of fighting back, American rebels not only embrace their disenfranchisement, but consider this defeat a victory. Now as then, many of them occupy city parks, while their overlords sneer down at them from surrounding bank towers.

On the edge of Chapman Square, I saw a young man writing with yellow chalk on the paved walkway:

Environmental / geopolitical / spiritual trends are increasing the importance of the task of restructuring / replacing / recycling our political / economic institutions. "Occupations" or "humanity hubs" can help us with this task by peacefully creating spaces for political / economic experimentation.

Above the northeast corner of this statement, he had written in turquoise chalk:

LOOK DOWN
I LOVE YOU.

No older than twenty-five, he had been homeless for a couple of years, he said, "I get by on food stamps, and I couch-surf. I don't really use money anymore."

"How long will you go on like this?"

"I don't know."

"You're young, so it's easy to tough it like this, but what if you get older? What if you get sick?"

"I don't know. I'll deal with it when I get there."

"You know, the Occupy movement made homelessness a model. That's what they were doing. They became symbolically and publicly homeless, but why should we occupy a park when they get to occupy everything else?! If all we're after are these parks, if we just want to become bums, then they're perfectly happy with that. We're not threatening them at all! We should threaten them, man! We shouldn't retreat into these parks. We should threaten them where they are!"

He smiled, didn't say anything and seemed anxious to get back to his chalk manifesto, so I shut down my rant and moved on. Let's not forget that *Time* magazine had "The Protester" as its 2011 Person of the Year, so if the mainstream media can chuckle and affectionately muss up your dreadlocks like that, it means you're no threat to the status quo. I know a middle-aged Wall Street denizen who used to drop by Zuccotti Park on his lunch breaks to hang out with the many cute protesters. It was almost as exciting as going to a go-go bar. Still gorging on Wall Street, he's fond of calling himself an "Occupy Wall Street veteran."

Walking south from Chapman Square, I stopped at Keller Fountain Park and sat next to a homeless man about my age, that is, fifty. Though he wore glasses, one lens was missing while the other was entirely wrapped, several times, with black electrical tape so that it bulged out like a vinyl tumor. He had a large plastic container of what looked like cooked macaroni, but its skimpy coating of tomato sauce had turned gray. With a plastic spoon he ate the sour-smelling dish. Though the high that day was 85°F, he had on several layers of grimy clothes, for it was just more convenient to wear everything he owned. What skin he showed on his arms and legs was splotched with reddened lesions in various degrees of freshness, crimson scabs, tiny eruptions of pus, now hardened, and bloody scratch marks. Even when he's caught in the rain, I doubt that much water can reach his skin beneath its permanent layer of greasy dirt.

Since the dude didn't feel like chatting, I moseyed on and ran into a shirtless young man with a 750ml bottle of Aristocrat gin. As he marched down the street, he raved and glared at passersby, then, still agitated, sat down on the curb for a few seconds, only to get up to splash on the sidewalk all of his remaining liquor, a good half bottle. That's roughly four bucks, I quickly calculated with genuine regret. Needless to say, he wasn't in a conversational mood.

Ah, and now, finally, we come to Bonnie, a sweet and most candid woman sixty-one years old. Though women on the streets tend to have more stuff than men, Bonnie had absolutely nothing beyond her orange sneakers, blue and white strap dress, necklace, ring and dirty pink jacket. As I walked by, she yelled, "Mister, can I please use your phone for a moment?"

"Sure."

She asked me to dial her boyfriend and mother several times, but no one answered. Bonnie left a message for her man, "Where are you? Are you mad at me?"

"Let's call him back later," I suggested. In the meantime, Bonnie told me her life story: She was born in Washougal, Washington, which is just northeast of Portland, "We're famous for our toilet paper. There's a paper mill in Camas. I worked there."

"What else have you done?"

"I was a makeup artist for Revlon. I modeled for this girl. She's an artist. I used to be so beautiful! You should have seen me! I was a cook. I've done just about everything."

"Were you a good cook?"

"Yeah. When I felt like it!" We both laughed. "For a year, I did that. I went from one job to the next. I was working sixteen hours a day, with an hour break in the middle. Then I went to college, for a while. I studied secretarial science. I worked four jobs while I was in college."

"You had no time to study."

"Yeah, I did. I got every single question on all my final tests perfect, because I had a baby and I wanted to take good care of her. My second husband hit her, and I didn't want to have a husband no more. He might hit me. I wanted to have a good job so I could take care of her."

"How many kids do you have?"

"Just two, but I also had three miscarriages and seven abortions."

"Seven abortions?! Some people die after just three or four."

"I know. My first one was the worst. My fever was up to 104 something. They hadn't gotten all the contents out of me, so I had to go into the hospital again."

"How old were you?"

"Twenty-eight."

"And when was your last abortion?"

"I'm not sure, but I was in my thirties. You know, what it is is I get pregnant real easy. I just kept getting pregnant. Once a woman gets pregnant, then her body is more prone to get pregnant again and again." Bonnie giggled.

"And three miscarriages?"

"Those came after the abortions."

"And your two kids, where are they now?"

"My son is in the Army, in Texas, and my daughter's in Seattle. She orders parts for Boeing. She's doing really well. My daughter just went to Italy with her husband."

"She can't help you out?"

"No, I'm too proud to go up there and beg."

"And your parents?"

"My mom is in Vancouver. My dad killed himself. My younger brother, too. He died just a year ago. The anniversary is coming up. I feel awful about it. If I had reached out to him more, maybe he wouldn't have died. My brother was just fifty-one when he hanged himself. He was a mechanic for the railroad, but he had a drinking problem, so they fired him, then his wife left. My father also worked for the railroad, but he was an engineer. My father was seventy when he shot himself."

"Why don't you go stay with your mom if she's in Vancouver? You know, just walk across that river?"

"She's loaded, too, but I can't rest if I go there. She's a go-getter. She always wants to do stuff so she won't leave me alone to just rest, and I can't detox if I'm around her. I have a drinking problem, you know."

"How often do you drink?"

"Every eleven or twelve days."

"Oh, that's not bad at all. You don't have a drinking problem!"

"Yes I do, because every time I drink, I get sick, and I need medication to come out of it. I've been to detox a bunch of times. I've been stripped naked and thrown onto the concrete floor."

"So you do have a drinking problem!"

"Yes, I do!" We both laughed. "But I have more problems than that. I'm also bipolar, and I have post-traumatic stress. Noises bother me. That's why I have to put these into my ears." As Bonnie showed me two skin-colored, molar-sized pieces of foam, I was surprised that she had had them on all this time. To stand life, Bonnie needs to have it muffled. "I was beat up a lot. My dad used to beat me real hard when I was a little girl. He beat me all the time. Messed me up."

"How many siblings do you have, Bonnie?"

"I have three brothers and two sisters. I'm the oldest. I took care of them."

"So you're like their mom?"

"Yes."

With her disabilities, Bonnie was receiving $1,500 a month in benefits, so that should have been enough had she been frugal, but she ended up homeless anyway. As someone with an alcohol problem and seven abortions, careful planning is not her forte, obviously, and she is bipolar, after all. Also, this is a culture where the advertisements, songs, movies and TV shows are constantly glamorizing and sexualizing all sorts of impulsive behavior, so though Bonnie may appear much different from the younger homeless of Portland, they're basically the same. Stumbling from dead-end jobs or no jobs at all, they're alienated, often addicted and can't see beyond their next feel-good moment. Last winter, Bonnie slept outside, "Oh, it'd get so cold, so it doesn't matter how good your sleeping bag is, and then it'd start to rain, and all these men would try to rape you."

If you had seen Bonnie inside, say, a bingo hall or a Denny's, you might mistake her for a Norman Rockwell grandma, but if you talked to her at length, you'd hear her laughingly ejaculate, "I'm *fooooucked*!" Of course,

Norman Rockwell types all over the country are also *fooooucked*. Bob, too, might be *fooooucked*, and he's as wholesome looking as can be. At this very moment, he just might be eating his own ass, seasoned with a bit of ketchup stolen from the local McDonald's. Moreover, should he need to wipe his buttocks as he's feasting on it, he can get free toilet paper from Bonnie's hometown, for it's a tradition to toss free rolls to cheering onlookers during its annual parade.

In Portland, I also met Sam, a thirty-five-year-old unemployed metal fabricator, welder and boat painter. Born in Laos, Sam came to the US at two years old, has lived all over this country and is now homeless. When moving around, Sam pushes an old man's walker with all of his belongings strapped to it.

With Sam, I entered Ming Lounge, a grubby bar in Chinatown, and there I talked to Laquita, an unemployed woman in her late thirties who's planning on starting a business recycling tires. She'd done her homework and was convinced she would succeed. After losing her electrician job in Texas, Laquita came to Oregon to take advantage of its more generous welfare provisions, and with the state's help, she had moved into a new apartment. Half-Belizian, half-American black, she spoke of retiring in Belize someday.

Ming Lounge's bartender, Britney, was born in Morgantown, West Virginia. After getting her bachelor's degree in agribusiness, she moved to Philadelphia, then Portland. She loves Portland, she said. Her boyfriend is raking in the bucks selling rubber fetish wear and rubber and titanium jewelry. Ah, so there is still manufacturing left in America! On second thought, though, I'm sure these tongue rings, skin eyelets, hider plugs, collars, cuffs, open-grid double-strap halter bras and penetrable thongs are all made in China. It really is over.

Along with the visible decay that can be seen in cities and small towns alike, there is a widespread malaise afflicting the American spirit, and this is most acutely felt among the younger set. If they have gone to college, then they are most likely crippled with insane debt while stuck in a job that doesn't require their overpriced yet diluted education, acquired with bankster loans. To make ends meet, they're living in a crowded, shared apartment or at home with mom and dad, again. As for the professions, many are rotten with fraud, corruption or other immoralities, what a quaint word, so that to hold even the lowliest job in the military, police, government, banking, accounting, insurance, health care, media, advertising or the academy, etc., is to swim among crooks and liars, and it's all too easy to become a cynical and sinister asshole yourself. In an image-dominated society, public relations is everything, so the most crucial task, always, is to maintain a sexy or dignified appearance, and to hell with what happens behind the scenes. In a Camden tent city, I met a young man who had wanted to be a policeman, but after a few months on the job, he just had to quit, "You don't even know how corrupt it is."

Living in such a sick climate, it's no wonder there is pervasive disaffection. The Occupy movement started by focusing on Wall Street, and that's where Herman Melville placed Bartleby. For reasons never explained, Bartleby the Scrivener became increasingly noncooperative at his job, so that "I would prefer not to" became his stock answer to each command from his mild-mannered and tolerant boss. Bartleby became so good at saying no, he finally said no to life itself. Even in beautiful Portland, many people have become Bartlebys.

It's not all roses here. Per capita, Portlanders ingest more antidepressants than residents of any other American city. They also commit suicides at a much brisker rate than the national average. Last year alone, five people jumped off Vista Bridge, and in 1998, a homeless, heroin-addicted young couple hanged themselves from the Steel Bridge. For almost an hour, they dangled in full view of thousands of downtown office workers, motorists and train passengers. From the man's 13-page suicide note, "I think I've decided on an old-fashioned public hanging . . . The Steel Bridge shall be my gallows." Ah, squirrelly Portland! Sexy and hip, you're not shy about showing the world what you have, whether in your many strip joints or even in death.

MINING WISCONSIN

8-13-14—Before we start, I must admit that I didn't set foot in Wisconsin this time, but only saw it from the train as I crossed it going west, then east. (I had been to Madison and Milwaukee before.) This, then, is really a train Postcard, but the long-distance train is a community in itself. In fact, Americans seldom have such thorough conversations as when they're trapped on a long distance train. If only more of us could be confined that way, we would relate to each other a whole lot better, but such a wish also conjures up citizens being packed into boxcars as they're sent to hard labor, or much worse. How many Americans will cross this country without seeing any of it?

Ah, the ecology of the long-distance train! If Lewis and Clark were alive, they would freak out over the outlandish fauna to be discovered on the Empire Builder! Where else will you find a woman trying to eat some very badly made, meatless fried rice, only to give half of it to a stranger, "The plastic spoon is clean. I wiped it off real good with a paper napkin." Since she couldn't afford the $7.25 for chicken and rice at the Spokane station, she had asked for just rice, but then it tasted "like popcorn," she discovered with a grimace. The other lady couldn't afford anything at all, however. Hence the leftovers with a used spoon.

Or take a young man from Missoula who was trying to hit on a woman by giving her a cup of instant noodles, "Yes, you can have it! I just ate one myself. It's pretty good! Really, you can have it." Tall and lanky, he wore a gray baseball cap backwards, a Marines jacket and charcoal-colored thrift-store trousers. Like his face, everything he had on was worn and faded. After spending $4.50 on those two cups of MSG-flavored ramen, he was left with just $13.

Sitting in the lounge car, the woman of his fancy was with three friends, two of them male, and though they didn't seem all that interested in his plight, the Missoula man kept sharing, "By the time I get to Fargo, hopefully it'll be night, so I can sleep at the station. After that, I'll find a shelter and stay there a week, maybe a month. It won't be my first time in a shelter. A buddy was supposed to put me up, but after talking me into coming, he stopped answering the phone and even changed his friggin' number, but I figure sooner or later I'll run across him in Fargo. I'll bitch-slap him! I had a place in Missoula, but I gave that up, so he definitely has an ass-kicking coming for leaving me on the friggin' street. I've spent all my money on this train ride, and I won't go back to Missoula, because there's nothing for me in Missoula. In Fargo, I'll take any job I can get, dishwashing, janitorial . . . I can't lift anything heavy because I had a car accident. In 2006, I had a seizure behind the wheel and cracked my skull, broke my back and a bunch of other bones.

"I have this bad habit of being in the wrong place at the wrong time, I guess. Funniest thing is, I got married in Lake Tahoe, California, then woke up the next morning on an Indian rez outside Minden, Nevada. How the hell did that happen?! My wife, this Indian woman, must have poisoned me. Twice, I've been on dialysis. I was down to 99 pounds, and I used to weigh 200. I was twenty-two, she was forty-six, and she died at fifty-three. Suddenly, I was living on this Indian reservation. Yeah, I quit drinking when I woke up and married to that!

"You're lucky to have someplace to go after getting off this train. I thought I had a place! I'm all right, though, I have thirteen bucks. I'm not worried. That's enough for a pack of smokes and a meal, then I'll check myself into a shelter."

Though train passengers are more affluent than bus riders, for sure, you'd be surprised by how many poor people you'll find on Amtrak, for some towns have no air or bus service, while on some other routes, the fare differences between bus and rail are minor enough that one might as well take the much more comfortable and civil train.

On the train, the top 20 percent or so go to the dining car for every meal, while the rest of us settle for the café lounge. Some skip eating and drinking altogether for their entire journey. Between Chicago and New York, I sat next to a friendly yet glum man who ingested nothing, not even a drop of water, for twenty-one hours, and near Clifton Forge, West Virginia, I overheard this dude boast that he had been starving for two days. He couldn't bring himself to cough up $6.25 for a damn cheeseburger, he said, so he was boycotting it out of principle. Who can blame him? Give me the Dollar Menu or give me death!

Going to your seat on a plane, you pass through the first-class compartment, and there you can see, very starkly, the larger, couch-like seats with no shared armrests, more ample leg room and much better dressed people who have gotten on before you. They will also be the first ones to jump off. On a train, however, the dining car is like a mythical realm to the bad-broth slurpers, with what's happening there only wafting downstream as improbable rumors crackle over the intercom: "Today's seafood catch of the day is a mahi-mahi filet, served with two sides, at $23.75. The Amtrak signature steak is $25.75 . . ." Yes, yes, I hear you, there are always rich and poor in any society that comes after hunting and gathering, but do mind that gap, eh!

Since they know what it's like to be ordered around, waitresses and bartenders tend to be the best tippers. Conversely, those who have only been waited on can be extremely demanding, if not rude, to the waitstaff. With their multiple requests, they will send a waitress scurrying back and forth to the kitchen, and they'll nonchalantly ask that a menu item be tailored. So fixated on getting their way, some won't relent even when they're on a train. A woman from Sharon, Massachusetts, complained to me about her dining car experience, "They only had one vegetarian dish, pasta with vegetables, so I ordered that, but I didn't want the pasta, only the vegetables, but when I asked the waitress to withhold the pasta, she gave me all this attitude! She said they were already made, and I could pick out the vegetables myself, but I didn't want to look at the pasta and be tempted to eat it! I've lost a lot of weight, you see, and I didn't want that pasta in front of me. Everything I said drove this psycho waitress nuts! When I asked for skim milk instead of whole milk for my coffee, she just glared at me, and after I had told her I didn't want a bun with my salad, she brought it out anyway! In fact, she brought out two! She was trying to get at me, you see."

When our train stopped in Milwaukee, I thought of Woodland Pattern, the best poetry bookstore in the entire country, and of Grace, who showed up there when I gave a reading in 2005. I had not held her since 1985. Giving me a tight hug, Grace said, "You haven't changed," then she stole one of the books I had brought for sale, I think. I can't blame her. Like so many of us, Grace had wanted to be an artist. Erasing Grace and Milwaukee, the train chugged and whistled its way to Portage, and that's where Kelly and his daughter got on.

With his body always tilting to the right, Kelly doesn't walk, he staggers, and that's how he entered the lounge car. Sitting across from me, Kelly had to strain to speak, and sometimes his eyes would shut, his head would droop forward and he'd nod off for ten seconds or more, "I was a sheet metal worker. My brother and I had a business. I didn't have insurance for myself since I hardly ever climbed up that ladder. I was trying to save some money, you know . . ."

"Kelly!" I had to grab his arm to wake the man up.

"It's my pain medicine. It puts me to sleep."

"You were saying you didn't have insurance?"

"Oh yes, so I fell thirty feet! I've had operations on my right knee, upper right arm and back. I'm always in pain. On top of that, my wife is bipolar. I'm messed up in the body, she's messed up in the head!"

"So where are you going on this train?"

"I'm taking my daughter on a trip. She's sixteen. I want to clear her head . . ."

"Kelly! You want to clear her head?"

"Oh yes, I want to remove her from the bad influences. It's impossible to raise a kid these days, because whatever you're teaching them, it's contradicted by the television and internet, so who do you think they're going to listen to? My daughter was fine until she discovered boys a couple of years ago."

"So where are you going?"

"We're going to Portland, hang out for a couple of days, then rent a car and drive down to San Francisco."

Though I could clearly see Kelly dozing off on Interstate 5, I only said, "Your daughter will love San Francisco! She hasn't been there, right?"

"She hasn't been anywhere. My daughter has only visited Chicago and Milwaukee. I thought she would enjoy this trip more, but she's been pretty blasé so far. She's at her seat, texting. I thought I was sitting next to a ghost, and that's why I came up to this lounge car."

"Maybe she'll get into it more after a day or two."

"I can only hope. My daughter needs to see how large this world is. We live in a tiny town where everybody's in everybody's business. People know exactly how much money you have, and so the rich kids hang out with the rich kids. If you're poor and you hang out with the rich kids, people would think you're just sucking up to them."

Hit the road and you're likely to learn a whole lot, but this can't happen if you keep your eyes welded to that tablet. From Clifton to La Crosse, the train passed several sand mines, and we also saw idle boxcars loaded with sand. The fracking boom in nearby North Dakota and elsewhere has ramped up sand mining considerably in Wisconsin. Along with jobs and revenues, this mining has also generated silica dust that causes lung cancer and silicosis, and the miles-long trains that rumble through cities and towns day and night disrupt traffic and sleep. Mining's economic benefits must also be revised downward, since automation has trimmed the workforce, and mining's boom-and-bust nature attracts transient out-of-state workers who take much of their earnings elsewhere. Finally, since mining is always a tremendous act of violence against the landscape, thousands of acres of verdant Wisconsin are being turned into waste land just so this American joyride can zoom along for a tad longer. Like North Dakota, Wisconsin is also a casualty of fracking, but don't tell this to Governor Scott Walker, for he's so gung-ho about sand mining, he's publicly thanked "God and the glaciers."

Just to stay chubby, we're eating the country itself, not to mention a good chunk of this earth, but this self-devouring orgy is clearly winding down, and as our world is tapped out, man will slide down the oily pole of modernity. With bombs and drones, then sticks and stones, everyone will fight everyone else for the remaining scraps.

On the train, I met a man from Racine who gave me a preview of what's coming. A Vietnam vet, George discussed what he had learnt about basic survival, but he only arrived at it via a preamble about a TV documentary, "If a story is passed from generation to generation, sometimes people put yeast in it, inflate it, sometimes it becomes astronomical, but PBS did such an excellent, extraordinary documentation, and that's why I love PBS. I think every American should give them something, because they'd go from nature to biology, oceanography, photography... You name it and PBS covers it."

Before I engaged George, he had been sitting there for maybe an hour, just staring out the window. A thin black man, he wore a sparse moustache and had on a "WISCONSIN" baseball cap. George started out speaking very softly, but gradually became more animated, "This show was about a Japanese who was living in a cave, and everybody thought, Oh man, this can't be, but the Vietnamese did it! This one gentleman. Cookie... I can't pronounce his name. Kekanazi? Cookienazi? It's so tremendous, his great desire to survive, I could feel it!

"So this man ate raw fish, he ate snails, anything that an American or average person would turn their stomach to or hold their nose and say, 'I can't eat that,' but I've learned in Vietnam, Don't say what you can't or won't eat, because if you get hungry enough, and if you're cut off from your supply, and your only means of survival is what God has put here on this earth, and you learn from the tribesmen and villagers of Southeast Asia or wherever... Man, you'll find some of the best eating in the world!

"I've eaten squirrel and water buffalo. I've eaten orangutan. We didn't have to find them, they found us. We'd go into a sector that was really theirs, and they'd be hanging out in the trees and looking at us. They weren't scared. The baby orangutans would be inquisitive, curious, like children, and as we set up our base camp, they'd wait until we had our backs turned to snatch something and run off! They'd steal our food and weapons. They might take an M16, and as large as their fingers are, if you have the safety off, their finger would get caught in the M16, and it would go off while they're up in the trees!

"We were invading their territory, so they had to be wondering, What are these strangers doing in my home? I'm not the invader, you are! You're destroying my lifestyle, my habitat, my food supply, and I just want to know what's going on down there? You have to look at it from an animalistic point of view."

To endure Vietnam, George had to adapt to its environment, and to survive in the jungle, he became a neo-primitive, but his quest for assimilation was so fierce, he even learned to speak Vietnamese and Loatian, "People think the only dimension that exists is what we can see, but I've learned from the Asians, from the Laotians, that's not true. I speak Vietnamese and Laotian. Something comes natural. Vietnamese is part Chinese, French and Japanese combined. You may be Oriental, but if you go to Spain, you might recognize a word here and there, and you'd be like, How do I know that word? So I listened to the Vietnamese talk, and soon enough, I could also say *la le, di di ma, di di ma wa*, you know what I'm saying?"

Actually, I had no idea what he had said, but not wanting to interrupt this man's train of thought, I betrayed neither mirth nor bafflement.

George, "If people keep telling you that you're going to die, that we're going to kill you, and if you give up your weapon, we'll treat you nice. If they repeat that over and over, you'll pick up the language too.

"I went to Cambodia and Laos. Being there, what I found as the greatest experience, more than the war itself, is talking to the people, and instead of spending my time going to the village to get, you know, I decided I want to get an education, and who's better to tell you about a situation than the average American, the average Laotian? They told me stories that were absolutely unbelievable."

Finding an eager listener, George expounded at length on numerous topics, including sagging pants, "Every time I see them I always get into an argument or a fight, even at my age, because I can't stand these ignoramuses. I'd say to them, 'Remember you're a man, and a black man, so pull your goddamn pants up! That's right, I'm talking to you! We didn't struggle all those years, didn't go to demonstrations and marches so you can humiliate all of us like that!' They're acting like fools and animals, man, like penguins, because that's not walking. They're wobbling! If you're black and you say anything bad about the black community, they'll call you an Uncle Tom, but you have to get through to these knuckleheads. Take the knockout game. There ain't nothing funny about that! Hitting old people from behind . . . You know that sixty-two-year-old man they hit in Philadelphia? They're lucky it was him and not me, because I'd have chased them down and pumped lead into their heads, then I'd call the police!"

George on the sad shape of the American Indian, "They're on everything but a horse." He spoke of a Cherokee coworker, "She escaped the rez at fifteen, ran off with a biker, a nut, and they still aren't married sixteen or seventeen years later. 'We're still getting acquainted,' she said. Acquainted! She can't be older than thirty-one or thirty-two, but she goes to the doctor more often than I do. She's having another back surgery this summer. I said to her, 'You have more pain, you go to more appointments than I do, and I'm sixty-two. I've been hit with shrapnel, had a concussion, had my legs messed up from jumping out of airplanes, had my rib broken, but you're in worse shape than me, and what have you done but ride around in a truck with your boyfriend? It just hurts me to see another suffering American, like you, not knowing what you're entitled to, so you should reconnect with your tribe to get your share of whatever compensation the tribe is getting from the US government.' She didn't appreciate me telling her all this, and even got mad at me, so she said, 'Mr. Shepherd,

I've got work to do.' I explained to her, 'Not once have I made a pass at you. Not once have I physically or verbally assaulted you, so why are you angry at me?' And she is a beautiful woman, but as good as she looks now, she must have been a superstar as a teenager!"

George knows something about getting his just compensation, for he had to fight the Department of Veterans Affairs for ten years to be classified as a victim of Agent Orange. Before this, he was only getting "kibbles and bits" in disability payments. America's neglect of her veterans is a disgrace, he said, "Why do we continue to spend money on murder and mayhem while our veterans sleep on the streets?" In spite of all this, George's patriotism is unalloyed, "This is the greatest country on earth, and there's nothing more beautiful than the sight of that flag flying. Each time I look at it, I just want to choke up. I knew in my heart I was born to be a soldier. I knew in my soul I was born to be a warrior. I also knew that God did not put me here to be dormant or a fool. When I was a kid, I didn't like cowboys and Indians, I played with a Sherman tank."

George signed up for an extra year of fighting in Vietnam, "I did it to save my brother, because I knew he wouldn't be able to take it. There's a law that said only one son from each family could be in Vietnam at a time. I had another reason, but it's something civilians will never understand. It's a burning desire called esprit de corps in the military, and in civilian life, it's called compassion. It's a love for those who have made the greatest of sacrifices so you, yourself, can go home.

"So you're home and you're walking around and you see the corner store, and you think of a restaurant you'd like to eat at, and everything is so nice, the trees, the vegetation, and you're thankful that God has granted you another day on this earth, and somebody you know waves at you, 'How you doing?' and you go, 'Hey, man, what's up!' and everything should be just fine, but it isn't, really, a pretty sight, because no one knows what you've gone through, and no one cares. How many beers can you have before you feel like killing yourself?"

George spoke of a Marine who served five tours, "On this fifth tour, he didn't come back. I went to his funeral, and it was a closed coffin ceremony. You see, people think there must always be a body inside that coffin, but sometimes a coffin is just for show. Lots of time, there's nothing to send back but some bone fragments, half a boot, bit of clothing, a Bible or dog tag, so whatever you have, you put inside that coffin. If you have nothing, then it's just an empty coffin that goes into the ground.

"The captain was married to an Eskimo, and each time we came over, she always treated us like she had known us forever. He had such a beautiful, happy, peaceful family, and his kids had so much manners and were so humble. I'm their adopted godfather. I'd kill a brick for one of them kids."

George spoke lovingly of his late wife, whom he was married to for thirty-three years, and of a grandson who was shot for trying to help a stranger, "He saw this man step on a woman's face, and he just had to do something, because that's the kind of man he was. That's how he was raised."

George's son graduated from Clemson, and he himself went to three colleges and a vocational school. He's also been jailed four times, however, "I didn't hurt anybody. One of my convictions was for writing bad checks." With his emphasis on family, education, discipline and personal improvement, George is typical of many working-class Americans, especially of his generation, but his enthusiasm for the military is also all too common. Firmly believing in the dignity and honor of serving his country, he ignores its contradictions and abuses, many of which he has seen firsthand. After shooting the shit with and shooting Southeast Asian villagers, tribesmen and orangutans, George came home as a good American soldier, and the same Communists he risked his life fighting are about to buy weapons from American manufacturers, and why not, since America is an equal opportunity death merchant that has armed just about every country, militia or drug gang. Just call this toll-free number!

Though America's ideology will gyrate, twerk or U-turn from moment to moment, her allegiance to war profiteering is unshakable, and as she destroys humanity, she speaks of civilization so constantly that the word itself has become suspect. "Democracy" and "freedom" she has long crapped on beyond recognition. From Portland to Williston, I sat behind a young man who spent all of his waking hours being mesmerized by a computer game. Candy, a gregarious woman with Sioux blood, asked him, "What are you playing?"

Without looking up, he growled, "Civilization Builder."

"So what's the point? Are you building up civilization from scratch?"

"No."

"Are you defending what you already have?"

"Sort of."

"Oh, I get it, you want to get a lot more!"

"Yeah."

Now, before you laugh at this young man's naked and childish admission to wanting more, remember that greed and lust for power are fairly universal traits that spread across the political spectrum, though only on the conservative end are they openly admitted to and even touted as virtues. The war instinct is also found in all surviving cultures, with tiny pockets of pacifism remaining thanks to the mercy or tolerance of their larger societies. Again, it is mostly those who self-identify as conservatives or traditionalists who openly embrace war as not only necessary for the survival of society, but as a crucible for the development of each individual's character. To them, a rejection of war is not just cowardly and unrealistic, but a refusal to, literally, become a man.

Exploiting these convictions, American war profiteers have few problems selling any war to the American public, and that's why you see the generic "Support Our Troops" stickers and signs everywhere, but what these unquestioning war supporters don't realize is that, in this endless war that's being waged by their masters, they're also collateral damage and enemy. Fighting against themselves, they'll wave the flag until they're bombed back to the Stone Age, perhaps by friendly fire even.

FREE GRUB IN JACKSON

10-6-14—Riding the train from Chicago to New Orleans, I impulsively got off in Jackson, Mississippi. I had never thought about visiting Jackson, never even seen a photo of it, so I had no idea what I'd encounter. In the train's lounge car, however, a boisterous game of dominoes, with much laughter and trash talking, already told me I was in the Deep South, and the towns glimpsed along the way, Tchula, Eden, Bentonia, spoke of a quietly dignified world that's also besieged and crumbling.

Jackson is no town, however, but the state's biggest city, and I couldn't quite recall Johnny Cash's smirking lyrics, "Well, go on down to Jackson, go ahead and wreck your health," as I trudged around a sterile downtown of massive parking garages and stultifying office buildings, banks and hotels. Everything was grimly functional, at best, or else abandoned. There was no art or flirtation, no life. Perhaps this is a mistake, I thought, but quickly dismissed the lame conclusion, for wherever there are people, there's beauty and instruction. Just keep walking! The disused Greyhound station had a meek sign announcing an architectural firm. Passing a forlorn men's clothing store, I noticed a security guard imposingly perched on a stool right in the doorway. Maybe they should build him a pillbox.

Having not eaten in sixteen hours or so, I was fantasizing deeply about any three-piece dark meat special with a biscuit thrown in, but I spotted no eatery, takeout or bar. Yes, there was a sushi palace, but it was closed on Saturday, not

270

that I was inclined to drag in my rank carcass. Having showered just twice in a week, I was not fit for any chichi sushi bullshit, and there was no way I'd turn my slim wallet inside out for a lacquered plate of Fukushima-irradiated or Corexit-seasoned fish. For such a price, I better get a boatload.

Snooping around, I paused to admire the rusting and boarded-up remains of the Sun-n-Sand Motor Hotel. Opened in 1960, it served liquor even before Mississippi finally repealed its alcohol ban in 1965. At the capitol, one block away, politicians would vote no to imbibing, then amble here to booze. With its googie sign and technicolored poolside lounge chairs, it was built for a groovy, spacey future that never arrived. The racial tension of the sixties culminated in the police killing of two black Jackson State students in 1970. White flight then commenced, suburban malls were built, so now, the empty and wrecked buildings are scattered throughout downtown, only to multiply as you stray north, but this decay is all too common across much of Mississippi, for many of its cities and towns are like quainter versions of post-industrial Detroit. This is the poorest state, after all, and the fattest, too, for obese and broke go chubbily hand in hand in this upside-down nation. Mississippi also just misses on being the least educated, so there goes the triple crown, goddamnit! Under a lovely sun, though, things do rot more beautifully than with dirty snow.

On a billboard with thirty-two women and a man, "Tyrone Lewis / Sheriff," who's actually depicted twice, small, then huge, there's this message, "Mother's Like You Shape Our Future." Of course, that apostrophe is wrong, but millions of Americans, even those majoring in English, routinely make that mistake these days, so it's no indictment of Mississippi. Across this sinking nation, we're just too glazed-eyed to give a fryin' okra! In any case, Sheriff Lewis has much more to worry about than bad English, for he's being charged with losing control of the Jackson prison. According to a grand jury report, the guards are terrified of their charges, and "the inmates seemed to be in control of the jail." Look closely, my friend, and you'll see that all the wheels are loose or already bouncing off this much abused and neglected vehicle. On a wall a few blocks away, there was Richard Wright next to one of his haikus: "There is where I am / Summer sunset loneliness / Purple meeting red." The writer's punctuation has been stripped away, but whatever, it's only a poem. On another wall were lurid portraits of "Shawn Earl" and "Pretty Boy," presumably victims of violence. In death, angel wings have sprouted from their painted persons. In black neighborhoods across this country, these memorials are ubiquitous, a funky form of folk art. Sunrise, sunset, sunrise, sunset, and so the beat goes on. Bang! Bang! Bang!

In 2013, Jackson attracted some rare national attention when it elected Chokwe Lumumba as its mayor (with 87 percent of the vote). A steadfast Black Nationalist, Lumumba had been vice president of the Republic of New Africa, a secessionist entity that would include Alabama, Georgia, Louisiana, Mississippi and South Carolina. Until this could be birthed, Lumumba wanted to solidify black political power in Mississippi, a state that already had the highest number of black elected officials nationwide. Though western Mississippi was overwhelmingly black, blacks only made up 40 percent of its population, so a way to remedy this, according to Lumumba, was to encourage massive black migration into the state. In practice, this would also mean a flood of whites fleeing it, for that's how it has worked all across this country up until now, though on a smaller scale, as in a single street, neighborhood or city.

Clearly, Lumumba saw blacks not as Americans but as yet another nation that had been terrorized and raped by America, so the only solution was to be liberated from it. In 1998, Lumumba spoke in Washington, DC, "We're here in the governmental center of the citadel of imperialism, here amongst these buildings which have been built off the blood of our people . . . and as we come into the city, we see the outskirts where the people live in poverty, where the buildings are crumbling and the people's lives are crumbling and we come and see these monstrous buildings fortified by our blood, fortified from the wealth that they have stolen not only from colonies all over the world but from the African colony, the Puerto Rican colony, and the Native American colonies that exist right here inside America . . . As we look back historically at this empire, we see how it has stretched out its tentacles all over the world, it has dug them deep into the veins of suffering people . . ." After only eight months as mayor of Jackson, Chokwe Lumumba died on February 25th, 2014, and since the cause of death, heart failure, wasn't immediately given, it fueled rampant speculation that he may have been offed by Uncle Sam.

Now, cynics might dismiss Lumumba's dream of a black homeland as a wish to create, say, another Liberia or Haiti, and they can also point to the tendency of successful blacks to move away from other blacks, a phenomenon that happens not just within national borders, but across them. A Republic of New Africa, then, will not only struggle to attract the best and brightest blacks, but may generate a steady stream of black refugees and immigrants of all levels.

Though what Lumumba advocated was voluntary segregation, it was the forced kind, ironically, that yielded the last era of black self-sufficiency and relative prosperity. When black expertise and money could not be leached from the community, there were black-owned businesses of absolutely every kind, not just those selling incense sticks, body oils and wigs. Just as the "free market" is destroying the American working class, it eviscerated the black community. Unfettered capitalism kills from the bottom up, but so does every competitive, cutthroat arrangement. If you're outsprinted by a blink, you're human garbage.

Lumumba's plan for black empowerment wasn't merely demographic, however, but included structural components such as more citizen involvement in bank, business and land stewardship. He also aimed to turn around a gravely sick culture, and in this, at least, he's not far from a conservative. In an interview with *Final Call*, Lumumba explained, "Rather than going to church, and yelling and screaming about it, complaining about it, rather than bad-mouthing the youth, my plan is to engage the youth . . . In the course of talking about what to do, you can always talk about some things that you shouldn't do. We're going to have summer youth programs here, and in those summer youth programs they're going to have a chance to do some manual labor, help pick up paper on the streets, but another three hours of their day is going to be spent learning skills . . . This is going to do a great deal to help change the culture."

What's most interesting to me about Lumumba's aspiration, however, is that it's mirrored by whites who long for white havens, although this wish might not be openly admitted to, especially if the wisher is a "liberal." Mouthing racial (as well as class) platitudes, this self-absorbed master of self-love recoils from all who differ from him to the slightest degree, although he'll put on a jazz record, of course, and scarf Ethiopian once a year. To stroke his twitchy conscience, he'll elect an Uncle Tom, twice even, and pretend that it ain't so. Though the working poor of any color have daily, direct experience of the multiculturalism espoused by the liberal affluent, their opinions on its pros, cons and limits are peremptorily dismissed from "enlightened" conversations. In any case, when nations crumble, they often crack along racial or ethnic lines, and there's no reason why it won't happen here, but since racial hatred is as barbaric as they come, I don't wish to live long enough to witness this catastrophe. From 1882 to 1968, white mobs lynched 539 blacks in Mississippi alone, the most in the entire nation, but now, there are white groups who keep tabs on the staggering number of black-on-white murders, maimings, rapes and recreational assaults. Seeing their share of the population decreasing relentlessly, they speak of a white genocide. As for the elites, though they don't welcome social unrest, since it's bad for business, they will benefit from increasing racial animosity since it distracts from the serial crimes they're inflicting on us all.

Beat, I hiked past boarded-up or burnt-out houses that were over-grown with weeds or vines, or impaled by gnarly trees. These were inter-spersed with well-kept homes, however, and when I saw a man striding out of one, I asked him to point me to the nearest beer trough. Lugging my backpack around, I had sweated away all my fluids. "I can't think of any that's open right now, but I'll sell you a Coors Light for a buck, and it's cold too!" Sounded fair to me, so I handed him a dollar.

So far, everyone I had seen was black, but presently, I came across a white-haired white man jabbing a long steel rod repeatedly into the ground of an empty dirt plot. At 80 percent, Jackson has the sec-ond-highest percentage of blacks of all American cities over 100,000 people. With 84 percent, Detroit is top.

"What are you looking for?" I shouted.

Lifting his bulbous-nosed, razor-nicked visage, the gent in pale gray T-shirt and dirty khaki pants slowly spoke. To let his thoughts coalesce, he'd often take a breather in mid-phrase. "Old bottles, usually. I've found clay marbles, and sometimes even coins from the Civil War."

"Wow, they must be worth a lot!"

"Not really. I do it for fun, not for profit."

When I told him I was from Philadelphia and had just gotten off the train, he counseled, "You should be careful walking around this neighborhood. There are lots of crimes around here, and drug dealing. Farish Street is kind of a bad deal, because they let it go so bad. I think you should head back downtown."

"But you're here!"

"Well, I'm a cop," he smiled and wiped his brows.

Before leaving the unarmed officer, I did extract from him directions to a nearby tavern, though with this warning, "It can get a little rough in there." Satisfied with the information, I went on my way. Farish Street turned out to be worse than advertised, with formerly handsome buildings now roofless and empty, their window and door frames left hollow or covered by warped or kicked-in plywood. Colorful, crude murals covered some of the sheets. The brick sidewalks, trimmed trees and stylish lampposts appeared to be recent, half-assed efforts at restoration, for they contrasted ludicrously with the unchecked vegetation gaining on the ruins. During segregation, Farish Street was actually one of the liveliest black business districts in the entire country, the equivalent of Memphis's Beale Street, but staring at it now, a visitor might hallucinate that this mess is somehow related to General Sherman's brief courtesy call to Jackson in 1863.

My hoppy oasis turned out to be a small red building with no name, just a Pabst Blue Ribbon sign dangling. Across from it, concrete foundations were all that remained of three houses. Though downtown was within sight, it looked like the sticks in the other direction, with more unkempt trees and grass than potholed and cracked asphalt. Outside the bar door, several people mulled around a charcoal grill redolent of smoked meat, yum, yum, and they all saw me march down the middle of the empty street. "This must be the place!" I shouted, and grinned quite inanely before entering an empty bar. Inside, the walls were also painted red, with here and there, a miniskirted or bikinied beer babe on a torn-edged poster. I spotted two small American flags, but no homage to Obama. A disco ball anchored the ceiling. Mirrors multiplied the room's dimensions, made it feel a tad bigger. Soon, the owner followed me in. In his mid-sixties, the mild man sported a white and magenta floral shirt and panama hat. Rewarding myself a bit, I shunned Pabst and Bud and ordered a Heineken, this joint's high-end offering. In many places around the world, an obvious stranger can expect to be fleeced, but here I was treated not just equally, which is all a man can ask for, but even quite generously, as I would find out.

Settled, I said to the owner, "Sir, I'd like to order a plate of whatever you're cooking outside."

"It's not ready," he answered, "and it's not for sale. You can go out and ask them, though."

I wasn't sure what he meant, exactly, but I ordered a bag of potato chips just to have something in my maw. "I walked a few miles," I continued, "but didn't see any bar. I just got off the train."

"We're the only one around here."

"So where's everybody, if you're the only one that's open?"

"A lot of them went to the football game."

"Jackson State is playing at home?"

"No, in Arkansas."

"People drove all the way to Arkansas?!"

"Sure did."

That's a seven-hour round-trip, but such is the devotion to the local team in many parts of America. In countless small towns, the streets are deserted if there's a high school football game many miles away. If only such unity and singularity of purpose could be deployed for anything other than cheering for touchdowns, we wouldn't be in such deep shit. Instead of columns of guerrillas, we have caravans of fans.

Every now and then, an old guy would mosey in, and he'd be dressed rather nattily in slacks, button-down shirt and a hat. According to several signs, even muscle shirts and backward caps were banned here, much less sagging pants. Starting a card game, the owner and a patron played mostly in silence, unperturbed by thumping music or television chattering, jingles and come-ons. Not just an old man's bar, this was an old-fashioned establishment, and all over its walls, aging itself was mockingly celebrated: "You're living in the Metallic Age: Gold Teeth, Silver Hair and a Lead Bottom," "LIFE is not passing you by, it's trying to run you over!" "Your motor is still running, But your warranty has expired!" "IF YOU WERE A CAR, YOU'D BE AN ANTIQUE!" "TOO OLD TO ROCK N ROLL, TOO YOUNG TO RANT 'N RAVE," "You're stuck between the 'Young and the Restless,' and the Old and the Senseless!" "OLDER THAN DIRT!"

Like old men everywhere, these guys couldn't avoid discussing their health and, by extension, diet. From where I sat, I could only catch an odd fragment here and there, something about eating only one meal a day, how catfish is preferable to shrimps, and how skinless hot dogs are best. After a lifetime of toil and near misses, a man is lucky to have all four limbs, a functioning brain and be outside earshot of Lil Wayne and such as he attempts to postpone his induction into the Greenwood Cemetery, not a long field goal away.

Older than bad luck, the men in the no-name bar remember only too well the day Medgar Evers was shot in Jackson, and how his fertilizer salesman killer wasn't convicted until three decades later. They shudder at the memory of the bloody Woolworth's sit-in downtown. Though they lived through Freedom Summer, and have helped to elect one black politician after another, they have come to realize the limitations, bordering on impotence, of the vote, for in Jackson, as in communities across America, incomes continue to dip, jobs disappear and young people are sent off to incomprehensible wars, while at home, robbing and killing have become a career choice for too many citizens.

Fed up with violent crimes, Jackson even elected one Frank Melton. In office from 2005 to 2009, this loose cannon liked to illegally pack guns, illegally carry a police badge and illegally lead drug raids and sweeps with a personal band of bodyguards and teens, many of whom had criminal records. Innocently dubbed "the Lawn Crew," Melton's posse once destroyed a purported drug den with sledgehammers, all without even a search warrant. Swinging with such glee, Melton slashed his hands with broken glass and had to be patched up at a hospital. Viewed as a folk hero by many Jacksonians, Melton never saw the inside of a jail cell, while others were nauseated enough by the mayor's antics to prevent his reelection.

Since another bag of potato chips wouldn't do it, I wandered outside to find a woman tending the barbecue. Again, I pleaded, "When you're done, ma'am, I'd like to buy a plate of whatever it is you're making."

"It's not for sale," she stared at me, "but I'll give you some!"

I had never been given a free plate of food in a bar, but that's exactly what happened about fifteen minutes later as the lady placed a Styrofoam container of sausage, pound cake and deviled egg in front of me, and this will remain one of my most memorable meals, I swear, since it was served up with such sweetness. This became the theme of the day, for on the way to catch my New Orleans bus, I was also given an excellent piece of fried chicken by a homeless man with tattoos all over his face.

"You eat it, brother. These church people just gave it to me. It's still hot, too! I've had enough, and was just going to throw the rest away."

I wish I had more to report about Jackson, but my time there was short, though considering what's lurking beyond the horizon these days, having little time anywhere might not be a curse. Still, there are plenty who can't wait for the fireworks to begin, for they think their daddy of daddies will emerge from the red, white and blue smoke. Just before I stepped on the bus, a balding white man with fresh scabs on his face, arms and legs begged money for his "seizure medicine." I gave him that, plus an extra buck. Jackson State ended up beating Arkansas–Pine Bluff 33–30, by the way, so life was good in Jackson, sort of, until the next tribal clash.

GROWING OLD IN OSCEOLA

10-11-14—The American presidential election is a drawn-out, byzantine process that involves precinct meetings, regional caucuses, state primaries and national conventions, all to give citizens the impression that their participation matters, for in the end, the lying buffoon who gets to stride into the White House has long been vetted and preselected by the banks, death merchants and brainwashing media that run our infernally corrupt and murderous country.

It's foolish to expect a system to allow anyone who threatens it to the least degree to rise to the very top, for all those who benefit from this system will do all they can to snuff out such a pest each step of the way. He'd be lucky to get a job teaching freshman English at the community college, and is as out of place in this bloody scheme as an Iowa beaver trapper at a Hamptons pool party. As for dissidents who get print space or airtime, they are but harmless, distracting foils or court jesters. Since voting cannot change the system but legitimizes it, voters become collaborators in all of the system's crimes, as well as their own destruction, for the system works against nearly all of them.

Don't tell this to Iowans, though, for they take the election farce very seriously, with intense and subtle debates among themselves and close listening to bullshitty speeches from the corporation-jerked marionettes. Earnestly playing along with this sick charade, Iowans do get to claim the national spotlight every four years, though, for it's here that the election "season" begins. Like a whistle pig, Iowa crawls out of its hole to tweet the worst possible omen to the rest of the country, "We have a new war criminal!"

Standing on its hind legs, the woodchuck screamed at me, "Oh, man, why be so negative?! And you ain't never even seen our flat, featureless landscape, our splendid collection of parking garages and parking lots known as downtown Des Moines, not to mention our poetry factory farm, the Iowa Writers' Workshop!"

All right, dude, I've atoned. I had been to forty-seven states, but Iowa wasn't one of them, so it was with a clearly prurient excitement that I crossed the Mississippi into Burlington, Iowa. From my train seat, I could marvel at its one-span suspension bridge, but the midget Statue of Liberty was nowhere to be seen, which just means I must detrain the next time. OK!

Encased by steel, I crossed Iowa entirely and didn't get off until my return trip, in tiny Osceola. With several first-rate colleges and consistently high SAT scores, Iowa once toyed with the nickname "A State of Mind," but decided to stay with the mysterious "Hawkeye State," a nonsensical allusion to a forgotten Sauk chief. Interestingly, the red man only makes up half a percent of the state's population, compared to 1.3 percent and 8.9 percent in neighboring Nebraska and South Dakota, respectively. Osceola is named after a Seminole chief, and though only six American Indians now live in Osceola, its high school athletes are nicknamed, what else, the Indians. The civic banners hanging all over the center of town read, "OSCEOLA / HOME OF THE INDIANS." Of course, the professional football team of Washington, DC, that bastion of some the most ruthless white men for 200-odd years now, is called the Redskins. Perhaps Beitar Jerusalem F.C. will change its name to the Jerusalem Arabs once the last Palestinian has been blasted from Israel. The keffiyeh can be incorporated into their uniform.

Hissing, the groundhog just delivered a flying reverse kick upside my head, "What's up with this Iowa-bashing bullshit, man?! Didn't we just invite you to do your silly and, I strongly suspect, drunken song and dance at Grinnell and Coe?!"

Alrighty, alrighty, land beaver! I'll introduce everybody to a super friendly quintet I met in Osceola: Kurt, a vending machine business owner; Monk, a retired sausage plant worker; Bubby, a woodpecker watcher; and Bill, an ex-Air Force sergeant, mailman and playboy. We'll get to them. Leaving the station, I walked down a dull stretch of Main Street, past Leslie's Dance Emporium, with its tumbling, clogging, jazz and hip-hop dancing classes; Casey's General Store, a chain gas station with convenience mart; La Pequeña Mexican grocery; a bowling alley; a bank. Finally, a large, leafy square opened up in front of me.

Most of Osceola's businesses were clumped around it, and on all the stores' plate glass windows, rah-rah slogans have been painted to cheer on the high school football team. Each was tailored to the business, for at the flower shop, it was "BLOOM UP A VICTORY." At the bank, "CASH IN A WIN." At the Chinese buffet, "STIR UP A VICTORY." Though the local boys had lost all four of their games, such civic enthusiasm did slather a festive coat over this tranquilizing village.

Hey, haven't you noticed that "village" is almost never used to describe any American settlement? Just about any flyspeck across this land is solemnly declared a "city," on government buildings, official stationery and cop cars, etc. Similarly, an American peasant is spiffed up as a "farmer" or "agricultural worker," and an American coolie who keeps rolling over his payday loan, dwells in a shared squat, has four broken teeth left and must take two subways and a bus to each of his three jobs is merely a "low-wage worker."

After futilely trying to find a diner, I settled for the Chinese belly stuffer, housed as it was in the Masonic Temple. The illuminated array was certainly cheap enough. At the next table, two women discussed difficult familial relationships and health hiccups. Compared to the egg drop, the hot and sour soup was perhaps the lesser of two evils, and after much deliberation, I elected the fried chicken over the clearly impeachable beef with broccoli. Looking for glasses to refill, the stoic waitress marched back and forth when not bitching about something over her cell phone. "Thanks a lot!" I waved at this suffering woman before dashing out the door for the West Side Tavern across the square. Over its entrance, there was a 3-D facsimile of a pool rack with crossed cues. I walked in.

To enter any unknown bar is to dive into an alien society, for here might be a meeting place for the local KKK, Hells Angels, Black Republicans, Born to Kill Vietnamese gang or, since we're in Iowa, Most Ancient and Hermetic Order of the Eternally Windswept if not Snowed-in Cable Subscribers. Luckily for me, though, the West Side turned out to be a most welcoming joint, for it took but a few seconds for the long-haired dude to my left to say, "How are you doing?"

"It's my first time here. I just got off the train. This looks like a great place to sit for a while."

"It's the only place to sit," he laughed and extended his hand. "I'm Kurt."

I told Kurt I was on my way to Des Moines, and had just been to McCook, Nebraska.

"You got any more of that?"

"What?"

"Coke."

"No, I said McCook, Nebraska."

"McCook, Nebraska?!"

"Yeah, I just went to McCook, Nebraska."

"Why?!"

"Just to see it."

"Dude," he said, and just shook his head. To flush Nebraska from his mind, Kurt then told me about his nine-year-old autistic daughter, "Just this morning, my daughter said, 'Dad, if you don't get me a pepperoni pizza right away, I'm going to call 911!' Isn't that hilarious?! She's smart, smarter than me, but her mind works differently. She has a different outlook."

"How does she get along with other kids?"

"Not very well. They tease her all the time, she gets into fights, but I don't blame them, because she's the one that's different."

"So she has no friends?"

"She has an invisible friend called Tails."

"Tails?!"

"It's from the Sonic video game. My daughter solved that in three days. It took me twenty years! My daughter's smart, but she just has a different outlook, that's all. She can read and understand all the words, but she can't make sense out of them."

It turned out that Kurt's not a native Iowan, "I'm originally from Austin, Texas. I got my girlfriend pregnant, or somebody did, but we moved up here to be close to her family."

"So now you're stuck here!"

"Oh no, man, a man ain't never stuck . . ."

"I don't mean that in a negative way. I mean, you like it here OK?"

"No, it's horrible."

"It's horrible?!"

"Yes, it's too windy, too cold, and you have all the politicians coming through, and they never stop coming. They're always coming through."

I paused to think about that for a moment. "Do you ever come out to hear the speeches, just to see what they're like?"

"No. Why, do you have someone you want to kill?"

When his phone rang, Kurt said to me, "It's my brother-in-law," then he answered, "What's up, big weed? Hey, fuckie! What's going on, man? I'm glad somebody is talking about me. Thanks for calling me and for saying all that. Yeah, you're the only who's wished me a Happy Birthday today. Hey, do you want to have sex later? Damn! I have the pill and the blanket, and a blow-up doll too if we get tired of each other."

After hanging up, Kurt explained, "My sister died in February. Me and my brother-in-law are real close. He's in Los Angeles."

"It's your birthday today?"

"Yeah, I'm fifty."

"I'm also fifty! Hey, what do you do, man? How do you make a living?"

"I own vending machines. Forty of them."

"Sounds like a pretty good business."

"It's enough to pay the bills, that's all. My machines are in four different counties, so I must drive all over. I leave the house at four each day, and am done by ten."

"Which means you're here by 10:15!"

"Yeah, that's about right."

"That doesn't sound too bad. I wouldn't mind it. Hey, can you, like, expand your business? Put in a condom machine at this bar?"

Kurt shouted to the bartender, "What do you think, Milt? Should I put a condom machine in this bar?"

Rearranging a half-drained bottle, the sixtyish man drily pronounced, "You must have sex to use a condom, and none of us has sex."

"None of these guys can even get it up anymore," Kurt informed me unsmilingly. "Iowa is just a bunch of old white farmers."

When Kurt went out the back door to smoke, I followed him outside and there, I met Monk. Lounging on a ratty armchair, he was chomping on some spareribs. Since the sun had dipped, the light had softened, and on the gravel, a bar patron had parked his John Deere mower, which Kurt found highly amusing. There were no commercial signs, hence no distracting language, and there were no sounds save for our talking. Across the street, the houses appeared well-maintained and peaceful.

I noticed that Monk had on two pairs of shorts, a stars and stripes one on the inside, and over that, one with the "Iraqi Freedom" military camouflage. Though Kurt had insisted to me that the economy was fine, and there would be no recession unless the Republicans returned to power, Monk had a different take, "In 1992, I already made $13 an hour at Jimmy Dean, the sausage plant. I was there for twenty years, but Jimmy Dean moved to Tennessee because they wanted to pay people $8 an hour."

"How old are you, Monk?"

"Sixty-five."

"Holy! You look about my age, man, and I'm fifty!" And it's true that the people I met in Osceola were remarkably youthful-looking. Perhaps the sodium acetates, natamycin, pimaricin, nisin, nitrites, potassium nitrite, sodium nitrite, itrates, sodium nitrate, potassium nitrate, sorbates, sorbic acid, sodium sorbate, potassium sorbate, calcium sorbate, sulphites, sulphur dioxide, sodium sulphite, sodium bisulphite, sodium metabisulphite, potassium metabisulphite, potassium sulphite and potassium bisulphite that are commonly used in meat processing have had a holistically curative effect in curing their still chattering carcasses.

Jimmy Dean abandoned Osceola in 1992, after its owner, the country singer, had sold his company to Sara Lee. Dean is most famous for "Big Bad John," a ballad about a mythic miner. "Like a giant oak tree," Big Bad John held up a groaning, sagging piece of timber so his fellow head-lamped moles could escape from a collapsing pit, but no Big Bad John showed up in 1992 when the sky fell on 380 Osceolia workers. This story has become all too familiar, all over, for such is the wondrous mobility of capital!

In 1995, however, Hormel bought the shuttered plant, expanded it and now employs 677 Osceolians. A single company can make or break such a village, and Hormel is now Osceola's savior, but it's not all corn syrup, honey, for the average hourly wage at Hormel's Osceola plant is, guess what, roughly $13 an hour, about what Monk made twenty-two years ago, even as the cost of everything has gone way, way up, especially housing and gas. In 1992, I could easily get a one-bedroom apartment in downtown Philadelphia for $500, but now, you must be prepared to fork over nearly three times as much.

"So you're retired now?" I asked Monk.

"Yeah, I get $1,500 a month in Social Security."

"That's not too bad!"

"No, it's not, and I inherited my house, so I don't have to worry about a mortgage. My heating bill, though, is very high. I'm thinking about using my fireplace more, but the problem with that is you just can't burn wood and step outside or go to sleep, since it might burn your entire house down!"

An indication of Osceola's relative economic health is the slow but steady increase in population over the last several decades. As for the newcomers, many of them are Mexicans. They make up roughly 20 percent of the population. Back in the bar, I talked to seventy-three-year-old Bubby. He said, "Osceola is sometimes referred to as Mexiola!"

"But I saw no Mexicans on the streets. Where are they? Do they ever come in here?"

"No."

"So where do they drink?"

"I have no idea."

From several stools away, someone shouted, "There was a Mexican bar, but it closed down."

Of course, people can just get buzzed at home, as Bubby often does while watching his bird feeder, "There's one who acts like he owns the damn thing! He'd chase all of the other birds away!"

"Males?"

"Yeah, he'd chase the other males away."

"What about the females?"

"The ones he'd mate with, you know, he'd let eat, but even then, he'd chase her away if he thought she had enough."

"What a bird!"

"The others, though, would work together to get their food. One would distract this dominant bird, get him to chase him, while his buddies would swoop in and eat. You look at them and wonder, how big can their brains be, and yet they're really smart. They know how to coordinate their actions so they can eat."

"That's amazing!"

"Yes, it is, and it's really relaxing to sit there and watch them. Of course, most of the time, I'm drinking a beer!"

It's exhilarating to know that these birds don't just wave cute signs while being penned in a free speech zone, and I seriously doubt if they vote every four years to have yet another shamelessly pompous, unctuous and speechifying bird crap on their heads while committing the most evil crimes in their name.

In my early twenties, I looked with a mixture of amusement and pity at the old men who sat nearly all day in the same bar every day, for it seemed so dull and defeated, but as I got older, I realized that these were the luckier ones, for at least they had enough money and health to hobble out of the house each morning, and after a lifetime of seeing, doing and having things done to you, it was enough to just be left in peace to stew, or to swap stories, jokes and innocuous observations. In Osceola, it was, "Yes, I saw Mary yesterday and I gave her a big old hug," which I found terribly moving, and I laughed uproariously at this, "The St. Louis Condoms might just go all the way. Condoms! Condoms! All the way!" Of course, having about two kegs in me didn't hurt.

Now, it is with a kind of terror that I introduce you to the most spectacular dude I met in Osceola, Bill the ex-mailman, Air Force sergeant and playboy. Arriving in an old white car with amber strobe light on top, Bill parked his trim form to my right, and though he turned eighty that day, the man looked twenty years younger, I swear, and his mind was revving (loudly) as he recounted to me highlights from his improbable life. Several times, I had to ask the other barflies, "Is Bill bullshitting me?" We began, though, very mildly.

"There used to be a bunch of bars around here, but now there are only four."

"There were twelve, Bill," someone chimed in.

"Why do you think that is?" I asked Bill.

"First of all, you can't smoke in a bar anymore, and then there's the internet. These days, people just like to sit home and watch movies on Netflix. I live in Woodburn, ten minutes away, and out there, there's not one bar left."

Besides Netflix, an early twenty-first-century American is also kept in quarantine by Facebook, Twitter, Tumblr and, of course, online porn. Kurt's daughter is hardly the only one with an imaginary friend. How many Tailses do you have? Outside, there may be war, riot, financial collapse, pestilence, record drought or fracking earthquake, but I can't even lift my head since my consciousness has been sucked into a screen, and my earbuds are rockin'. I don't even know what's going on in my room, much less outside.

"So how many people are in Woodburn, Bill?"

"Two hundred and fifty. There's a fellow who wants to reopen a bar that's closed down, but I think that's a stupid idea. It's mostly just old people out there, and most of them don't drink beer. The young people have moved away. There's nothing out there. I have all the beer at home, and I have a couple of friends with lots of beer at home, and they have garages, so we just have parties and drink beer. This fellow can have Willie Nelson at his new bar twice a week, and no one will come out. Of course, I first went to the bars to, you know, pick up chicks, but I'm eighty now, so it ain't so easy anymore."

"You can still try!"

"Oh, I have had more than my share, believe me."

"Happy Birthday, Bill!" Bubby yelled out. "We're in the same category, buddy, but I'm not sure I'm going to last that long."

Standing by the front door, Kurt cheerfully added, "I'm definitely not going to make it to 80. My wife keeps asking me where I want to be buried."

"Today is my birthday," Bill continued, "Tomorrow is the day I got married to my first wife, and also when my second wife died, of cancer."

"So is that a happy or sad day?"

"Neither. I first got married when I was twenty-seven. She and I got along fine, mostly. She had two brothers. One offered to give me a blow job, he died of AIDS, and the other shot at me as I was driving down the Interstate. He was a real piece of shit."

"Did he have a reason to shoot you?"

"I was getting a divorce from his sister. He hanged himself before I could get even. The other guy was, you know, a queer. I turned him down."

"That sounds just terrible!"

"I've had an interesting life." Then, "Have you heard of Orson Welles?"

"Sure."

"Orson Welles was living in Paris, and he tried to hook up with the Queen of Montparnasse, but she didn't care for him. Astrid was her name, as in asteroid. A gorgeous blonde, she's a legend and friend of Françoise Sagan. I went with her for about three months. This is what she said about Welles, '*Il est un gros cochon*.' She called him a big fat pig, but she liked me because I was good-looking."

"Were you?"

"Yes, I was a stud! I've never had my eyes wide open. The girls here said I had bedroom eyes. They thought it was very romantic. Once, while I was on leave, I had three girlfriends named Lois."

"So, ah, was Lois a very popular name around here?"

"No, they were in three different towns."

"Maybe you were just attracted to women named Lois?"

"I don't think so. It just happened. One Lois was to keep, one was to screw and one was to, I can't even remember now. The first Lois was the prom queen and a good girl, so we just dated."

"So who do you sleep with now?"

"My dog!" Bill laughed. "Ah, he's a great toy terrier! If I stay in bed for twenty-four hours, he stays right there with me." The evocation of this pooch cheered him up, and Bill smiled to himself for a moment. Then, "He's a funny dog. When I sing 'Blue Eyes Crying in the Rain,' he sings along. Ooh, ooh! He enjoys it."

Collecting Social Security and a pension from the Postal Service, Bill's budget is definitely not pinched, for he talked of owning two houses, although the second, he bought for only $18,400 two years ago, this being Woodburn, Iowa. Also, "I like to collect things. I have thirty guns, including three AK-47's, but I haven't fired any of them."

"Why not?"

"Just don't feel like it. I was the best shot in the Air Force. I also own seventy guitars, and when I get drunk, I play all of them at once!"

Walking by, Kurt said, "Bill was a mailman for fifty years. No one dared to cross him."

"If you pissed him off," I laughed, "would he throw your mail away?"

"I don't know. You ask him!"

"So how long were you in the service, Bill?" I asked.

"Four years. I was in Korea, then France. I really wanted to go to Rio de Janeiro or Bavaria."

"That would have been fun! So did you fight in Korea?"

"No. By the time I got there, the war was over. Something happened, though, that bothers me to this day. Me and another GI were in this jeep when we saw a tree lying across the road. It was an ambush, you see, so we jumped out, and I must have shot the guy because he stopped. Or maybe I didn't kill him, maybe I didn't kill anybody. For eighteen years, I didn't think about this, but then I started having nightmares."

"You feel bad about killing the guy who tried to kill you?"

"Yes, I feel very bad. I was having these nightmares and couldn't sleep, so I started to think about going back to that spot to say a prayer for this guy and apologize. It's probably just a big parking lot."

"And for eighteen years, you never thought about this at all?"

"No. I must have had PTS, whatever the hell they call it, and there's something else that came back. There was a nurse on the air base, and he was cleaning his pistol, a .45, and I was right there. As I went out the door, I saw him, and he was cheerful because he was cleaning his gun, but after I closed the door, I heard a bang! I looked in and saw the blood. Thump, thump, thump, these three guys came running down the hallway, and I said, 'Hey, I didn't do it!' The nurse had shot himself, by accident, and I feel terrible about that too."

"But you had nothing to do with it!"

"It doesn't matter. He was just this kid, and he had no need for a weapon anyhow. There was no reason for him to have a gun, much less cleaning it. He was on a base and well-protected."

Bill's dad died at nearly ninety-nine, so he feels like he has a few more miles to ride yet on his golf cart, which he does with noisy glee. "When I shout 'Whoaaa, whoaaa,' people think I'm saying, 'Whore! Whore!' Of course, in Korea, you could get one for about 10 cents." Nutty as ever, Bill spoke of some recent pseudo-sexual experiences which I won't recount here, for I want to be welcome the next time I step inside the Westside Tavern. There's no guarantee, though, that the old man will be there. "When I'm done, I want my ashes to be scattered at the exact spot where I was born."

After leaving the bar, I passed a tiny boxing gym and saw a scrawny Mexican kid working the speed bag. On the wall were the flags of Mexico and the USA. Four blocks away, I then crossed paths with two Mexican teens playing guitar and accordion as they walked along.

"You guys going to a party?"

"No, we're coming from one!"

Unlike too many city kids, these boys didn't try to look tougher or older, which is excellent, really, for there's plenty of time left to be older, if they're lucky enough, that is, to be allowed to mature without being blasted from this earth, either domestically or at some far-flung "theater." As for Osceola, its fortunes are contingent on the rest of the country's increasingly strained ability to bring home the bacon.

SQUATTING IN NEW ORLEANS

10-15-14—This time, I got to New Orleans on a bus named Mega, and it also dropped me off at Elysian Fields. In Nola, there's a street called Arts, so of course there has to be one named Desire, and Tennessee Williams clearly saw the two as intertwined, thrusting and plunging their bodies against each other. Of course, death will interrupt this coupling not just finally but every step of the way.

Across the avenue, there was Gene's Curbside Daiquiris, with its colorful All Night Long, Suicide, Sweet Dreams and What the Fuck rum concoctions, etc., and on this side, there's the Phoenix Bar, home of the Bears and Bear Trappers Social Club. If I was into hidemen, I could have headed to the second floor to be chained, strapped, whipped and have my parts serviced or abused to my heart's desire, all while being showered with titillating insults. At street level, however, there's no hint of this theatrical decadence, and since Elysian Fields has eight lanes, including two for parking, it's mostly just cars zooming by endlessly, as they do all across this land.

I came to New Orleans to hang out with Brooks Johnson and his crew of squatters, see how they were scraping by on the fringe of a fringe city. Son of poet Kent Johnson, twenty-nine-year-old Brooks is struggling to stay afloat as he finds his way as a writer, artist and man. Half an hour after my evening arrival, we were sitting on the tailgate of his canopied, beat-up pickup truck. Drinking Coors, we chattered. Before this, we had only met in Chicago in 2009.

"So how are you making a living, man?"

"I'm doing housepainting and plumbing, but I was tutoring for Delgado Community College. They let me go."

"Why?"

"They never said. They were just kind of dicking me around. They'd say they had the budget to hire me, and then no, and then yes, and then no."

With so many humanities majors desperate for teaching jobs, colleges can afford to dick around just about everybody, even very accomplished candidates with multiple degrees.

"So how did you hook up with a contractor?"

"A lot of my friends work with this lady, Carol. She doesn't have her license or anything. She hires punks and queers. I do housepainting, plumbing and demo shit. I work off the books, have to, because this is the only way for me to make OK money. I don't think I'll ever be able to pay back my student loan."

"How much do you owe?"

"$12,000, so it's not too bad, comparatively."

"But it's still bad, because before you know it, it will become 20!"

"Totally! And it's like, fuck, I've gotten just one job from my degree, and it paid $12 an hour for twenty hours a week."

When a thumpingly raucous bus drove by, we had to pause. Here, you can rent a "party bus," and at the high end, it's like a 40-foot-long limousine with a granite-top bar, leather seats, flat-screen TV, disco lighting and brain-damaging sound system. The cheapest version seems no more than an old yellow school bus with a boom box. Since I don't understand the allure of being trapped with a fixed cast of people inside a very narrow, loud and expensive moving bar, you won't find me booking a party bus anytime soon. Still, it was charming to catch a glimpse of the laughing and hollering young people with their heads stuck out the windows.

"What did you major in?" I resumed.

Laughing, Brooks confessed, "English and art history."

"There you go," I laughed along with him, "It is pretty funny."

"It's hilarious! It's like a fuckin' scam. They got me! It's based on a lie. It's like, you can go to college, borrow this money, get a job and make it back."

"For pointing some of that shit out, I can't get hired now. I kept saying how problematic this whole setup is. Since you're the paying customer, the professor will pretend that you're some kind of a genius, that everyone's a genius. He'll flatter you to keep you hooked."

"Yeah, totally. They have to keep you tied in and borrowing from the banks."

I taught creative writing at Bard, Penn, Montana, Naropa and Muhlenberg. It's not that people shouldn't study English, art history, ceramics or creative writing, etc., but they shouldn't be juked and jived about their dismal prospects while being fitted with a bankster shackle around their callow neck, and if they suck at what they do, and I mean really, really suck, then they should be told to cut their losses right now, rather than be led on so cynically by those who are only pretending to be nurturing. It's you, young man or woman, who are supportive of your professors' salaries, not to mention the bulging bureaucracy above them.

"The last thing you want to do is to scare them away," I continued. "Let's say they're not doing the work, let's say they're really stupid or whatever, but you can't warn them about how precarious their future is because you'll be losing customers for the fuckin' corporation!"

"Exactly, and the other part of it is, I liked that job a lot because I could be real with people. It's the kind of dynamic education where you can be personal, one-on-one, and talk about life and what's going on."

I chuckled, "But you're not supposed to talk about life, man! That's why it's called a campus. You're not supposed to point to anything outside, since it will scare the students! You weren't a good soldier, man!"

"Exactly, and that's why I was getting the stink eye from the other instructors. Another thing is, I didn't have a shower for a long time. We were squatting and didn't have running water, so we were just drinking rainwater from a rain barrel, but finally, we got our shit together, so we're stealing water now. It's insanely easy! There's a water meter in front of every house, so all you need is a copper pipe, a right-sized gasket and a water key from Home Depot. There's a trick to it, but it's very simple."

"Can you steal electricity?"

"That's a lot harder, and dangerous. What we have is a temporary electric pole. After we paid the tax lien on the property, we became its caretaker, so now we're legal with the electricity."

The property, a double shotgun, is owned by one Rufus Rose, a black man in his eighties. Before the first squatter moved in, it had been left empty for six or seven years and was falling apart, with a leaking roof, sinking foundation and wrecked walls. Since Rose ignored his taxes for years, the squatters could claim the property by paying the city $1,200, but this modest sum is also all Rose needs to reclaim his house, and once he does that, these benign anarchists, or obnoxious spongers, depending on your point of view, can be booted out within a week. Instead of paying up, however, Rose tried to get the city to help him demolish the property, and he also came by give the squatters a piece of his mind. The old man bought houses when they were dirt cheap, and he owns a bunch.

The white squatters moved onto this all-black block in the Eighth Ward one by one, and now there are five of them, four males and a female. When their neighbors saw them come in, there was widespread suspicion and even hostile looks, for who knew what these grungy types were up to, but all negative feelings have dissipated. "People have even given us food," Brooks said. "One lady brought us spaghetti. Another gave us yaka mein. We've also brought food to our neighbors, and I've done a couple of easy repairs for them. You know, basic neighborly stuff." After taking over the house, the squatters have put in a new roof, painted the front in cheerful colors and fixed this and that to make the dwelling more habitable and not an eyesore.

In *Streetcar*, Williams writes, "New Orleans is a cosmopolitan city where there is a relatively warm and easy intermingling of races in the old part of town," and this appears to hold more than six decades later. Of course, the city now has a black majority, but its current mayor, Mitch

Landrieu, is white, and Laudrieu's father, Moon, also a mayor, is remembered for his fight in the sixties against segregation. One can assume that those who can't stand blacks, punks, queers or Vietnamese, etc., have removed themselves from New Orleans or never cared to live there in the first place, for this has long been one of the most eclectic and iconoclastic cities in all of America.

As for squatting, New Orleans has the tradition of the Batture Dwellers. Most numerous during the Great Depression, these are the poor and hardy folks who squat on a precarious strip of land between levees and riverbank. Technically dwelling on the Mississippi itself, their homes are not just ramshackle stilted shacks and houseboats, but also fairly spacious and sturdy cottages. When a storm comes, the river swells and I picture a couple lying on a bobbing bed while, next door, a cursing old fart stands belly-button-deep in a turbulent pool that's garnished with Mardi Gras beads, aluminum cans and driftwood. "Oh shit," he mutters.

Tennessee Williams never squatted in New Orleans, but he did skip out on his landlord, if we're to believe the account in his autobiographical "The Angel in the Alcove," "When I finally left there I fooled the old woman. I left by way of a balcony and a pair of sheets. I was miles out of town on the Old Spanish Trail before the old woman found out I had gotten past her."

Now, it's clear that this Postcard is anchored by the theme of petty criminality, with the implied justification that one's soul, not body, cannot be sustained any other way, for if a person squats, defaults on a bank loan, steals water or software, he's not trying to gain riches or comforts, but merely a bit of breathing room for his mind and spirit. Working at a restaurant and writing mostly on weekends, Tennessee Williams still couldn't make rent so had to hightail from his landlady, but the eventual results are so nourishing for the culture, no one would think of faulting the genius. Most turnstile-jumping or train-hopping young writers, though, won't yield even a single sharp sentence. Still, we must let as many of them go at it as possible, for not only may a Tennessee Williams emerge from the fray, but the much dimmer lights can also illuminate a basement or storefront theater for a moment or two. In any case, it's the local culture that will sustain us, and not the calculatingly concocted poison that's beamed relentlessly from the brainwashing centers!

"So what brought you down to New Orleans?" I asked Brooks.

"I've been trying to come down here for years. I rode a freight train down, like, eight years ago."

"All the way down?"

"Most of the way down. I got to Memphis, but they pulled me off and put me in the Shelby County Jail for a couple of days. They gave me time served."

"What did the judge say?"

"Basically, get the fuck out of here!"

"Was there a moral lecture?"

"Yeah, it was like, 'You guys are living all wrong,' that kind of stuff. It was my first time being in a jail. When I first went in, I was worried, like, oh shit, it's going to be all race-ganged-out, but it was chill. Memphis is really a prison town. It's either you're a guard or you go to jail. That became clear really quick, and my worry about the race gang thing wasn't real at all, because people were really helping us out."

"They could tell you were just kids, right?"

"For sure, they were super cool about it. After we were charged, we were put in this holding cell, and I was almost in a prison riot, because they kept pushing people in until there were, like, seventy of us in this small room. People had to stand on these benches. Two guys were standing on the toilet."

I roared at this detail, and Brooks laughed too. I said, "I'm sure it wasn't too funny then."

"Fuck no, it was hot as hell! There were four dudes in the corner having a really serious conversation, then one of them said, 'All right, if they put anybody else in here, we're going to grab the fuckin' guard and hold him until they let us out!' It was one of those moments where it's like—"

"Enough is enough!"

"Yeah, enough is enough. I knew I was supposed to be out soon, but

I had to be down with this, although I might have had to stay there for a lot longer."

"You didn't want to be the lone pussy!" I laughed.

"Hell, no! You have to go all the way with it! Thing is, they didn't put another person in and they let us out in about five minutes. It's insane, man, but it's not funny, really, especially with the women. Two of my friends, Candy and Vanessa, were kept at this prison that's way out of town, and when they let you out, it's at a time when no bus is running, you can't get a cab and it's a long walk to get anywhere, so women will walk down this road—"

"Holy fuck!"

"Yeah, and a car might stop to offer them a ride, but lots of time it's an undercover cop who would arrest them on prostitution charges, and send them right back."

"Why?! That's bizarre, isn't it?"

"It is super weird."

"I half expected you to say the guy was going to rape them, or make a deal, you know, like if you suck my dick, I let you go."

"Maybe that happens too, but from the stories my friends were told, it's about revenue for the city."

"So they're just eager to keep people in?"

"Yeah."

"I had a Philly friend. She tried to be a prostitute but wasn't successful. I guess she just wasn't good-looking enough. She studied printmaking, by the way, and was pretty good too. Anyway, her first potential client was this Japanese guy who slammed a door in her face, so her pimp wasn't too happy about that. Not knowing what to do, she just walked down the street, you know, and when she saw a cop car, she waved or some shit because she thought the cop would rescue her, but the cop then tried to fuck her, so she had to jump out of the car and run away from him! That's the easiest thing, you know, because if you're a prostitute and a cop fucks you, who's going to care?"

"Exactly. Cops are predators, man. They got a gun. They got everything."

In Tennessee Williams's "The Poet," a wandering, scrounging poet is occasionally raped when he sleeps outside, and though this leaves "his clothing torn open and sometimes not only a dampness of mouths on his flesh but painful bruises," the poet doesn't feel "any shame or resentment." In "The Alcove," Williams describes himself being more or less raped by a fellow tenant, a tubercular young artist who coughs up blood. It's telling that Williams would depict the poet as a raped and battered being, but in a 1981 interview with the *Paris Review*, Williams also spoke of the "terrible indignities, humiliations, privations, shocks that attend the life of an American writer," and this from a time when a serious artist like him could still be a national figure. Many of Williams's plays were adapted for Hollywood or television. Arthur Miller wrote screenplays, married Marilyn Monroe and the TV movie of his *Death of a Salesman* drew 25 million viewers on CBS in 1985. I'm citing relatively recent examples to show that it wasn't all that long ago when we still had functioning synapses between our ears. Jackson Pollock was profiled in *Life* magazine, and Steinbeck and Salinger were read by high school kids. Now, they have never heard of Mark Twain or think he might be a country singer, for in these gleefully illiterate and belligerently philistine United States, there is only a minuscule, coterie audience for any of the high arts, and this has been arrived at by design, of course, because it's a lot easier to rob and manipulate an idiotic population. Though we have a vast cultural heritage, it's being buried deeper and deeper, like a forgotten time capsule, while on the surface, blathering morons of every type are being pumped up and feted on a revolving stage.

Driving away from Elysian Fields, Brooks mentioned that a cop had been shot just outside Gene's Po-Boys two weeks earlier. Both killer and cop were black. Half a mile away, the shooter had killed another man at a party. New Orleans's murder rate is consistently about seven times the national average, and since 1985, it has led the nation in murders for twelve different years. In 2014, only 121 people have been killed through October 15th, however, so that's a considerable dip from the all-time high of 424 in 1994. Most of the time, New Orleans is the Big Easy, with old men playing dominoes beneath trees, chickens crossing roads, slow walking, outdoor drinking and slurry trombones, but then the shots would ring out. Among states, Louisiana has had the most murders per capita for twenty-five straight years. It is also the third-poorest.

The latest murder involves two men and a woman. The shooter is the father of her two kids, while the victim was someone she "knew through a current sexual relationship." Drunk, the hapless fornicator came by to borrow a scale, which was fine, but when he started to "squeeze" her, he was shot.

Leaving Marigny, we went to Fairgrounds, and at the Seahorse Saloon, I met one of Brooks's squatmates, Heather, as well as his boss, Carol. In her mid-sixties, Carol was a very large woman with an extremely well-developed beer belly, but I shouldn't talk, for my nickname during my housepainting days was "Pol Pot Belly," I kid you not. (Screw you, Hank, for giving me that moniker, though I wish you happy boozing and health wherever the hell you are.) Carol also had a very masculine voice, and as I shook her hammering hand, I actually thought she could be a man.

Raised on a small farm in Oklahoma, Carol was slim and pretty in youth, with the photos to prove it too. She married, had children, divorced, quit drinking, then came to New Orleans at age forty-two. Carol hadn't been in a bar in years, so was rather subdued this evening, but her pool game sure hadn't left her, for she simply kicked Heather's and Brooks's asses in quick succession. Clownish with a cue, I didn't dare challenge her.

In her early thirties, Heather's from a tiny village in South Dakota. She had on a black cap, black wig, black and tan top, black shorts, black fishnet stockings and black shoes, with just about everything quite weathered, like a beat-up barn. Granting her bits of good luck, a tiny horseshoe pendant rested on her sternum. At seven o'clock from her right outer canthus, there was also a single French quotation mark, elongated and facedown, but I forgot to ask her what it meant. Like Brooks and, in fact, all of the other squatters, Heather studied English in college. Paired with a fiddler, Heather plays guitar and sings in a plaintive, sometimes cracked voice, and the music is a combination of Appalachia and Dylan from his *Desire* album. They've performed at the Mudlark, a hub of underground arts. At the Seahorse, though, I hadn't known that her lyrics tended to be queer, and so I asked if she had ever been married. "Look at me!" She guffawed. "Do I look like I've been married?"

"I don't know! What does a married face look like?"

That night, I was given my own room at the squat, and though the sheet was stiff with old sweat, I was grateful to be taken in and horizontal. In the middle of the night, I had to get up, and since I didn't know that the toilet was inside, and the shower a makeshift stall outside, I groped my way out to stand among the banana tree and chicken coop, beneath a crescent moon. With the weather so balmy, I felt I could kiss the equator half a world away.

At Brooks's age, I lived over a print shop in a space that was so poorly insulated, I froze my nuts off through two winters. It was almost as bad as sleeping outside, but with the smell of a kerosene heater plus chemicals from downstairs, not to mention the unceasing grinding of gears during the daytime. My sculptor roommate had two cats that didn't seem to like the maddening cold any better than us, and when Betty, a scrawny oxicat, fell sick, Jay promptly suffocated her under a pillow, then threw her out with the trash.

As an unknown painter in Greenwich Village in the late thirties, Franz Kline survived mostly on sugar and coffee, so it was definitely not a good idea when a friend asked Kline to take care of his German shepherd. Starving, the dog tried to eat a bar of soap and died, which prompted Kline to remark, "It just shows you that a bohemian is someone who could live where an animal would die."

To eat at all, bohemians must be extra resourceful. Before New Orleans, Brooks spent a couple of months in the California desert, and there he learned to catch pheasants with a box trap, "All you need is a box, twig, rope and some breakfast cereal." It's a simple, almost childish skill, yet most of us don't know it, and of course few can feather and gut a chicken. Perhaps they can set this up as a four-year, fully accredited program? Borrowing $100,000 from Bank of America, a student can major in gizzard removal.

Squatting or no, one still has to make a living, and Chris, the thirty-two-year-old head of this crew, runs a tour guide business. Starting from The Sweet Palate, tourists are led through the French Quarter or nearby cemeteries, and they pay whatever they feel like at the end, which usually ranges between ten and twenty bucks. Originally from Milwaukee, Chris is a playwright and fiction writer.

Rhode Island-born Nolan, in his early twenties, is a poet who admires Frank O'Hara and Kenneth Koch. This summer, he went to Humboldt County in Northern California to trim marijuana. Paid $200 a pound, he averaged one and a half pounds per day, working twelve hours. Listening to Books on Tape, he endured this tedious task for three weeks. "It's crazy to be in a room with thirty pounds of weed, and the illegality of it all also bothered me. It's still a felony in California to grow that much weed, so even though I was just a trimmer, I don't think I'm going to go back." Since logging is dead in Humboldt County, pot growing is the meat, skin, heart and backbone of the local economy, and for pot prices to stay high, its cultivation has to remain illegal. What you have, then, are a bunch of towns where just about everyone is a criminal, and they want to stay that way forever just to survive.

Connecticut-born Sergio, in his early twenties, is also a poet. In a red bathrobe, he sat with the others on an old, frayed couch to watch a movie. I didn't talk to him. Without cable television, the squatters get their screen fix by staring at videos. There were about seventy in the house.

In the end, though, there is no romance in going without a proper shower, stove or heating system, but one must handle it with resilience and even defiance and humor should that become one's lot, and of course, poor artists are just a tiny fraction of the millions of Americans who have gone neo-primitive, and this number will only spiral up. Missing a few utility payments, one will be plunged into the dark and cold, but at least there won't be anything left in the refrigerator to go bad. Rotting slums, ragged trailer parks and tent cities already dot this "greatest of countries."

For a contrast to Brooks, let's check out, briefly, his girlfriend, Shira, from Brooklyn Heights. Twenty-four years old, Shira studied media arts at NYU and has already published a well-received comic book. Besides drawing comics, Shira also plays bass in punk bands and does performance art. Though only working part-time in a library, she lives in a Mid-City apartment that costs $1,100 a month. Clearly, Shira's much better situated and more advanced artistically than the others, but she also comes from a completely different background. Her mom is a noted modern dancer, her brother a rising star in Hollywood and her dad was a publishing executive.

Burning to make art, poor kids ignore or are ignorant of the fact that it's essentially a rich man's game, but as Tennessee Williams observed, "If they're meant to be writers, they will write. There's nothing that can stop them. It may kill them." Further, if a poor kid can tough it out somehow, he has stories to tell and experiences to relate that his more privileged peers have only read about.

In 2011, Brooks Johnson and another cultural guerrilla staged a demonstration at a Raúl Zurita reading at the Poetry Foundation in Chicago. Flyers were handed out and two banners were unfurled from a balcony, "WHAT WOULD HAVE HAPPENED IF EMILY DICK-INSON HAD BEEN PRESCRIBED PROZAC?" and "VIVA CADA." The Prozac dig refers to the Poetry Foundation being funded by the maker of Prozac, Cialis and the autism-causing thiomersal. At the end of America, poetry is supposed to put you to sleep with a hard-on. Also, the Poetry Foundation's president was John Barr, a former investment banker and leading figure in energy deregulation. Such a sick knot of symbolism deserved to be mocked, but the Poetry Foundation was certainly not amused. They called the cops.

Soon, too soon, it was time for me to leave, and before I went to the station, I sat for a while at Canal and Basin, right in front of the Simón Bolívar statue. As I ate some leftover Mexican meat balls, a black man in his mid-sixties, sitting on a nearby bench, started a conversation, "I have a new apartment, and it only costs me $300 a month!"

"Where?"

"Three blocks from here."

"Sounds way too cheap!"

"I'm in this program. It's brand-new too, with a dishwasher and every-thing."

"Damn!"

"You damn right! You see that hotel there? People pay $150 just to sleep there for one night. That's insane! I can't imagine spending that kind of money, and for what?! All you're going to do is shit, piss and lie down, and before you know it, it's time to check out! It's insane, I tell you. I'd rather sleep outside, on this bench."

"I hear you."

"I'm thinking of renting my room out. For $300, you can stay in my room for two weeks!"

"Then where would you sleep?"

"On the couch, but you can have the rest of it, and I won't get in your way. I'll be gone most of the day."

"It's a pretty good deal."

"You need a room?"

"I'm leaving town."

"How about $20 for just tonight?"

"I'm leaving, and I'm kind of broke too."

"You don't have $20?"

"Actually, no," and I really didn't. I had $19 which must last for the next forty hours.

"I'm down to three bucks myself," my new friend commiserated. "I want to buy a bag of weed, but I'm $2 short."

"When will you get more money?"

"The first! That's three days from now. I'm on Social Security. I get $800 a month. I'm all right. I have some sausage and bacon cooked up at home, and I also have beans and rice with some butter in it. I'm all right."

"Do you drink?"

"Very little. I know a place on Bourbon where you can get three cans of Budweiser for five bucks!"

"And how much weed do you smoke?"

"Just two bags, though sometimes I buy me a $10 bag."

When a woman walked by, he shouted, "How are you doing, baby?" She ignored him. Turning to me, he growled, "She ain't from here. People down here are friendly."

Though in his sixties, he was remarkably trim yet muscular, and to show off his physique, the old man wore a low-cut lead-colored tank top, with an open indigo-and-white-striped shirt draped over it. Pop was stylin', to tell you the truth.

"This chick I know can't pay her phone bill," he continued. "She's $66 short, so she said, if I gave her that, we could have sex."

"How old is she?"

"Thirty-two, and she's pretty good-looking too. She works at a strip club."

"But you only have three bucks, though."

"I wouldn't anyhow. I have never paid for sex!"

"That's pretty good!"

"All night long, they walk up and down Canal, trying to sell their pussies, while on Bourbon, they're just trying to give it away! A woman can only do two things, sell it or give it away! I have never paid for sex!"

Most men have a hard enough time giving it away, much less selling it, and there's no transcendence in their in-and-outs, but Oliver Winemiller, Tennessee Williams's New Orleans gay prostitute, is described as not just a sexual but psychic savior, and even a Christlike figure, "To some he became the archetype of the Savior Upon the Cross who had taken upon himself the sins of their world to be washed and purified in his blood and passion." Handsome yet missing an arm through a car accident, Winemiller is also compared to "a broken statue of Apollo," but more than Jesus or Apollo, Winemiller is really a reincarnation of Bras-Coupé, a New Orleans slave turned bandit. Considered an avenging hero by blacks, and a demonic terror by whites, Bras-Coupé first became notorious for his dancing in Congo Square. A place for slaves to let loose once a week, Congo Square was an intensification of those qualities we've come to associate with New Orleans, wild, unassimilably alien, joyous but also seething. After he was shot by whites and lost his arm, Bras-Coupé got even by leading a growing band to rob and kill whites. The fictional Winemiller, on the other hand, kills only one rich guy, a yacht owner who has hired him to have sex in front of the camera. Denied ownership of their bodies and treated like meat, they both retaliate and are punished by death. New Orleans is itself a maimed yet transcendent whore, and unlike Las Vegas, it is essentially real.

In New Orleans, Amtrak and Greyhound share the same building, and with so much traffic passing through, I simply assumed the station would be open all night, but when I got there around 10:40 p.m. for my 7 a.m. departure the next day, they wouldn't let me in, so I ended up, only too appropriately, sleeping on concrete under the Pontchartrain Expressway. Using a corner of my backpack as pillow, I curled up clutching my camera bag and managed to sleep fitfully until 5, when the station finally opened. Around 3:30, a man lay down a few feet from me, which was not remarkable in the least, since we gave each other added security. A mugger would hesitate to approach a group of sleeping homeless, since there's a pretty good chance someone is not quite sleeping, and may even have his eyes wide open in the dark. What was remarkable was a man who appeared out of nowhere to place a jacket under the sleeping man's head, since he didn't have anything to use as a pillow. Done with this task, he simply disappeared, and if I were a liar, I'd even add that he had one arm.

HANGING ON IN TAYLOR

11-30-14—The sixteen-year-old's consciousness was percussive with recorded music, as usual, when the train slammed into him, and it's not clear, even now, if it was suicide or merely absentmindedness that killed this boy. (To have your inner life constantly stunted or suffocated is already a form of death, but had he lived, this incipient man may eventually have outgrown his three-chord addiction.) Home in Taylor, Pennsylvania, Chuck Orloski was already in bed when he received the call to drive four hours to that ghastly site where it was his job to clean up the unholy mess. Like a mortifying penitent in an impossibly long church, Chuck knelt on lumpy or jagged track ballast and inched along for half a mile to pick up five perfectly aligned teeth still embedded in gums, a spleen and so many other bloody bits as his supervisor stood over him with a flashlight. It took eight hours to scrounge all that could be salvaged from this exploded human form. Ah, but the pay was half-decent! Or $23.75 an hour, to be exact.

On another occasion, Chuck and his coworkers removed blood-splattered boxes of frozen crinkle-cut french fries that had tumbled out of a tractor-trailer lying on its side, mangled, at the bottom of a leafy embankment. There is so much fluid inside each of us. It was football season and Penn State won that weekend, if memory serves. The dead driver was a seventy-year-old man who had lived in his cab. Wifeless, he covered his personal space with naked crotch shots of various ladies. What others hazily consign to mental albums, he made concrete and permanent, or at least much more so than his flesh. Staring nostalgically at a Kodak labial flare, did the pay-by-the-half-hour Don Juan even recall the smoky, drunken or drugged smile that came with it? Nodding off at the wheel, perhaps he was dreaming of a truck stop angel.

A constant phrase among Chuck and his coworkers was, "Eat some shit!" This rallying cry steeled them as they dealt with yet another toxic or bloody horror. "Eat some shit!" they'd grumble at each other as they tried to remove a chemical spill from the freeway or the lovely suicide's splattered brains from a motel bed, floor and wall. Heading to a hellish scene, Chuck often clutched his rosary. Knowing it wasn't easy to find another job that paid $23.75 an hour, Chuck toughed it out and tried his best to ignore the abusive and, at times, psychotically menacing behavior from two of his bosses, but what else could he do? Like employees everywhere, Chuck just ate shit and grinned. In March, however, they fired him anyway. Chuck emailed me, "The termination is actually a 'mercy killing' of sort. Two decades of 24/7 emergency responses have gotten the best of my mental health, and the ruthless branch manager took every shot he could at me. At age 62, in life's 9th inning, I can start collecting Social Security and maybe unemployment money for a while—must learn how the freaking system works."

A month later, Chuck reported, "I am looking at PA Employment office training to become a 'Certified Nursing Aide.' The State will pay the full-cost for this, capped @ $5,000. Colleges charge on average $30,000 to become an Licensed Practical Nurse, and at age 62, it makes little sense to take a college loan for this endeavor. I'd really like to do something to help people & make some money, and IDEALLY of course, avoid management tyrants. If this nursing deal does not pan out, I plan to get a bus driver endorsement on my Class B Commercial Driver License. Anything but re-entering life as a 24/7 emergency spill responder. F#@uck that."

Alas, Chuck became a school bus driver, but this happy ending is blighted by the fact that his pay is just over a quarter of what it used to be, and when there's a snow day, like tomorrow, Chuck doesn't get paid at all. Such jobs used to be unionized and well-compensated, but in today's economy, a man must leap at any bone that's flung his way. Meanwhile, Chuck's wife, Carol, is still stricken by rheumatoid arthritis, lupus and carpal tunnel syndrome. For four decades, Carol was a waitress.

With jobs so scarce, workers have even less leverage against asshole bosses or managers, and starting one's own business is hardly a solution, considering how many of them have been wiped out by huge corporations. On Main Streets across America, countless mom-and-pops are left vacant or replaced by chain stores.

A year and a half ago, I went to see the Orloskis, stayed at their house and wrote about it. Chuck told me much about Scranton and Taylor, recounted his grandfather's life as a coal miner and even took me to see his mother-in-law, Florence, who had spent half a century as a seamstress. I talked to Chuck's older son, Daniel, who wished CVS, the chain drug store on Main Street, would give him more hours. Chuck's other child, Joseph, was lost to the television.

Last week, I visited the Orloskis again, and since I got in before Chuck was finished with his driving, I left downtown Scranton and headed south. The Scranton area is populated mostly by Irish, Polish and Italians, with an influx in recent years of Mexicans, Puerto Ricans and Dominicans. It is still overwhelmingly white, and though very poor, much safer than others of similar size. In 2012, there was no murder in Scranton proper, population 76,000, and just one each for 2013 and 2014.

With so much barbarity in the nightly news, our capacity to be outraged has been diminished to an alarming degree, and one has to wonder at what point, exactly, will we cease to be civilized or even socialized? Two recent crimes shook the Scranton area. In June of 2013, a Taylor woman and her two daughters were charged with starving her retarded son to death. Though thirty-one years old, he weighed only 69 pounds and had open sores all over his body, with bones showing in places. Interviewed by the police, the fifty-nine-year-old seemed unaware of her likely jail stint, for she asked if she'd still receive her dead son's Social Security checks of $1,042 a month. To those closest to him, Robert Gensiask was little more than a fetid cash machine. Locals were also astonished by the huge size of the three women.

In May of 2014, a sixteen-year-old, Aazis Richardson, called for a cab at 3 a.m., then shot the driver, Vincent Darbenzio, twice in the back of the head "because he didn't listen" to Richardson's driving instructions.

"Is that a reason to kill someone?" a reporter asked.

"To me it is," the soulless-eyed, sullen young man coolly blurted.

"Do you have anything to say to the victim's family?"

"Fuck them."

In Scranton, the "We Buy Gold" shops are everywhere, so it's obvious its population is going broke, and on the wire fences of electrical substations, there are all these signs showing handcuffs, and:

Our metal in your hands?

Their metal around your wrists

REWARD

PPL Electric Utilities is offering a reward of up to $1,000 for information that leads to the arrest and conviction of anyone responsible for stealing copper wire, or other materials, from any of its facilities.

Stealing wire from electrical facilities and equipment is dangerous!

Severe injuries or death could result.

Needing quick cash, Americans are stripping the greatest nation on earth's infrastructure. A 2013 headline from CNBC: "Copper theft 'like an epidemic' sweeping US."

Most of the houses in Scranton are still well-kept, however, and there is no trash or graffiti to speak of. It was extremely cold that day and with the topography somewhat hilly, I soon got tired of traipsing around, so I asked a man sitting in a parked car to point me to the nearest bar. He suggested Bacwals, which I misheard as Back Wall, and this evoked, somehow, the famous Goya execution scene . . .

I opened the door, saw only old men, heard no music, yeah, then discovered that each pint of Yuengling would only set me back two bucks. Thank you, Lord! Though Ben Franklin never declared, "Beer is proof that God loves us and wants us to be happy," it's still an insight worthy of Poor Richard. Settled, I dialed Chuck to tell him where I was, but Carol answered, so I talked to her for a bit. Since my last visit, the Orloskis had given up their cell phones.

Old-timers who had known each other forever, they talked about how much things used to cost, how you could get a beer and hot dog for only 25 cents at a long-dead bar, and how at another joint, three beers were also a quarter, as were two boiled eggs, "Though I only bought one at a time for 15 cents. I still don't know why. Maybe I'm stupid."

A gent with a lingering Irish brogue came in, "How come it's so hot in here?"

"It ain't hot," the short, white-haired bartender responded. "The heat's not even on."

"It's your testosterone," said a man in a baritone drawl. "It's your hormones."

"Testosterone?! I lost that a long time ago!"

"How about your brain?"

"That too. I ain't got nothing left."

"You've gained a lot of weight, that's for sure."

"You know what it is? It's my hernia."

"I have a hernia too, but I don't look like you."

"I have five hernias!"

"Five! You go to the hospital all the time. Why don't you have them removed?"

"They can't be taken out. I just take these pills for the pain, that's all."

"Drink more of that!"

"I do."

"Eat right."

"I'm seventy years old. I don't give a shit what I eat."

"Go to a good doctor. Go to Dr. Frankenstein!"

"Hey, I wouldn't want him to turn me into you!"

A man came in wearing an ushanka, which prompted Baritone Drawl to exclaim, "Holy Jesus!"

"No, it's only me!"

Brogue, "That's just his hair."

Eventually, I talked to Brogue and found out that he was in the Navy during the Vietnam War and has two grandchildren who're half-Chinese. When our conversation strayed into politics, he declared, "We shouldn't have two parties in this country, because they cancel each other out and nothing gets done! I think we should only have one party."

When Brogue complained about Obama's immigration diktat, I pointed out that the Executive Office shouldn't be able to start wars either, but he disagreed, "The president is the commander-in-chief, so he can start wars." Then, "What really gets me are the freeloaders. There is a segment of the population who think they're still living on the plantation. They want the government to do everything for them!"

Like a cruise vacation or the gulag, slavery is also an all-inclusive package, I suppose, but though crudely put, Brogue's assessment of black dependency doesn't differ essentially from the analysis of Thomas Sowell, a black conservative. Seeking to explain the much higher level of achievement among West Indians as compared to American-born blacks, Sowell pointed out a key difference in their histories, "Unlike slaves in the United States, who were issued food rations and were often fed from the common kitchen, West Indian slaves were assigned land and time to raise their own food. They sold surplus food in the market to buy amenities for themselves. In short, West Indian Negroes had centuries of experience in taking care of themselves, even under slavery, as well as experience with buying and selling . . . They had the kind of incentives and experience common in a market economy but denied American slaves for two centuries."

With this in mind, what does that say about the state of all Americans as more become dependent on government and private charities just to eat from day to day? Even many of those with jobs can't get by without food stamps, church pantries or soup kitchens, and with self-employment harder to achieve than ever, we're also being corralled into a new kind of plantation. A system that prevents you from fishing will throw you a fish bone. Economically castrated, we're also losing our basic rights. Down into slavery!

Speaking of free food, the owner of Bacwal's came in and gave everyone a peanut-sprinkled and chocolate-dipped ice cream cone, and a patron also brought a large box of bagels, "My brother works in a bakery. They'd have just thrown them away. They're still excellent, though. Take as many as you want!" He even had paper bags to put them in.

The man to my right, Larry, filled me in on his life, "I've always had two jobs, but I lost them both five years ago."

"What did you do?"

"I fixed dentist equipment and was a deliveryman. My wife also had two jobs. She worked in a cafeteria and a nursing home."

"Did she lose her jobs too?"

"She quit one. After working in the cafeteria for twenty-five years, she was only paid $9.25 an hour, and her boss was an asshole. Now, I'm a school crossing guard. I only work an hour a day. My wife does the same. Together, we make $40 a day."

"Wow, man, that's nothing!"

"It's enough to pay for the groceries and taxes. They've gone way up!"

"You don't pay rent?"

"No, I own my own home. I got a good deal, though. It's my grandma's, and we were already living in it when she died. In her will, she left it to my dad, me and my brothers, so I paid them $25,000. Even before that, though, I paid rent. I had to get married at eighteen because I got my girlfriend pregnant. She was a year older than me."

"She was the older woman!"

"Yeah, she took advantage of me! But it's worked out. We're still together, and I'm fifty-nine."

"You look good!"

"I'm going to the doctor tomorrow. I haven't seen one in eight years."

"I haven't seen one in a lot longer than that. Is anything wrong with you?"

"I don't know. I'll find out tomorrow."

"You come here every day?"

"Most days."

"How about your wife?"

"No, she doesn't drink at all."

"She's never been to this place?"

"Never, and I wouldn't want her to see it. I mean, just look at it!"

"It's not so bad. One thing, though, I've been here for about three hours and haven't seen a single woman. At least your wife doesn't have to worry about you hitting on women!"

"And the women who do come in here, you wouldn't want to hit on anyway, believe me!"

Finally, Chuck came in, "You know, I've been a hermit and haven't been out in weeks!" After a beer and a quick game of pool with one Dana, whom Chuck met at the jukebox, we left for Taylor. In her "HOOPS FOR TROOPS" T-shirt, Dana appeared as schlocky as the rest of us, but she was in fact a lawyer. She also volunteered, quite unprompted, that she had been the live-in lover of Jason Miller, the Pulitzer-winning playwright of *That Championship Season*, by far the most famous literary work about Scranton.

"It's weird, ain't it, Chuck, that she just told us that?"

"And he was a lot older too."

Trim, youthfully dressed, with his Eagles cap, round glasses, salt-and-pepper soul patch and often smiling, Chuck exuded a serenity that belied the considerable amount of stress he'd gone through the last several years, what with losing his job and Carol's deteriorating health, among many other worries. Three weeks earlier, he had written to me, "I try to be a gentleman but fail. My mind, body and spirit have gone through dramatic changes since 1952, and I still do not understand what brought me to be a school bus driver and maker-of-response to your email." Like many others, like me, Chuck's surface equanimity and good humor rest on a quivering bedrock of bewilderment, frustration, sadness, dread and not a small bit of anger.

Fifty of his sixty-two years, Chuck Orloski has spent in the Scranton area, where he was born, so he has seen a vast cast of characters evolve. As we drove or walked around over two days, Chuck kept running into old faces. In a bank parking lot, Chuck waved at a funeral director, then said to me, "I should ask him for driving work over Christmas. I must have an income for those two weeks I have off." Then, "You know, when my dad died, we didn't have enough money for the funeral, so we had to pay him back a little at a time."

Chuck stopped his car to say hello to a confused-looking man, "Hey, Sal!"

After I was introduced, the unsmiling man asked, "Taking pictures?"

"Yeah, just for fun!"

"Nothing wrong with that."

Chuck jumped in, "Hey, Sal, can I buy you a coffee?"

"Sure," and so Chuck handed him a buck.

Driving away, Chuck explained, "Sal is a little slow. People help him out. He used to hang out all day at this diner, Sluckie's, but it has shut down."

"It was weird to see him just standing there like that," and it was bitterly cold that afternoon, in the low 20's.

"He has nowhere to go!"

There is almost no foot traffic on Taylor's Main Street and no tavern left in this entire borough of 6,200 souls. One evening, we popped into an Italian restaurant and bar in neighboring Old Forge and found ourselves the only customers. "It's the day before payday," the bartender explained. "This place used to be jumping," Chuck told me. "I could have become its manager had I married the owner's daughter. He liked me a lot. I was dating her."

Ever since Carol got too sick to work five years ago, the Orloskis have had to resort to the food pantry at St. Ann's, their parish church. In an email, Chuck elaborated, "My company's family health insurance also skyrocketed to $14,000 a year. Ever the stoic, Carol used to make light, insisted, 'We'd be O.K. financially were it not for the need to EAT.' The cost of food also skyrocketed." For the last five months, Chuck has also been a volunteer, at least two days a week, at St. Francis of Assisi Soup Kitchen. It's a bright, cheery place that serves over 200 people each day at lunch, plus dinner three nights a week. Most of the folks who eat there aren't homeless, just poor, and during my visit, I saw people of all ages, including small kids. Entire families would come in, as well the odd street walker in her skimpy outfit. No one is turned away. Many would show up half an hour beforehand and wait just inside the door. That day, lunch was pierogies, cheese pizza, fruit salad and bread, with everything freshly made.

When Chuck greeted an old lady he had given a jacket to, she told him its texture chafed her skin, and on top of that, it had to be dry cleaned, so he promised to find her another one. Chuck is always giving stuff away, and this time, like the last, I had to restrain him from stuffing my backpack with all sorts of gifts, but since he was so relentlessly giving, I went home with a Phillies baseball cap, Phillies knit cap and a book.

I was hoping to see Jack, whom I had talked to during my last visit, but he wasn't around. Busted with two thousand kilograms of pot, yes, two tons of ganja!, Jack was locked up for twenty-two years, but now he had a paid job at St. Francis of Assisi. Both Chuck and I marvel at Jack's absence of bitterness. When I howled at "two tons," Jack cracked up too.

On the day I left, there was the Santa Parade in downtown Scranton. I'm very fond of homespun, small-time parades where crude floats roll by, kids perform basic dance steps that even I can pull off, sort of, and one civic group or another in casual clothes simply march and wave. I also like the goofiness that's also often on display, and in Scranton, it was three ducks in a cage being pushed by a waddling woman, sombrero-wearing donkeys, humans transformed into walking Christmas presents, an inflated Statue of Liberty that struggled to stay upright, teen girls in "I LOVE MY JOB" sweatshirts and a puffy and glowering Ronald McDonald who was clearly in the last stage of a psychotic breakdown.

Chuck's younger son, Joseph, was one of four young people carrying a banner for the Pennsylvania State Police. Since I saw him in 2013, Joseph has matured into a solid young man with two part-time jobs, at a supermarket and video game store, and he has a plan for the future. Dating the daughter of a state trooper, Joseph also wants to be one, although it will take five years of studying. Meanwhile, his brother Dan is majoring in psychology at Keystone College, where he lives on campus, though each weekend he comes home to work at CVS, a job he has had for over two years. Dan wants to eventually get a master's in head shrinking, which worries Chuck, naturally, but if that's the young man's passion, who's to stop him? With this economy being strangled and disemboweled, just about every profession is endangered, so there's no surefire career choice. The bottom line is we have too many people going to college, and doing so will also weigh down your future if it entails crippling loans. Still, there are many social benefits to attempting a higher education, for it's good for any young person to be liberated from parents and home. Removed from one's upbringing and its stifling thought patterns, one can sample new ideas, hair colors, spiked cocktails, what's left of free love and personalized or unprecedented sexual orientations, for example, and with the right instructors, one can also learn how to write in loopy, looping and ungrammatical sentences.

Although Dan has received financial aid, including a grant from the Office of Vocational Rehabilitation due to his cerebral palsy, he will still owe $40,000 by the time he graduates in May of 2015. Dan's among the millions of poor Americans who are led to believe a college education at a second- or third-tier school, at whatever cost, will still lead, inexorably, to a brighter future. Although they are merely businesses that must compete with each other for customers, colleges pose as life mentors and nurturers to their students, and in this disguise, steer millions of wide-eyed marks towards the rapaciously criminal banks. Marketing has become an American college's first order of business, not education.

This year, Keystone charges $21,750 in tuition and fees. In comparison, UPenn docked $9,600 for the same in 1984, so for the current cost of a Keystone education, one could attend an Ivy League school for two years, with enough bouncing coins left over for many cases of beer and bong hits. UPenn's tuition and fees are now $47,668. Of course, wages haven't increased fivefold in thirty years. The obscene overpricing of a diluted education is yet another sign that we're failing future generations. To stuff the pockets of a few smirking old farts and their precious scions, countless young people are maimed.

The Orloski household now has three working adults, but only one car, and the buses barely run in Taylor, so on many days it's a Chinese fire drill just to get everyone to where they need to be on time. Chuck also has an old motorcycle, but it's not practical to use in winter.

Behind Joseph at the Santa Parade was an old military truck carrying Tiffany Dickson, widow of Bryon K. Dickson II, a state trooper recently killed by Eric Frein. During the forty-eight days when hundreds of cops searched for the murderer, they managed to accost a man who somewhat resembles Eric Frein dozens of times. "I lost count after twenty," James Tully told ABC News. Frein is six three with a pudgy face, and Tully five nine with a narrow face, but they're both very pale, and that's close enough to account for the law enforcement confusion.

One day, Tully was stopped seven times altogether. Exasperated, he took to wearing a reflective vest plus lanyard with his driver's license and work ID. One has to wonder, though, what kind of police intelligence and coordination can fail to figure out that the same poor schmuck they stop, day after day, on the same road, is not the cop killer-survivalist they were looking for? During Tully's most harrowing encounter, a screaming, camouflage-dressed man pointed a rifle at him as he ordered Tully to lie on the ground, face down, with his arms spread out. Kneeling on Tully's back, the presumed cop yanked Tully's IDs from his neck. "Good thing it had a break away clasp or he would have choked me," Tully said to the *Pocono Record*, "From the minute I saw him with that gun I thought, let me survive this."

His ordeal far from over, Tully added, "I'm worried about what is going to happen with the next one. Is he going to shoot first and ask questions later?" With our cops known to pump a dozen bullets into a suspect within seconds of spotting him, then, with guns still trained, handcuff the bloody corpse, it's not too paranoid a fear. With such police tactics at home, it's no wonder why we're so popular as liberators worldwide! To show even more unequivocally that he was not the fugitive, Tully should have decked himself in feathers and sequins, like a mummer, then strutted down the side of the road strumming a banjo. Actually, that's a terrible idea, for the authorities could cite said instrument as the rationale for splattering him. "Dressed in colorful camouflage to blend with the autumnal foliage, suspect pointed an object with barrel and stock, just like any assault rifle, at our peace officers. Ignoring our telepathic instructions, suspect then charged forward while screaming 'Oh, dem golden slippers!'"

The reason why Tully was always walking around and ready to be pounced on by cops was because he had no car. Each day, he spent four hours trekking to and from work. Living in a badly laid out country that's unraveling economically, many Americans are already familiar with Tully's one-manpower, sweating-and-huffing, uphill or through the rain, sleet, hurricane or snow, leg-it-out commute, and these ranks will only balloon. Tully's story does have a happy ending, however, for a neighbor organized an online fundraising that netted him $23,025.15. A local church also raised $985. With contributions from well over a thousand people, Tully is now driving, with money left over for insurance and gas.

Walking for many blocks along the parade route, Chuck would ask the cotton candy, hot dog or toy vendors how business was going, and they all said it was terrible, no one was buying anything, and it's true we only saw one kid getting his face sticky with cotton candy and another blowing into a plastic horn. Nobody was buying nada!

For two decades now, it's traditional to head into the Steamtown Mall after the parade, so that's what we did. Just outside, we saw a shabbily dressed old guy fish a cigarette butt from a standing ashtray. "How are you doing today?" Chuck said, for he greets everybody, but the dude didn't respond. Walking inside, we found the mall to be nearly empty, with over two-thirds of its retail spaces vacant. In the remaining stores, still brightly lit, employees stood staring out at nothing.

"This was the centerpiece of Scranton's urban renewal," Chuck explained. "This place used to be packed. Let's go find Santee Claus." (Yes, that's how Chuck pronounces "Santa.")

If this was the downtown mall after a big parade, just outside, I can only imagine what it looks like at midday during the week. A naked Miley Cyrus could twerk her ass off and no one would notice. Just five years ago, hundreds of teenage girls swarmed into Steamtown to scream lovingly at a baby-faced Justin Bieber.

Hey, here comes Santee Claus! With no kids lining up to see him, the rotund fellow in the rather mangy outfit was wandering around this still sparkling, well-maintained yet comatose temple of shopping. Cerulean banners with graphic snowflakes streamed from the cathedral-high ceiling. In the abandoned stores' windows, cheerful tableaux had been set up to shoo away the gloom. In one, disco-dancing John Travolta, Mr. Spock, Kermit the Frog and a cruise ship pinup tried to perk us up. In another, there were Captain America, Indiana Jones and Ecto-1, the Ghostbusting car. Meandering through the American ruins, we shall be comforted by shards and peeling evocations of American pop icons. Classic rock songs will be our dirges. "Ooh baby, it's a wild world!" Across this Potemkin nation, faux frontage has become a thriving business, for we're still the world leader in illusions, after all, though our top hat, red cape and white gloves have become seriously threadbare. Soon enough, we'll be booed off the stage, if not arrested, put on trial, then lined up in front of a firing squad.

Looking bored, Santee only grinned when bumping into a rare window-shopper. I greeted him, "How are you doing, sir?"

"Call me Santa," he whispered, winked, smiled.

Santee has worked at this mall every Christmas, ever since it opened in 1993. Business started to dip in 2000, but things didn't get awful until five years ago, "It's bankrupt. The banks own it now. In the past, the rent was so high here, it was unbelievable. For a kiosk like this," he pointed, "you had to pay eight to ten grand for the Christmas season, for three months, and you had to pay it up front."

"When was this, Santee?" Chuck asked.

"Nineteen ninety-six, -seven . . . This place is so boring, teenagers don't even come. Sometimes they throw coins at me from the second level!"

"Why?!"

"Because they're teenagers. The last three weeks before Christmas, it will get a little busy, mostly because of me."

"But how come the kids aren't here now?" I asked. "We thought you'd be mobbed!"

"People are afraid to come inside. There used to be a lot of homeless, you know, and crimes."

"Inside here?"

"Yes, and down in the basement. There was a rape down there."

"Rape?!" Chuck blurted. "How come we didn't hear about it?"

"They had to keep it quiet."

The dying mall has attracted some odd tenants, such as a satellite branch of the public library and an office of the State Attorney General's Child Predator Unit. As malls die across the country, we'll see many kinds of creative repurposing. Already, there are churches and casinos inside half-dead malls, so why not massage parlors, detox centers, transient hotels, haunted houses, prisons, petting zoos or putt-putt golf courses (covering the entire mall)? Leaving Santee, Chuck and I wandered into the food court, where only three of twelve restaurant slots were still occupied. On the back wall of this forlorn and silent space was a mural put up by Boscov, the mall's main tenant. Titled "B part of your community," it reads:

KINDNESS COUNTS / PLANT A TREE / MAKE A
DONATION / HELP A NEIGHBOR / VISIT THE
ELDERLY / HOPE / ADOPT A PET / DRIVE A HYBRID /
PICK UP TRASH / VOLUNTEER / CONSERVE ENERGY
/ RECYCLE / JOIN SOMETHING / PAINT A MURAL /
HUG SOMEONE / SMILE / DRINK FILTERED WATER /
GIVE YOUR TIME / USE SOLAR ENERGY / FEED THE
HUNGRY / ORGANIZE A FUNDRAISER / CREATE
AWARENESS / FIX A PLAYGROUND / START A CLUB
/ BABYSIT

These empty recommendations are about as effective as "Just Say
No," I'm afraid. As the CIA pushed drugs, the first lady chirped, "Just
say no!" And since everything in the culture, car, iPad, iPhone, television, internet, Facebook, Twitter and shopping mall, etc., is designed to
remove you from your immediate surroundings, it will take more than
cutesy suggestions on walls to rebuild communities. Also, the worse the
neighborhoods or contexts, the more hopeful and positive the slogans.
Starved of solutions, we shall eat slogans.

Chuck and I approached a man sitting by himself. Fifty years old, Bob
looked nearly a decade older. A Scranton native, he had gone to Las Vegas
to work as a cook at the MGM Hotel. Making $20 an hour, Bob was
doing fine until disaster struck, "I had a stroke and a heart attack. I lost
my memory for a while. It's coming back . . ."

"Did you have health insurance?" I asked.

"No, I turned it down."

"How long did you work for MGM?"

"Two years. I was working in the Rainforest Cafe. Huge place, lots of
people."

"Did you save money while you were there?"

"No! I gambled and I partied."

"Oh shit!"

"God bless you," Chuck added.

All this time, Bob was listening to the Penn State–Illinois game on a tiny transistor radio. As Illinois prepared to kick the winning field goal, we stopped to listen. Game lost, I continued, "Do you have an income, Bob?"

"No, I'm applying for Social Security but it will take a while, though. I will probably have to get a lawyer."

Though Bob has family in the area, he's sleeping in a shelter and takes his meals at St. Francis and the Rescue Mission, "You stay for the service, then they feed you."

"What if you don't stay for the service?" I asked.

"Then they don't feed you," Bob laughed. "They have good food there, too, they feed you good."

"What if you fall asleep during the service? Will they notice?"

"I don't think they care about that, but they do give you coffee as soon as you come in."

Attached by a footbridge to the Steamtown Mall is an impressive railroad museum that's just as moribund, unfortunately, thanks to poor management. The locomotives on display are relics from a time when Scranton was a major mining and industrial center. The magnificent wealth of the US, at its peak, came largely from its ability to extract hydrocarbons from its own (and many other people's) soil. As these finite resources are depleted, the country's fortunes must decline, and it doesn't help that much of our manufacturing base has been exported, leaving cities like Scranton husks of what they used to be. If you don't make shit, you ain't gonna have shit to buy nothing, excuse my Scrantonese. Driving through a particularly desolate part of town, Chuck summed it up, "There is nothing but shit jobs! College graduates are fighting each other over shit jobs!"

I'll end with an account from Carol. Before I came up, Chuck said Carol's condition had deteriorated, so I feared seeing her emaciated or even bedridden, but Carol was her usual feisty self. One afternoon, as Chuck was out on his bus run, I sat at the Orloskis' kitchen table as Carol cooked. "Carol," I began, "you told me a story last year about a stomach wound the size of a grapefruit. Who was that?"

"Ah, Chuck's father! He was in a car accident, and he had a wound in his stomach the size of a grapefruit."

"I remember you telling me about how miraculously it healed?"

"Yes, it was this large wound that you could look into. I could see the inside of his stomach."

"And it was your job to take care of it?"

"Yes, they gave me a solution to apply each day, and as I cleaned the wound, I could see it healing itself from the inside out. The skin grew back from the inside out!"

"That's incredible!"

"Yes, it was, and the skin and everything grew back out, little by little, until he was almost normal again. His stomach smoothed itself out. Now, how did it know to do that?!"

No serious wound can heal, however, if you don't tend to it, but according to our rulers and their media magicians, there is not even a nick on these Disunited States of Dying Malls. Daily, we're told that unemployment is down, inflation is actually too low, the recovery is picking up speed, and soon enough, we'll be energy-independent. With life so good, it's unclear why food stamp usage is at a record high and more and more adults are forced to live with their parents. As we stagger into 2015, however, watch for this rosy pornography to freeze, then black out finally, for our supernaturally levitating stock market will certainly rediscover gravity, and our relentless provocation and demonization of Russia will climax in either a suicidal war or end, more mercifully, with us a humbled and shunned nation. Already, many of our peripheral allies are decoupling from our "leadership." If only Americans themselves could do the same.

SMUG BUBBLE WASHINGTON, DC

3-11-15—For nearly four years, I lived just twenty miles from Washington, in Annandale, Virginia, and I worked in DC for nine months. From my home in Philadelphia, I've also gone down to Washington at least a hundred times, so this metropolis should not be alien to me, and yet no American city is more off-putting, more unwelcome, more impenetrable, and this, in spite of its obvious physical attractiveness, and here, I'm talking mostly about its Northwest quadrant, the only part visitors are familiar with, and where commuters from Virginia and Maryland arrive daily to work.

Even though it's the world's foremost generator of mayhem, Washington is supremely tranquil and orderly. With its wide streets, unusually wide sidewalks, many leafy squares and the vast, magnificent Mall, DC is the ultimate garden city. It's greener than Portland, Oregon. It's also a showcase for culture. All of its publicly owned museums don't charge admission, a unique arrangement not just in the United States but likely worldwide, thus the unwashed masses can stream into the National Gallery to admire the only Leonardo in the Americas, fifteen Rembrandts, twelve Titians, four Vermeers and two Albert Pinkham Ryders. A laid-off factory worker or brain-damaged war veteran can stuff his face with Bonnards, Degas, Canalettos and Morandis, then pick his crooked teeth with a Renoir or Cassatt. If still not sated, he can hobble over to the Hirshhorn, Freer or National Museum of American Arts for more artistic nourishment to heft up his mind and bevel down his rough edges.

Washington museums feature almost no local artists, however, for this is a profoundly uncultured place, paradoxically. Nothing germinates here but power. (The only DC artists I can think of are Kenneth Noland and Morris Louis, two innocuous painters whose canvases are designed for corporate lobbies.) Unlike in New York, Chicago, Los Angeles, San Francisco or even Philadelphia, there are no first-rate galleries of contemporary art here. The politicians, lawyers, lobbyists, military types and spooks who dominate DC have loads of money, but they are all culturally conservative. Elites everywhere tend to be that way, sure, but DC is a magnet nonpareil for those who crave power and can think of nothing else. They are here to gain and barter influence, not to be distracted or pestered by art that hasn't been curated, many times over, to be palatable to the status quo. Even art from many decades ago can threaten and disturb, and that's why the caustic social commentaries of Max Beckmann or Otto Dix, for example, are safely kept in storage and rarely dragged out for public contemplation. As this nation normalizes legal sadism, Leon Golub's images of torture will not be on display. Here, why don't you ogle these colorful blobs of nothing by some garbage painter!

Other capital cities have rich artistic heritages, but not Washington, for it was conceived only to be a center of power. Built up almost entirely from scratch, it's the ideal American city, literally, with just about every aspect of it carefully calibrated, and almost nothing that's organic or spontaneous. Its oldest section, Georgetown, was a major slave-trading center, as was Alexandria, just across the Potomac. Providing quaintness, fine dining and shopping, Georgetown and Alexandria give tourists a much needed breather from the oppressive monumentalism of downtown DC.

After its founding, Washington itself became a major slave trading center, and one must remember that Washington, the president, inherited 10 slaves at age eleven, had 50 slaves before he married Martha, and owned 123 slaves when he died. (Martha and her children from another marriage had 195 more slaves.) Ben Franklin, by contrast, never owned more than a handful, so it was much less painful for him to release his two slaves, and he only did this at age seventy-nine, three years before his death. For much of his life, Franklin only objected to slavery because it was bad, well, for white people, for it made them arrogant and lazy, he claimed. Plus, it wasn't too wise an investment, and to bring resentful blacks into your household is a pretty stupid idea, Franklin pointed out, and here he was thinking of the domestic slaves common in the North, not the platoons of field hands that an oligarch like George Washington could whip into inhuman productivity in the South.

In 1987, I worked as a loose-leaf filer in Washington. I had just quit college and was sleeping on my aunt's living room floor in Annandale. My daily task was to file thousands of pages into binders in law libraries. With a coworker, I would walk from law firm to law firm, and sometimes take the Metro to go as far out as Bethesda, Maryland. Before this job, I didn't even know that many of these 13-story buildings in downtown were law offices. Since no building in Washington can be higher than the Capitol, the tallest all have 13 floors. Due to superstition, however, many elevators display a "14" button after "12." Washington Circle, Dupont Plaza, Logan Circle, Mount Vernon Square and the White House do make an inverted pentagram, but that evilness, if you believe in such things, was part of the original plan, and has long been enshrined by concrete, asphalt and tradition.

My job was very low-paying yet exacting, and we had to work at breakneck speed. Wearing rubber finger grips, we had to zero in on thousands of tiny numbers to make sure no page was inserted wrongly. Rushing, I ran into a glass partition once, but the secretaries, paralegals and lawyers near me did not laugh. For months, a law librarian kept calling me "Kim," and I never bothered to correct him. I had no time to lose. It didn't matter. We were just rushing in and out and not a part of any firm. Though at the very bottom of the legal hierarchy, loose-leaf filers still had to look somewhat professional, and so I bought five polyester dress shirts and four pairs of old man's pants from Sym's, the discount clothing store.

Hard as I tried, though, mistakes were inevitable, for no man is a machine. After one screwup, my supervisor enunciated to me, "Here at Bartleby Temp, we don't tolerate mediocrity," and she said the last word so carefully, drawing out each syllable, one might think she had just learned it herself. The name of the agency is made up, by the way, for I can no longer remember it. What I do recall, however, is a coworker's dazed face as he emerged from a book stack. Of course, I had to be equally stultified. Our eyes had to be equally glazed.

After work, I socialized with a couple of guys, but there was no place for us to go, really, not on our budget. Unlike in Philadelphia, there were no corner bars where regular joes in goofy T-shirts and worn baseball caps could whoop it up. In downtown DC, the only taverns catered to the executive types, and the city has become even more exclusive since. With a more bloated federal government, Washington is even richer now, even as the rest of the country has become destitute. Just about every expensive house, car, tie, loafer, call girl, gigolo and martini in DC is being paid for, one way or another, by Joe Six-Packs from across this nation. Elected officials come here to feast on illicit money, for you must be daft to assume American graft is limited to campaign contributions. They legalize some corruption to trick you into thinking that's all there is. In any case, the only other American oasis that's similarly thriving is Manhattan, for that's where our banksters and presstitutes dwell. Everybody else is going to hell.

As a loose-leaf filer, I belonged to that servant class in DC that helped it to function without knowing hardly anything about it, and there was absolutely no hobnobbing with the higher-ups, for with their conservative haircuts, perfect teeth, gym-finessed body and expensive, carefully coordinated outfits, not to mention a confident, upright bearing and honking voice, I'm not kidding, they knew exactly who they were and who they cared to associate with.

One of my coworkers was a tall black guy who was having the time of his life, however. During lunch, I asked Bill what he'd done that weekend, and the mellow, soft-spoken man closed his eyes and sighed, "I had sex. Lots of it. There are so many good-looking guys here. They must be busing them in. I've never had so much sex in my life. I'm getting a little tired of it, actually." Hearing that, I felt anguished and embarrassed, for I had gotten nothing in months, but looking defeated is no way to hook up with any woman, and I had never felt worse in my life. I was socially displaced. Once, a female coworker, a native of Ethiopia, freaked out at a reception desk because she felt disrespected, but I was right there and saw nothing. I don't blame her, though, not at all, for it was all too easy to feel intimidated or paranoid. Like much of Northwest DC, these swank law firms are designed to exude authority.

Earlier this month, I was in DC for a day and decided to check out Arlington, just across the Potomac from Georgetown. As a teenager, I had gone there to watch kung fu movies, and during my filing clerk days, I'd eaten at a Vietnamese restaurant near the courthouse. It was a rather seedy five-table affair at the back of a grocery store. Its wallpaper showed a snowcapped mountain and waterfall. Pointing to it, a middle-aged white guy shouted, "Don't drink the water!" He looked as if he was about to sob. The other eaters ignored him. Smiling, the waiter informed me in Vietnamese, "He comes here all the time. He fought."

Arlington used to have these rather grim apartment buildings, cheap motels and the businesses that catered to such residents, but now it is all spiffed up and gentrified. All the tacky shops on Wilson Boulevard are gone. Its funk purged away, Arlington has become as sterile as downtown DC. The same process has been repeated all over the area. The smug bubble has enlarged itself. In downtown, there was Sholl's Colonial Cafeteria at 20th and K, and in the eighties I'd go there for its cheap prices and humble atmosphere. Once I even took Bill, the sex machine. At Sholl's, the emphasis was on comfort food, with meat loaf, breaded fish, overcooked spaghetti, soft green beans, soft carrots and mushy spinach, and an assortment of pies, that kind of stuff. With its many elderly diners, Sholl's had to be mindful of their false teeth and receding gums, not to mention their mournful and exhausted jaws. Anything too hard, such as fresh piece of celery, might just lay them out on the floor. Sholl's was so cheap, even the homeless ate there. At each table, there was a prayer card and on the walls, framed photos of the pope. Most of the servers appeared to be immigrants from Central America. In the forties, Sholl's was one of the first DC eateries to serve whites and blacks equally. Alas,

Sholl's is no more, and it was finally out of business by the dip in tourism after September 11th of 2001. Even without that incident, I don't think it would have survived to this day anyway.

Seeing next to nothing in Arlington, I got on the Metro and headed to Southeast Washington. Crossing the Anacostia River, you enter another DC altogether. Almost everyone here is black, and Washington itself is still half black. Just a few decades ago, it was 70 percent black, however. Back then, Washington had the highest murder rate in the entire country, and its basketball team was called, appropriately enough, the Bullets. DC hoopsters have been rechristened the Wizards, but a more appropriate name would be the Missiles or the Drones, methinks.

Frederick Douglass spent eighteen years in Anacostia, and this was also where disgruntled WWI veterans and their families set up a shantytown as they demanded to be paid, early, their promised bonuses. This was during the height of the Depression and they were starving. Responding to their pitiful pleas, the federal government sent in General MacArthur with troops, cops and six tanks to chase them all out and burn down their encampment. During various clashes around DC, four protesters were killed and over a thousand wounded. On the government side, sixty-nine cops were hurt.

One must remember that Washington itself was founded after the US government had stiffed its own soldiers even before the War of Independence, its very first war, was over. In 1783, roughly five hundred troops besieged Congress, then based in Philadelphia, to demand to be paid. A bunch of weasels even then, the congressmen delegated youngish Alexander Hamilton to schmooze and jive with the angry soldiers. Just give us some time to hash this out, he begged them, but these congressmen then tried to arrange for troops to come in to snuff out the mutiny. Had they succeeded, you would have American soldiers firing on American soldiers, which was exactly what happened later in DC. Leery of more incidents like this, the weasels slithered south to erect their ideal city.

I walked a couple of miles through Anacostia and saw a handful of takeout eateries selling Chinese, chicken or fried fish. One was named "Chicken, Beans and Bones." Geez, I wonder how much they charge for a whole skeleton? I poked my head into a Korean-owned dry cleaner and noticed the bulletproof plexiglass had vertical slits just wide enough for articles of clothing to be handed in or out. I passed Union Town Tavern, which looked surprisingly chichi for this rather dismal hood. It turns out they have new owners, for the previous is in the slammer for possessing 65 kilograms of cocaine. That's enough to coat several Christmas plays! Enterprising Natasha Dasher was just thirty-six at the time of her arrest. Though Anacostia has more than 50,000 people, Union Town is its only full service restaurant or sit-down bar. Folks here just go to the liquor store for a tall can or 40-ounce bottle.

Many of the businesses on Martin Luther King Boulevard, Anacostia's main drag, had small posters commemorating the late Marion Barry, a popular black mayor who was busted for smoking crack. Jailed for just six months, Barry still managed to make the news when he was charged with having a woman sucking him in the prison waiting room. After release, Barry was elected to City Council, then became mayor again. A folk hero, at least to DC's black community, Barry is the only Washington mayor to serve four terms, or sixteen years, doubling his nearest rivals, so he must have done some things right.

Historically, blacks gravitated towards Washington because federal hiring practices were much less discriminatory than in the private sector, then when affirmative action kicked in, blacks became favored in getting not just government jobs, but contracts, and there are more of those in DC than anywhere else. (A side consequence of such wrongheaded racial redress is that a recently arrived tycoon from Nigeria or, hell, even China, can now be certified as a minority contractor, and the requirement that one must be at least 25 percent nonwhite also sends many whites to dig up their Cherokee, Sioux or Navajo ancestors.) With numbers came political power, but local politics or demographics have no influence on what really runs DC, for here is the dark, evil heart of an empire with an unprecedented global reach. In spite of our current, half-black president, blacks are the tiniest cogs of this sinister machinery, but so are most of us. Blacks may be hired as cops and firemen, but they can't touch the biggest criminals and pyromaniacs that huddle daily on Capitol Hill.

In any case, the members of the black underclass that perform menial tasks downtown live in neighborhoods like Anacostia. They don't drink in downtown bars either, and I doubt many of them go to the museums, not unless they work there. In 1990, there was an Albert Pinkham Ryder retrospective at the National Museum of American Arts, which is off the Mall and not often visited. Having all of these galleries practically to myself, I kept studying a magnificent Ryder that had not just one but four cows. Squinting, I kept moving closer, then back, closer, then back, and often I had to tilt my head a certain way to avoid the glint off Ryder's thickly layered linseed oil. After nearly a century, hairline cracks spider webbed across the canvas. If man could live off minutely modulated ultramarine blue, burnt sienna and olive green, I'd have ballooned to about 600 pounds, but that was then. I've stopped going to museums. Everywhere I go now, I simply roam the streets.

"Why are you taking so long to look at that?" It was the security guard, a smiling black lady of about thirty-two.

"Um, it's very rare to see all of this guy's paintings in one place. I may never get a chance to look at this painting again. I came down all the way from Philadelphia to see this."

"That's a painting?"

"What do you mean?"

"You said painting. That's a painting?"

"Uh, yes, it's an oil painting."

"I thought it was just some picture."

"No, no, this is an oil painting, and it's old too. There's only one of this."

"Really?!"

"Yeah, and this guy is good. He's a very good artist."

"Listen, come here," and she led me to a small fountain that had been set up just for this exhibit. In the small pool were four fish.

"See that one," she continued. "Can you see that his colors are slightly different than the others?"

"Now that you've said it, yeah, I do see it. He looks a little bit different than the other three fish."

"You damn right he does!" she laughed, "and those fish know it too, and that's why they've been attacking him all day long."

"Oh, man."

"Yeah, I have to do something about this. Soon as my shift is over, I'll tell them to get that fish out of here. I don't want to see him dead."

"It's great you noticed that."

"How can I not notice it? I stand right here all day!"

Indifferent to pictures on walls, that lady was sensitive to many other things and realms, and the fish drama she saw was, to her, an all-too-familiar allegory. Most of us, though, can only bend our neck a certain way, so will only notice what we're determined to see.

It was dark by the time I headed to Union Station, but on the way there, I happened to catch a group of people, mostly Jews, protesting Netanyahu. Bibi was inside the Convention Center to give a speech to the American Israel Public Affairs Committee. Though he was scheduled to address Congress the next day, many of our senators and congressmen also showed up for this event to earn extra ass-kissing points.

Protesters are a regular feature of DC and the locals barely see them. In front of the White House, sometimes you see two unrelated protests marching within sight of each other. Oddballs also appear, such as a man who protested supermarket coupons. DC's most unusual protester, however, is Concepcion Picciotto, for she's been living in a tiny tent, directly across from the White House, for thirty-four years now. Born in 1945, this diminutive native of Spain's main targets are the innumerable war crimes of the United States and Israel, which she calls Israhell. Picciotto is the first, last and ultimate Occupier.

A much more recent addition to the streetscape just outside 1600 Pennsylvania Avenue is Yusef, a beefy, red-bearded Muslim with "NO GOD EXCEPT ALLAH MUHAMMED A MESSENGER ALLAH" painted in white on the back of his black polyester coat. In 2011, I had seen him in a sort of flasher's overcoat and no visible pants, but earlier this day, he had on a beige pair, though with the legs cut off to expose his ankles.

Yusef isn't objecting to American atrocities against Muslims, but the various deviations, according to him, from true Islam. Thus, his denunciations of vaccines, tunnels (because they block sunlight), movies, television, "picture makers" (which I take to mean painters and photographers) and even electricity. This didn't prevent him from asking me, in accented English, what time it was. As we talked, a middle-aged female tourist pushing a stroller glared at him, but when I inquired if people had given him trouble, Yusef merely said, "I'd rather not talk about it."

Even more than Concepcion Picciotto, Washington's many homeless are its most damning and enduring protesters against this city's parasitic affluence, smug criminality and vapid culture of faux refinement. Numbering more than 7,000 as of May 2014, very few beg openly, thanks to DC's severe law against panhandling, but they are visible enough even during the day. To escape the cold wind, some sit or sleep, all wrapped up, in the entrance of the McPherson Square Metro station, just three blocks from the White House. Keeping reasonably inconspicuous, they rest in the many squares and parks.

At night, though, when the day-tripping tourists and commuting workers are all gone, they emerge to claim their sleeping spots all over downtown, including up and down Pennsylvania Avenue, the capital's grand boulevard. They lie on church steps, grass strips, in doorways and behind hedges, some with crutches or a wheelchair next to them. Rolled up in whatever will hold body heat, including gray packing blankets, they curl up within sight of the Smithsonian museums and the Capitol. Inside the National Gallery, there's Hieronymus Bosch. Outside, there's this!

At Union Station, this nation's most regal train and bus depot, they lie on the circular stone bench around the handsome fountain outside, while during the day they wander in to embarrass travelers with their grimy, smelly clothes and sometimes delirious monologues. They don't pull wheeled luggage but, limping in, cradle trash bags with both arms. Like zombies, hoboes or war refugees, they peer into shops with names like Jois Fragrance and L'Occitane en Provence. Signs on Union Station's large, platform-like seats, "THANK YOU FOR NOT RECLINING."

Wearing a leopard print dress, with much of her face covered by a cappuccino-colored shawl, a slim black woman in her late forties rocked back and forth as she unleashed an incontinent stream of invectives against unseen foes. Her hands could not have been more beautiful. She reeked of urine. "You betrayed me, you betrayed God, you betrayed this government. That's not the right protocol! You can't treat people like that. Turn in your badge, you're a threat to national security! I'm going to have a heart attack if you don't do so by morning. The heart has to be right place for socialism! You think you can just kill everybody but you yourself will be bombed! You're nothing but a traitorous person. There's no effort or sincerity, there's just treason! You're all bad people here. You ain't got no evidence. You can't do that to me! It's perjury you committed. I command you to turn in your badge. We're going to meet in court!" Every five or ten seconds, she punctuated her litany with a five-note riff of scatting, "Toot too too too too."

Washington was designed to be a perfect square, and it was until Alexandria broke away. When the Interstates were built, "the Beltway" was added to encircle DC. What you have, then, is a broken square surrounded by a near perfect circle. Flying in, most visitors land at Dulles or Ronald Reagan airports, so from their rented car or hotel shuttle, all they will see coming in is an elegantly manicured, dignified and affluent landscape. In DC itself, they will be lavished with magnificent monuments and arts, much of it free of charge, and just about every turn of the neck is rewarded with a grand vista. If this is their only exposure to the United States, then this country is truly a utopia of handsome, well-dressed people who cherish the arts, fine dining and well-made cocktails. The grit, squalor and menace of Washington are well off the beaten track and hardly exist, really, compared to other American cities, and even during its bloodiest years, the bullets didn't fly in downtown DC. As for the homeless, they're shooed away from tourist attractions and don't really assert their presence until nightfall.

All capitals strive to be showcases, sure, but very few, or perhaps none, are as successful at blocking out its nation's true ugliness and failures. This sleight of hand, though, also works on many of the residents of this near perfect square inside a near perfect circle. The hell they've created keeps seeping in, however, and soon enough, it will overwhelm, if not explode, this Potemkin village of a city. This smug bubble will burst.

JIM THORPE, WAR AND THE LIBERAL ARTS
IN CARLISLE

3-29-15—Invited to give a reading at Dickinson College, I came to Carlisle, a town of 19,000 people thirty miles from Harrisburg. Arriving by train, I passed Amish country and saw plows being pulled by horses. On extremely long clotheslines, single-colored clothes fluttered in the wintry wind. Rising high and lithographed against the pale sky, they resembled subdued prayer flags. A white-bearded man under a straw hat waved. Lancaster, Elizabethtown, Middletown. Had I sat on the opposite side, I would have been browbeaten by the looming nuclear reactors of Three Mile Island.

I have always been struck by how calm and sane Amish children look. On another occasion in Harrisburg, I marveled at the serene, nearly beatific way a teenage Amish girl prepared my sandwich. Each movement was economic yet unharried, and she even smiled, ever so subtly, at the tomato, lettuce, onion and roast beef. She was at one with the fragrant white bread. If you travel by train often, you will have many opportunities to observe Amish families, for they don't fly. With their emphasis on God, family and community, they're traditional in every way, and you can even call them reactionary for their resistance to progress. Indifferent to this fleeting mania that's exhausted the earth and brought humanity to the brink of extinction, the Amish are content to come, till the field and lie beneath, and though they have their dogmas, they don't seek to impose their ways on you.

No subscribers to any global system, the Amish believe that each community should create its own mores and regulate itself. It's fair to say, though, that they have only survived thanks to the forbearance and mercy of the state, for this state can suddenly decide to press-gang them into a preemptive war, outlaw their horse and buggies or even ban them from selling unpasteurized milk, the last of which has happened several times recently. If the French can criminalize the burqa, then perhaps Amish suspenders are an intolerable threat to public order? Never underestimate the perversity of the state. Communist governments hounded feminine clothes, shoes, cosmetics and even hairstyles out of existence.

The Amish, then, can be deformed or even snuffed out at any moment, as has happened already to many similar communities worldwide. Should the Amish way of life become contagious, the state will certainly see them as a cancer. Immune to all propaganda, they are also the worst consumers. As the state unravels, however, the independence, resilience, simplicity and sanity of the Amish should serve as a model for the rest of us deranged Americans. There are those who point to the failings of individual Amish as evidence that their wholesome image is a fraud, but domestic violence, incest, drug use and cruelty to animals can be found within any community. The Amish's biggest flaw, I think, is their principled abstention from the use of force in all situations, for that can only lead to their doom and martyrdom.

Dickinson had sent a car to pick me up, and during the thirty-minute drive to Carlisle, I had a most enjoyable chat with its driver, Melanie. In her early fifties, Melanie had gotten a bachelor's in American Studies from Dickinson and a master's from the University of Maryland. She then worked at Planned Parenthood and another nonprofit that helped battered women, "I thought I would be among feminists, but they weren't really feminists, and that's why I became a massage therapist. I did that for nineteen years."

"Why did you quit?"

"Oh, the stress of it became too much, and I also had some health issues. I like this job driving for the college because it's very flexible. My partner teaches Judaism and Hebrew at the school. She's also a writer."

"What does she write?"

"Novels and poems. She's only had a few poems translated into English. She writes in Hebrew."

Melanie and her partner go to Israel twice a year, "My dad loves my partner and loves Israel. When I first got involved with my partner, my dad said, 'Anytime you want to go to Israel, I'll pay for your ticket,' but after my fifth trip within three years, my dad told me, 'I didn't know you were going to commute to Israel!'"

Melanie's dad is also a writer. "One of his books is called *Stalking the Antichrists*."

"Wow, that sounds cool. Who are the antichrists?"

"American presidents."

"I'm not going to argue with that!" We both laughed. "But which presidents?"

"Mostly recent ones."

"What about the early ones? What about George Washington?"

"I don't know. The book is over 600 pages and it's kind of a mess. My dad can use an editor."

"What about his other books?"

"Another is called *It Can Happen Here: A Fascist Christian America*, and that's 500 pages. He's also written a book called *Birding and Mysticism: Enlightenment Through Bird Watching*."

"Wow, your dad sounds like a fascinating guy. I'd love to hang out with him. Is he in Carlisle?"

"No, Florida."

Later, I'd try to find the man's writing online, and the only piece that turned up was a Daily Kos article, "Ukraine: Why All Options Are Not on the Table." That's the clearest part, I'm afraid, for the rest is an impenetrable thicket of diaristic jottings and stray thoughts, much of it typed in caps. Never stingy with hostile comments, readers are nearly unanimous in their ridicule of this former naval intelligence officer.

Entering Carlisle, we drove past helicopters, artillery pieces, tanks and a bunker. Constituting the Army Heritage Trail, it's on the grounds of the United States Army War College. Alongside Dickinson College, it dominates this quiet town. Here converge not just American senior officers, lieutenant colonels and up, but those from dozens of other countries. They come to learn the American ways of war.

For its size, Carlisle has a large and active downtown. There are nice bars, coffee shops and a Thai, a Belgian and a Japanese restaurant, though the last, Issei, is half-Vietnamese. After coming to the United States as a refugee, Long joined the US Army and went to Okinawa, where he met his future wife, Naomi. Just outside downtown, there's also Proud to Serve Mini-Mart and Deli, and here it's the wife, Barb, who's the Army veteran, and she had to go to Morocco to meet the love of her life, Rachid. On an oblong sign, there's an American flag surrounded by these words, "Proudly Served Our Country. Now Proudly Serving Our Community. A VETERAN-OWNED BUSINESS." Inside the store, there are photos of local veterans and a six-foot-two Statue of Liberty. Unlike provincials in other countries, many small-town Americans have traveled across the globe, though usually only after being drilled in firing automatic weapons, throwing hand grenades and in hand-to-hand combat. They come back with tales, a blood-splattered conscience, a more sophisticated palate, dogged nightmares, trinkets, half a body, a spouse, or an unspeakable face. Thousands return as absolutely nothing.

Outside downtown, the fast-food joints and strip malls show up and the houses gradually become less quaint. Nondescript apartment blocks edge in. Like other small towns, Carlisle used to have its factories but the only manufacturing that remains is Frog Switch, a maker of manganese steel castings. Carlisle Tire and Rubber Company, founded in 1917, drew down its operation, then finally moved to Jackson, Mississippi, in 2010 for cheaper labor costs. Masland Carpets, founded in 1866, went to Alabama.

The war and liberal art colleges, then, are Carlisle's chief economic engines. Colonels and generals do have wads in their deep pockets, and

Dickinson College students aren't too broke either, for the tuition there for 2015–16 is $49,014, with room and board $12,812, books $1,090 and health insurance $1,822 more. Even without beer, liquor and weed expenses, prerequisites for a well-rounded college experience, it costs over $65,000 to spend nine months in Carlisle. Though many students do get financial aid, many don't, such as the 7 percent who arrive from forty-four foreign countries.

Most college students are transients. Wanting to meet more rooted locals, I asked my student hostesses, Mary and Laura, to point me to "an old man's bar, where old guys go to drink away their social security checks."

"There aren't any, really," Mary answered, "but Alibis might be the closest to that." A senior, Mary's writing a thesis on Ezra Pound and J.R.R. Tolkien. Also a senior, Laura is focusing on Edna St. Vincent Millay.

With two hours to kill before my reading, I slipped into Alibis and found it too nice to be a dive bar. It had fourteen draft beers, most of them microbrews or imported. A pint of Yuengling, though, was only $2.50, so I ordered that. Not yet happy hour, this spacious pub was practically deserted. The only other patrons were three people who sat to my left, so let's meet them, eh?

Thirty years old, Heather's a single mom with a daughter entering puberty. (Before Heather ordered her rum and Coke, the bartender actually carded her, which made her gush, "Thank you!") Born in Carlisle, she has also lived in Gettysburg and Hanover, the latter nearly two hours away, a big move. A lifelong waitress, Heather's unemployed but is trying to find work as a medical assistant. For the last seven months, she's applied at every doctor's office, clinic and hospital in the area.

"They all want a year plus experience, but how am I going to get experience if you don't give it to me?"

"So how many applications altogether? Fifty?"

"At least!"

Heather's mom is fifty-seven and has been waitressing since she was sixteen. "She's the best waitress I've ever met, my mom. She's amazing."

"Where does she work?"

"Denny's, but she has also worked at Bob's Big Boy for like fifteen years, and she was at Eat'n Park. She was the shift manager there. She was the head waitress."

Heather recounted being fired from her last waitressing job, "I was working at Denny's, and there was this party of seventeen people. I worked my ass off and they left me a one dollar and one penny tip."

"I thought you were going to say a dollar per person, which is bad enough."

"I can deal with that. That's like 10 percent. Some people give you 20, some 10, but these people just left me a dollar and a penny!"

"That's unbelievable! Was there any problem?"

"No, I thought I did a great job. I thought I was going to get a great tip. I was so pissed off, I took that money, ran outside to the parking lot, gave it to the lady and said, 'I think you need this more than I do!'"

"And what did she say?"

"I don't know, because I turned right around and went back inside. They fired me on the spot."

"I don't know if I could have controlled my temper either. That's really fucked up what they did."

"Totally!"

"I mean, that extra penny is like an extra fuck you!"

Next to Heather was Steve. Twenty-seven years old, he had on a brown shirt and a deep green tie, not his usual togs, because he had just been to court. Nearly three years ago, a second-floor windowpane landed on Steve's leg as he was walking by. He showed me a long scar on his calf. Though Judge Guido fell asleep at the bench that morning, the jury seemed sympathetic to Steve's plight, he said, and the case was scheduled to be wrapped up the next day. Steve's lawyer had tried to settle out of court with the building's owner but the man refused.

"I should get at least $10,000, I hope. Knock on wood."

"That's not a whole lot for all the shit you went through."

"No sir, but I'll be glad to have it."

"I mean, the medical bills, the pain, the aggravation. I don't see how you won't get it."

"Thank you." Steve smiled and shook my hand, as if for luck. "If I do get it, and you come by tomorrow, I'll buy you lunch!"

"You don't have to do that, but I'll come by just to see how it turns out."

Steve has toiled and sweated in kitchens, which he didn't like at all, and at the Amazon warehouse. Since it paid $12 an hour, Steve thought it was a pretty good job, and he only quit because he could earn more as a construction worker, so that's what he's doing now, swinging his hammer. Being an Amazon grunt can be so grueling, and it can get so hot inside that warehouse, workers sometimes pass out. When I brought this up, they both said yeah, that's just how it is.

Unlike Heather, Steve has never strayed from Carlisle, "I have a high school diploma, no children, but I can't even move anywhere."

"It's hard, man. You can't just pick up and leave. Usually, you have to know someone somewhere."

"Yes sir, and I'll be honest with you, it also comes down to your piss. If you smoke marijuana, you're an evil person in this world. If you smoke marijuana once in your life, you're screwed."

We all laughed. I said, "I know a guy who sells piss, though. That's a business, man. You should just drive around construction sites and sell piss!"

Heather, "I don't smoke pot. I should sell my piss!"

Sitting with Heather and Steve was Austin, and though he seemed comfortable enough, he hardly spoke. Unlike the others, Austin was black, but it was clear he was Steve's close friend. Blacks make up only 7 percent of Carlisle's population, and the eastern part of town is even dubbed Carlem, as in Carlisle and Harlem. This odd tidbit I only found out the next day, when I returned to congratulate Steve on his windfall. Steve never showed up, however, so I talked to Brandon, the bartender.

Brandon came to Carlisle from Shippensburg, twenty miles south. Although this town of 5,500 also has a college, it's only a state school and much cheaper. The economy really sucks there, Brandon said, and its alcohol and drug problems, heroin and meth, are much more serious.

Shippensburg's furniture, engine and pump factories are all gone. "We do have six bars," Brandon advertised. "I think you'd like them!"

In his late twenties, Brandon considers himself supremely lucky to sling beer five nights a week. Sharing a house with two roommates, Brandon only pays $400 a month, plus utilities, and he lives close enough to amble to work. Though business seemed awfully sluggish during my two visits to Alibis, Brandon said Dickinson students do surge in late at night, especially on weekends, and, get this, the War College sometimes conducts classes inside the bar, "They show up early in the morning and use that space there. We even have a screen so they can project their lectures."

"Do they drink during class?"

"No, but many will drink right afterwards."

I'd imagine the colonels and generals to be decent tippers, at least more so than a white-haired man who shows up in Alibis each day to order a double shot of DL Franklin for $5. Knocking it down, he shambles out without leaving a penny. It's unclear why he doesn't just buy a liter for $15 or so and drink it at home. He obviously has very little money. When I was there, he was paying for his vodka fix with quarters, dimes and nickels. It took him longer to count out his change than to swill his liquor.

In small towns across America, you have this basic scenario of little or no manufacturing left, so the locals must scramble for service jobs that often don't even pay the bills. In Carlisle, I saw Help Wanted signs at Wendy's, Papa John's and a hoagie shack. At High and Hanover, a rather haggard long-haired man was dressed as the Statue of Liberty to advertise Liberty Income Tax Service. Paid $8 an hour, he had to constantly switch directions to wave a sign at onrushing traffic. With earphones plugged to heavy metal, he would sometimes strum this sign as if it were a guitar. Outside a Sunoco gas station, an old white man sat on the curb, begging. He was balding, stooped and had white paper napkins tucked into the back of his pants. A black man gave him some change.

So we've become a nation of burger flippers, burrito rollers, taco stuffers, cocktail mixers, surly cashiers, personal care assistants, dog walkers, sign-waving Statues of Liberty and, whether on sidewalks or more discreetly, beggars. It sure doesn't sound like a superpower to me but, ah, when you still have the most bellicose military on earth, you can extort plenty of merchandise from your vassal states. Here, just take this shipload of Federal Reserve notes that are freshly excreted, ever so liberally, by Janet Yellen. You want more? There's plenty more where that came from!

To postpone that fearful plunge into that vicious battle royal of the job market, you can also matriculate, check into a coed dormitory and buy yourself a bong. Borrowing from banksters, however, you will be mortgaging just about the rest of your life, and at Dickinson, I met a student, let's call him Tim, who was glad to be only $50,000 in debt by the time he graduates. A friend of his already owes $240,000.

"He should have just bought a house," I said, "and rented out rooms!"

"I know." Tim does have a plan, though, to not only be debt free but loaded within a few years. "I'm twenty-two now, but I want to have a $80,000 BMW by the time I'm twenty-five."

A native of Yonkers, Tim grew up with his mom, a cafeteria worker, and his grandma, a nurse for sixty years. Tim's dad abandoned the family, so he has never seen him. He does have a rich uncle. Tim's plan is to create an app that would facilitate academic cheating. Bumbling students can use Tim's service to find ghostwriters for their term papers. Since Tim will dock 10 percent from each transaction, this will net him at least half a million bucks during his first year, he calculates. He has invested $8,000 into this venture, hired a South Asian fellow student to write the codes and talked to a lawyer to make sure he won't end up in the slammer. Tim won't be cheating himself, he explained, but only creating the means for others to succeed academically. If you're going to be suffocated with debt, you might as well get an A. With his new wealth, Tim will see the rest of this vast country, at last, for he's never been west of Pittsburgh. He kept asking me about California and the Pacific Northwest. Since the BMW X6 M can go from zero to 60 mph in 3.9 seconds, Tim can see himself flying into nirvana in no time flat.

"I've tried a lot of things. I'm always trying something new. I wanted to be a musician. Now I want to be a professional, you know, weightlifter. There's always something I want to do. I'm always jumping from one thing to another. It's a bit scary. What if I never settle down? I started a clothing brand."

"What happened with that?"

"It went really well. I made $7,000 in a month. People were really into my hats, and they're still asking me about them, but I stopped to concentrate on my app."

At Dickinson, Tim is majoring in studio art, but it isn't clear if he's a painter, sculptor or printmaker. Tim couldn't tell me. He also said he's interested in writing. If you were really cynical or realistic, you could say that it doesn't matter one bit what Tim's artistic goals are, for he won't come anywhere close to reaching them. But that's the eternal sadness and futility of the arts. For one can spend one's entire life, and not just a few years, to produce less than nothing. For all of one's hopes and sacrifices, one may not even end up as a minor pest. The difference these days, though, is that one must pay grandly just to dabble.

Unlike the Amish, who frown upon personal exaltation, the rest of us are conditioned to bare our teeth, claw and kick ass, for we must destroy all competition, we're convinced, to prevent ourselves from being chewed up, then spat out. Fairly or by cheating, we must win at all costs. This mindset has become so ingrained, we hardly notice it, but in the annals of human history, no culture has exalted individual achievement as much as the Greco-Roman lineage we've inherited. Yes, others record their great thinkers and artists, but the West remembers even its fastest runners, longest jumpers and best boxers. There is no Indian or Chinese equivalence of Chionis of Sparta, Diagoras of Rhodes, Milo of Croton or Theagenes of Thasos. Sima Qian paid no attention to any muscleman.

This introduction of ruthless competition into all realms of life has allowed the West, or more specifically the white man, to dominate the world for many centuries, and his very disunity in Europe ratcheted up his competitiveness. Competing against other white men, he innovated, conquered, slaughtered and came to believe, almost too inevitably, that he was the perfect man, perhaps even the only true man.

After so much blood and laughter, however, the white man's hegemony is finally waning, and just as we can discuss peak oil, peak water or peak sand, it's not inappropriate to speak of peak white man. The white man's paling, though, has less to do with his constitutional decline than with the fact that others have learned how to play the same nasty games he himself has set up.

An early omen of the white man's less than superman status happened right in Carlisle, for it was here that Jim Thorpe first established his legend. As a student at the Carlisle Indian Industrial School, Thorpe excelled at just about every sport, and in football, he led the Indians to victories over powerhouses Harvard and Army. A contemporary newspaper headline, "Indians Scalp Army 27–6." After Thorpe won gold medals in the decathlon and pentathlon at the 1912 Stockholm Olympics, he was universally recognized as the world's greatest athlete.

Around this time, white America was also tormented by Jack Johnson. Not only was Johnson beating up white men, he was having sex with plenty of white women. (Thorpe himself married three white women.) White rage hounded and ultimately ruined Johnson, but it mostly spared Thorpe because, after all, Thorpe wasn't coldcocking one white man after another, and he didn't have a reputation as a serial bedder of white women. His transgressions weren't as viscerally offensive. Plus, the contrast between Thorpe and a white man wasn't as great. He was half-white, one must remember.

Black, white, brown or yellow, anyone who's dwelling within these Disunited States will be thoroughly nicked up, if not buried alive, from the coming collapse and turmoil, and it's telling that our final chapter started with a double castration when the twin towers fell, broadcast live to the entire world, and that one of our bravest dissidents, Bradley Manning, also wishes to have nothing between his legs, and that our present-day Jim Thorpe, one Bruce Jenner, also dreams of the day he will finally be emasculated. Don't worry, it's coming.

PARCHED CALIFORNIA

4-23-15—Decades ago, I'd show up weekly to clean the Philadelphia apartment of a California transplant. Daughter of a Hollywood executive, Jacqueline confessed she had to escape California because "California women are too beautiful." To save her self-esteem, she had to flee to Philadelphia.

Ah, California as the perfect state with the most beautiful people! In spite of mudslides, wildfires and many blasé places like Bakersfield and Fresno, California, still captures the imagination of not just Americans, but foreigners. With its elaborate landscaping, it imitates Hawaii, even as Hawaii mimics California by laying on strip malls and freeways. Much of California, though, is no tropical paradise but a desert that's running out of water, and its freshwater crisis has become so severe, it has made salient a hushed-up concept, namely the fact that there are limits to growth, and that all resources can become scarce if not run out completely.

Newly condemned and mocked for their swimming pools and golf courses, Californians are lashing back by charging, rightly, that other Americans are no less profligate. Though less than 5 percent of the world's population, Americans burn up 26 percent of its oil and 27 percent of its natural gas. Our houses are larger than anyone's and still expanding. We have more cumbersome cars than fat drivers. So what, I can hear some of you saying. If we can afford it, then it's no one's business, but the problem is we haven't been able to afford any of this for a while now. We are the world's biggest debtor nation, lest you forget.

Coming into the Bay Area this month, I saw mostly prosperity, however. From San Francisco down into San Jose, there is one affluent city after another, while on the East Bay, there are a few pockets of destitution and squalor, but nothing compared to the hundreds of miles of decay that mark the Rust Belt, for example. Even Oakland is rapidly gentrifying, and becoming very expensive, with the average rent for a one-bedroom going for an astounding $3,078! That's more than three times what I must cough up, with much anxiety and bile, in Philadelphia, and I get two rooms. In this sinking economy, how does the Bay Area become ever more spiffy?

Two years ago, I talked to Hung, a Vietnam-born Chinese living in Milpitas, and he dismissed my grim assessment of the US economy as nonsense, "The Chinese and Indians are coming over. They have money and skills. They will keep this economy going."

"What about the locals?" I asked. "Won't an influx of rich foreigners hurt the poor here?"

"No, these Chinese and Indians will create jobs."

"But they will also jack up real estate prices!"

"Which is good!"

"Not for a renter, though. It's already too expensive to live here. I mean, look at all the homeless in the Tenderloin."

"You will always have bums. In every society, there are winners and losers. Those bums should be put in work camps and made to be productive."

We were standing in a two-story extension Hung was adding to his home. In the main house, Hung's aging parents sat mostly in silence on matching recliners. The Mexican construction crew was out to lunch.

It is estimated that nearly 20 percent of the homes being sold in the Bay Area are being snatched up by foreign buyers, paying cash, with about half of them Chinese. In Palo Alto, one of the toniest Bay Area cities, Chinese alone are responsible for more than a quarter of real estate sales.

In adjacent Los Altos, the most expensive housing market in the entire country, Chinese buyers don't shy away from mansions that cost several million dollars, and instead of haggling down, they often pay more than the list price, sometimes hundreds of thousands more, just to get what they want. Sometimes a Chinese buyer would buy without having seen the property in person, and he might leave his new home empty for months after purchase. In China, the land under each house cannot be owned outright but only leased from the government for seventy years, with terms for renewal uncertain, and it wasn't so long ago that private property was seen as the ultimate evil. To protect their wealth, then, the richest Chinese are buying in California. Ken DeLeon advertises in China, then guides visiting Chinese on a tour to inspect palatial homes. To move them around, he has bought not just a Mercedes van but a plane, on which two number 8's in Chinese have been affixed for luck. To appeal to Chinese buyers, realtors have also asked municipalities to remove the number 4 from certain addresses. In Chinese, "four" sounds like "death."

When the Chinese first came to California in the mid 19th century, they weren't so feted. Though welcomed by white bosses for their cheap labor, they were despised by the white working class for taking away jobs. Groups such as the Anti-Coolie Association and the Supreme Order of the Caucasians sprung up to oppose the Chinese presence. Organized labor was their sworn enemy. In 1887, Denis Kearney of the California's Workingmen's Party gave this address:

> Our moneyed men have ruled us for the past thirty years. Under the flag of the slaveholder they hoped to destroy our liberty. Failing in that, they have rallied under the banner of the millionaire, the banker and the land monopolist, the railroad king and the false politician, to effect their purpose.
>   . . . They have seized upon the government by bribery and corruption. They have made speculation and public robbery a science. The have loaded the nation, the state, the county, and the city with debt. They have stolen the public lands. They

have grasped all to themselves, and by their unprincipled greed brought a crisis of unparalleled distress . . .

Land monopoly has seized upon all the best soil in this fair land. A few men own from ten thousand to two hundred thousand acres each. The poor Laborer can find no resting place, save on the barren mountain, or in the trackless desert. Money monopoly has reached its grandest proportions. Here, in San Francisco, the palace of the millionaire looms up above the hovel of the starving poor with as wide a contrast as anywhere on earth.

Sounds like, well, today, so the playbook hasn't changed, but whereas the American working man now rails against illegal immigrants from Latin America and cheap "slave labor" in Asia, poor white Americans back then felt threatened by the Chinese that were employed all over the West in every sector, mining, railroad, construction, agricultural and domestic help. Kearney:

To add to our misery and despair, a bloated aristocracy has sent to China—the greatest and oldest despotism in the world— for a cheap working slave. It rakes the slums of Asia to find the meanest slave on earth—the Chinese coolie—and imports him here to meet the free American in the Labor market, and still further widen the breach between the rich and the poor, still further to degrade white Labor.

These cheap slaves fill every place. Their dress is scant and cheap. Their food is rice from China. They hedge twenty in a room, ten by ten. They are whipped curs, abject in docility, mean, contemptible and obedient in all things. They have no wives, children or dependents.

They are imported by companies, controlled as serfs, worked like slaves, and at last go back to China with all their earnings. They are in every place, they seem to have no sex. Boys work, girls work; it is all alike to them.

The father of a family is met by them at every turn. Would he get work for himself? Ah! A stout Chinaman does it cheaper. Will he get a place for his oldest boy? He cannot. His girl? Why, the Chinaman is in her place too! Every door is closed . . . We are men, and propose to live like men in this free land, without the contamination of slave labor, or die like men, if need be, in asserting the rights of our race, our country, and our families.

California must be all American or all Chinese. We are resolved that it shall be American, and are prepared to make it so. May we not rely upon your sympathy and assistance?

Fueled by such sentiments, a host of laws were passed against the Chinese that forbade them to become citizens, testify against whites, bring their wives over, marry white women, carry goods using a shoulder pole, live in a crowded room or even dig up the bones of their dead to send back to China. Chinatowns were burnt down and Chinese killed. In 1877, the *Chico Enterprise*, a newspaper still publishing, warned that eaters of produce picked by Chinese might contract leprosy or diphtheria since these fruits and vegetables had been fertilized by Chinese excrement.

The Grass Valley Union, also still extant, warned against hiring Chinese domestics. "After establishing himself, the China boy goes to making up his wages. He steals a little every day, and packs his plunder off to his bosses or his cousins. The sugar does not last as it used to, and the tea disappears rapidly. Pies and chops and pieces of steaks have the same course; yet that young heathen looks so innocent and is so saving when he is watched that he is never suspected." How unfair that white girls had been bumped out by these devious aliens! "He underbids the girls, ruins their reputations as workers, robs his employers to make up his wages and is a cheat and a fraud from top to bottom."

One of the Chinatowns that were burned down by white arsonists was in Pacific Grove, just over an hour from San Jose. In 1978, I saw a spectacle there that was so strange, I kept doubting myself with each remembrance. As the entire town of 15,000 people, nearly all of them white, sat on a beach after dusk, half a dozen white girls dressed as Chinese fairies danced on a barge. All around them, Chinese lanterns bobbled on the darkened sea. Dance over, there was a fireworks show. Writing this Postcard, I researched and found out, finally, that it's called the Feast of the Lanterns, and this festival was started at exactly the same time Pacific Grove chased out, very violently, all of its Chinese more than a century ago. Whites got rid of the Chinese so some of them could become somewhat Chinese once a year.

In the Bay Area, many whites are becoming Chinese in earnest. In San Francisco, there are no less than five Chinese immersion prekindergartens, with most of their pupils non-Chinese speakers at home. At Presidio Knolls, for example, only 25 percent of the students are Chinese-Americans. Paying a dizzying $23,150 annually, students start as young as 2.4 years old, and for those enrolled in kindergarten to second grade, it's $23,500. At the Chinese American International School, tuition is $25,800 for pre-kindergarten through eighth grade. There, half the school day is taught in Mandarin, the other half in English. Nineteen percent of its students are Caucasians, with 41 percent more multiethnic. Hispanics and blacks make up 1 percent each. At the Chinese Immersion School at DeAvila, the aim is to have its students become fluent in Cantonese, Mandarin and English. To compete in the Pacific Century, it's best to speak two Chinese languages, *ni ting de dong ma?* If you can only tweet in withered English, ur fckd.

California's orientation towards the East has its basis in trades. If China, Hong Kong and Taiwan are counted as one unit, then greater China is California's biggest customer, to be followed by Mexico, Canada, Japan and South Korea. Each year, the Chinese increase their purchase of California computers, electronics and agricultural products, but it's not all good thanks to the crippling drought that may only get worse. You see, it takes a gallon of water to produce a single California almond, and 25 gallons to make a bottle of Napa Valley wine. The Chinese are in love with both. CNN quotes Linsey Gallagher of the Wine Institute, "Even in remote parts of China, people know about Governor Arnold Schwarzenegger, *Baywatch*, the Golden Gate Bridge, and it's always a positive association."

The Chinese aren't just guzzling California wines, they're buying California wineries. Yao Ming leads the way. From his company's website, "In November 2011, Yao Ming, global humanitarian and recently retired NBA star, announced the establishment of his new Napa Valley wine company: Yao Family Wines." Forced to take brief showers, leave their cars unwashed or even swapping their beloved lawns for cacti, tumbleweed, snakes and scorpions, many locals are grumbling about depleting the state's precious water so Chinese can munch on roasted almonds and sip an aromatically oaky Cabernet Sauvignon from the Golden State. In a recent article, the *Anderson Valley Advertiser* points out that 70,000 acres in Sonoma County are allotted to wine grapes, with only 12,000 for all other food crops. Such a mono culture is a disaster, it warns, "If California's drought continues, famine may follow."

For some, California's water crisis would be instantly solved if the state curbed or even banned such water-intensive crops as almonds, alfalfa or tomatoes, etc. All over the Central Valley, millions of acres already lie fallow, however, with thousands of workers idle. Unless heaven's floodgates were to swing wide open really soon, then, a mass exodus will certainly commence. Will Californians be the first American climate change refugees? Anticipating an influx into the Pacific Northwest, a University of Washington professor of atmospheric science, Cliff Mass, jokingly suggests that a fence be built around Oregon and Washington. This will also keep out other Americans fleeing intensified hurricanes, hellish heat waves and seawater flooding into their living room. Speaking of fences, commentator Fred Reed has also predicted that as Hispanics become ever more dominant in California politics, its southern border will be patrolled even more laxly, resulting in a de facto merger with Mexico.

On my recent California trip, I had neither the time nor the money to stray beyond the Bay Area, and so I encountered mostly happy, confident people. A friend in Fremont even insisted that this whole drought business is but a scare tactic to jack up his water bill. "See those hills," Giang pointed to Pleasanton Ridge. "Are they green?"

"Yes."

"Did anyone water them?"

"No."

Giang laughed with deep satisfaction. The fact that it rained hard during two days of my five-day stay further proved, in his mind, that this drought brouhaha is nothing but a Jerry Brown con game.

"I should have taken a photo of you all dripping wet from walking in the rain!" Giang added, still laughing. In his defense, I can only speculate that my friend's not all there thanks to a recent, drawn out divorce, loss of home, suicide attempt and a three-year spell of unemployment that, mercifully, has just ended.

It is all too easy to be upbeat in the Bay Area, however, especially if you're in Silicon Valley. Trekking through Santa Clara, Cupertino, Sunnyvale, Mountain View, Fremont and San Jose, I saw mostly neat, beautiful homes with well-kept landscaping. Cheery Cupertino High School contrasted so sharply with the grate-windowed, prison-like complexes common to Philly, I had to stop and stare. With an average SAT score of 1832, it's not even the best public high school in town. By comparison, the average score for South Philadelphia High, the one closest to me, is 1045. Cupertino is 63.3 percent Asian, and the star of Cupertino High's basketball team is six-foot-four junior Ajaypal Singh. He's averaging 17.5 points, 6.5 rebounds and 1.7 blocks per game.

At the East West Bookshop in Mountain View, there are notices for lectures with names like "I'm Not Dead, I'm Different" and "My View from Heaven: Life After Death." Like California itself, some Californians are smirking at physical limits. We're not dying of thirst, we're different. With its posh restaurants and cafés, downtown Mountain View exudes wealth. At Scratch, which advertises "comfort food," a "Midwestern meatloaf" goes for a mere $19. Outside Xanh, an upscale Vietnamese joint, I spotted a notice in Spanish offering a kitchen job.

Help Wanted signs are all over the South Bay, in fact, especially at fast-food outlets. At Ike's Love & Sandwiches in Santa Clara, the large "NOW HIRING" poster features a vaguely Asiatic Uncle Sam, with "WE WORK FOR TIPS, AND PHONE NUMBERS!" Plus "Medical/Dental Benefits." The California minimum wage is $9 an hour, and since most of these jobs only start out at that or a tad more, they have a hard time attracting workers. With competition for diners so fierce, however, bosses can't offer better. Immigrants tend to open restaurants, and the South Bay is carpeted with reasonably priced Chinese, Vietnamese, Indian and Mexican eateries.

Coming from a city that's 44 percent black, I also noticed the scarcity of blacks in Silicon Valley. The largest ethnic group in Santa Clara County is Asian, at 34.1 percent, to be followed by white at 33.9 percent and Hispanic at 26.8 percent. Blacks make up only 2.9 percent. As in every other place across this entire country, Hispanics claim the more physical jobs that once went to blacks, just as Chinese used to bump out the lowlier whites. As for the tech jobs, they are dominated by Asians and whites, which makes perfect sense, since these are also the best engineering students anywhere. At super competitive Thomas Jefferson High School for Science and Technology in suburban Washington, 70 percent of the class of 2019 are Asians. In a mixed-race society, the vocational aptitudes of each ethnic group become sharply contested, then delineated against each other. Of course, individuals should always be judged singly, and these larger patterns are not etched in stone. In San Francisco, Tibetans and Central Americans are said to make the best nannies.

Americans remember well that nightmarish time when just about every American company outsourced its customer service to India, which gave rise to the term "cyber coolies." If one had to ask one's bank or cable company a question, one would be routed to a "Stephanie" or a "Beth" who was actually a Nisha or a Jyotsna in Bangalore. Though Jyotsna was trying her best to sound Midwestern, the conversation would quickly turn awkward, if not aggravating for both sides. "Excuse me, but can you repeat that?" Less conspicuous was the hiring of Indian engineers, and that too ran into problems. The challenge of having Americans and Indians working together in different time zones proved too much of a hassle, thus many outfits tried to send American managers overseas, but since few were willing to go, it was decided that Indian IT workers would be brought here.

Ultimately, the reason why so many Indians are thriving in Silicon Valley is their unmatched computer prowess. The CEO of Adobe and cofounder of Hotmail are Indians, as is the Google executive overseeing Android, Chrome and Google apps. Outside California, the top man at Microsoft is also Indian. One morning I went to Fischer Park in Fremont and saw that nearly all of the tennis, basketball and volleyball players were Indians. At the jungle gym, all the kids were Indians. Mostly draped in saris, their grandmoms and moms stood nearby. A couple of blocks away, there's Bombay Pizza House, "Home of the Curry Pizza!"

With no college degree, no science, no math, no coordination, no rah-rah team spirit, no charm, no looks, no nothing, I wouldn't last half a second in Silicon Valley, and hiking all over, I also spotted quite a few souls who had been spat out by this sunny, mild yet merciless environment. The Jungle, a massive tent city in San Jose, has been cleared, but each night, there are around five thousand San Joseans sleeping outside, though they are scattered at roughly two hundred spots and less visible. California itself has more homeless people than any other state, and 4.3 percent of its schoolchildren, incredibly, don't have stable or adequate housing. These kids must sleep in a shelter, a single room with their parents and siblings, a garage, a car or a tent. Fully 10 percent of school kids in Sunnyvale, in the heart of Silicon Valley, fall into this miserable category. Needless to say, they aren't likely to be immersed in any subject, much less Chinese.

Meanwhile, luxury condos and homes keep springing up, for besides the infusion of Chinese money, our inflated stock market is benefiting, especially, the many high-profile, sexy companies that dot the Bay Area, such as Apple, Adobe, Google, Yahoo!, Facebook, PayPal, Yelp, Netflix and Twitter, etc. Outside of Manhattan, no other region has gained so much from the banksters' quantitative easing. When this stock mania crashes and burns, the Bay Area will also be charred.

Meanwhile, everything seems to be improving, and Twitter has even moved its headquarters into the Tenderloin, San Francisco's most wretched neighborhood. Located right downtown, in the shadow of City Hall, it's inevitable that this pocket of transient hotels, urine-reeking sidewalks, thousands of homeless, bodegas and cheap Vietnamese eateries would be gentrified. One night, I found myself in The Basement, a hip, happening new bar at Taylor and Turk. It's co-owned by Lieu, someone from my high school in East San Jose, although we didn't know each other then. Though roughly my age, fifty-one, Lieu looks so young, he's probably carded at every bar not his own, and with my white hair, I'm like his granddad.

The Basement used to be occupied by Club 222, with the legendary Black Hawk right next door. (It's now a parking lot.) Musicians from Miles to Dizzy used Club 222 as a greenroom before they exited it through the back to enter the jazz club. At The Basement, all the beers are microbrews, with nothing under $5. Lieu doesn't want the Tenderloin's riffraff to wander in to order a can of Bud or Miller. "This neighborhood is moving up," he said.

"Ah, man, won't you miss people defecating on the sidewalks?"

"Get that shit out of here!"

This night, there was a comedy open mike. I asked Lieu if the poetry slam crowd had approached him.

"Yes, but I turned them down."

"Why?"

"Poets don't drink enough."

That's a sure sign of a collapsing society! The two bartenders were young, pretty women, one white, one Chinese. The Basement also has a hunky Swedish guy to attract the ladies. Leaving The Basement, I reentered the Tenderloin proper and promptly saw a young yet haggard white woman, in tight jeans and no shoes, just socks, flashing for a black man leaning against a frail, half-dead tree. Seeing me, she smiled most crookedly, ran up, turned around, pulled down and leaned over to display her cheeks. Trying to panhandle from me, an older black woman screamed at this exhibitionist to shoo her away. With yuppies and hipsters invading the Tenderloin, it's hoped that scenes like this will gradually disappear from San Francisco, but if the economy collapses, and it will soon enough, you will see this spread all over.

Ah, California, you will turn bone-dry and shirk off your weeping children by the millions! Announcing the state's first ever mandatory restrictions on water usage, Governor Brown reminded us, "For over ten thousand years, some people say twenty thousand years, people lived in California, but the number of those people were never more than 300,000 or 400,000, as far as we know, and they lived much simpler, and they were able to move when a drought occurred, or fires occurred. They could cope. Now, we're embarked upon an experiment that no one has ever tried, ever, in the history of mankind, and that's 38 million people, with 32 million vehicles, living at a level of comfort that we all strive to attain." Weaned from abundant resources, we will have to strive to attain less.

In a country where political speeches, elections and even terrorist attacks are but elaborate theatrical productions, California is the longest show running, designed to convince everyone everywhere, and even Californians themselves, that here is the epitome of the American Dream, and that it's surfing along just fine. Just outside the spotlight, however, are all sorts of frightful omens. The next act will be a scream.

DEAD CENTRALIA

6-28-15—Just as there are so many ways for a man to die, there are countless methods for a place to be destroyed. Unlike a dead man, however, a wrecked city or country most often doesn't disappear entirely, but lingers on as a shadow or zombie, or it becomes an entirely different place. Most American cities have become zombies, while the country itself is a swearing, staggering, fist-waving zombie with a gazillion cruise missiles strapped to its bloated and festering carcass.

Come up to Northeast Pennsylvania, my friend Chuck Orloski urged, and he'll show me Centralia. Fifty-three years into its famous coal mine fire, this dead town only has three houses left from over five hundred, and out of its seven churches, only one is standing. Its current population is 6, and its last unpaid and unofficial mayor died in May of 2014 at age ninety. Centralia does have a fire station, however, and inside its municipal building, there's a bar that opens twice a month for old-timers to drop by and reminisce. Also, Centralia's four cemeteries still honor reservations. Forced to flee, many come back to lie down. Dead, they can reclaim their community.

Chris Perkel and Georgie Roland made a searing documentary on Centralia, The Town That Was, and in this 2007 film, one meets fascinating John Lokitis. With its population down to a dozen, Lokitis tried to maintain normalcy by mowing acres of grass, painting benches and, most absurdly and heartbreakingly, hanging candle, tree and lantern decorations from utility poles each Christmas. By refusing to let comatose Centralia die, Lokitis was hoping against hope that it could be revived, but, alas, Lokitis himself was evicted in 2009 and his memory-laden house torn down. Following Lokitis around, the camera often lingered uncomfortably on his face after he had stopped talking, as if expecting this sad yet defiant man to break down. Every now and then, Lokitis would chuckle nervously. Combating nature, fate, the damned government and time itself, Lokitis couldn't will the Centralia story to a different outcome.

Taking a bus from Philadelphia, I met Chuck in downtown Scranton, but before he arrived, I had time to grab a very sad fish sandwich at Curry Donuts. The other patrons did cheer me up, however. Copiously inked and in daft or menacing T-shirts, they guzzled Mountain Dew, greeted each other and jived. Sitting alone, a squinting black man wore cheap plastic glasses sans nose pads and a once-orange T-shirt that declared, "YOUR MOM WAS HERE." Pushing a stroller, possibly the shortest woman I've ever seen came marching in and grandly announced to the frazzled cashier, "We're having lunch!" Visibly and audibly ecstatic that the fish sandwich with fries special was just $4.99, she ordered the dismal meal I just had. Standing outside the plate glass window, a young man in a white muscle T spat extravagantly between puffs of American Spirit. I never knew a seemingly healthy body could generate so much phlegm.

Joining Chuck and me on the trip to Centralia was Jack. Sixty-five years old, Jack has had a turbulent life and was locked up for twenty-two years altogether for dealing drugs. He has at least eleven children by eight women. When not chasing pink sweatpants, Jack works at a soup kitchen. A man who has never been in battle or jail can feel inadequate in the presence of one who has. It is as if true manhood consists of a capacity to endure endless humiliation and pain. It is this psychology that is exploited by the softest of men to convert millions of other men into draft animals and soldiers.

Running from the Scranton police, Jack settled in Fishtown in Philadelphia. Living within sight of a police station, in fact, Jack did honest construction work, but on cold nights, he would let a young prostitute in. In exchange for warmth and crack, she would give Jack some attention. By four in the morning, she wasn't likely to hook up with another john anyway.

"Isn't it funny, Jack?" I said. "These girls come in from all over, small-town New Jersey, Kansas, and they end up in Kensington, which is like the worst fuckin' neighborhood in the world—well, the country—so they have to act all tough and shit, but they're not."

"They're not."

"They're just kids."

"Yeah, they're just kids, and I knew what they wanted, you know. I'd get them a bundle of crack, two bundles. I didn't give a shit. I was making 16, 17 an hour under the table, and my rent was only 300 a month. I didn't care too much what they looked like. The backs of their heads looked good to me."

Always looking, Jack was constantly pointing out notable sights to Chuck and me as we were driving. No square inch of soft flesh escaped his attention. A thickly built man, Jack has a Jesus tattoo on his barrel chest. In any fight, you'd want him on your side.

In this region, the landscape has no dramatic markers. There are no snowcapped peaks or wide rivers spanned by spectacular bridges. Everything is tranquil. For a century and a half, however, there was much drama below. To keep America heated and lighted, an army of men and boys toiled in virtual hells, with many of them blown up or crushed. From 1877 to 1940, 18,000 died in Pennsylvania coal mines.

Three miles from Centralia is Ashland, and we stopped here to examine an unusual statue. Like nearly every town in coal country, Ashland is almost entirely white. God, family and country are their holy trinity. Each man is expected to go to the war(s) of his generation. If returning in one piece, no matter how truncated, he has earned himself a stool at the VFW Legion. In such a town, flags and patriotic declarations are everywhere, and war memorials, often with a piece of artillery, torpedo or even tank, are conspicuous. Ashland's most prominent monument does not feature soldiers, however, but a symbolic mother. A bronze rendition of the famous Whistler painting, it rests on a stone pedestal that reads, "MOTHER. A MOTHER IS THE MOST SACRED THING ALIVE."

After his mom died in 1992, Chuck went to this statue to recite a Hail Mary. There, he thought of her last, troubling decade when she often clawed herself bloody or yanked her hair out, so much so that she had to wear a wig in public. Climbing down the monument's steps, Chuck was suddenly accosted by an old, limping woman. "They should call that Our Lady of Memory," she barked. To honor the mother, then, is to acknowledge our roots and history. It is to define, as best we can, who we really are.

On the edge of Ashland, we met up with Remo. An old Teamster friend of Chuck, he would show us Centralia, his hometown. White-haired and -mustached, Remo had a dog tag and pair of glasses dangling from his neck. A second pair perched on his hunting cap. Six eyes, this man had. In two cars, we drove into the "outskirts of hell," as it's described in a 1981 newscast. Are you ready for toxic steam to crawl up your legs and into your nose? Perhaps you will be sucked into an inferno, as happened to twelve-year-old Todd Domboski, though, unlike him, no miraculous hands will pluck you out at the last second. Into hell you will go.

Photos of Centralia posted online are often taken in winter, to emphasize its desolation, but the town I saw was mostly green trees and shrubs, and lording over this verdant expanse was a beautiful white church on a hill. Outside the fire zone, the Assumption of the Blessed Virgin Mary has not been razed. Completed in 1912, it was one of the first Ukrainian churches in the US. For its construction, each family in the congregation contributed $50, or $1,290 in today's dollars. Remo was married here, and his dad and maternal grandparents are nestled in the soil out back. When he and his ma die, they will join them. Thanks to lung cancer, Remo only has one bronchus left. The church's steep steps pose a unique challenge for pallbearers. Remo joked of hearing many a dead man's head bouncing against the coffin as it's tilted upward. Though there are no more Sunday services, weddings and funerals are still performed here. Mostly funerals.

Under a red granite slant headstone, Nicholas and Mary Bazan rest. Outliving her husband by thirty-eight years, Mary died only in April of 2015. Having moved to Highlands, North Carolina, Mary knew she would come back to a plot she and her husband had paid for decades earlier. Such fidelity to man, memory and land has become much rarer, no doubt, though we blithely call it freedom. When not blown hither and thither like husks, many of us still disown everything.

Remo showed us another cemetery, Odd Fellows. The fatal fire started right next to it in 1962. As a teenager, Remo and his buddies would get it on with their girlfriends among the tombstones. The hellish heat from below kept those young entangled limbs on the surface balmy even in winter. A mile away, snow may be falling, but here they could disrobe under the stars.

"You could walk around with no shoes on. It was like the beach."

"Remo, didn't you feel guilty having sex next to a bunch of crucifixes?" I asked.

"It's only a sacrilege if you're sober. It's not a sacrilege if you're drunk."

We all laughed. "You didn't feel funny having sex on top of grandmas and grandpas?"

"I crossed myself before I did it."

I, too, have a teenage cemetery (sorta) sex story. Perhaps it is an archetypical scenario. Above an astronomical mound of bones, we make love. Bones against bones, on top of bones.

Chuck and Remo worked together as dockworkers for Roadway Express for a decade, so they have plenty of shared memories. As we walked around, they brought up many frightful characters. They spoke of an intimidating ex-Marine who had the disconcerting habit of suddenly grabbing another man's genitals or kissing him. Suspected of stealing guns from the dock, the nut squeezer even smooched an FBI agent. He finally killed himself with a .357.

A company executive would ask odd sexual questions during job interviews. "Do you like to wear your wife's panties?" He claimed it revealed personality traits.

Irked at a newly hired supervisor from Boston, a black worker showed his sullen mamba to this annoying gent as he was talking on the phone. Traumatized, the man quit. This reminds me of a white friend's take on a famous Robert Mapplethorpe photo, "That's every white man's biggest fear. To see a huge black penis from some guy in a suit."

"Isn't it weird, Chuck," I said, "the guy's reaction? I think it's incredible he would let go of his job over that."

"I used to see black penises all the time," Jack added. "They were all lined up in a row. In the shower."

Once, Remo grabbed the neck of a foreman but was not fired. Unionized and in skilled jobs, workers obviously had more leverage then. Now, you can be fired with no pretext, for there's plenty of fresh meat waiting just outside the door.

Done with what's left of Centralia, we all went to Dorko's in Mount Carmel, four miles down Route 61. Remo's wife bartends here, and this is where he goes regularly to chat and sometimes to play shuffleboard or shoot darts. Remo's health prevents him from downing the cheap Yuengling. A while back, a reader complained that I was talking to too many folks in bars, but lady, people the world over talk to each other while drinking. It's called socializing. At its peak, Centralia had a population of 2,761 but 27 bars, so go back to your chatroom, lady, and leave me to my fermented hop and Remo to his spring water. We're talking.

Wine in, words out, goes a Vietnamese saying. In Dorko's, I talked to a man who had lived in half a dozen countries during his Army stint. He spent three years in Italy, loved it, and almost married a woman there. He still thinks the USA is best, however, "We have the most freedom."

"Ah, man, don't you love the Italian food, people and pace of life? Italians taught me how to live, I'm not joking." I spent two years in Certaldo, the birthplace of Boccaccio. "The health care, too, it's a lot cheaper there. If I had the money, I'd live in Italy."

"I still prefer it here, because we have the most freedom."

"They have all the freedom that we have!"

"No they don't."

"What are you talking about?"

"They can't own guns like we do."

"That's it?!"

"Yup."

In the American West, you have thousands of towns quickly settled, then quickly abandoned. In China, there are grandiose urban projects that can't find enough commercial or residential tenants. Founding Israel, Jews evicted Palestinians and razed their villages. When borders shift or political systems change, entire towns evacuate. People have always had to flee for their lives, but in modern times, the scale and range of refugee flows have become unprecedented and truly staggering. A refugee at age eleven, I slept in a tent in Guam, an Army barrack in Arkansas, then lived in Washington, Texas, Oregon, California and Virginia before graduating from high school. Such rootlessness is hardly unusual. When in Hanoi, however, I feel strangely at home, though I have never spent more than two weeks at a time there. It's not just the accent, my mother's, but a deeper resonance that comes from millennia of settlement by my kind. The entire Red River Delta has more gravity to me, but less so Saigon, my birthplace. Vietnamese haven't been there as long. That said, I'm best adjusted to Philadelphia and can negotiate its maze better than any other place's. My primary language is still English. I'm a Philadelphian.

With ghost towns all over, why should Centralia fascinate? First off, it's extremely rare to see Americans fleeing en masse from a place, and here they're even doing it permanently. An American refugee is still a very rare breed. Secondly, there are layers of symbolism to this catastrophe. Nourished by coal, this town has been destroyed by it. It's a man-made ecological disaster that destroys a man's home and all that he cherishes. Beneath a thin crust of it's-a-wonderful-life normalcy, there's a bubbling hell threatening to swallow everyone up, and you have to be an extremely smug American to be oblivious to this plot. Centralians also resent having their history and identity being reduced to a final disaster, and this happens, by the way, to all of history's losers. Just think of the American South or South Vietnam. Soon, you too will know the feeling. All Americans are Centralians.

Stories make a place. Without stories, there is no place, but without place, there can still be stories. If your stories are not organically grown, but imposed on you by those who hate everything about you, then you're virtually dead.

After the last Centralian has come home to be buried, the town will be just its cemeteries and a section of lost road. Buckled and cracked, it's filled with graffiti, much of it erotically inspired. Above bones, we screw, until we too become lost words. O mother of memory, forgive us for what we've already forgotten.

POSTSCRIPT: A POEM

State of the Union

Shovel-toothed, funky in profile,
I, John Dodo, am a son of Camden.
Beneath boasting of a city invincible,
I'm two boarded-up windows. I am a
Well-painted mural of kaput industries.
Who touches these, touches my void.

Once I shoveled coal, tamed pig iron,
Strung bridges. Erected. Now I strut
Up and down Broadway, dazed,
Fingering coins, aiming for chicken.

Pants low-slung, crack peeping,
I'm son of Bethlehem. I peddle
Christmas mart, push Sands.
I patrol dying mall in Buffalo.

At dawn, in McArthur Park,
Los Angeles, I piss and scratch.
Legless, I buff Hollywood
Plaques, pose as monster
For tourists who undertip.

I push charity condoms, body oils,
High-class-looking purses, low-class,
High-definition porn, incense and sox.

Lying on news, ads and cardboard,
I browse, RECOVERY IS ON COURSE.
BUM SIGHTINGS DOWN. LATTE SALES UP.
BRITNEY SEEN IN ODD-COLORED SHOES.
JUSTIN ALARMS FANS WITH FAKE HAIRCUT.

As I sleep, an asswipe sneaks
Photos, then gives me a buck.
Strung-out, I will suck and fuck,
Excuse me, until I get my fix.

Like a cliché, I press nose
Against steakhouse glass.
Soon I will break that glass.